Michael Ferrebee Sadler

**The Epistles of St. Paul to Titus, Philemon and the Hebrews**

With notes critical and practical

Michael Ferrebee Sadler

**The Epistles of St. Paul to Titus, Philemon and the Hebrews**
*With notes critical and practical*

ISBN/EAN: 9783337318277

Printed in Europe, USA, Canada, Australia, Japan

Cover: Foto ©Lupo / pixelio.de

More available books at **www.hansebooks.com**

THE EPISTLES OF ST. PAUL

TO

# TITUS, PHILEMON

AND THE

# HEBREWS

WITH NOTES CRITICAL AND PRACTICAL

BY THE REV. M. F. SADLER

LATE RECTOR OF HONITON AND PREBENDARY OF WELLS

LONDON

GEORGE BELL AND SONS

1898

First published Nov., 1890.
Reprinted 1892, 1896.
Re-issue, 1898.

# INTRODUCTION TO THE EPISTLE TO TITUS.

THE Epistle to Titus is, taking into account its shortness and the fact that there is no doctrine depending upon its sole testimony, as well attested as any one of the Apostolical epistles.

It is mentioned in the Muratorian fragment in the words "Verum ad Philemonem unam, et ad Titum unam et ad Timotheum duas." (Westcott on "Canon," p. 529.)

One passage is quoted twice by Irenæus, "But as many as separate from the Church, and give heed to such old wives' fables as these, are truly self-condemned, and these men Paul commands us 'after a first and second admonition to avoid.'" ("Against Heresies," I. cap. xvi., 3, and also III. cap. iii., 3.)

By Clement of Alexandria it is quoted at least nine times. One will suffice, "Epimenides the Cretan, whom Paul knew as a Greek prophet, whom he mentions in the Epistle to Titus, when he speaks thus, 'One of themselves, a prophet of their own, said, 'The Cretans are always liars, evil beasts, slow bellies.'" ("Miscellanies," I. 14.)

By Tertullian at least twelve times, as "To the pure all things are pure, so likewise all things to the impure are impure, but nothing is more impure than idols." ("De Corona," 10.)

There are undoubted reminiscences of the Epistle in the Apostolic Fathers, as in Clement of Rome, chap. ii., "Ready to every good work;" chap. xxvii., "Nothing is impossible for God except to lie;" chap. lviii., "Chose us through Him to be a peculiar people."

"If the Epistles to Timothy are received as St. Paul's there is not the slightest reason for doubting the authorship of that to Titus. Amidst the various combinations which are found amongst those who have been sceptical on the subject of the Pastoral

Epistles, there is no instance of the rejection of that before us on the part of those who have accepted the other two. So far indeed as these doubts are worth considering at all, the argument is more in favour of this (the Epistle to Titus) than of either of the others. Tatian accepted the Epistle to Titus and rejected the other two. Origen mentions some who excluded 2 Tim. but kept 1 Tim. with Titus. Schleiermacher and Neander invert this process of doubt in regard to the letters addressed to Timothy, but believe that St. Paul wrote the present letter to Titus. Credner, too, believes it to be genuine, though he pronounces 1 Tim. to be a forgery and 2 Tim. a compound of two epistles." (Howson in "Dict. of the Bible.")

## LIFE OF TITUS.

Abundant mention is made of Titus in the Epistles of St. Paul, but none whatsoever in the Acts of the Apostles. Some have made a difficulty of this even to the extent of supposing that he is one of the stated companions of St. Paul (as Timothy) under another name. But such difficulty could only have arisen from forgetting the extremely fragmentary nature of the narrative in the Acts of the Apostle; for eight at least of the Apostles are not mentioned after the first chapter. St. John is not mentioned after the third chapter; nearly twenty years of the life of St. Peter are dismissed with a single notice in chap. xv., and years of the life of St. Paul—three particularly in Ephesus—have not a single word respecting them.

The first notice of him is in Gal. ii. 1-3, and from this we gather that he was wholly of Gentile extraction, and not, like Timothy, Jewish in regard of one of his parents. So that St. Paul resisted the Judaizers who insisted on his circumcision.

The other notices are in 2 Corinthians, and indicate a confidence in him and a personal affection towards him, not inferior to that which St. Paul entertained towards Timothy. It appears that fearing the effect of the severe tone of his first Epistle on the Corinthians, he had sent him to Corinth to bring him word as to how they took his censures, and his anxiety respecting this was such that he forsook for the time a most promising work at Troas (2 Cor. ii. 12), and went forward to Macedonia to meet Titus and receive his report. He did meet him and was more than comforted;

he rejoiced exceedingly at the account which Titus gave him of the obedience, "the fear and trembling" with which he was received (vii. 13-15).

But besides this Titus was entrusted with another mission of a different character. He was to further the collection for the poor saints of Judæa which lay so near to St. Paul's heart. He "desired Titus that as he had begun so he would finish in them the same grace," viii. 6. From this we gather that he had initiated the matter, and he carried it out with an earnestness which left nothing to be desired on the Apostle's part. "Thanks be to God which put the same earnest care into the heart of Titus for you. For indeed he accepted the exhortation, but being more forward, of his own accord he went unto you" (viii. 17, 18). And at the conclusion of the chapter he describes Titus as his partner and fellow-helper. Next, then, to Timothy, of all his companions and fellow-soldiers, Titus was the one in whom he had the most confidence. And lastly, when he is indignantly repudiating the slightest attempt of self-seeking in this matter of the collection, he associates Titus with himself as being both of them imbued with the same unselfish spirit. "Did I make a gain of you?... I desired Titus and with him I sent a brother. Did Titus make a gain of you? walked we not in the same spirit? walked we not in the same steps?" (2 Cor. xii. 17, 18).

Then comes the present Epistle, addressed to Titus as "his own son after the common faith," and leaving him in Crete with the same commission as he had given to Timothy, to act as bishop or overseer, to ordain elders or bishops, to teach the various classes, aged men, aged women, young women, young men, servants or slaves.

Towards the conclusion there is another slight historical notice, that Titus on the arrival of Artemas or Tychicus should join the Apostle at Nicopolis (iii. 12), and the last allusion to this companion of St. Paul is to be found in his last letter, a little before his martyrdom, viz., that he had been sent on some mission to Dalmatia. 2 Tim. iv. 10.

The pastoral directions in the Epistle are, in an abbreviated form, the same as those in the first Epistle to Timothy. There are, however, in the second and third chapters respectively, two doctrinal statements of the first importance, that in ii. 13 of the Divine Glory of our Lord, "The glorious Epiphany of the great

God and Saviour of us, Jesus Christ," and in the third there is a short epitome of the whole work of salvation. There is our natural depravity, "We ourselves were sometimes foolish, disobedient, deceived." Then there is the manifestation of the grace of God, "After that the kindness and love of God our Saviour . . . not by works of righteousness which we had done, but by His mercy he saved us." Then there is the instrumentality of the Sacramental system, "by the font of New Birth," then the "renewing by the Holy Ghost," then our justification by grace and heirship, and then the necessity of good works to crown all.

Much, then, of what is both ecclesiastical, doctrinal, and practical is compressed into the few verses of this short Epistle. It is the summing up of St. Paul's rule and teaching, and loving regard for his fellow workers. In it, as in all he wrote, shines forth his faith, his hope, his charity.

# INTRODUCTION TO THE EPISTLE TO PHILEMON.

THE Epistle to Philemon is reckoned amongst St. Paul's in the Muratorian fragment, "Verum ad Philemonem unam, et ad Titum unam," &c. It is also mentioned by Tertullian as being allowed as genuine by Marcion. Eusebius also reckons it amongst the Epistles of St. Paul when he speaks of their number as fourteen, (including, of course, to make up this number, the Epistle to the Hebrews), and is quoted twice by Origen.

Indeed, it is impossible to conceive on what ground an Epistle not containing a single dogmatic statement, and entirely occupied with a private personal matter, can be supposed to have been forged.

The Epistle tells its own story. Philemon was a man of wealth and consideration, at Colosse. He was converted to Christianity by the ministration of the Apostle, for in pleading for Onesimus Paul reminds Philemon how he owed to him even "his own self."

Philemon had a slave, Onesimus, who ran away from him, and it is not improbable, took some of his master's goods with him in his flight. This slave came in contact with the Apostle as he preached whilst he was a prisoner in Rome, and was converted, and became a Christian and a member of the Church. He appears to have been a man of talent or aptitude, for he was valuable to the Apostle as ministering to St. Paul in the bonds of the Gospel so well that in the view of the Apostle his services would have been equivalent to those of Philemon, no doubt an educated, as well as a zealous man. What this diaconia consisted in we cannot exactly say, but it cannot have well been private or domestic service, for it would hardly have been expected that Philemon would have rendered that to the Apostle; it must have been Church service, reading, looking up converts, preparing them for Baptism and the reception of the Eucharist, and such things.

But St. Paul distinctly recognized that Onesimus, though a member of the Church, and so of Christ, was yet, according to human laws, the property of his master, and so he would do nothing in this matter without the full approbation of Philemon. He sends the runaway back to his master with a letter permeated with the tenderest feeling towards the offender, and the most loving courtesy to him who had rights of life and death over him, and yet without the slightest assertion of Apostolic authority, though he reminds him that he might have properly exercised such. But even in this he pleads for what is to Philemon's benefit, "without thy mind I would do nothing that thy benefit (kindness) should not be as it were of necessity, but willingly." It would scarcely be thought that Philemon should require pecuniary compensation for any loss which he had sustained, but to meet even that case St. Paul signs, as Lewin expresses it, a promissory note for the amount, whatever it might be: "'If he hath wronged thee, or oweth thee aught, put that on mine account; I, Paul, have written it with mine own hand, I will repay thee." Hitherto he had asked for Onesimus' *pardon*, but he gently insinuates what he would not directly ask, that Philemon should give him his *freedom;* for the following words cannot but imply this:—'I know that thou will also do more than I say.'" (Lewin's "Life of St. Paul.")

The Epistle to Philemon is a private letter, and it may be asked, indeed, it has been asked, why a letter on such a subject should have been admitted into the Sacred Canon. We answer, because of the extreme importance of the subject. It had to do with the most delicate and difficult, and we may add the most dangerous, of all the relationship that the Church for some centuries had to face, the relations of slaves to their masters. If the relations of Christian slaves to their Christian masters required to be approached with such delicacy, what care must have been required in keeping a *modus vivendi* in the case of heathen families.

Now this Epistle would teach that whilst the rights of property, however harsh, were to be respected, yet that the Christian slave was to be considered and treated as a member of Christ, just as much as the Bishop himself; and if he was deprived of the enjoyment of the means of grace, that the Christian community should subscribe to the utmost of their power to purchase his freedom.

But there is another reason which, we say it with all reverence, was very probably in the mind of the Spirit, when He caused that this letter should be included in the Canon of Scripture. This letter, so full of sympathy and Christian love to a penitent member of the Mystical Body, so full of delicacy and urbanity to his Christian friend and fellow-labourer, is the letter of one who is described by the Spirit as "breathing out threatenings and slaughters against the disciples of the Lord," who described himself as "exceedingly mad" against the followers of Jesus. What a transformation! How has the ravenous beast become a lamb? It is true that years had intervened, but years of heathenism would not have so transformed the persecutor. It was Divine Grace—the Spirit of Jesus. The considerations brought to bear upon Philemon are not natural, but spiritual—no rights of man, no natural equality of mankind, but the fact that "in Christ there is neither Jew nor Greek, Barbarian, Scythian, bond or free, but Christ is all and in all."

The Epistle to Philemon was in all probability written at the same time as that to the Colossians, as we learn from Coloss. iv. 7, 9. "All my state shall Tychicus declare unto you, who is a beloved brother and a faithful minister and fellow-servant in the Lord . . . with Onesimus, a faithful and beloved brother, who is one of you."

If he was the co-bearer of the Epistle to the Colossians he would naturally carry the letter of the Apostle to Philemon, a citizen of Colosse.

# INTRODUCTION TO THE EPISTLE TO THE HEBREWS.

## TO WHOM WAS THE EPISTLE SENT?

OF the many questions which the varied phenomena of the Epistle to the Hebrews suggests, the first is that of the persons to whom it was written.

There are three considerations which must be taken into account in attempting to answer this question.

(1.) The first, that it was written to a Church wholly, or almost entirely, composed of Jews. There is not the least hint of the intermixture of any Gentile element, and in this it stands in contrast with almost all the other Epistles. Every Epistle of St. Paul, as well as that of St. Peter I., recognizes that Jews and Gentiles were side by side in the Church.[1] It is true that in the Epistle General of St. James there is no recognition of the presence of Gentiles, but the two cannot be compared. The Epistle of St. James, in its precepts, is entirely general. If we had not the allusion to the "twelve tribes" in the first verse we should not know that it was written to Jews, whereas the Epistle to the Hebrews is upon Judaism, upon the meaning of its rites and the shortcomings of its priesthood, in comparison with the fulness of the Priesthood of the Eternal Son which superseded it.

It is scarcely possible, then, to suppose that, if there had been any Gentile element in the Church or Churches to which it was addressed, this element should have been altogether ignored. A great part of the trial of the Jewish Christians in any mixed Church was that they should cheerfully acknowledge the equality of all men in Christ—that in Christ Jesus there was neither Jew nor Greek, but Christ all and in all.

I grant that what I am now asserting is not an absolute certainty. For some wise and good reason the Holy Spirit may have led the writer to ignore altogether the presence of Gentiles in the Unity of the One Body; but it seems to me extremely unlikely, and that consequently, if the Epistle is addressed to some local church, as it seems to be, the place of this church must be in Jerusalem—or in some contiguous part of Palestine.

Among possibilities, it may have been addressed to some isolated colony of Jews, who were able to shut themselves up from all outward communication, even with believing Gentiles, but it is extremely improbable that if such a community existed, such a document would have been addressed to it.

2. Then the Epistle seems to have been written to Jews who yet continued under the ministrations of the Jewish Priesthood. They had hitherto participated in the services of the Jewish Temple; they were now to be deprived of this, either by the cessation of these ministrations by the destruction of the temple and altar, or by excommunication on the part of the Jewish ecclesiastical rulers.

Now the significance of this can be best brought out by comparing the teaching of this Epistle with that to the Galatians. In the Epistle to the Galatians the converts are warned of the danger of apostatizing from Christ through the machinations of Judaizers. But what Judaizers? Evidently those of the Synagogues, not of the temple. Throughout the Epistle to the Galatians there is no warning whatsoever against Jewish sacerdotal pretensions. Not a word is said respecting altar, tabernacle, or temple, or veil, or sprinkling of blood, and such things. The Judaism which was a snare to them was that of the synagogue, not of the Temple. It put forth the perpetual obligation of circumcision, of the keeping of Jewish days of observance ("ye observe days, and weeks, and months, and years"), and differences between meats, whereas the Epistle to the Hebrews says little of this, and is mainly occupied with the ministrations of the High Priest, and his entrance into the most holy place with blood of others, not his own. With this it contrasts the entrance of the Great High Priest of Christians into the heavenly Holy of Holies, and our entrance into the same by "the new and living way which He hath consecrated for us through the veil, that is to say, His flesh." This seems as if the recipients of the Epistle were living in close proximity to the celebration of the most characteristic rites of Judaism, and that (though they were believers) the old ritual, though it was all fulfilled in Jesus, exercised a strange fascination over them—they were all "zealous for the law," as it yet was observed in the temple ceremonial.

These two considerations seem to prove almost beyond doubt that the Hebrew Christians who received this Epistle formed part of a Church entirely Hebrew in its membership, and living under the shadow of the Temple, or, which is practically the same, were living at such a distance from Jerusalem, that they could easily attend the yearly festivals.

There is another fact also which points in the same direction. The teaching of the Epistle is founded entirely on that of the Old Testament. It is the old covenant, the old law, the old figures, the old examples, the old prophecies regenerated. There is absolutely nothing new. Even the New Covenant is in one of the old prophets. There seems to be no special revelation, as there is in that to the Ephesians. It is the interpretation of the old, shedding on it a new light, quickening it with a new life, applying it afresh to altered circumstances, but the substratum is the Old Testament. Of course this is true in a sense of all Christianity—all its truths are everlasting, because all are in the eternal counsels of God. Now when we turn to the Epistles to the Ephesians, Philippians or Thessalonians, we perceive a great difference. There is the constantly recurring new phrase "in Christ Jesus." There is the new Headship of the Church, the new Body, the new ministry, the new oneness or bond of union. All this points to the fact that this Epistle is written to a Church still retaining as a Church its traditions, even to a certain extent its separation, and doing this at that time lawfully, but still the word might come, if it has not already come, "Let us go forth to Him without the camp, bearing His reproach." A Christian Jew in Corinth, or Ephesus, or Rome had not to "go out" as a Jew in Jerusalem had. From the stand-point of his countrymen, in Judea at least, he was already more than half without, and the step seems to be small, and the courage required for it insignificant, compared to what it was at Jerusalem.

## AUTHORSHIP.

The Epistle to the Hebrews is quoted as Scripture by the first Christian Father in point of time whose work has come down to us, viz., Clement of Rome, who wrote, as most agree, not later than A.D. 96.

"By Him the Lord has willed that we should taste of immortal knowledge, who being the brightness of His majesty, is by so much greater than the angels, as He hath by inheritance obtained a more excellent name than they. For it is there written, 'Who maketh His angels spirits and His ministers a flame of fire.' But concerning His Son the Lord thus spake, 'Thou art my Son, to-day have I begotten thee.'" There are at least thirteen references in Clement's Epistle. He quotes three or four times the text, "Moses was faithful in all his house." He quotes so remarkable a place as Heb. xi. 37, "Let us be imitators also of those who in goatskins and sheepskins went about proclaiming the coming of Christ" (xvii.).

Ignatius quotes the Hebrews in his Epistle to the Trallians: "Be ye subject to the Bishop as to the Lord, for he watches over your souls as one that shall give account to God" (ch. ii.); and again in the same Epistle, "Sat down at his right hand, expecting till His enemies are put under His feet;" and to the Smyrneans he quotes the phrase of "how much sorer punishment, suppose ye, shall he be thought worthy?" &c. (ch. ix.).

In Justin Martyr, Dial. cvi., there seems a clear reference to Heb. ii. 11, 12, "And that he stood in the midst of his brethren the Apostles . . . and when living with them sang praises to God, as is made evident in the memoirs of the Apostle. The words are the following, 'I will declare thy name unto my brethren,'" &c. And again, the only place where our Lord is called the Apostle of the Father is in the Epistle to the Hebrews, and Justin, in Apology I., ch. xii., calls Him "the Apostle of God the Father." Again, "But your ears are shut up and your hearts are made dull. For by this statement, 'The Lord hath sworn, and will not repent, Thou art a priest for ever,' with an oath God has shown Him on account of your unbelief to be the high priest after the order of Melchisedec" (Dial., ch. xxxiii., referring to the Hebrews vii. 17-22). Again, Heb. ix. 13, 14, "And who no longer were purified by the blood of goats and sheep, or by the ashes of an heifer." Again, Dial. lxvii., "Likewise I said, did not the Scripture predict that God promised to dispense a new covenant besides that which was dispensed on the Mount Horeb? This, too, he replied had been predicted. Then I said again, was not the old covenant laid on your fathers with fear and trembling, so that they could not give ear to God?

He admitted it. What, then, said I, God promised that there would be another covenant, not like that old covenant," &c. (Dial., ch. lxvii., comp. Hebr. viii. 9-10, 12).

Again, referring to Melchisedec, Justin says, " Melchisedec, the priest of the Most High, was uncircumcised ; to whom also Abraham, the first who received circumcision after the flesh, gave tithes, and he blessed him ; after whose order God declared by the mouth of David that he would establish the everlasting priest." (Dial. xix.) Again, Dial. cxiii., "This is he who is the King of Salem, after the order of Melchisedec, and the Eternal priest of the Most High God." And lastly, there seems a reference to Heb. vi. 18, in the words, "proclaiming thereby that all who through Him have fled for refuge to the Father constitute the true Israel." (Dial. cxxv.)

Clement of Alexandria quotes the Epistle to the Hebrews about thirty-five times. He several times quotes the first words of the Epistle, "God also at sundry times and in divers manners," in Miscell. i. ch. iv. 5, ch. vi. 6, ch. vii. He cites i. 3, "The express image of the glory of the Father." (Miscel. vii. 10.) "We then, according to the noble Apostle, desire that every one of you show the same diligence to the full assurances of hope." (Miscell. ii. ch. xxii.)

Irenæus, on the contrary, does not clearly quote the Epistle once. In a fragment found by a learned Lutheran in the Royal Library of Turin, there is an extract in which Heb. xiii. 15, " Let us offer the sacrifice of praise, that is the fruit of the lips," is quoted, but many hold it to be doubtful. But there is a reference to a lost book of Irenæus in Eusebius, bk. v., ch. 34, which runs thus, " A book also of ' various disputes ' [was written by Irenæus] in which he mentions the Epistle to the Hebrews."

Tertullian mentions the Epistle to the Hebrews, but distinctly ascribes the authorship to Barnabas as the companion of St. Paul: " There is extant withal an Epistle to the Hebrews under the name of Barnabas, a man sufficiently accredited by God, as being one whom Paul has stationed next to himself in the uninterrupted observance of abstinence. ' Or else, I alone and Barnabas have not we the power of working.' And of course the Epistle of Barnabas is more generally received among the Churches than the Apocryphal Shepherd of adulterers. Warning accordingly the disciples to omit all first principles, and strive rather after perfection, and not lay again the foundations of repentance from the works of the dead, he says, 'For it is impossible that they who have been once illuminated, and have tasted of the heavenly gift,'" &c. ("De Pudicitiâ," ch. xx.)

We now come to Origen. He constantly quotes the Hebrews as the work of St. Paul. Thus in the the second chapter of the "De Principiis": "The Apostle Paul says that the only begotten Son is the image of the invisible God ... and when writing to the Hebrews he says of Him, that He is the brightness of His glory, and the express image of His person." Again ("Contra Celsum," v. 4), "We indeed acknowledge that 'the angels are ministering spirits,' and we say that 'they are sent forth to minister for them who shall be heirs of salvation.'" Again, "For the word is used by our Paul in writing to the Corinthians, who were Greeks, and not yet purified in morals, 'I have fed you with milk.' ... How the same writer, knowing that there was a certain kind of nourishment better adapted to the soul, and that the food of these young persons who were admitted was compared to milk, continues, 'And ye are become such as have need of milk and not of strong meat.'" (Heb. v. 12, 14; "Against Celsus," iii. 53.) Again, "And it is in reference to this Jerusalem that the Apostle spoke ... ye are come, says he, unto Mount Zion, and unto the city of the living God" ("Against Celsus," vii. 29).

There is no quotation from the Epistle to the Hebrews in either Cyprian or Hippolytus.

Such, then, are the references to the Epistle in the Ante-Nicene Fathers. They one and all prove its canonicity—that it had a place assigned to it in the list of books of Scripture, being fitted by the inspiration of the Holy Ghost to be appealed to as profitable for doctrine, for reproof, for correction, for instruction in righteousness.

But when we come to consider the authorship of this document, we are face to face with a very difficult problem indeed, such as forced a man like Origen to say: "Who wrote it God only knows."

These doubts have principally come down to us in notices in Eusebius. The Ecclesiastical History of Eusebius is in a great measure a literary history, and particularly the writer takes every pains to illustrate the history of the doubtful books, showing by whom they were acknowledged or quoted, and by what churches received or rejected.

In book iii., ch. iii., we read: "The Epistles of St. Paul are fourteen, all well known and beyond doubt. It should not, however, be concealed that some have set aside the Epistle to the Hebrews, saying that it was disputed as not being one of St. Paul's Epistles; but we shall in the proper place also subjoin what has been said by those before our time respecting this Epistle."

In book vi., ch. xiv., we read respecting Clement of Alexandria: "The Epistle to the Hebrews," he asserts, "was written by St. Paul to the Hebrews in the Hebrew tongue; but it was carefully translated by Luke, and published among the Greeks. Whence also one finds the same character of style and of phraseology in the Epistle as in the Acts." "But it is probable that the title 'Paul the Apostle' was not prefixed to it. For as he wrote to the Hebrews who had imbibed prejudices against him, and suspected him, he wisely guards against diverting them from the perusal by giving his name." A little after he observes: "But now as the blessed Presbyter (Pantænus) used to say, Since the Lord who was the Apostle of the Almighty was sent to the Hebrews, Paul by reason of his inferiority, as if sent to the Gentiles, did not subscribe himself an Apostle to the Hebrews; both out of reverence for the Lord, and because he wrote of his abundance to the Hebrews, as a herald and Apostle to the Gentiles."

Again, book vi., ch. xx.: "There is, besides, a discussion which has come down to us of Caius, a most learned man, held at Rome in the time of Zephyrinus against Proclus, who contended for the Phrygian Heresy, in which, whilst he silences the rashness and daring of his opponents in composing new books (of Scripture), he makes mention of only thirteen Epistles, not reckoning that to the Hebrews with the rest, as there are even to this day some among the Romans who do not consider it to be the work of the Apostles."

And with respect to the opinion and testimony of Origen, Eusebius gives the following extract from Origen's "Homilies on the Hebrews". (now lost): "The style of the Epistle with the title 'to the Hebrews' has not that vulgarity of diction which belongs to the Apostle, who confesses that he is but rude in speech, that is, in his phraseology. But that this Epistle is more pure Greek in the composition of its phrases, everyone will confess who is able to discern the differences of style. Again, it will be obvious that the ideas of the Epistle are admirable, and not inferior to any of the books acknowledged to be Apostolic. Everyone will confess the truth of this who attentively reads the Apostle's writings." To these he (Origen) afterwards adds: " But I would say that the thoughts are the Apostle's, but the diction and phraseology belong to someone who has recorded what the Apostle said, and as one who noted down at his leisure what his master dictated. If then any Church considers this Epistle as coming from St. Paul, let it be commended for this, for neither did those ancient men deliver it thus without cause. But who it was who really wrote the Epistle God only knows. The account, however, that has been current before us is, according to some, that Clement, who was Bishop of Rome, wrote the Epistle; according to others that it was written by Luke, who wrote the Gospel and the Acts."

Nothing can be gathered with any certainty from the silence respecting names of Ecclesiastical writers, such as Clement of Rome and Justin. Justin, in fact, never alludes to any New Testament writer by name, but it is quite another matter when such writers as Clement of Alexandria and Origen attempt to account for the difference of style between the Epistle to the Hebrews and those Epistles of St. Paul, which are undoubtedly his and his alone, by supposing that St. Paul originally wrote the Epistle in question in the Hebrew, and St. Luke translated it into Greek, and when Origen tells us that some suppose it to have been written by Clement of Rome, and that Tertullian ascribes it to Barnabas.

Nobody can read together the Epistle to the Ephesians and that to the Hebrews without observing the marvellous contrast, if, as Origen says, " he is able to discern the difference of style." Whence this difference in the style of two documents commonly ascribed to the same author? The extracts in Eusebius show that this phenomenon was observed from the first, for if observed by Clement and Origen it is tantamount to having been observed from the first, and that it was ascribed to the fact of a sort of double authorship, the one, St. Paul, furnishing the ideas, the other, whoever he was, the phraseology and language.

Now one thing is to be noticed connected with this authorship, that, notwithstanding this discrepancy, the authorship is ascribed to St. Paul; another may have written it, but from his dictation; another may have translated, but in some real sense it is assumed to be his.

Now I do not think that this discrepancy—not only in style and phraseology, but in ideas—has been in the least exaggerated; on the contrary, it seems to me to have not been sufficiently noticed and dwelt upon. Consider the following:

The High Priesthood of the Eternal Son is the theme of the Epistle to the Hebrews; one really may say to the exclusion of every other, till we come to the eleventh chapter. There it is dropped, to be resumed again before the conclusion at xiii. 8 and following. Now the Eternal Priesthood of Christ is not once mentioned in any of the thirteen Epistles of St. Paul, or in fact in any book of the New Testament, except in this solitary Epistle. The Mediatorship of Christ is mentioned abundantly, as for instance in 1 Tim. ii. "There is one God, and one Mediator," &c., but not under priestly forms. The Mediatorship of Christ pervades the Epistle to the Hebrews, but only under the priestly form. Even in xii. 24, where only it is specifically mentioned under the name of Mediatorship, it is "Jesus the mediator *of the New Covenant*," not as in 1 Tim. ii.: "There is one Mediator between God and men, the man Christ Jesus."

Now when we turn to the Epistles of St. Paul, especially those to the Romans, Corinthians, and Galatians, we find them pervaded with the Mediatorship of Christ, but not once in the form in which it appears in the Epistle to the Hebrews. In the acknowledged Pauline Epistles the Mediatorship acts through the Risen and Glorified Head, who does not pass into a heavenly Holy of Holies to act there as a priest, but is exalted at once to the right hand of God, and acts there as a federal Head of the Church, a Second Adam, having all His people joined together in the Unity of His Body—a Mystical Body. Thus in Coloss. ii. 19: "The Head, from which all the body by joints and bands having nourishment ministered, and knit together, increaseth with the increase of God." Thus again, Ephes. i. 23-24, and iv. 15, 16, and v. 23, 30. Also Rom. xii. 4, 5, and 1 Cor. xii. 12-27.

Now this is undoubtedly the closest form which Mediatorship can assume—those for whom the Lord mediates are in Himself as the members of His Body; the mediation is the conveyance of grace and nourishment from Himself as the Head to the members of His Body, as in the most mysterious sense "in" Him. Compared to this idea the mediation typified by the Jewish high priest is external, but though external it is indispensable, for the mediation of the head of the mystical Body does not imply forgiveness through the constant application of the Atoning Blood. I mean it does not imply it so visibly, as it were, or so graphically as the mediation of our Epistle does. So that, when it is said that the Epistle to the Hebrews contains the ideas of the Apostle, as in the words of Origen, " I would say that the thoughts are the Apostle's, but the diction and phraseology belong to some one who has recorded what the Apostle said," this must be taken with some reserve, for the figure under which the mediatorship of Christ is presented to us throughout the Epistle to the Hebrews is the High Priest entering into the Holy of Holies with His own Blood ; whereas the figure under which mediation is presented to us in the thirteen Epistles of St. Paul is Christ the Head of a Mystical Body, and we in Him receiving grace, as the members of a body receive life and sensation from the head.

Throughout such Epistles as those to the Romans, Corinthians, Galatians, and Ephesians, mediation through the exalted Head of the Mystical Body is undoubtedly considered to be the highest result of redemption, whereas throughout the Epistle to the Hebrews the entrance of our High Priest into the presence of God is as undoubtedly considered to be the highest result of Redemption.

Now if they were written altogether by the same author, *i.e.*, St. Paul, or if the same author furnished the ideas, how is it that he has left the idea of Headship of the Mystical Body in and under Christ out of the Epistle to the Hebrews ? I desire to say it with the greatest reverence, he must have done violence to himself in so doing. For consider, the inherence of all men, Jew and Gentile, in Christ, was St. Paul's special doctrine. It was the mystery hid from ages and generations, and now made known to him and his brother Apostles and prophets (Ephes. iii. 5, 6) by the Spirit. Even justification by faith was subordinate to it. How is it that it is kept out of the Epistle to the Hebrews, and apparently another result of Redemption put in its place ?

If St. Paul either wrote the Epistle or furnished its ideas, this exclusion must have been of set purpose.

The Apostle was led by the Spirit to write to his brethren the believing seed of Abraham to convince them that they had the completion of their law in Christ. Now the gathering together in one of all things in Christ was in a manner extraneous to their law. There was no type of it at all equivalent to the type of the Lord as the Priest after the order of Melchisedec. It may have been that two such co-ordinate results of redemption as the entrance of the High Priest into heaven and the gathering together of all things in Christ, could not in that age of the Church be held in their integrity by either Hebrew or Gentile believers.

So that we can reverently imagine the Apostle giving direction to one of his disciples that he should prepare a short treatise in which nothing should interfere with the Hebrew conception of the high priest entering into the Holy of Holies as the acme, as it were, of the Jewish ritual, and that he should expand and extend this so as to lead up to the great High Priest entering once into the heavenly holiest with His own Blood. This was accomplished, and the Apostle himself then added to it, as it were, a postcript (xiii. 17, to end), identifying the whole with himself, making it his own, and taking the responsibility of its teaching. Who was this to whom the Apostle entrusted this great work? Tertullian, living at the end of the second century, without hesitation fixes on Barnabas, indeed seems to make him the independent author. In modern times Apollos has been named. He was a Jew born in Alexandria, and so presumed to be well acquainted with the writings of Philo. He was an eloquent man, and parts of this Epistle are of surpassing eloquence. He was "mighty in the Scriptures," and the Epistle shows a remarkable aptitude in bringing whatever is typical of the work of Christ to bear on his great subject; but the fatal objection to both Apollos and Barnabas is this, that they occupy far too independent a position as regards St. Paul. If either of them had written the Epistle, his name would have come down to us, for the name of the writer was evidently known to the persons to whom it was sent. But the name of Barnabas was only connected with the Epistle by one writer, Tertullian, living at a great distance, and the name of Apollos was never connected with it till the time of Luther. Besides this the Church of Alexandria would have claimed it for him as he was their countryman. The authorship or part authorship is mentioned both by Clement of Alexandria and Origen in connection with St. Luke. Clement says that St. Paul wrote it in Hebrew, and Luke translated it into Greek; and Origen writes that some ascribed it to Clement of Rome, and others to St. Luke. St. Luke's name seems to me to accord best with the fact that it was written under the direction of St. Paul. He did not occupy so independent a position with respect to St. Paul as either Barnabas or Apollos did, and the vocabulary agrees marvellously with that of

Luke. I will conclude with the words of two very eminent men, the one a Protestant, the other a Catholic, both concurring in the opinion that the authorship is St. Luke's, under the direction of St. Paul.

Delitzsch concludes his notes (p. 407) with the words : " The opinion which in the course of our commentary has more and more approved itself to our mind, is simply this, that the Epistle is not written by the hand of Paul, and bears the stamp of St. Luke's more than of St. Paul's style. It breathes Paul's spirit, but it does not speak Paul's words. From verse 18 to the conclusion he quite inclines to Paul's method. And be it directly or indirectly it is Paul's own peculiar Apostolic parting blessing and salutation with which, in verse 25, his doctrinal parentage in Paul is finally sealed " (vol. ii. p. 407, Clark's " Foreign Theological Library ").

In Dollinger's "First Age of the Church," we read: "The Epistle to the Hebrews, *i.e.*, the Jewish Christians of Palestine, coincides in date with the latter years of the Apostle's life. It is clear from internal evidence that it was not written before the year 63, or after 69. It is addressed to men familiar with the Levitical service and rites of the temple, and living in its neighbourhood, so that the Jewish worship and priesthood still exercised their full influence over them. Their church had existed a long time. Their original ministers and teachers were already dead, and their death could be held up as a pattern to survivors from the unshaken constancy with which they died for their belief (Hebr. v. 12; xiii. 7). A second generation of Christians had grown up, but they were in imminent peril of falling away from Christ and returning to Judaism. Some had already forsaken public worship. There is no reference in any other Apostolical Epistle to the danger here mentioned of apostasy to Judaism, and blasphemy against Christ. This state of things had now appeared for the first time in Judæa, and especially at Jerusalem, caused apparently by the hostility of the unconverted Jews, and the fear of exclusion from the Temple worship. But it is a mistake to affirm, as has often been done of late, that the author of the Epistle required an entire separation from the Jewish religion. He would not have done that incidentally in a couple of passing words, but would have explained his grounds at length. As long as the temple stood, no Jewish Christian was required to abjure Levitical worship. But the writer points out the superiority of the New to the Old Covenant, with its purely transitory and symbolical character, the dignity of Messiah, and the prerogative of the New as compared with the Old Testament revelation, and that the offering of Christ precludes all need of further offering for sin. The form of an Epistle only comes out towards the end of the document; the earlier portion is more like a treatise, carefully tracing out the chain of argument, and elaborating the subject with a more systematic arrangement than is found in any other Apostolical Epistle, not without some display of oratory. It was written originally not in Aramaic, but in Greek. It bears no Apostle's name, and cannot, in its present form, be the work of Paul's hand, though breathing his spirit. We cannot indeed urge, as has often been done, the passage speaking of the salvation first proclaimed by the Lord being handed down to us by those that heard it as conclusive against his authorship (Heb. ii. 3). For that is said in the name of the community addressed, and it would have been very far-fetched and gratuitous for the Apostle, who in fact had not heard the preaching of Jesus directly, to insert a saving clause, 'I have indeed received an inward revelation from the Lord.'

"But there are other proofs that he did not write the Epistle. The author invariably follows the Alexandrian version, even when differing completely in sense from the Hebrew (see Hebr. x. 5, especially), whereas Paul does not keep strictly to it, but much oftener translates for himself; secondly, Paul always named himself at the beginning of his Epistles; and lastly, the style is more polished, and flows more evenly and smoothly, but is less precise than Paul's, where the thoughts seem often to be struggling with the language, and the tone is less dialectical and more rhetorical, betraying a philosophical education.

"Nevertheless, the tradition of the Eastern Church, followed afterwards by the Western, has recognized the Apostle Paul as the principal author of the Epistle. It was attributed to him by the Syrian and Alexandrian Churches, those nearest the community it is addressed to, but the general belief was that he had not written it with his own hand, but used the services of another, either Luke or Clement. Clement of Alexandria's idea, that Luke translated the Apostle's Hebrew into Greek, is quite untenable, for the Epistle betrays clearly enough its original Greek composition, and Paul's friend or disciple must have contributed more to the authorship than mere translation. Clement of Rome cannot be regarded as the writer or joint writer, for then it would be the more unintelligible how the Epistle came to be so long rejected or ignored in the Roman Church, and the difference between this Epistle and his to the Corinthians is too great for both to be by the same author, besides that the use made in the latter of this one is further evidence against it. Tertullian's assertion that Barnabas is the writer stands quite alone. Nor is there any trace or hint in the ancient Church of the conjecture that Apollos wrote it; and as nothing more distinct is known of Apollos, it is a mere makeshift. It continues therefore to be the most probable view, that Luke wrote the Epistle under St. Paul's inspiration, and to this the most ancient tradition points." (Dollinger's "First Age of the Church," i. 109, Oxenham's translation.)

The divergence between Eastern and Western Christendom upon the authorship and canonicity of this Epistle is very remarkable. In noticing the agreement of the Eastern fathers upon this question, I have not yet appealed to the testimony of Cyril of Jerusalem. The Epistle, as almost all agree, was written to the Christian Jews of Jerusalem and those Palestinian Jews that could come up to the feasts, and Cyril unhesitatingly ascribes it to St. Paul. He flourished about 340. He ascribes to St. Paul fourteen Epistles (Lecture x. 18). He takes as his text for his fifth lecture Heb. xi. 1, 2, and for his eleventh Heb. i. 1, 2; altogether he refers to this Epistle nearly forty times, and in a considerable number of places refers to it as written by the Apostle just as he quotes the Romans as written by the Apostle, and in several places names St. Paul as the Apostle.

In the Western or Latin Church it seems not to have been received by the Church till shortly after the times of Jerome and Augustine. Though both these fathers constantly refer to it as Apostolical, they also, in referring to it, seem unwilling to pronounce absolutely on its authorship. A large number of quotations from Jerome implying some doubt or hesitation are given in Alford's introduction to this Epistle, pp. 23 to 25, second edition; one will suffice : "Relege ad Hebræaos Epistolam Pauli, sive cujuscumque alterius eam esse putas, quia jam inter ecclesiasticos sit recepta."

Augustine seems more confident respecting its Pauline authorship, as is manifest from the references in the same introduction, pp. 28, 29: "Audisti exhortantem Apostolum" (Serm. lv. 5); "audi quod dicit Apostolus" (Serm. lxxxii. 11). But in "De

Civitate Dei," xvi. 22 : "In epistolâ quæ scribitur ad Hebræos, quam plures Apostoli Pauli esse dicunt, quidam vero negant."

In accounting for the adverse testimony of the Western Church, it has been suggested that the Church of Cyprian's time was unwilling to receive it because it was thought to favour the harsh doctrine that those who had lapsed should not be restored to Church fellowship, as in chap. vi. 4, 5, 6, and x. 26. If sinners who have fallen after Baptism or conversion are excluded from grace, of course they must be excluded from Church communion. That the Epistle was received as a part of Scripture in the time of one of the first Roman bishops, a contemporary of St. Paul, is certain, and that Justin Martyr, who wrote and was probably martyred in Rome, quoted it as Scripture is equally certain, and yet Cyprian evidently considers it as not a part of the Canon. Irenæus, a Bishop of Gaul, does not refer to it; but it is a singular fact that as far as I can see, he never refers to our Lord's priesthood, just as St. Paul does not throughout the whole of the thirteen epistles.

The matter is deeply mysterious, but nothing can upset the fact that the Eastern Church—the Church best able to judge respecting such an historical matter as the authorship, considering that if not actually written by St. Paul, it was written under his direction or his influence, or his inspiration.

## DATE OF WRITING.

All agree that it was written some time after the liberation of St. Paul after his first imprisonment, and before the destruction of Jerusalem. Wordsworth supposes it was written about A.D. 64. Howson in Smith's "Dictionary of the Bible," about 63; Alford between 68 and 70; Westcott between 64 and 67. If it was not written under the influence or inspiration of St. Paul, it can only be fixed as written before the destruction of Jerusalem in 72.

## ANALYSIS OF THE EPISTLE.

i. 1-3. The Son of God equal in nature with the Father.
By whom He made the worlds (æons).
The brightness of His glory. The express image of His Person (or Essence).

## THE EPISTLE TO THE HEBREWS.

4-12. The Son of God greater than the angels.
Let all the angels of God worship Him.
Of the Son He saith, Thy throne, O God, is for ever and ever.
Thou, Lord, in the beginning hast laid, &c.

13-14. The Son, supreme Ruler under the Father. The angels only ministering spirits.

ii. 1-4. Our greater responsibility because of the Divine greatness of the Son.

5. The οἰκουμένη not under the angels,

11-14. But under the Son. Made Son of man in order that He might partake of flesh and blood,
And so taste of death for every man, and so

17-18. be a merciful and faithful High Priest.

iii. 1. The Apostle and High Priest of our profession.

2-6. Greater than Moses, being the Owner and Master of the house of God.

iii. 7, iv. 8. Greater than Joshua, as He leads His people into their true and eternal rest.

iv. 12. The Word of God.

v. 1-3. The great high priest, though the Son of God, must be of the same nature as ourselves.

4-6. Must be chosen of God.

7, 8, 9. Must learn obedience by suffering.

10. Cannot be of the order of Aaron, but must be of the order of MELCHISEDEC.

v. 11-14. Digression respecting the danger which the
vi. 1-13. Hebrews were in through their dulness, yet they needed encouragement.

20. Resumption of the doctrine respecting Melchisedec.

vii. 1-3. Superiority of the priesthood of Melchisedec to that of Aaron, in that he was made like unto the Son of God.

4, 5, 9. Received tithes from Abraham.

6-7. Blessed Abraham as being the greater of the two.

vii. 11. According to Psalm cx. another priest is to arise after Melchisedec's order.

## INTRODUCTION TO

- 20, 21. Which priest is made with an oath, and so is superior to the Aaronic priests, who are made without oath.
  - 23. The Aaronic priests were removed by death.
  - 28. The priesthood of the Son everlasting and unchangeable.
- viii. 1. The sum, or principal thing.
  - 1. We have an high priest—set on the throne of God.
  - 1. The minister of the true tabernacle.
- 6, 7, 8. The Mediator of the New Covenant.
  - 8. The New Covenant foretold by the prophets.
- ix. 1. The first covenant—its sanctuary and its furniture.
  - 2. The sanctuary consisted of two parts.
    - (1.) The Holy place, into which the priests constantly entered.
    - (2.) The Holy of Holies, into which the High Priest alone entered once a year.
  - 7. Not without blood.
  - 8. Signifying the imperfection of the Atonement.
- 11, 12. But Christ, with His own Blood, entered once for all into the Heavenly Holy of Holies.
  - 24. No repetition of His Sacrifice.
  - 25. He hath put away sin to the Sacrifice of Himself, and so has not continually to offer Himself.
  - 26. Will return a second time, not as did the Jewish High Priest, but without sin unto Salvation.
- x. 1, 3. In the law a remembrance (or *anamnesis*) of sins once a year.
  - 4. Because the blood of bulls and of goats cannot take away sins.
- 5, 6, 7. This can only be by the surrender of a most holy will.
  - 7. So the great High Priest has a Body prepared for Him, in which He comes to do the will of God by surrendering it.
  - 10. By which will, *i.e.*, by the offering of His Body in accordance with the will of God,
  - 14. We are sanctified once for all.

## THE EPISTLE TO THE HEBREWS. xxix

   21. The new and living way through the veil, *i.e.*, His flesh.
19, 20, 21, 22. By this we must draw near.
  25, 31. A second digression on the danger of Apostasy,
   32. And yet ending with encouragement.
   36. Need of patience.
  xi. 1. What is faith?
  2-40. Examples of faith overcoming the world.
  xii. 1, 2. The cloud of witnesses encourage us while we look to Jesus.
   5-12. The need of chastening.
   14. Follow peace and holiness. Example of Esau.
   18. Ye have not come to Sinai.
   22. Ye have come to Mount Zion.
   25. And yet ye are not safe. Ye may refuse him that speaketh.
   28. And that this be not so, hold fast grace.
  xiii. 1. Precepts of Holy Living.
   1-4. Be loving, hospitable, sympathising, chaste, open handed, contented.
   7. Remember your former teachers.
   9. Be established with grace.
   10. We have an altar.
   12. Jesus suffered without the gate. Let us bear His reproach.
   18. The Apostle asks their prayers.
   20. The Apostle's prayer for them.

# THE EPISTLE TO TITUS.

# A COMMENTARY.

## THE EPISTLE TO TITUS.

### CHAP. I.

PAUL, a servant of God, and an apostle of Jesus Christ, according to the faith of God's elect, and ᵃ the acknowledging of the truth ᵇ which is after godliness;

ᵃ 2 Tim. ii. 25.
ᵇ 1 Tim. iii. 16.
& vi. 3.

---

1. "*Paul, a servant of God, and an Apostle of Jesus Christ.*" He usually styles himself the servant (or slave) of Jesus Christ; here the servant of God.

"You observe," says St. Chrysostom, "how he uses these expressions indifferently, sometimes calling himself the servant of God, and sometimes of Jesus Christ; thus making no difference between the Father and the Son (of course as regards the dignity and perfections of their Divine Nature)."

"*According to the faith of God's elect, and the acknowledging,*" &c. Most commentators agree in interpreting this "according to" (κατὰ), as meaning "with a view to," "in furtherance of," the faith or belief of the elect of God in the hearts of men. St. Paul was a servant of God, and an Apostle of Jesus Christ, in order that those chosen by God might hold the faith "once for all delivered to the saints," and realize it in all its fulness, for such seems to mean the word "acknowledging." It is the full or perfect knowledge. Still we must remember that all truth has not only to be embraced by the soul, but to be acknowledged in the face of the world.

"*Which is after godliness.*" All parts of the truth, every aspect of it, every principle which it embodies, is designed to

**4**  IN HOPE OF ETERNAL LIFE. [TITUS.

‖ Or, *For.*
c 2 Tim. i. 1.
ch. iii. 7.
d Num. xxiii. 19. 2 Tim. ii. 13.
e Rom. xvi. 25. 2 Tim. i. 9. 1 Pet. i. 20.
f 2 Tim. i. 10.
g 1 Thess. ii. 4. 1 Tim. i. 11.

2 ‖ ᶜ In hope of eternal life, which God, ᵈ that cannot lie, promised ᵉ before the world began;

3 ᶠ But hath in due times manifested his word through preaching, ᵍ which is committed unto me

2. "Before the world began." Literally, "before eternal ages."

---

bring us to God, and to His obedience, and so is "according to godliness."

2. "In hope of eternal life." "In hope," that is, "resting on," "animated by" the hope of eternal life.

"Which God, that cannot lie, promised before the world began." "That cannot lie." This has been supposed to be interjected, as it were, because of the besetting sin of the Cretians (verse 12); but may it not be a reminiscence of such words as "The strength of Israel will not lie nor repent" (1 Sam. xv. 29)?

"Promised before the world began." A promise implies not only a promiser, but a person to whom the promise is made. To whom was the promise made? Evidently to the Eternal Word— the Second Person in the Godhead in the view of His Incarnation and consequent Reconciliation of all things to God. Note here the anxiety of the Apostle to shew that the Gospel, and what it involved, "the bringing of all men to God" (John xii. 32), was no new thing, but was in the counsels of the Blessed Trinity from all eternity. This was, of course, in answer to his unbelieving countrymen, who rejected it because, in their eyes, it was new: whereas their Prophets, their Psalmists, their wise men, all revealed it as the purpose of God—hidden in one sense, but to be revealed in its time.

3. "But hath in due times manifested his word through preaching." "In due times," after all expedients, the natural light, the law, philosophy, had been tried and been found utterly wanting to provide a remedy, when the chosen people had most deeply revolted, and the iniquity of the Amorites, *i.e.*, of the Gentiles, was full, then God made known the true and only possible remedy —the preaching of the Gospel.

"Through preaching," through heralding. Chrysostom has a fine passage noting the distinction between preaching and teaching.

[h] according to the commandment of God our Saviour;

4 To [i] Titus, [k] *mine* own son after [l] the common faith: [m] Grace, mercy, *and* peace, from God the Father and the Lord Jesus Christ our Saviour.

[h] 1 Tim. i. 1. & ii. 3. & iv. 10.
[i] 2 Cor. ii. 13. & vii. 13. & viii. 6, 16, 23. & xii. 18. Gal. ii. 3.
[k] 1 Tim. i. 2.
[l] Rom. i. 12. 2 Cor. iv. 13. 2 Pet. i. 1.
[m] Eph. i. 2. Col. i. 2. 1 Tim. i. 2. 2 Tim. i. 2.

---

4. "Mine own son."  "My true child."
"Mercy" omitted by ℵ, C.; retained by A., K., L., and most Cursives.

"For as a herald proclaims in the theatre in the presence of all, so also we preach; adding nothing, but declaring the things which we have heard. For the excellence of a herald consists in proclaiming to all what has really happened, not in adding or taking away anything. If, therefore, it is necessary to preach, it is necessary to do it with boldness of speech. Otherwise it is not preaching. On this account Christ did not say, '*Tell it upon the housetops,*' but '*preach upon the housetops,*' shewing by both the place and the manner what was to be done."

Bishop Wordsworth has a long and able note upon "His word" as meaning the Personal Word, the Logos, to which I refer the reader, and it seems more consonant with the sentence "manifested His word through preaching."

"Which was committed to me," *i.e.*, with which I was entrusted "according to the commandment of God our Saviour." When was the commandment given? The voice of the Father was never heard, but the word of the Son to St. Paul was "Depart, for I will send thee far hence to the Gentiles;" but all God's providence with respect to St. Paul, from his separation in his mother's womb onwards, was by the ordination and direction of God to bring about that he should be the Apostle of the Gentiles.

4. "To Titus, mine own son after the common faith." His own genuine son, not according to the flesh, but according to the faith, the one faith, "the faith once for all delivered to the Saints." It seems the same idea as he expresses in 1 Corinth. iv. 15: "In Christ Jesus I have begotten you through the Gospel."

"Grace, mercy, and peace." The word "mercy" seems doubtful, as the reader will see by the critical note. Still, if it be rejected, we have to face the question how it is that St. Paul twice sends to Timothy a greeting which includes mercy, and to Titus one

5 For this cause left I thee in Crete, that thou shouldest ⁿ set in order the things that are ‖ wanting, and ᵒ ordain elders in every city, as I had appointed thee:

ⁿ 1 Cor. xi. 34.
‖ Or, *left undone*.
ᵒ Acts xiv. 23. 2 Tim. ii. 2.

---

from which mercy is omitted. None of the commentators seem to entertain the question.

"Observe also how he offers the same prayers for the teacher as for the disciples and the multitude. For, indeed, he needs such prayers as much, or rather more, than they, by how much he has greater enmities to encounter, and is more exposed to the necessity of offending God. For the higher is the dignity, the greater are the dangers of the priestly office" (Chrysostom).

"From God the Father, and the Lord Jesus Christ our Saviour." This is also one of those (we may say) innumerable places which assert the Proper Deity of the Son of God; for how can grace and peace be invoked in the same breath from the Creator and a creature?

5. "For this cause left I thee in Crete, that thou shouldest." We learn from this that after his first imprisonment, Paul and Titus preached the Gospel in Crete, and made many converts; in fact, from the words "in every city," we should suppose that the island was permeated with Christianity. But the Church, though planted and rooted, was not yet organized, and St. Paul left this work to Titus whilst he himself went to other regions to lay the foundations of Churches, or to oversee them.

We are not, however, to suppose that this under Paul and Titus, was the first planting of Christianity in Crete. On the contrary, there were among the devout men who received the witness of the Holy Ghost, "Cretes and Arabians" (Acts ii. 11), and such we may be sure would proclaim among their countrymen both the teaching of the day of Pentecost, and the Death and Resurrection of Jesus, which was its root; and besides, one of the qualifications of the presbyters or bishops whom Titus was to appoint, was that they should have "believing children," which postulates some length of time for the bringing up of children in their own faith.

"That thou shouldest set in order the things that are wanting." This is a plain proof that St. Paul did not consider that each congregation of Christians was independent, so that it should organize

6 ᵖ If any be blameless, ᵠ the husband of one wife, ʳ having faithful children not accused of riot or unruly.

7 For a bishop must be blameless, as ˢ the steward of God; not selfwilled, not soon angry,

p 1 Tim. iii. 2, &c.
q 1 Tim. iii. 12.
r 1 Tim. iii. 4, 12.
s Matt. xxiv. 45. 1 Cor. iv. 1, 2.

---

itself, but each one had to receive its organization and ministry from him through Titus his delegate.

6. If any be blameless, the husband of one wife, having faithful children," &c. This and the two next verses are the reproduction of the directions given to Timothy (iii. 1): "A Bishop then must be blameless, the husband of one wife, given to hospitality . . . not given to wine, no striker, patient, not a brawler," &c.

"Having faithful children not accused of riot," &c. This refers to the children; the children of the man who is to be appointed overseer are not only to be Christians, *i.e.*, believers, but creditable and respectable. Chrysostom remarks: "If he cannot keep in order those whom he has had with him from the beginning, whom he has brought up, and over whom he had power both by the laws, and by nature, how will he be able to benefit those without? For if the incompetency of the father had not been great, he would not have allowed those to become bad who from the first he had under his power. For it is not possible, indeed it is not, that one should turn out ill who is brought with much care and has received great attention . . . It, occupied in the pursuit of wealth, he has made his children a secondary concern, and not bestowed much care upon them, even so he is unworthy."

7. "For a bishop must be blameless, as the steward of God." A steward is one who has the goods or estate of another committed to him, and the Christian minister has the truth of God and the administration of the Christian Sacraments committed to him, that he should disburse them, "Who is that faithful and wise steward whom his Lord shall make ruler over his household to give them their portion of meat in due season? (Luke xii. 42). For the exposition of this character of the Christian minister see notes on 1 Tim. iii. 1-8.

"Not self-willed." He must have a deep conviction that he may be mistaken. Oliver Cromwell wrote to the Presbyterian ministers of Edinburgh: "I beseech you in the bowels of Christ, think it

- not given to wine, no striker, " not given to filthy lucre;

8 ˣ But a lover of hospitality, a lover of ‖ good men, sober, just, holy, temperate;

9 ʸ Holding fast ᶻ the faithful word ‖ as he hath been taught, that he may be able ᵃ by sound doctrine both to exhort and to convince the gainsayers.

---

ᵗ Lev. x. 9.
Eph. v. 18.
1 Tim. iii. 3, 8.
ᵘ 1 Tim. iii. 3, 8.
1 Pet. v. 2.
ˣ 1 Tim. iii. 2.
‖ Or, *good things.*
ʸ 2 Thes. ii. 15. 2 Tim. i. 13.
ᶻ 1 Tim. i. 15. & iv. 9. & vi. 3. 2 Tim. ii. 2.
‖ Or, *in teaching.*
ᵃ 1 Tim. i. 10. & vi. 3. 2 Tim. iv. 3. ch. ii. 1.

---

possible you may be mistaken." And yet when a man's conscience unites with the word of God in assuring him that he is right in his determination, and he has the support of those who are equally honest and enlightened with himself, he must be fearless in his course of action.

"Not given to wine." St. Paul could scarcely have written this if he had thought that asceticism was the true perfection of the ministerial life.

"No striker." He should do all things by admonition or rebuke, but not by insolence. What necessity, tell me, for insult? He ought to terrify, to alarm, to penetrate the soul with the fear of hell. But he that is insulted becomes more impudent, and rather despises him that insults him. "Nothing produces contempt more than insult; it disgraces the insolent person, and prevents his being respected as he ought to be." (Chrysostom.)

8. "But a lover of hospitality," &c. It is one of the questions asked of the bishop about to be consecrated whether he will show himself gentle, and be merciful for Christ's sake to poor and needy people, and to all strangers destitute of help? Sometimes incumbents of small benefices, and very generally curates, are poor and needy people, and would be thankful for that hospitality which some bishops show abundantly and others do not.

"A lover of good men." Rather, a lover of what is good.

"Sober." That is, under self-control.

"Just." Not given to favouritism—doing nothing by partiality.

9. "Holding fast the faithful word as he hath been taught," &c. The faithful word is in all probability the form of sound words of 2 Tim. i. 13, but some suppose it to be the faithful sayings which are cited in the Epistles to Timothy.

"As he hath been taught" should rather be rendered, "ac-

10 For ᵇ there are many unruly and vain talkers and ᶜ deceivers, ᵈ especially they of the circumcision:

11 Whose mouths must be stopped, ᵉ who subvert whole houses, teaching things which they ought not, ᶠ for filthy lucre's sake.

ᵇ 1 Tim. i. 6.
ᶜ Rom. xvi. 18.
ᵈ Acts xv. 1.
ᵉ Matt. xxiii. 14. 2 Tim. iii. 6.
ᶠ 1 Tim. vi. 5.

---

cording to the teaching," that is, according to the original teaching of the Apostles—the principles of the faith which they impressed upon all the churches when they first founded them.

"That he may be able by sound doctrine both to exhort and to convince." Rather that he may be able both to exhort in the sound doctrine and to convince—rather to convict, *i.e.*, of saying what is false—the gainsayers, that is, those who contradict the truth.

Notice how so early as this men were directed back to the original teaching. Thus St. John: "Brethren, I write no new commandment unto you, but that which ye have heard from the beginning" (1 John ii. 7). Even in this first age anything new was considered false. St. Paul took every pains to prove, not only that he preached the original Gospel, but that he said no other things than what were written in the law and in the prophets.

10. "For there are many unruly and vain talkers and deceivers, specially," &c. To the bitter end they of the circumcision were the opponents of this Apostle and of his doctrine. They resented the freedom of the Gentiles, which St. Paul proclaimed everywhere. They would have all men to be Jews, as narrow, as carnal, as much slaves to the letter as they themselves were. Such men were "vain talkers and deceivers." We can imagine how they could quote text after text of the Old Testament to uphold the permanency of the law: and yet all to no purpose, to no purposes of holiness and truth, for the spirit of both dispensations was against them.

11. "Whose mouths must be stopped." How were the mouths of these men to be stopped? By sound argument, of course, by the setting forth of the faithful word; but also, we doubt not, by authoritatively interdicting them from speaking in the Christian assemblies, by deposing them as heretics from the ministry.

"Who subvert whole houses." By creeping into them and

12 ᵍOne of themselves, *even* a prophet of their own, said, 13 This witness is true. ʰWherefore rebuke them sharply, that they may be ⁱsound in the faith;

ᵍ Acts xvii. 28.
ʰ 2 Cor. xiii. 10. 2 Tim. iv. 2.
ⁱ ch. ii. 2.

The Cretians *are* alway liars, evil beasts, slow bellies.

---

leading captive the silly women (2 Tim. iii. 6). The words can only refer to stealthy, creeping, underhand ways of propagating schisms.

"Teaching things which they ought not, for filthy lucre's sake." St. Paul, a discerner of spirits, knew the secret motives of these men, and exposed them.

12. "One of themselves, even a prophet of their own, said, The Cretians," &c. The spirit of poetry and that of prophecy are akin, and so the Apostle quotes the Cretian Epimenides as a prophet. It is remarkable that Cicero (cited in Alford) mentions him as a prophet. "Qui concitatione quadam animi, aut soluto liberoque motu futura præsentiunt, ut Baris Bœotius, ut Epimenides Cres." ("Cicero, de Divin." i. 18.) He was born at Phæstus, and lived at Gnossus in Crete, in the sixth century before Christ. The whole line is said by Jerome to be taken from the Chresmi of Epimenides. (Speaker's Commentary.)

"The Cretians are always liars." This part of the verse is quoted in Callimachus in a Hymn to Zeus. The Cretians had a tomb of Jupiter, as if he was mortal and had died, and Callimachus praising him as immortal naturally cited this as a proof of the falsehood of the Cretians.

"Evil beasts." Rather, fierce wild beasts.

"Slow bellies." Indolent and gluttonous.

13. "This witness is true," &c. We have the character of the Cretians testified to in heathen authors, as Livy and Polybius, as being what is described by the Apostle. Several instances are cited by Alford in his Prolegomena to this Epistle.

"Rebuke them sharply." Their disposition was forward, deceitful, and dissolute. Such characters will not be managed by mildness, therefore "rebuke them" sharply. Give them, he says, a stroke that cuts deep.

"That they may be sound in the faith."

14 ᵏ Not giving heed to Jewish fables, and ˡ commandments of men, that turn from the truth.

15 ᵐ Unto the pure all things *are* pure: but ⁿ unto them that are defiled and unbelieving *is* nothing pure; but even their mind and conscience is defiled.

ᵏ 1 Tim. i. 4.
& iv. 7. 2 Tim.
iv. 4.
ˡ Isa. xxix. 13.
Matt. xv. 9.
Col. ii. 22.
ᵐ Luke xi. 39.
40, 41. Rom.
xiv. 14, 20.
1 Cor. vi. 12.
& x. 23, 25.
1 Tim. iv. 3, 4.
ⁿ Rom. xiv. 23.

---

14. "Not giving heed to Jewish fables," &c. If they are sound in the faith, if they hold firmly the great truths of the Gospel— the Incarnation, Death, and Resurrection of the Son of God—they will have no taste for Rabbinical traditions, and will take no notice of such contemptible matters. Such things can only "turn from the truth" by fixing the mind upon what is false and degrading.

The same with "the commandments of men." These may be the commandments respecting meats in Leviticus, from the observance of which the Gentiles had been emancipated, and which when reimposed upon them were so done by mere human authority, and were on the same level with any purely human precept. The observance of such commands, as much as the giving heed to traditions, turns from the truth. It is part of a decayed and vanishing system, and interferes with the obedience to a nobler and purer one.

15. "Unto the pure all things are pure, but unto them that are," &c. There can be no doubt but that the primary allusion here is to defilement by meats forbidden by the Judaizers. It is a parallel passage to Rom. xv. 20: "All things are pure, but it is evil for that man which eateth with offence." The defiled and unbelieving are those who are not purified by the reception of Christian truth, and whose consciences are yet under bondage to the Levitical system, and not made free by the law of Christ. Such persons are under the constant apprehension of sinning in matters of meats, drinks, washing, &c. The thorough cleansing by the Spirit, and the hearty reception of the truth of Christ, would place them in a sphere above such doubts and misgivings.

But the sentiment of the Apostle is of the widest application. It is literally true that to the pure all things are pure. Things which suggest thoughts and deeds of impurity do not suggest impurity to them. Their mind's vision turns away from impurity,

16 They profess that they know God; but °in works they deny *him*, being abominable, and disobedient, ᵖ and unto every good work || reprobate.

° 2 Tim. iii. 5. Jude 4.
ᵖ Rom. i. 28. 2 Tim. iii. 8.
|| Or, *void of judgment*.

and is not contaminated by it: whereas to the defiled the most innocent words and things suggest sin and evil.

"Even their mind and conscience is defiled." Their mind, their memory, their imagination, dwells upon what is bad. Their very conscience—the judge within them—is blunted, and has lost its power of instant decision and direction in the right path.

16. " They profess that they know God; but in works they deny Him," &c. Some suppose that this is an allusion to the claim of the Gnostics to a superior knowledge of God, but it seems to be capable of the widest application. All Christianity is based upon the confession of a creed of definite truth respecting God, and His Son, and His Spirit. No such profession of the lips can be of any avail unless it is lived to: and they who live evil lives deny God, and undo all the effect of their profession.

"Being abominable and disobedient, and to every good work reprobate." No words worse than these could be applied to the lives of the heathen : and yet this is all said of unworthy Christians.

## CHAP. II.

ᵃ 1 Tim. i. 10. & vi. 3. 2 Tim. i. 13. ch. i. 9.

BUT speak thou the things which become ᵃ sound doctrine :

1. " But speak thou the things which become sound doctrine." " Speak thou." The " thou " is emphatic, and is contrasted with the " vain talkers and deceivers " of the last chapter. " Whatever others teach do thou teach," &c. The sound doctrine of the Incarnation and Atonement has teaching which becomes it, which is fitting to it, and this fitting doctrine is the holiness and goodness of the daily Christian life in the Church, in the family, and in private.

2 That the aged men be ‖ sober, grave, temperate, ᵇ sound in faith, in charity, in patience.

3 ᶜ The aged women likewise, that *they be* in behaviour as becometh ‖ holiness, not ‖ false accusers, not given to much wine, teachers of good things;

4 That they may teach the young women to be

‖ Or, *vigilant.*
ᵇ ch. i. 13.
ᶜ 1 Tim. ii. 9, 10, & iii. 11. 1 Pet. iii. 3, 4.
‖ Or, *holy women.*
‖ Or, *make-bates*, 2 Tim. iii. 3.

---

4. "Teach;" *i.e.*, school, train.

2. "That the aged men be sober," &c.—*i.e.*, to be vigilant (νηφαλίους). Their mere age is not to be relied upon as putting them above the necessity of constant watchfulness.

"Grave" (σεμνούς). Serious, as becomes those who have one foot in the grave.

"Temperate." Rather, sober-minded and self-restrained.

"Sound in faith, in charity, in patience." All these faculties of the soul or spirit are to be in healthy activity, the sound faith will strive to realize the whole Christian faith which is set before it in the Christian Revelation, the charity will embrace all the brotherhood, the patience will receive submissively all the dispensations of God.

3. "The aged women likewise, that they be in behaviour as becometh holiness." "That they," as the revisers have it, "be reverent in demeanour." The word "as becometh holiness" has somewhat of a priestly sound, and may properly be rendered (as Alford) "reverent in deportment."

"Not false accusers." If they are not to be false accusers, *i.e.*, slanderers, they must not be busy-bodies, or tale-bearers, or fond of gossip, for these things naturally, indeed one might almost say inevitably, lead to slander.

"Not given,"—the original is, not "enslaved" to much wine.

Wine, it is to be remembered, was not then so much a luxury as with us; nor was it ever strengthened with alcohol, as with us.

"Teachers of good things." Not only of Christian or Scripture truth, but of its application to all family and private life, as appears from the next verse.

4. "That they may teach the young women to be sober," that is, "to be self restrained and discreet." "Teach" is rather

| Or, *wise.*
d 1 Tim. v. 14.
e 1 Cor. xiv. 34.
Eph. v. 22.
Col. iii. 18.
1 Tim. ii. 11.
1 Pet. iii. 1, 5.
f Rom. ii. 24.
1 Tim. vi. 1.
| Or, *discreet.*

g 1 Tim. iv. 12.
1 Pet. v. 3.

‖ sober, <sup>d</sup> to love their husbands, to love their children,

5 *To be* discreet, chaste, keepers at home, good, <sup>e</sup> obedient to their own husbands, <sup>f</sup> that the word of God be not blasphemed.

6 Young men likewise exhort to be ‖ sober minded.

7 <sup>g</sup> In all things shewing thyself a pattern of

---

5. "Keepers at home." א, A., C., D., E., F., G., read, "workers at home;" but H., K., L., P., and most Cursives read as in Rec. Text.

"train," and there seems an allusion to the Σωφρονισταί of the Greek cities. So Wordsworth, "This rather agrees with the sort of duties here inculcated, in which the learners must be disciplined or trained, rather than be merely taught by word of mouth."

5. "To be discreet, chaste." Again the oft repeated word, σώφρων. Our "prudent" seems to come nearest to it.

"Keepers at home." Some read, "workers at home," but the meaning is the same. Those who work at home are keepers of their homes.

"Obedient to their own husbands, that the word of God be not blasphemed." Which it would be if the reception of Christianity loosened family ties, and was supposed to release from family obligations, and to undermine due subordination in the household.

6. "Young men likewise exhort to be sober minded," *i.e.*, (as before) "to be self-restrained." Most of the ancient commentators refer the precept to sensual lusts. Thus Chrysostom: "Nothing is so difficult at that age as to overcome unlawful pleasures:" but may it not be capable of a wider application? Certainly at the present day it requires to be applied to the whole tone of mind, and even religious behaviour of young men. The Apostle's exhortation should now be turned thus "Say nothing to feed their vanity. Be careful not so to address them as to make them conceited, overweening, priggish, self-asserting." Such a precept, so rendered, should be written over the doors of young men's Christian associations, and places where Bible-classes for the young are held.

7. "In all things shewing thyself a pattern of good works." St. Paul deems it necessary not only to instruct Titus as to what he is

good works: in doctrine *shewing* uncorruptness, gravity, ʰ sincerity,

8 ¹ Sound speech, that cannot be condemned; ᵏ that he that is of the contrary part ˡ may be ashamed, having no evil thing to say of you.

9 *Exhort* ᵐ servants to be obedient unto their own masters, *and* to please *them* well ⁿ in all *things ;* not ‖ answering again ;

ʰ Eph. vi. 24.
ⁱ 1 Tim. vi. 3.
ᵏ Neh. v. 9.
1 Tim. v. 14.
1 Pet. ii. 12,
15. & iii. 16.
ˡ 2 Thess. iii. 14.
ᵐ Eph. vi. 5.
Col. iii. 22.
1 Tim. vi. 1, 2.
1 Pet. ii. 18.
ⁿ Eph. v. 24.
‖ Or, *gain saying*.

---

7. "Sincerity" omitted by ℵ, A., C.; retained by K., L., and many Cursives.
8. "Of you." ℵ, C., D., E., F., G., K., L., P., most Cursives, Ital., Vulg., Syriac, read, "of us." A. reads "of yon."

to teach; but also to remind him that he must teach it by his life. Men in the highest ecclesiastical positions seem to require to be put in mind of the obligations of the every day Christian life.

"In doctrine shewing uncorruptness, gravity," &c. Let there be in thy teaching no taint of the errors, Judaical or Gnostical, against which thou hast to warn others. Do not attempt to meet heretics or false teachers half way. Let thy teaching also be free from anything approaching to levity or joking. Ever bear in mind the unspeakable greatness of the truths thou hast to deliver.

8. "Sound speech, that cannot be condemned." By whom? Evidently only by those who from their greater knowledge and holy Christian character have a right to judge. Critics, of course, there will always be whose judgment is generally, so far as its peremptoriness is concerned, in inverse proportion to their capability of forming a right one.

"That he that is of the contrary part may be ashamed, having no evil," &c. Affording, as Chrysostom says, no pretext to those who are willing to censure.

9. "Exhort servants to be obedient to . . . God our Saviour in all things." This is another direction respecting servants or slaves that they are to be taught to be submissive and obedient. That there are so many declarations of the same sort is perhaps to be accounted for by the danger into which Christian slaves would fall when they learnt the absolute equality of all men in the sight of God, all equally the work of God's hands, all equally redeemed, and, if Christians, all equally partakers of the one Baptism, and the Body and Blood of Christ. Such would naturally ask, If we

Marginal notes:
o Matt. v. 16.
Phil. ii. 15.
p Rom. v. 15.
ch. iii. 4, 5.
1 Pet. v. 12.
‖ Or, that bringeth salvation to all men, hath appeared.
q Luke iii. 6.
John i. 9.
1 Tim. ii. 4.

10 Not purloining, but shewing all good fidelity; °that they may adorn the doctrine of God our Saviour in all things.

11 For ᵖ the grace of God ‖ that bringeth salvation ᑫ hath appeared to all men.

11. See marginal reading.

are all equal in such extraordinary benefits, ought we, the people of Christ, to be subject to the caprice of men? To this St. Paul in effect answers, "For the Gospel's sake you must, for no greater argument could be alleged against the Gospel by the heathen than that it released slaves from their obligation to obey their masters."

Not only are they to be obedient, but to shew a cheerful obedience; "to please them well in all things," which would be impossible if their service appeared forced or constrained. Thus Chrysostom: "For if (the slave) restrain not his hand or his unruly tongue, how shall the Gentile admire the doctrine that is among us? But if they see their slave, who has been taught the philosophy of Christ, displaying more self-command than their own philosophers, and serving with all meekness and goodwill, they will in every way admire the power of the Gospel."

"Not answering again," *i.e.*, "not contradicting." The Syriac (quoted by Ellicot) seems to mean, not thwarting or setting themselves against their masters' plain wishes or orders.

10. "Not purloining," which must have been a very common sin amongst a class (as Chrysostom tells us) not as a rule instructed in morals, and so exposed to temptation all through the day.

"Shewing all good fidelity, that they may adorn the doctrine," &c. If any imagine that slaves were too harshly treated in being thus required to submit implicitly to heathen masters, it should be remembered that Christ promised by the mouth of this very Apostle that He would reckon all obedience, not only to the good and gentle, but also to the froward, as done to Himself: no promise can be more express than that of Ephes. vi. 8: "With good will doing service (as the servants of Christ) as to the Lord, and not unto men, knowing that whatsoever good thing any man doeth, the same shall he receive of the Lord."

11. "For the grace of God that bringeth salvation hath appeared

CHAP. II.]     DENYING UNGODLINESS.     17

12 Teaching us ʳ that, denying ungodliness ˢ and worldly lusts, we should live soberly, righteously, and godly, in this present world;
13 ᵗ Looking for that blessed ᵘ hope, and the

ʳ Luke i. 75.
Rom. vi. 19.
ˢ Eph. i. 4.
Col. i. 22.
1 Thess. iv. 7.
ˢ 1 Pet. iv. 2.
1 John ii. 16.
ᵗ 1 Cor. i. 7.
Phil. iii. 20.
2 Pet. iii. 12.
ᵘ Acts xxiv. 15. Col. i. 5, 23. ch. i. 2, & iii. 7.

---

12. "World." "Age" and "aiōn."

to all men." There is some doubt as to the rendering. The exact order of the words is, "For there hath appeared the grace of God (the grace) bringing salvation to all men." When St. Paul wrote, the grace of God had not been manifested to all. But it brought salvation within the reach of all, before it was manifested to each man. So that the translation of the latest revision is probably the correct one. "The grace of God hath appeared, bringing salvation to all men." So also Ellicott and Alford. The grace of God not only offers salvation to all men, but its first word is the assurance that Christ died as an atonement for the sins of all men.

12. "Teaching us that, denying ungodliness and worldly lusts," &c. This is the intent of the Gospel, this is the purpose of the coming of Christ. This is set forth in the Hymn of Zacharias: "That He would grant unto us that we, being delivered out of the hands of our enemies, might serve him without fear, in holiness and righteousness before Him all the days of our lives." Unless this is fulfilled in us Christ has, as yet, come to us in vain.

"We should live soberly, righteously, and godly, in the present world." How often do we pray for this! "Grant, O most Merciful Father, for His sake, that we may hereafter live a godly, righteous, and sober life."

13. "Looking for that blessed hope, and the glorious appearing of the great God and our Saviour Jesus Christ." "The great God and our Saviour Jesus Christ" seems, according to the Authorized, to indicate two Divine Persons—the First and Second Persons of the Trinity; but looking to the original, and taking it with exact literalness, we should render the passage: "Looking for the blessed hope and Epiphany of the glory of the great God and Saviour of us, Jesus Christ,"—the great God and Saviour of us being, in such case, indubitably the same Person Who is both the great God and our Saviour. Thus it was understood by the Fathers, whose ver-

C

glorious ˣappearing of the great God and our Saviour Jesus Christ:

<sup>a</sup> Col. iii. 4.
2 Tim. iv. 1, 8.
Heb. ix. 23.
1 Pet. i. 7.
1 John iii. 2.

For examination of the "great God and Saviour of us," see below.

nacular was the Greek. Thus Clement of Alexandria: "This Word then is the Christ, the cause of both our being at first (for He was in God) and of our well-being. This very Word has now appeared as man. He alone being both—both God and Man . . . according to that inspired Apostle of the Lord. The grace of God which bringeth salvation . . . and appearing of the glory of the great God and our Saviour Jesus Christ." ("Exhortation to the Heathen," chap. i.) Again, Hippolytus: "In order that, maintaining the faith that is written and anticipating the things that are to be, thou mayest keep thyself void of offence, both towards God and man, looking for that blessed hope and appearing of our God and Saviour." ("Treatise on Christ and Antichrist," chap. lxvii.) Athanasius: "The Son is called the great God" ("Treatise on the Essence of the Father, and Son, and Holy Spirit," quoted in Wordsworth). Again Chrysostom: "Looking for the blessed hope and the glorious appearing of our great God and Saviour. Where are those who say that the Son is inferior to the Father?" And Theodoret: "But he called Christ the great God, convicting the heretics of blasphemy."

But another—and almost, one may say—overwhelming reason is that the word Epiphany, or Manifestation, or Appearing, is said many times of Christ, never of the Father. We have St. Paul himself saying of the Father, "Whom no man hath seen nor can see" (1 Tim. vi. 16). The Epiphany, for which the Christian is directed to look, is always that of Christ to judgment. It is true that Christ shall appear in His own glory, and in that of His Father, but the Father invests the Son with His glory, in which the Son appears, the Father Himself not appearing.

It would seem, then, that there could be no doubt about the rendering; but Dean Alford has argued, principally from the use of the term God our Saviour, as applied to God the Father in the Pastoral Epistles, that the "great God" applies to the Father, and Saviour to the Son. I do not think, however, that his reasoning is conclusive, particularly when we consider that there is no

14 ʸ Who gave himself for us, that he might redeem us from all iniquity, ᶻ and purify unto himself ᵃ a peculiar people, ᵇ zealous of good works.

15 These things speak, and ᶜ exhort, and re-

ʸ Gal. i. 4. & ii. 20. Eph. v. 2. 1 Tim. ii. 6.
ᶻ Heb. ix. 14.
ᵃ Exod. xv. 16. & xix. 5. Deut. vii. 6. & xiv. 2. & xxvi. 18. 1 Pet. ii. 9.
ᵇ Eph. ii. 10. ch. iii. 8.
ᶜ 2 Tim. iv. 2.

---

Epiphany of the Person of the Father to be expected: the Epiphany of the Son is in the glory of the whole Trinity. But, as the Dean says, whichever way it is taken, it is decisive in favour of the Godhead of Christ. If in the way of our authorized translation, then the Son of God shares fully in the Epiphany of the glory of the Father, which implies His equality with the Father, for God has emphatically said that He will not give His glory to another: and if the title, the Great God, is given to the Saviour, then it is only what was given to Him long before by St. Thomas, "My Lord and my God," and by Isaiah in prophecy, when he spoke of Him as "The mighty God."

14. "Who gave himself for us, that he might redeem us from all iniquity." The redemption is twofold in its application to us. It redeems us both from the guilt and the power of iniquity.

"And purify unto himself a peculiar people." A people of possession. The phrase is taken from Deut. vii. 5: "The Lord thy God hath chosen thee to be to him a peculiar people" (λαὸν περιούσιον), a people by purchase peculiarly His own. This also is an incontrovertible proof of the Godhead of Jesus Christ: for by His Redemption He purchases Christians to be His peculiar people, just as the God of the Old Testament purchased the Israelites to be His purchased possession.

"Zealous of good works." "Dost thou not see that our part is necessary, not merely work, but zealous: we should with all alacrity, with a becoming earnestness, go forward in virtue." (Chrysostom.)

15. "These things speak, and exhort, and rebuke with all authority." "These things." That is, the Advent of Christ in glory, and His Redemption of us by the shedding of His Blood.

"And exhort and rebuke"—*i.e.*, apply them in the way of exhortation.

<sup>d</sup> 1 Tim. iv. 12. buke with all authority. <sup>d</sup> Let no man despise thee.

---

"And rebuke." Exhort all the flock to be influenced by these greatest of things—rebuke them if they come short.

"Let no man despise thee." Titus being probably an older man, he omits "thy youth," which he mentions in the corresponding message to Timothy.

## CHAP. III.

<sup>a</sup> Rom. xiii. 1.
1 Pet. ii. 13.
<sup>b</sup> Col. i. 10.
2 Tim. ii. 21.
Heb. xiii. 21.
<sup>c</sup> Eph. iv. 31.
<sup>d</sup> 2 Tim. ii. 24, 25.
<sup>e</sup> Phil. iv. 5.
<sup>f</sup> Eph. iv. 2.
Col. iii. 12.

PUT them in mind <sup>a</sup> to be subject to principalities and powers, to obey magistrates, <sup>b</sup> to be ready to every good work,

2 <sup>c</sup> To speak evil of no man, <sup>d</sup> to be no brawlers, but <sup>e</sup> gentle, showing all <sup>f</sup> meekness unto all men.

---

1. "Put them in mind to be subject to principalities and powers, to obey magistrates," &c. These injunctions were probably much needed both at that time and in that country. The Jews were in a state of rebellion everywhere, and the Cretians were ill-affected to their conquerors the Romans, and were always a turbulent and disaffected race.

"To obey magistrates" signifies to be obedient. These precepts were for the temporal advantage of the Cretians, for what benefit could they get by rebellion against the crushing power of the Roman Empire?

"To be ready to every good work." In such a context this must mean every good work of patient submission.

2. "To speak evil of no man," &c.—*i.e.*, very probably (from the context) to take no part in seditious harangues against the powers that be.

"To be no brawlers"—*i.e.*, not to be contentious (so Revisers).

"But gentle, showing all meekness unto all men." He here

3 For <sup>g</sup> we ourselves also were sometimes foolish, disobedient, deceived, serving divers lusts and pleasures, living in malice and envy, hateful, *and* hating one another.

4 But after that <sup>h</sup> the kindness and ∥ love of <sup>i</sup> God our Saviour toward man appeared,

5 <sup>k</sup> Not by works of righteousness which we

<sup>g</sup> 1 Cor. vi. 11. Eph. ii. 1. Col. i. 21. & iii. 7   1 Pet. iv. 3.
<sup>h</sup> ch. ii. 11.
∥ Or, *pity*.
<sup>i</sup> 1 Tim. ii. 3.
<sup>k</sup> Rom. iii. 20. & ix. 11. & xi. 6.   Gal. ii. 16. Eph. ii. 4, 8, 9. 2 Tim. i. 9.

---

3. "Sometimes;" that is, "aforetime—in times past."

seems to have in mind the contentious character of the Cretians—they were, according to their own prophet-poet, "savage wild beasts" (κακὰ θηρία, i. 12). And so for their own temporal and eternal good the Apostle would have them to be, by God's grace, the very opposite of this.

3. "For we ourselves also were sometimes foolish, disobedient, deceived," &c. Whom does he allude to when he speaks of "we ourselves?" The words of the original are very emphatic. No doubt he means the unconverted Jews. The Jews in the time of our Lord were emphatically an adulterous generation. They were like the Cretians in turbulence and sedition. Josephus speaks of Jerusalem as a most wicked city. The Apostle here associates himself with his unbelieving countrymen as one of them, though personally even in his unconverted state he had "lived in all good conscience towards God."

4. "But after that the kindness and love of God our Saviour toward man," &c. "God our Saviour" here is God the Father: "God so loved the world that he gave His only begotten." As the Father is the fountain of Deity, so He is the fountain of love. The Redemption by the Son is through the love of the Father.

5. "Not by works of righteousness which we have done, but by his mercy he saved us," &c. The Jews, and those who are Jewish minded, would come setting forth their former innocence of life, their keeping the law of the ten commandments from their youth up, as the reason why they should partake of the benefits of Christ's Redemption; but supposing that men desire salvation who have not lived innocent lives, and who have not kept the law, what then? Why then comes Salvation by Mercy. "By his MERCY he saved us." Salvation is to be of grace, so that they who

have done, but according to his mercy he saved us, by

---

have lived evil lives may come for salvation, and not be deterred by the thought of the evil of the past.

By (διὰ) the washing, or rather font, or bath, or laver, the word λουτρὸν signifying not the act of washing, but the bath or font in which the person is washed, and so certifies that this place does not allude to an internal or subjective act of God upon the mind or will only, but to an act of God that cannot be dissociated or disjoined from an outward visible λουτρὸν or font or bath.

This happens to be the only place where St. Paul uses the word new birth or regeneration, and he associates it with an outward application of water, which takes place at the very beginning of the Christian career. But is it not too much to say even of an ordinance or Sacrament ordained by Christ Himself that God "saves us by it?" No; because the Apostle supposes that it is with Titus as with the Corinthians: "I speak as to wise men, judge ye what I say." St. Paul was not so insensate as to say, or Titus to believe, that Baptism redeems us, or that it turns a bad man into a good one, or that those once baptized will never fall away; but what he means is that God the all-wise uses the time of Baptism, or the hand of the baptizer, or the formula, embodying the name of the ever-blessed Trinity, as the means by which He first applies Redemption.

The doctrine of Baptismal Regeneration, or of engrafting into the Body of Christ by Baptism, is perfectly consistent with common sense, and is in accordance with what every one of us does in everyday life. Suppose that a man desires to engage a servant, he gives to that man at the time he engages him everything needful to the man to enable him to fulfil his service: but supposing that the servant required some sort of extra strength or help, and the master who desired to engage him was able to give him such internal strength or help, surely he would do so. What would be the use of putting a man into a position of trust, and giving him instruments or tools to enable him to fulfil the service of trust if he had no strength to do so? Now this is the theory or idea of Baptismal Regeneration. God, if His word is to be believed, desires the services (to say nothing higher) of all men. Of all men, that is, to whom by His providence He brings the message

¹the washing of regeneration, and renewing of the Holy Ghost;   ¹ John iii. 3, 5. Eph. v. 26. 1 Pet. iii. 21.

---

of salvation. The lowest idea of Baptism is that it implies an engagement to serve God, and in the first age of the Church followed immediately upon the reception of the Gospel message, because the message of Salvation could only come to any man by the providence of God, and the mere fact of its coming to any man was to assure him that he must no longer serve God's enemy, but must now henceforth serve God. But this is not all. Suppose that a man was desirous of engaging a servant, who on account of parentage, or from misconduct of his parents or of himself, was under a disability. Surely *if the engager of the servant was able* he would remove the disability at once, at the first. Now this God, according to the Church view, does in Baptism, because Baptism is the beginning, the door—in fact, that beginning of all beginnings, the Birth. But (and we must now face objections) is it possible that God should, as the Apostle says, save us by such a thing as Baptism? is it not too simple, too common, too little thought of? It seems a mere nothing. Well, that depends upon whether God is a God Who chooses things which are not to bring to nought things that are. But what, after all, is Baptism? Is it the act of a registrar, or of a policeman, or of a justice of the peace, or even of the head of the family? No; it is the act of the minister, or quasi-minister of an institution, of which it is much too little to say that it is unique in this world. There can be no similar institution in the universe, for in this world only did the Son of God become Incarnate, that He might found in it the Church, which He hath purchased with His Blood. Baptism is a part of an institution which the Eternal Son of God came to establish, which He established in order that men might be so united to Him as to be members of a Body, of which He is the Head, against which the gates of Hell are not to prevail—that is, it is to last till His Second Coming. Is there any difficulty to a believing mind in thinking that at the time when a mortal enters such an institution he should be gifted with grace to fulfil its obligations?

But we are pertinaciously reminded that the Baptism spoken of in the New Testament is that of Adults. To this we answer, it must

6 ᵐ Which he shed on us † abundantly through Jesus Christ our Saviour;

ᵐ Ezek. xxxvi. 25. Joel ii. 28. John i. 16. Acts ii. 33, & x. 45. Rom. v. 5.
† Gr. *richly*.

be so in any place where the church is a missionary body which has not won the society of the country to its belief; but when this is the case we ask, Does the Saviour desire that children should be brought up in his service, or only embrace it at some future time of life? There can be but one answer to this question. Every word which the Saviour says of little children would lead us to believe that He values their spiritual well-being, and looks for their services quite as much as much as He does for those of believing adults.

The only answer worth anything which can be alleged against all this is Calvinism. Calvinism teaches that God does not desire the services of all men—only of a very small number; and so Baptism, in the vast majority of instances, is no sign of God's good-will, no call to serve Him, and so consequently is not accompanied with any grace for the due use of which the person baptized can be held responsible.

We have no reason then to restrict, or fritter away, the meaning of this place. It teaches the same doctrine as Romans vi, that we are mystically and sacramentally buried with Christ by our Baptism into His Death, that "like as Christ was raised again from the dead by the glory of the Father, even so we also should walk in newness of life."

"And renewing of the Holy Ghost." The washing, or bath of regeneration, takes place once for all: the renewing of the Holy Ghost is a constant daily work in those who retain the grace of their Baptism or in those in whom it is revived after they have fallen from it. Thus, in the Collect for Christmas Day, "Grant that we, being regenerate and made thy children by adoption and grace may daily be renewed by thy Holy Spirit;" and so in the Epistle to the Ephesians, "That ye put off concerning the former conversation the old man, which is corrupt according to the deceitful lusts, and be renewed in the spirit of your mind" (iv. 22).

6. "Which he shed on us abundantly through Jesus Christ our Saviour." The first outpouring of the Holy Ghost on the Day of Pentecost was a very abundant one. It was the fulfilment, at least in its beginning, of one which was prophesied of as very abundant: "I will pour out my Spirit upon all flesh" (Joel ii. 28). The

## JUSTIFIED BY HIS GRACE.

7 ⁿThat being justified by his grace,° we should be made heirs ᵖaccording to the hope of eternal life.

8 ᑫ*This is* a faithful saying, and these things I will that thou affirm constantly, that they which have believed in God might be careful ʳto main-

ⁿ Rom. iii. 24. Gal. ii. 16.
ᵒ ch. ii. 11.
ᵒ Rom. viii. 23, 24.
ᵖ ch. i. 2.
ᑫ 1 Tim. i. 15.
ch. i. 9.
ʳ ver. 1, 14.
ch. ii. 14.

---

8. "Constantly." Revisers translate this "confidently." Vulg., "confirmare."

Apostles in the Acts and in their Epistles always speak and write on the supposition that the Holy Ghost is poured out plentifully rather than sparingly; and their great anxiety seems to be that men may retain the grace and live to it and not grieve the Spirit—and their anxiety never is that they may receive Him as for the first time.

"Through Jesus Christ our Saviour." This may either mean that Christ on the day of Pentecost sent Him forth from the throne of God according to His promise. "The Holy Ghost whom I will send unto you from the Father," or it may mean simply "for the sake of." The former is preferable.

7. "That being justified by his grace," &c. That is, being both considered and made righteous. Justification is the being grafted into Christ so as to be made partakers of His life. It is a matter of the bestowal of life, rather than of imputation (see my notes on Rom. viii. 3, 4; Gal. iii. 21; and Excursus on Justification at the end of volume of notes on Romans).

"Heirs according to the hope of eternal life." "Heirs." The object of the mercy according to which God saved us by the washing and renewing and consequent justification was that we should be heirs of an eternal inheritance, but as we are not put into present possession of this inheritance we are made heirs according to the *hope* of it. Before we can enter upon it there is need of patience, (Rom. viii. 20-25), and of unweariness (Gal. vi. 9).

8. "This is a faithful saying, and these things I will that thou affirm," &c. This "faithful saying" is that which he had just enunciated, that the kindness and love of God our Saviour saved us according to His mercy by the bath of New Birth, and the renewal of the Holy Ghost. This is not to be kept in the background, or only mentioned now and then, but to be affirmed constantly

tain good works. These things are good and profitable unto men.

9 But [a] avoid foolish questions, and genealogies, and contentions, and strivings about the law; [b] for they are unprofitable and vain.

[a] 1 Tim. i. 4. 2 Tim. ii. 23. ch. i. 14.
[b] 2 Tim. ii. 14.

---

in order that they who have once believed may be careful to maintain good works.

This seems to contradict the opinion, so often asserted, that they who have believed will of necessity do good works. According to the Apostle it is not so. The connection between belief and good works is often, but by no means always maintained. Believers have constantly to be reminded of the first truths of Redemption, and how the holding of these first truths puts them under every obligation to maintain good works: but the good works do not follow necessarily. Look at all the Epistles of this great Apostle, how they set forth the loftiest views of Justification and Election and being "in Christ," and yet the latter part of almost every Epistle is occupied with enforcing the lowliest duties.

" These things are good and profitable unto men."

9. " But avoid questions, and genealogies, and contentions," &c. " These," *i.e.*, the practical application of the great truths, are profitable, " but avoid foolish questions."

Such as that with which a certain lawyer approached the Saviour: "Master, which is the great commandment of the law." Since all the law comes from God, it is trifling to ask which is greatest, since all have to be received and obeyed. The mere asking such questions shews that those who asked them had no just perception of the law.

"And genealogies." " Genealogias intelligit Judæorum et Judaizantium, qui a puero ita hisce student ut ab exordio Adam usque Zorobabel omnium generationes ita memoriter velociterque percurrant, ut eos suum putes nomen referre, inquit Hieron." (Cornelius à Lapide.)

" Strivings about the law." Strivings in most cases to make void its application to themselves, as in Matth. xv. 1-9.

10. A man that is an heretick after the first and second admonition reject .... condemned of himself." A heretic, in the language

10 A man that is an heretick [u] after the first and second admonition [x] reject:

11 Knowing that he that is such is subverted, and sinneth, [y] being condemned of himself.

[u] 2 Cor. xiii. 2.
[x] Matt. xviii. 17. Rom. xvi. 17. 2 Thess. iii. 6, 14. 2 Tim. iii. 5. 2 John 10.
[y] Acts xiii. 46.

---

10. "*An heretic.*" Not so much a holder of false doctrine as a maker of divisions, but the two seem inseparable.

of the New Testament, does not signify a man holding false opinions, so much as a man who chooses for himself some sect or party to which he attaches himself. It consequently means schismatic rather than heretic. The Pharisees were an αἵρεσις not so much because of the falsehood of what they held as because they separated themselves from the body of the Jews in order that they might, as they thought, be more strictly holy. The heretic in this place would mean the sectary, the man who separated himself from the Catholic Body and attached himself to a body more or less external to it.

"After the first and second admonition reject." There can be no doubt that this "reject" means to reject or cut off from the body over which Titus presided. It is not, of course, addressed to Titus as an individual that he should eschew the company of the erring person—but as the highest Church officer of Crete acting for the Apostle who had himself in very fearful terms formally excommunicated heretics (1 Tim. i. 20).

11. "Knowing that he that is such is subverted, and sinneth, being condemned of himself." In that age the mere fact of separating from the main Christian body was self-condemnation. It was not merely setting his own opinion above that of the Church, but allowing his own private opinion to undo as far as possible the unity of that Body. For the sake of maintaining his own idea in some point he set at naught the express desire and prayer of Christ that His Church should be one (John xvii. 21).

It is plain that we cannot apply this in our time to separation from any national branch of the Catholic Church in the same way as the Apostle did in his time; for the Church was then in manifest connection with the Apostolic fellowship, and the sin of separation was wholly on the side of the separating body, whereas in this day the cause of the schism may be, in part at least, on the side of the

12 When I shall send Artemas unto thee, or *Tychicus, be diligent to come unto me to Nicopolis: for I have determined there to winter.

13 Bring Zenas the lawyer and ᵃApollos on their journey diligently, that nothing be wanting unto them.

*Acts xx. 4.
2 Tim. iv. 12.

ᵃActs xviii. 24.

---

original body, as many of the highest Churchmen of our own day have confessed.

12. "When I shall send Artemas unto thee, or Tychicus, be diligent to come," &c. This place shews us that St. Paul yet retained the apostolic oversight of the churches in his own hands. Titus was not as yet to remain permanently in Crete, but to rejoin the Apostle after he had sent either Artemas or Tychicus to him to take his place in the oversight of the Cretian Church. Artemas is the shortened form of Artemidorus. He is not mentioned elsewhere in the New Testament. Tychicus is mentioned frequently, as in Acts xx. 4; Ephes. vi. 21; Col. iv. 7. From 2 Tim. iv. 12 we learn that he was sent to Ephesus, no doubt to take the place of Timothy, whom St. Paul wanted to be with him.

"Nicopolis." It is uncertain where this was, as there were three cities of the name. Probably a city of Macedonia or Epirus. We find from 2 Tim. iv. that Titus was gone, no doubt by the Apostle's direction, to Dalmatia, and Nicopolis would be on his way from Crete to Dalmatia.

13. "Bring Zenas the lawyer and Apollos on their journey diligently." Zenas contracted from Zenodorus. The word "lawyer" may either signify that though of Greek extraction he may have been an advocate in the Roman courts, or that he was a Jew who was formerly one learned in the Jewish law, and so was useful in opposing the teachers of the Jewish law, who would impose it on the Gentiles. I should think the former by far the more probable conjecture.

"Apollos." This man, eloquent and learned in the scriptures, was apparently one of St. Paul's staff, and at his beck and call. Titus was to bring him to the Apostle as one who could command his services.

"That nothing be wanting unto them."

14. "And let our's also learn to maintain good works for neces-

14 And let our's also learn ᵇ to ‖ maintain good works for necessary uses, that they be ᶜ not unfruitful.

15 All that are with me salute thee. Greet them that love us in the faith. Grace *be* with you all. Amen.

ᵇ ver. 8.
‖ Or, *profess honest trades*, Eph. iv. 28.
ᶜ Rom. xv. 28. Phil. i. 11. & iv. 17. Col. i. 10. 2 Pet. i. 8.

¶ It was written to Titus, ordained the first Bishop of the church of the Cretians, from Nicopolis of Macedonia.

---

sary uses," &c. It has been conjectured, and with some degree of probability, that this injunction was given in order that the Christians in communion with Paul and Titus (our's) should be liberal in contributing to the expenses of the journey of Zenas and Apollos; and certainly St. Paul would not lay the burden of a journey in which "nothing was to be wanting" on Titus alone. The reader will remember how Gaius, to whom St. John wrote his third Epistle, is commended for "doing faithfully what he did to the brethren and to strangers," and "bringing them forward on their journey after a godly sort."

15. "All that are with me salute thee. Greet (or salute) them that love us in the faith." One with us in holding the one faith in a clear conscience. If any are not in faith, *i.e.*, not holding to the faith, they are heretics, are dividing the Church, or are factious. They are not to have part in the salutation until they repent.

"Grace be with you all." Grace is invoked upon all without restriction, because all, especially those who are declining from faith and love, need it.

# THE EPISTLE TO PHILEMON.

# THE EPISTLE TO PHILEMON.

PAUL, <sup>a</sup> a prisoner of Jesus Christ, and Timothy our brother, unto Philemon our dearly beloved, <sup>b</sup> and fellow-labourer,

2 And to *our* beloved Apphia, and <sup>c</sup> Archippus <sup>d</sup> our fellowsoldier, and to <sup>e</sup> the church in thy house:

<sup>a</sup> Eph. iii. 1.
& iv. 1. 2 Tim.
i. 8. ver. 9.
<sup>b</sup> Phil. ii. 25.
<sup>c</sup> Col. iv. 17.
<sup>d</sup> Phil. ii. 25.
<sup>e</sup> Rom. xvi. 5.
1 Cor. xvi. 19.

2. "*Our beloved Apphia.*" So K., L., most Cursives, Syriac; but א, A., D., E., F., G., P., 17, 31, &c., read, "our sister."

1. " Paul a prisoner of Jesus Christ." He does not style himself, as in most other Epistles, Apostle, because, in the request he is about to make respecting Onesimus, he sets aside all Apostolical authority in order that Philemon's kindness might not be " of necessity, but willingly."

But he styles himself "prisoner," one in bonds, that one in bonds on behalf of the whole Church might the better intercede for one in private bonds, for one in bonds in an ordinary household.

" Philemon our dearly beloved and fellow-labourer." Probably he was one of St. Paul's band of fellow-labourers who at times brought him accounts of the neighbouring churches, as did Tychicus and Epaphras.

2. "And to our beloved Apphia." Some of the leading MSS. Vulgate, &c., read " to our sister." Apphia was most probably the wife of Philemon. Bishop Lightfoot supposes, from local inscriptions, that it was a Colossian rather than a Roman name.

"And Archippus our fellowsoldier." Mentioned in Coloss. iv. 17, " Say to Archippus, Take heed to the ministry which thou hast received in the Lord that thou fulfil it."

"And to the church in thy house." This does not mean the members of his private family who might be Christians, but to the

D

3 ᶠGrace to you, and peace, from God our Father and the Lord Jesus Christ.

4 ᵍI thank my God, making mention of thee always in my prayers,

5 ʰHearing of thy love and faith, which thou hast toward the Lord Jesus, and toward all saints;

6 That the communication of thy faith may become effectual ¹ by the acknowledging of every good thing which is in you in Christ Jesus.

ᶠ Eph. i. 2.
ᵍ Eph. i. 16. 1 Thess. i. 2. 2 Thess. i. 3.
ʰ Eph. i. 15. Col. i. 4.
¹ Phil. i. 9, 11.

---

6. "In you." So ℵ, F., G., P., many Cursives, f, g; but A., C., D., E., K., L., about fifty Cursives, read, "in us."

Church assembling in one of the larger rooms in his house, which he devoted to the use of the Christians for their public assemblies.

3. "Grace to you, and peace, from God our Father and the Lord Jesus Christ." We gather from this that he began all his letters, whether public or private, with this invocation.

4. "I thank my God, making mention of thee always in my prayers." What a list of persons for whom he daily entreated God must St. Paul have had! If he thus prayed especially for this convert in the comparatively small city of Colosse, what numbers must he have mentioned in Corinth, in Ephesus, in Philippi, in Thessalonica? And notice how in these supplications for private persons he mentions thanksgivings. He remembers not only their wants, but the blessings already bestowed upon them.

5. "Hearing of thy love and faith, which thou hast toward the Lord," &c. The "faith" is generally explained as referring to the Lord, the "love" to the saints. But surely the Lord must not be excluded from the love of Philemon. Faith may be exercised towards the saints, for Philemon might have faith in the genuineness of the work of Christ within them, and in their persevering to the end.

"Hearing of thy love." Wordsworth with great probability supposes that he had heard of it from Epaphras who was of Colosse but was then at Rome.

6. "That the communication of thy faith may become effectual," &c. There is some doubt respecting the allusion in the word "communication." It is the same word as is translated

7 For we have great joy and consolation in thy love, because the bowels of the saints ᵏ are refreshed by thee, brother.

8 Wherefore, ¹though I might be much bold in Christ to enjoin thee that which is convenient,

9 Yet for love's sake I rather beseech *thee*,

ᵏ 2 Cor. vii. 13.
2 Tim. i. 16.
ver. 20.

¹ 1 Thess. ii. 6.

---

7. " We have." So K., L., most Cursives, Syriac ; but ℵ, A., C., F., G., P., 17, 73, 74, 80, 137, f, g, Vulg., Copt., Arm., read, " I had."

" fellowship " in Acts ii. 42, and in 2 Cor. xiii. 14, " Fellowship of the Holy Ghost," and in 1 Cor. x. 16, " The communion (or participation) of the Blood and Body of Christ." It may mean that the imparting to others of their faith (when they see the fruits of it) may be effectual, &c. ; or " communication " may be taken as meaning distribution. If Philemon loved the saints he would distribute liberally to their needs. Both senses are true : faith " may become effectual by the acknowledging of every good thing." In the eyes of St. Paul it was needful, not only that there should be secret good in a man, but that it should be acknowledged on all hands as good springing from the grace of God and Christ, somewhat analogous to " Let your light so shine before men, that they may see your good works, and glorify your father which is in heaven."

7. " For we have great joy and consolation in thy love, because the bowels," &c. When we heard that the hearts of the saints are refreshed by thy acts of goodness, we joyed and were consoled at the news ; for we rejoice in all things which contribute to the good of the fellow-members of the same body of Christ. " Whether one member suffer all the members suffer with it, or one member be honoured all the members rejoice with it " (1 Cor. xii. 26).

8. " Wherefore, though I might be much bold in Christ to enjoin thee," &c. He here alludes to his apostolical authority, which would authorize him to command Philemon, in a case like this, to do what was fitting ; but he would have no good work done by constraint, and so he proceeds,—

9. " Yet for love's sake I rather beseech thee, being such an one as Paul the aged," &c. Love of long friendship, love of a Christian to his fellow Christian, love of a convert to his spiritual father, love of a lover of the Lord to his Lord's ambassader and representative.

being such an one as Paul the aged, ᵐ and now also a prisoner of Jesus Christ.

ᵐ ver. 1.
ⁿ Col. iv. 9.
º 1 Cor. iv. 15.
Gal. iv. 19.

10 I beseech thee for my son ⁿ Onesimus, º whom I have begotten in my bonds:

11 Which in time past was to thee unprofitable, but now profitable to thee and to me:

---

"Being such an one as Paul the aged." It seems to take away all the tenderness and beauty of this appeal by rendering the words "Paul the aged" as signifying "Paul the ambassador," as some do.

"The aged." He was what the ancients considered as old in years, being at least sixty, and was very probably, owing to "his labours more abundant," older in constitution. Such a multitude of anxieties and endurances as are recounted in 2 Cor. xi. 23-30, must have told upon him, and exhausted his manly vigour.

Aged, and a prisoner for the Master. The words would bring to Philemon's mind how hardly St. Paul's body could endure the rigours of a Roman prison.

10. "I beseech thee for my son Onesimus, whom I have begotten," &c. The words of the prisoner Paul touched him, and converted him to Christ. Though all glory must be given to the grace of God by whomsoever and whensoever spoken, yet it seems a greater than ordinary thing to yield obedience to the words of a prisoner in chains.

It is to be remarked how the name of him for whom he is interceding comes the last, as if he would use every motive to pity before he would name his name. "I beseech thee for my child, whom I have begotten in my bonds, Onesimus" (Revisers).

11. "Which in time past was to thee unprofitable, but now profitable," &c. One who had it in his mind to run away from and at the same time rob a good master, must have been "unprofitable;" but now "profitable";¹ "for if thou receivest him again he will serve thee as a Christian servant is bound to do, not with eye-service as pleasing men, but in sincerity of heart as to Christ."

---

¹ Many of the commentators notice here a play upon the words. Onesimus signifies "profitable." In his heathen state his name belied his character. When he became a Christian he became really Onesimus.

12 Whom I have sent again: thou therefore receive him, that is, mine own bowels:

13 Whom I would have retained with me, ᵖ that in thy stead he might have ministered unto me in the bonds of the gospel:

14 But without thy mind would I do nothing; ᑫ that thy benefit should not be as it were of necessity, but willingly.

ᵖ 1 Cor. xvi. 17. Phil. ii. 30.

ᑫ 2 Cor. ix. 7.

---

12. Revisers translate, "Whom I have sent back to thee in his own person." The Greek omits "do thou receive him" (προσλαβοῦ).

"Profitable to me." I have his prayers, I have the miracle of his conversion, as setting forth the grace of God. I have another son in the faith, I have another jewel in my "crown of rejoicing" (1 Thess. ii. 19).

12. "Whom I have sent again: thou therefore receive him as," &c. "As mine own bowels," *i.e.*, either "mine own offspring." compare Gen. xv. 4, or "my own heart."

13. "Whom I would have retained . . . . in the bonds of the gospel." What is this ministering? No doubt it is aiding Paul in his ministerial work, or he would not have said, "In thy stead." It is scarcely to be supposed that Philemon would have ministered to St. Paul in the capacity of a domestic servant; and if Onesimus was to have ministered to the Apostle, it was to supply the absence of Philemon in being St. Paul's deacon.

14. "But without thy mind would I do nothing," &c. Here, no doubt, the Apostle recognizes the claims of Philemon as a master on his slave.

"That thy benefit should not be as it were of necessity, but willingly." On that account he sent Onesimus back again; for if he had retained him, it would seem that there was a sort of compulsion exercised on Philemon to lend the services of Onesimus to the Apostle.

There must have been something peculiarly thorough in the conversion of Onesimus, if the Apostle should so desire him to be near him.

15. "For perhaps he therefore departed for a season," &c.

15 ʳFor perhaps he therefore departed for a season, that thou shouldest receive him for ever;

16 Not now as a servant, but above a servant, ˢa brother beloved, specially to me, but how much more unto thee, ᵗboth in the flesh, and in the Lord?

17 If thou count me therefore ᵘa partner, receive him as myself.

18 If he hath wronged thee, or oweth *thee* ought, put that on mine account;

ʳ So Gen. xlv. 5, 8.
ˢ Matt. xxiii. 8. 1 Tim. vi. 2.
ᵗ Col. iii. 22.
ᵘ 2 Cor. viii. 23.

---

15. "That thou shouldest receive him;" rather, "have him as thine own."
16. "As a servant;" rather, "as a slave."

"Perhaps." It may be that the providence of God suffered him to flee from thee, that he might come under the more powerful influence of the Word, and so be restored to thee, not in the flesh only, but in the spirit—not for a time only, but for ever, in the participation with thee of eternal life.

16. "Not now as a servant, but above a servant, a brother beloved," &c. Perhaps St. Paul here asks for the manumission of Onesimus.

"A brother beloved," not only to the Apostle, but much more to Philemon, could hardly continue in servitude. He must be a freeman if he is to assist Paul as his brother in the Gospel in the stead of Philemon.

17. "If thou count me therefore as a partner, receive him as myself." "A partner." This may be either a partner or co-partaker in the faith of the Gospel, or in the work of the ministry—most probably, I think, the latter.

18. "If he hath wronged thee, or oweth thee ought, put that on mine account." From the doubtful way in which this is put, it may not be quite certain that Onesimus, on his flight from his master took away with him any of his master's goods, but it is not at all improbable.

Some see in the words, "put that on mine account," a tacit reference to the Great Imputation. The verb is only used elsewhere in Rom. v. 13.

19 I Paul have written *it* with mine own hand, I will repay *it*: albeit I do not say to thee how thou owest unto me even thine own self besides.

20 Yea, brother, let me have joy of thee in the Lord: ˣ refresh my bowels in the Lord.     ˣ ver. 7.

21 ʸ Having confidence in thy obedience I wrote  ʸ 2 Cor. vii. 16. unto thee, knowing that thou wilt also do more than I say.

---

20. " In the Lord." So E., K., most Cursives, Vulg. (Am.); but ℵ, A., C., D., F., G., L., P., a few Cursives, d, e, f, g, Goth., Syriac, Copt., Arm., read, " in Christ."
21. "I wrote unto thee" may be translated, " I write." He alludes to the present letter.

19. " I Paul have written it with mine own hand, I will repay it." Some suppose that these words show that St. Paul wrote this short Epistle himself, and did not dictate it as he did others; and there is the more likelihood of this, inasmuch as the whole letter is occupied with a private personal matter. Others imagine that at this point St. Paul took the parchment out of the hand of the amanuensis, and wrote the promise of repayment himself.

"Albeit I do not say to thee how thou owest unto me even thine own self besides." Very pregnant words indeed. He that accepts the Gospel of Christ is made the true possessor of himself. Before this his soul was enslaved to evil, so that, humanly speaking, it would have been better for him if he had not been born. Now his true being is restored to him, so that by God's grace he can fulfil that purpose for which he was created and redeemed—the glorifying of God in his whole self—in his body and in his spirit, which are God's.

20. " Yea, brother, let me have joy of thee in the Lord: refresh my bowels," &c. " Joy of thee in the Lord," &c. In that thou doest what thou doest through the grace of Christ, through His dwelling in thee, and particularly thou imitatest Him in the breaking of bonds and freeing the captive.

"Refresh my bowels." Fill my heart with joy when I see the grace of Christ in thee.

21. "Having confidence in thy obedience I wrote unto thee," &c. If St. Paul had thought Philemon a churlish, hard man, he

22 But withal prepare me also a lodging: for *I trust that ᵃ through your prayers I shall be given unto you.

23 There salute thee ᵇEpaphras, my fellowprisoner in Christ Jesus:

24 ᶜMarcus, ᵈAristarchus, ᵉDemas, ᶠLucas, my fellowlabourers.

*Phil. i. 25. & ii. 24.
ᵃ 2 Cor. i. 11.
ᵇ Col. i. 7. & iv. 12.
ᶜ Acts xii. 12, 25.
ᵈ Acts xix. 29. & xxvii. 2. Col. iv. 10.
ᵉ Col. iv. 14.
ᶠ 2 Tim. iv. 11.

---

would not have written such a letter, but he knew him to be a kind, considerate man, and so he would be ready, not only to comply, but to go beyond the expressed desire of the Apostle. Notice the word "obedience." It is the only one in the letter which implies Apostolic authority, but it *is* in the letter, and justly reminds Philemon that it was no ordinary servant of Christ who was making the request.

22. "But withal prepare me also a lodging." St. Paul's personal wants in the way of accommodation would be very small. But it is certain that as the Apostle of Christ he would desire to get as many to hear him as he could, and to receive "all that came in unto him," as he did at Rome (Acts xxviii.) He must have room for preaching and teaching.

"For I trust that through your prayers I shall be given unto you." This letter, then, must have been written shortly before he was set at liberty. Notice how much the Apostle relied upon the prayers of his children in Christ, here for his liberty, and in Philip. i. 19, for his salvation even, or at least for what would further it.

23. "There salute thee Epaphras, my fellowprisoner in Christ Jesus." What had occasioned the imprisonment of Epaphras we know not. Some suppose that he voluntarily got himself to be the companion of Paul in his bonds, in order that he might the better minister to his wants.

24. "Marcus, Aristarchus, Demas, Lucas, my fellowlabourers." These are the same as send salutations in Colos. iv. The exception is Jesus, the Son of Justus, who was probably unknown to Philemon.

The mention of these names shows that the Epistle was written at the same time as that to the Colossians.

25 ᵍ The grace of our Lord Jesus Christ *be* with your spirit. Amen.   ᵍ 2 Tim. iv. 22

¶ Written from Rome to Philemon, by Onesimus a servant.

---

25. "The grace of our Lord Jesus Christ be with your spirit. Amen." "Your" is the plural personal pronoun (ἡμῶν), and implies that the Apostle sent the benediction to all in Philemon's household.

# THE EPISTLE TO THE HEBREWS.

# THE EPISTLE TO THE HEBREWS.

## CHAP. I.

GOD, who at sundry times and ᵃ in divers manners spake in time past unto the fathers by the prophets,

ᵃ Num. xii. 6, 8.

1. "Who at sundry times." "Multifariam," Vulg. Revisers, "God having of old spoken unto the fathers in the prophets," &c.

1. "God, who at sundry times and in divers manners spake in time past unto the fathers by the prophets." This treatise on the supreme excellence of the dispensation of the Eternal Son begins with setting in contrast the varying and so imperfect nature of previous revelations of God through His servants, with the oneness and perfection of that which He made through His Son.

The teaching is identical with that of the Lord's parable of the wicked husbandmen. The Lord of the vineyard during a long series of ages sent His servants, and last of all He sends His Son, saying to Himself, "they will reverence my Son." They have abused and murdered My servants, but My Son is so infinitely above any created servant of mine, that they cannot withhold worship from Him.

"At sundry times and in divers manners." Almost all expositors and translators agree in rendering the first of these adverbs by "in many parts," or "in many portions." Thus Westcott, "in many parts;" the Revisers, "by divers portions." The Variorum N. T. strictly "in many parts," but practically "at many times." Bishop Wordsworth, "in many portions."

But is this rendering intelligible to the great part of English readers? Neither the words "parts" nor "portions," exhibit the underlying truth, which is the piecemeal, fragmentary nature of the revelations through the prophets. May we not assert that the real meaning is best suggested by such a phrase as "in a fragmentary manner?" Compared to the Revelation of Himself and His Father by the Incarnate Word, the notices of His Coming and Kingdom in the prophets are the most disconnected possible. Thus, assuming that the object of all God's revelations to His chosen people was to prepare them for the Christ, see how fragmentary they are! One in the Book of Proverbs sets forth His being with God before the world was made; another in Isaiah sets forth His Birth of a Virgin; another in the same prophet, His sufferings as a sin-offering; another in Psalm cx., His Ascension and Eternal Priesthood. But all these are detached one from another. As they lie embedded in the various books, there is no connection between any two, whereas in the Gospel the fragments or detached portions all fall into their places, and form one harmonious whole.

"In divers manners." God spake to Abraham and to Moses face to face, as a man speaketh to his friend. God spake to Aaron and his successors by the mysterious Urim and Thummim. He spake in David apparently through the inspiration of the poet—in Solomon in the inspiration of Aphorism—in the Prophets by a certain Divine afflatus, which compelled them (sometimes against their will) to say, "Thus saith the Lord"—to Daniel in visions of the night season.

And this speaking to the Fathers by the prophets was of old time, in time past, from the beginning of the race. He spake to Adam and Eve in paradise, to Enoch, to Noah, to Melchizedec, and to Job; but now in the end of these last times, in the fulness of time, He has spoken to us by the Son. This speaking of God in Jesus is in the greatest possible contrast with all former messages from God. In all former revelations the presence of God was but for a time. The presence of God, if we may say so most reverently, "came and went." *Now*, in the Son of Man, it was an abiding presence, and a full and perfect manifestation. When men saw Him they saw God. "He that hath seen me hath seen the Father." When men heard Him they heard God. When men, His chosen ones, handled Him, they "handled of the Word of Life!"

And His revelation of Himself and of His Father was not fragmentary, not indirect, not in various ways, as by visions or dreams, not at times, but direct, and at all times. His Father had given

Chap. I.]      HEIR OF ALL THINGS.      47

2 Hath <sup>b</sup> in these last days <sup>c</sup> spoken unto us by his Son, <sup>d</sup> whom he hath appointed heir of all things, <sup>e</sup> by whom also he made the worlds;

<sup>b</sup> Deut. iv. 30
Gal. iv. 4.
Eph. i. 10.
<sup>c</sup> John i. 17.
& xv. 15. ch. ii. 3.
<sup>d</sup> Ps. ii. 8.
Matt. xxi. 38.
& xxviii. 18.
John iii. 35.
Rom. viii. 17.
<sup>e</sup> John i. 3.
1 Cor. viii. 6.
Col. i. 16.

2. "Hath in these last days." "Hath at the end of these days" ($\dot{\epsilon}\sigma\chi\acute{a}\tau o\upsilon$ instead of $\dot{\epsilon}\sigma\chi\acute{a}\tau\omega\nu$), so א, A., B., D., E., K., L., M., P., most Cursives, &c.
"The worlds." The "ages" or "æons."

Him what He was to say: "The Father which sent Me, He gave Me commandment what I should say and what I should speak" (John xii. 49). And so His whole Life and teaching was the Revelation of the unseen God. Neither did His teaching close with His Resurrection, "I have given them Thy word" (John xvii. 14). If it be said that after His Ascension it was the Holy Ghost which instructed the Apostles, we reply that He said of the Spirit, "He shall not speak of Himself, but whatsoever He shall hear (in the eternal counsel of the Trinity) that shall He speak" (John xvi. 13).

2. "Hath in these last days." Properly, "at the end of these days," *i.e.*, at the end of the Old Dispensation. ("The law and the prophets were until John.")

"His Son, whom he hath appointed heir of all things, by whom also he made the worlds." The word "Son" is without article. The bare literal rendering is in "a son," but this cannot be, unless it be understood that there is no pause between "Son" and "whom he hath appointed heir of all things." It is not any son, the first even of created or adopted sons, but that Son who as a true and proper Son ($\ddot{\iota}\delta\iota o\varsigma$) is the heir of all things, and enters upon the inheritance, if we may so say, both by right and by appointment.

"Heir of all things," not that the Father parts with the possession of all things, but he commits all rule over them, all direction, all providence, as he has committed all judgment of intelligent creatures, to the Son. ("All things are delivered unto me of My Father," "All power is committed unto me in heaven and in earth," "By Him all things consist.")

"By whom also he made the worlds." This exceedingly important assertion of the Divine Glory of the Son, seems, as it were, by the way, and it is to be remembered that the heirship of the Lord is always stated in the New Testament to be the outcome of His Redeeming work: "Became obedient unto death, even the

3 ᶠ Who being the brightness of *his* glory, and the express image of his person, and ᵍ upholding

ᶠ John i. 14.
& xiv. 9.
² Cor. iv. 4.
Col. i. 15.
ᵍ John i. 4.
Col. i. 17.
Rev. iv. 11.

3. "The express image of his person." Revisers, "the very image of his substance;" Vulg., "figura substantia ejus."

death of the Cross, wherefore God also hath highly exalted him, and given," &c. (So also Ps. ii. 8, viii. 6; Isaiah liii. 12; Ephes. i. 20, 22.)

"The worlds," not the spheres or heavenly bodies merely, but the ages and all existing in those ages. The making of the solid worlds, and even their inhabitants, would not include the supra mundane essences, the "all things invisible as well as visible"; whereas the making of the ages expresses all that exists in all time in the spiritual as well as in the material universe.

3. "Who being the brightness of his glory" ($ἀπαύγασμα$). It is a mistake, I think, to render "brightness" by effulgence, because the common use of the word is narrowed to signifying material brightness. Such brightness does belong to God, for he "dwelleth in the light which no man can approach unto;" and this surpassing splendour is what the Lord alludes to when He speaks of Himself coming in "His own glory, and that of His Father, and of the Holy Angels." Such ineffable brightness the Lord manifested at His Transfiguration, and when He appeared to St. Paul, and when He was seen by St. John. But if the moral attributes of God are a part of His glory, then the life of Jesus, and indeed His whole redeeming Work, is the shining forth of the glory of God; and if God's Almighty Power is part of His glory, then Jesus in His wonderful works which He did is the shining forth of it, as he said respecting the raising of Lazarus, "Said I not unto thee that if thou wouldest believe thou shouldest see the glory of God?" (John xi. 40). If it is the glory of God to create, then when the Son of God made the worlds He was the splendour of the glory of God. The brightness of His glory is expressed by the "light of light," "lumen de lumine," $φῶς\ ἐκ\ φωτὸς$ of our Creed. The Father is the Fountain of Light. He is called by St. James, "The Father of lights;" and the Son is the shining forth of the light in which the hidden Deity is discerned. ("In Thy light shall we see light," Ps. xxxvi. 9.)

all things by the word of his power, ʰ when he   ʰ ch. vii. 27. & ix. 12, 14, 26.

"The express image of his person," rather, "the express image of his essence or substance." St. Paul speaks of Christ as the "image of the invisible God," but here the Apostle speaks of a something far more like God. God is supposed to impress His hidden Deity with all its attributes on a substance which will receive the impression, as the wax of a seal will, and render the exact likeness to him who looks on it. Nothing can be more perfect than the resemblance of the impression of the seal on the wax to that which impresses it, and this is employed to denote the exact reproduction of all that is in the Father in that Son on Whom He has stamped His likeness.

"Of his person." "Person" does not here mean the outward person, but the innermost essence: hypostasis means something put under, or existing under something. Hence it signifies the very substance or essence of a thing, that unseen reality of which the outward form is the expression. If it be lawful then to say so, the Son is not the image or manifestation of the attributes of God, but of God Himself, the secret essence of which his attributes are the manifestations.

It denotes the closest resemblance conceivable. It answers to the Logos or Word; for as the Word reveals the innermost thoughts of the man, so the Word, or Son of God, reveals all that is in God to His creatures.

"And upholding all things by the word of his power." "Upholding all things." Thus Coloss. i. 17, "He is before all things, and by him all things consist," *i.e.*, hold together, are continued. "Upholding" is properly "bearing all things," not merely sustaining them, but bearing them on in their progress to the accomplishment of the Divine purpose. So Westcott. In the Clementine Liturgy there is a suggestive passage: "Thou, O eternal God, didst make all things by Him, and by Him too dispensest Thy providence over them; for by the Same that thou broughtest all things into being, by Him Thou continuest all things in well being."

"By the word of his power." As the word of the Father is all powerful so is that of the Son, but it is to be noticed that the term "word" is not the same as that in John i. 1. It denotes rather,

had by himself purged our sins, [1] sat down on the right hand of the Majesty on high;

[1] Ps. cx. 1.
Eph. i. 20.
ch. viii. 1. & x. 12. & xii. 2.
1 Pet. iii. 22.
[k] Eph. i. 21.
Phil. ii. 9, 10.

4 Being made so much better than the angels, as [k] he hath by inheritance obtained a more excellent name than they.

5 For unto which of the angels said he at any

---

3. "Purged"—"made purification of;" "purgationem peccatorum faciem," Vulg.

the command. "The choice of the term as distinguished from λόγος, marks, so to speak, the particular action of providence." (Westcott.)

"When he had by himself purged our sins." "By Himself," *i.e.*, "not by the blood of goats and calves, but by His own Blood."

"Purged," rather "made purification of"—a much more sacerdotal expression. He once for all made the sacrificial purification or atonement which He through His ministers afterwards applies.

"Sat down on the right hand of the Majesty on High." Majesty embodies the ideas of greatness and mightiness. Its application now to supreme rulers has somewhat obscured its meaning as applied to the Father.

"On the right hand." From all eternity He was in the bosom of the Father; and having assumed our human nature, a nature under the conditions of time and space, at a certain moment He took His seat at the right hand of God, *i.e.*, in the highest and most honourable place in the Universe. In answer to His own prayer He was then glorified by His Father "with the glory which He had with Him before the world was." He is visible in heaven now as the Lord of all things, of the angelic hosts—"angels, and authorities, and powers being made subject unto him."

4. "Being made so much better than the angels, as he hath by inheritance," &c. The name of angels, signifying messengers, is an honourable name, but it is that of mere servants, whereas Jesus, both as to His Divine and human Nature, inherited the name of Son. An anticipation of verse 14, "Are they not all, (even the highest of them), ministering spirits?"

5. "For unto which of the angels said he at any time?" It is plain from this that no reference to the temporal David in this

time, ¹Thou art my Son, this day have I begotten thee? And again, ᵐI will be to him a Father, and he shall be to me a Son?

¹ Ps. ii. 7.
Acts xiii. 33.
ch. v. 5.
ᵐ 2 Sam. vii. 14. 1 Chr. xxii. 10, & xxviii. 6. Ps. lxxxix. 26, 27.

verse for a moment crossed the Apostolic mind. He looked upon the words as applicable solely to the spiritual David, David's greater Son.

"This day have I begotten thee." This is applied by the Apostle in Acts xiii. 33 to the Resurrection of Christ, because His Resurrection from the dead was, as it were, His new Birth. He received then Life from the dead, a new Life. "In that He died He died unto sin once, but in that He liveth (with His Resurrection Life) He liveth unto God" (Rom. vi. 10).

"This day." This word "day" has been explained with reference to His Eternal Generation, as the day of Eternity—the everlasting "now" in which God dwells. The Son is not begotten in time which passes away, but in eternity which abides. We can have no conception of this, because we are under the conditions of time and space, which God is not under. So far as regards our Lord's human nature, we should have understood the words "This day have I begotten thee" of what is related in Luke i. 35, but the words of the inspired Apostle are express in referring it to the Resurrection of the Lord.

"And again, I will be to him a Father, and he shall be to me a Son?" God said this apparently of Solomon, but really of the greater than Solomon (ii. Sam. vii. 14, also Ps. lxxxix. 26, 27). But it was said of Solomon only as the type of the Messiah. It was only very partially true in him. It was not fulfilled in him. Solomon, the wisest of men, the greatest of the Kings of Israel, failed miserably in his high mission, and what was said to him passes to that Son of his who did not fail in *His* mission. Of Him only was it true in the highest sense; but what we have now to do with is that it was said to no angel. Whatever might be the sense of God's love vouchsafed to the angelic natures it never reached this. It was said only to Him of Whom it could be absolutely and eternally true.

6. "And again, when he bringeth in the first-begotten into the world, he saith, And let all the angels of God worship him." There is nothing corresponding to this in the Hebrew Old Testa-

§ Or, *When he bringeth again.*
n Rom. viii. 29. Col. i. 18. Rev. i. 5.
o Deut. xxxii. 43, LXX. Ps. xcvii. 7. 1 Pet. iii. 22.

6 ‖ And again, when he bringeth in ⁿ the first-begotten into the world, he saith, ᵒ And let all the angels of God worship him.

---

6. "And again, when he bringeth in;" or, "he again (a second time) bringeth in;" but no good sense can be made of this translation, though it is grammatically preferable.

ment, but in the Septuagint at the beginning of Deut. xxxii. 43 we have the words inserted "Rejoice, ye heavens, with him, and let the angels of God worship him," but the context in either the Hebrew or in the Septuagint does not seem in the least degree Messianic. On this account it has been supposed that the Apostle quotes Ps. xcvii. 7, "Confounded be all they that worship carved images and that delight in vain gods, worship him all ye gods," all the former part of the Psalm referring to a manifestation of the glory of Jehovah which can only be fulfilled in His Son, Who alone of the Persons of the Trinity will be actually manifested, and here the Septuagint instead of "all ye gods," reads "worship him all his angels." It is possible that the writer may have had in his mind both these passages, and, as some suggest, feeling the difficulty of citing a place which was not in the Hebrew, may have supplemented it by the Greek of Ps. xcvii.

But what is meant by "And again when he bringeth in the first-begotten into the world"? Here we have to notice that the proper rendering is "when he *again* bringeth in," the "again" to be taken with "bringeth in," and is referred to the second coming, when undoubtedly the angels of God will form His retinue; and so, no doubt, will bow down to Him; but this, though great names may be cited in its favour, seems extremely unsatisfactory. The words, "bringing in the first-begotten into the world," seems certainly to refer to His Incarnation or Birth, and seems unsuitable to His coming for Judgment, when God will not bring Him, but when He will come from God out of Heaven; and the term "first-begotten" is never associated with Christ as the Judge, and seems only capable of being applied to the Incarnation or the Resurrection. On the whole I cannot but think that we must look to the fulfilment of this assertion in Luke ii., when at the coming in of the Holy Child into the habitable world, or οἰκουμένη, the angels appeared

Chap. I.]                    HIS ANGELS SPIRITS.                    53

7 And †of the angels he saith, ᵖ Who maketh his angels spirits, and his ministers a flame of fire.

† Gr. *unto*.
ᵖ Ps. civ. 4.

---

as a vast multitude, and sang "glory to God in the Highest." This appears upon the whole by far the least objectionable explanation, the term "God" being equally as applicable in the believer's mind (and the Epistle was written for believers) to the Son as to the Father.

7. "And of the angels he saith, Who maketh his angels spirits, and his ministers a flaming fire." The word translated "angel" (מַלְאָךְ) and that translated "spirit" (רוּחַ) have different meanings, or rather each of them has a gradation of meaning; the first signifies "messengers," thus in 1 Sam. xi. 3, "Give us seven days that we may send messengers," &c., and in 2 Sam. xi. 19; "And (Joab) charged the messenger, saying." Then it rises in meaning so as to be applied almost exclusively to the angels as messengers of God. All that we know about the angels is simply that they are God's messengers, though of course they are His messengers, not merely to utter verbal messages, but to assist the people of God in time of need.

And so the word translated "spirit" (רוּחַ) has a lower and higher meaning—its lowest being breath, or air, or wind, and its highest being the Spirit of God Himself (Psalm li. 11, 12 Isaiah lxiii. 10, 11).

It is not improbable that in the Psalm as originally composed, both words have the lower meaning, "Who maketh his messengers winds," because the whole psalm is a hymn glorifying God for His operations in nature; but if we are to render the word מַלְאָךְ as signifying an intelligence, then we must perforce translate it by "spirit," if we would not fall into the absurdity of asserting that the glorious creatures who ministered to the Lord and were present at His sepulchre, were mere wind or air.

"And his ministers a flame of fire." This is parallel to the first clause, and like the first clause it cannot degrade these glorious intelligences into mere unconscious elements, such as fire is, but must imply something respecting their attributes or properties, as, for instance, that they have the penetrating, the enlightening, the purifying, or if need be, the consuming properties of fire. Or may

q Ps. xlv. 6, 7.   8 But unto the Son *he saith,* q Thy throne, O

---

it not signify what St. Paul alludes to when he speaks of " angels of light," or when his enemies beheld St. Stephen, they saw his face illuminated as it had been the face of an angel, *i.e.*, resplendent, or when St. Peter was delivered from prison by an angel, it is said " a light shined in the prison ? "[1]

8. " But unto the Son, he saith, Thy throne, O God, is for ever and ever." There can be no reasonable doubt of the correctness of this translation, as it appears in our authorized. God (Elohim, Ὁ Θεός) is in the vocative, as is required by the sense. There can be no reason for translating it otherwise, except a dogmatic one on the side of Socinianism. Throughout the Book of Psalms (Septuagint) the nominative, as far as I can find, is always used for the vocative, nor is there a single instance of the vocative of Θεός (Θεέ) being used. It is understood as a vocative in the Chaldee Targum, " Thy beauty, O King Messiah, is more excellent than that of the sons of men ; the spirit of prophecy is given unto thy life, therefore Jehovah had blessed thee for ever. The throne of Thy glory, O Jehovah, standeth for ever and ever: a righteous sceptre is the sceptre of Thy kingdom. Because that Thou hast loved righteousness and hated wickedness, therefore Jehovah Thy God, hath anointed Thee with the oil of gladness more abundantly than thy fellows." The fact that the Targumist substitutes Jehovah for God in verse 7, shows that however he understood the place, he did not understand the word " God " in a lower sense, as if it meant either judge or angel.

The ancient Greek translator, Aquila, renders the Hebrew by Θεέ. Justin Martyr, in his dialogue with Trypho, quotes this

---

[1] We can scarcely understand how any one can uphold the idea that angels should be made winds, *i.e.* made into winds, or made of wind, and yet a very learned commentator on this Epistle quotes with apparent approval the opinion of a Jewish theologian (?) that "angels were supposed to live only as they ministered." In a remarkable passage of Shemoth R. the angels are represented as "new every morning." " The angels are renewed every morning, and after they have praised God they return to the stream of fire out of which they came." Again, another, Ehrard, is somewhat more cautious : " The angels, at least a class of them, are regarded as δυνάμεις of God, *i.e.* as personal creatures furnished with peculiar powers, through whom God works wonders in the kingdom of nature, and whom He accordingly makes to be storm, winds, and flames of fire, in as far as he lets them, so to speak, incorporate themselves with these elements and operations of nature." The reader will notice that there is "great virtue" in the author's "as far as" and "so to speak."

God, *is* for ever and ever: a sceptre of † righteousness *is* the sceptre of thy kingdom.

9 Thou hast loved righteousness, and hated

† Gr. *rightness*, or, *straightness*.

passage as said to the Son : "It is not on this ground solely I said that it must be admitted absolutely that some other one is called Lord by the Holy Spirit besides Him Who is considered Maker of all things, not solely by Moses, but also by David. For there is written by him, 'The Lord said to my Lord, sit on my right hand until I make thine enemies thy footstool,' as I have already quoted, and again in other words, 'Thy throne, O God, is for ever and ever. A sceptre of equity,'" &c.

Again, the writer of the Epistle is now occupied with proving that the Lord has a super-angelic nature, which, of course, can be only the Divine, and if any of the expedients for translating the quotation so that it should not be spoken of and to the Divine Son Himself, such as "God is thy throne," or "thy throne is the throne of God," are possible, his intention in quoting the passage would be frustrated, for God is the support of the throne of every righteous ruler. Instead of making the Son higher than the angels, it would make Him no better than a virtuous human monarch. And again, as Alford remarks, "It would not suit the decorum or spirit of the passage."

"A sceptre of righteousness is the sceptre of thy kingdom." Righteousness, literally straightness. Compare another Messianic Psalm, lxxii., "He shall judge thy people with righteousness;" Isaiah xi. 5, "Righteousness shall be the girdle of his loins, and faithfulness the girdle of his reins;" and Jer. xxiii. 5, "The righteous Branch." It seems as if the Messiah was contrasted with all other kings, as the only one absolutely and perfectly righteous.

9. "Thou hast loved righteousness, and hated iniquity; therefore God," &c. This is said of the Messiah as man. When He became man He became a creature of God, so that God was henceforth not only His Father, but His God ("I ascend unto my Father and your Father, and to my God and your God"). As man, not merely as the Supreme God, he loved righteousness and hated iniquity, and so God rewarded Him as He has promised to reward us, if we love righteousness and hate iniquity. He thus shares in our reward, and so in all respects He is One with us.

iniquity; therefore God, *even* thy God, ʳ hath anointed thee with the oil of gladness above thy fellows.

ʳ Isa. lxi. 1.
Acts iv. 27, &
x. 38.
ˢ Ps. cii. 25,
&c.

10 And, ˢThou, Lord, in the beginning hast laid the foundation of the earth; and the heavens are the works of thine hands:

---

"Therefore God, even thy God, hath anointed thee with the oil of gladness," &c. Some would render this, "O God, thy God," making the first Θεος vocative, as in verse 6, but it is doubtful. The Targum translates as in our version, the first "God" as the nominative. What is "the oil of gladness?" Undoubtedly that Spirit of God by which the righteous are enabled to rejoice in God.

When did God thus anoint Him? Not at His Baptism, for then He was anointed to suffer, but on the day of His Triumph, when all suffering was over for ever. He Himself recognizes this joy, and assures us that, if we continue His, we shall partake of it, when in the parable He promises to say to those who have made their calling and election sure, "Well done, thou good and faithful servant, enter thou into the joy of thy Lord" (Matth. xxv. 21).

"Above thy fellows." Applied to a supposed earthly monarch, this may mean "Thy fellow monarch," but as applied to the Christ, it may have the widest application. Thy fellows, *i.e.* fellow-men; thy fellows, those whom the King calls not servants, but friends.

10. "And, Thou, Lord, in the beginning hast laid the foundation of the earth," &c. It is somewhat difficult to decide on what grounds the Apostolic writer quotes the first verse of this Psalm as addressed to the Son, as the whole seems addressed to the God of Israel, *i.e.*, as is supposed, to the Father, and there is no introduction of a Divine Person of Whom or to Whom it can be said, "God, even thy God, hath anointed thee." There is one ground which has not, as far as I have seen, been sufficiently considered, which is this. It was a rooted principle in the mind of the Apostolic writer, that God created the worlds by His Son. This is asserted almost at the very beginning of the Epistle, "By whom also he made the worlds." Whom then would the writer have in his thoughts when he made the second allusion to creation, "Thou, Lord in the beginning ... the heavens are the works," &c.? No doubt

11 'They shall perish; but thou remainest; and they all shall wax old as doth a garment;

ᵗ Isa. xxxiv. 4. & li. 6. Matt. xxiv. 35. 2 Pet. iii 7, 10. Rev. xxi. 1.

the Word, the Eternal Son. We are not to suppose that so believing a writer could hold such an idea loosely, asserting it in the most absolute way in one verse, and then dropping it at a few verses afterwards. We do not sufficiently realize what is necessarily implied in the fact that Jesus, the Son of God, is the Word by Whom all things were made. It necessarily carries with it a reference to the Eternal Word in every place, either in the Old Testament or in the New in which reference is made to creation. In the act of creation, the Father can never be contemplated without the Son, as the Apostle says, "One God the Father, from whom are all things, and we unto him. And one Lord Jesus Christ, through whom (δι οὗ) are all things" (1 Cor. viii. 6). Such assertions as John i. 3, can never be as if they were unwritten. They attribute to One Who was known amongst men as Jesus, and submitted even to death upon the Cross, in order that He might suffer the extremity of human shame and weakness, a pre-existent Nature which was One with the Divine Nature, and in and by which Nature He manifested the power and wisdom of God by creating all things. And precisely the same reasoning applies to the word Saviour. The God of Israel seems far more jealous that no one should share the name of Saviour with Him, than He is that no one should be called a creator besides Himself. And yet the New Testament is written to reveal to us that Christ is the Saviour. How can we reconcile the two Testaments? In this way only, that God saves us by His Son. The Son only became Incarnate, but it was by the will, the power, the desire, the self-abnegation of the Father, that He saved us by His Death and Resurrection. So that when we read in Isaiah xliii., "I am the Lord thy God, the Holy one of Israel, thy Saviour;" or in Hosea xiii. 4, "Thou shalt know no God but me, for there is no Saviour besides me," the true believer who has any grasp whatsoever of the Catholic Faith applies the saying to the Father and to the Son—not indifferently, by any means, but simultaneously, as it were, the Father as the supreme Decreer, the Bringer about, the Sender of Salvation, and the Son as the Agent of it. If it be asked, can we believe that the citation of "Thou, Lord, in the beginning hast

12 And as a vesture shalt thou fold them up, and they shall be changed: but thou art the same, and thy years shall not fail.

13 But to which of the angels said he at any time, "Sit on my right hand, until I make thine enemies thy footstool?

<sup>u</sup> Ps. cv. 1.
Matt. xxii. 44.
Mark xii. 36.
Luke xx. 42.
ch. x. 12.
ver. 3.

12. "And as a vesture shalt thou fold them up." So A., B., K., L., M., P., most Cursives, Syriac, Copt., Arm.; but ℵ, D., d, e, f, Vulg., read, "shalt thou change them."

---

laid," &c., would be understood by the Hebrews as referring to the Son, we reply that that depends upon how they were taught. If they were taught the truth that "by His Son God made the worlds" very sparingly, very infrequently, very reservedly, it is probable that they would not; but if they were taught it as a fundamental principle, that what the Father did in the past eternity He did by His Son, then they would assuredly see in such a citation only what was natural.

And there is another reason also why the Apostolic writer should cite this place as referring to the Second Person, and that is, that it is so emphatic a declaration of His unchangeableness. The reader will remember how full this Epistle is of the unchangeableness of the work of Christ. "Thou art a priest for ever after the order of Melchizedec," v. 6, vi. 20; vii. 3, "abideth a priest continually;" vii. 16, "after the power of an endless life;" vii. 24, "This man, because he continueth ever, hath an unchangeable priesthood;" 25, "He ever liveth;" 28, "The Son who is consecrated for ever more," viii. 7, x. 12, 13, 14; and above all, xiii. 8, "Jesus Christ, the same yesterday, to-day, and for ever." Again, "Here we have no continuing city;" xiii. 20; again, "the everlasting covenant," xiii. 20. We see, then, how to a believing generation the citation of the place as fully applicable to the Eternal Son, would present no difficulty whatsoever.

"As a vesture shalt thou fold them up." In the Hebrew it is "As a vesture shalt thou change them, and they shall be changed," which agrees better with the parallelism.

13. "But to which of the angels said he at any time, Sit on my right hand?" The whole verse reads, "The Lord said unto my Lord, sit thou on," &c. The Person of whom this verse was said

14 ¹ Are they not all ministering spirits, sent ¹ Gen. xix. 16. & xxxii. 1, 2, 24. Ps. xxxiv. 7. & xci. 11. & ciii. 20, 21. Dan. iii. 28. & vii. 10. & x. 11. Matt. xviii. 10. Luke i. 19. & ii. 9, 13. Acts xii. 7, &c. & xxvii. 23.

was, as our Saviour implies by his question, David's Lord in the highest sense of Lord, as David's Master and Possessor; compare Rev. xxii., "I am the root and the offspring of David."

We may also infer from this first verse that the whole Psalm was said to no mere creature. If such words as, " Sit thou on my right hand," were never said to any angel, neither could they have been said to any king—not to David—neither could they have been said to Solomon, nor to any earthly sovereign whatsoever.

14. "Are they not all ministering spirits?" Spirits must here mean spiritual or incorporeal beings, and rules the meaning of spirits in verse 7.

"Ministering," λειτουργικὰ, "liturgical." The words, λειτουργὸς and λειτουργία and λειτουργεῖν throughout this Epistle, have to do with divine service in the sense of worship. Thus x. 11, "Every priest standeth daily ministering;" also viii. 6, "Now he hath obtained a more excellent ministry" (that is, than that of the Jewish high priest); and ix. 21, "The vessels of the ministry," &c. The word then seems to look to those functions of the angels which are described in the book of Revelation, standing at the altar, offering incense, and such things. So that, taking the first half of the verse alone, it would seem to refer to what is usually called divine service, and the latter part of the verse is not at all against this, for the words " to minister" is not the same as in the first clause, and signifies a different sort of service (diaconia), and is applied to the assistance of the faithful in their conflicts and difficulties, so that the verse may be paraphrazed: "Are they not all liturgizing spirits —spirits who when in heaven are employed in the worship of heaven, but are sent at times from that exalted worship for purposes of ministry on the behalf of those who shall be heirs of salvation."

The angels of God are constantly described as ministering to the Son of God in His human nature. They ministered to Him after His temptation. One strengthened Him to support Him in His agony. They roll away the stone from the sepulchre. And as they minister to Him, so do they to the members of His Body, the Church. Even respecting little children, He says, "In heaven

forth to minister for them who shall be ʸ heirs of salvation?

ʸ Rom. viii. 17.
Tit. iii. 7. Jam.
ii. 5. 1 Pet. iii. 7.

their angels do always behold the face of my Father which is in heaven" (Matt. xviii. 10). And their ministrations continue unto this day. Those who refuse to accept any account, however well authenticated, of a special intervention from a higher sphere, on the express ground that there can be no higher sphere, no intelligences above the human, no powers above those which man can see or feel or handle, have to explain away an enormous number of facts which can only be accounted for by the assumption that there is a supreme Will and Intellect, and that there are gradations of beings between that Supreme Being and us who can act upon us, or for us, or perhaps against us, according to His Will or Permission.

## CHAP. II.

THEREFORE we ought to give the more earnest heed to the things which we have heard, lest at any time we should † let *them* slip.

† Gr. *run out as leaking vessels.*

1. "Let them slip." "Be diverted from them," Alford; "pereffuamus," Vulg. See below.

1. "Therefore we ought to give the more earnest heed to the things," &c. "Heard," that is, as verse 3 shows, the things heard in the preaching of the Lord Jesus and His immediate followers.

"Lest at any time we should let them slip." The word for "slip" ($\pi\alpha\rho\alpha\rho\rho\upsilon\tilde{\omega}\mu\epsilon\nu$) seems to mean to drift past the point we aim at. The metaphor is taken from ships which from the flux or reflux of the waves, or from the winds, are often hindered from reaching the port. Revisers translate "lest haply we should drift away from them." So Westcott, "Lest we be diverted from them." Alford, "miss them."

2 For if the word ª spoken by angels was stedfast, and ᵇ every transgression and disobedience received a just recompence of reward;

3 ᶜ How shall we escape, if we neglect so great

ª Deut. xxxiii. 2. Ps. lxviii. 17. Acts vii. 53. Gal. iii. 19.
ᵇ Num. xv. 30. 31. Deut. iv. 3. & xvii. 2, 5, 12. & xxvii. 26.
ᶜ ch. x. 28, 29. & xii. 25.

2. "For if the word spoken by angels was stedfast." "Stedfast," *i.e.*, abiding firm, and therefore not to be disobeyed with impunity.

"The word spoken by angels." There was a tradition among the Jews, which receives its confirmation from at least two other passages in the New Testament besides this (Acts vii. 53, Gal. iii. 19), that the law was in some sort given by the hands of angels, or through their intervention. There is no mention of this in the account of the giving of the law in Exodus, but there is a significant allusion to the attendance of angels at the giving of the law in Deut. xxxiii. 23, "Yea, he loved the people: all his saints are in thy hand, and they sat down at thy feet." As Ebrard shows, the saints or holy ones are clearly to be distinguished from the people or tribes of Israel, and are the angels. So also in Psalm lxviii., "The chariots of God are twenty thousands, even thousands of angels: the Lord is among them as in Sinai, as in the Holy Place." These references may be said to make up what is wanting in the account in Exodus, and to bear out what is taught us by this place and the other two before cited.

"And every transgression and disobedience received a just recompense," &c. The historical parts of the books of Moses are full of the speedy vengeance executed on the people in the wilderness after every act of disobedience, till all the males above twenty-one who came out of Egypt were cut off. Thus in 1 Cor. x. 6-10, they who lusted, they who committed idolatry, they who committed fornication (in idolatrous worship), they who tempted the Lord, they who murmured, were all summarily cut off.

3. "How shall we escape, if we neglect so great salvation?" "How shall we escape?" The certainty of the temporal judgment which followed close upon every transgression in the case of the Israelites, was a certain assurance of the vengeance which in another world would overtake those who had been careless about the claims of Jesus, the Son of God, upon their hearts and lives.

salvation; ᵈ which at the first began to be spoken by the Lord, and was ᵉ confirmed unto us by them that heard *him*;

4 ᶠ God also bearing *them* witness, ᵍ both with

ᵈ Matt. iv. 17. Mark i. 14. ch. i. 2.
ᵉ Luke i. 2.
ᶠ Mark xvi. 20. Acts xiv. 3, & xix. 11. Rom. xv. 18, 19. 1 Cor. ii. 4.
ᵍ Acts ii. 22, 43.

---

"So great salvation." Great in its Author Who is the Son of God incarnate; awfully great in the means by which it was purchased, even the Blood-shedding and Death of the Lord of glory; great in its proclamation, even by the power of the Holy Ghost; great in its issue, even the renewal of body and soul, so that the redeemed should be equal to the angels, and be the sons of God for ever.

"Which at the first began to be spoken by the Lord." This is translated by Wordsworth, "Which having received the beginning of its utterance through Him Who is the Lord." It did not come through angels or even through prophets, but through the Lord Himself. "Never man spake like this man." Such was the impression made by the words of the Lord upon His enemies; and He says Himself, "If I had not come and spoken unto them, they had not had sin" (John xv. 22).

"Was confirmed unto us by them that heard him." Compare, "He (the Holy Spirit) shall bring all things unto your remembrance, whatsoever I have said unto you" (John xiv. 26). The Gospels are the accounts of the life, words, and acts of Christ, and were written by them that heard Him. St. Matthew heard Him; St. Peter heard Him, and speaks to the Church through St. Mark; St. John heard Him. St. Luke bears witness to the fact that *they* delivered them to the Church who, "from the beginning were eyewitnesses and ministers of the word," and that he himself had had perfect understanding of all things from the very first (Luke i. 2, 3).

"God also bearing them witness, both with signs and wonders," &c. Rather "God also bearing co-witness," or "bearing witness together with them." Compare, "The Spirit of truth which proceedeth from the Father, he shall testify of me, *and ye also shall bear witness*, because ye have been with me from the beginning" (John xv. 27). God never would have sent them to bear witness to a salvation wrought by One Who was to all outward seeming a mere Jew, and yet His own Son incarnate, crucified, risen, and

signs and wonders, and with divers miracles, and ‖ ᵇ gifts of the Holy Ghost, ¹ according to his own will?

5 For unto the angels hath he not put in subjection ᵏ the world to come, whereof we speak.

‖ Or, *distributions*.
ᵇ 1 Cor. xii. 4, 7, 11.
¹ Eph. i. 5, 9.
ᵏ ch. vi. 5.
2 Pet. iii. 13.

ascended, unless He had accompanied such a word with assurances direct from Himself of its truth, and those assurances were "signs and wonders," which must direct attention to the speaker's message if he performed such things. The salvation which the first preachers proclaimed was salvation through a crucified Jew, Who after He had risen again did not show Himself to the world, but only to a very select few, which few were His witnesses to the world: but witnesses of what? Not to the truth of certain platitudes respecting virtue, but to the fact that the Unseen God was only to be approached through this crucified Jew; that His Death was the propitiatory sacrifice for all sins, and His Resurrection the pledge from God Himself that His Life could henceforth be communicated to us for the eternal life of soul and body.

In order that men might be brought to listen to such a message (I mean at the first), it must be witnessed to by signs (σημείοις).

The raising of a dead body, for instance, was a sign that the truth of the message was attested by the Lord of life and death.

"Wonders" (τέρασιν) which rivetted attention, and which could not be explained on any merely natural principles, *i.e.*, by any known laws of nature.

"And with divers miracles," rather "with divers powers," such as the power of speaking intelligently in tongues which men had never learnt, and which men would require months, perhaps years to master; or of prophesying, *i.e.*, declaring that things would come to pass which no foresight would enable the utterers to foretell.

"And gifts of the Holy Ghost," rather distributions (compare 1 Cor. xii. 11). "One and the self-same spirit *dividing* to every man severally as he will."

5. "For unto (the) angels hath he not put in subjection the world to come," &c. There are many intimations in Scripture that in old time the kingdoms of the world were put under the guardianship of angels. Thus, Daniel x. 13, a mighty angel is represented as saying, "The prince of the kingdom of Persia withstood me one and twenty days: but, lo, Michael, one of the chief princes came to

6 But one in a certain place testified, saying, ¹What is man, that thou art mindful of him? or the son of man, that thou visitest him?

7 Thou madest him ‖ a little lower than the

¹ Job vii. 17. Ps. viii. 4, &c. & cxliv. 3.
¶ Or, *a little while inferior to.*

---

help me," &c.; again, "there is none that holdeth with me in these things but Michael your prince," x. 21, also xii. 1, "Michael shall stand up, the great prince which standeth for the children of thy people." In the Septuagint of Deut. xxxii. 8, we read "When the most High divided the nations, when He separated the sons of Adam, he set the bounds of the nations according to the number of the angels of God." And very likely the writer of this Epistle had this in his mind rather than the Hebrew text as we have it now. So that in a sense, and to an extent we know not, the angels administered the providence of God over the kingdoms of this world, but it was not to be so in the kingdom of the Messiah, for that is the meaning of the "world to come," and so he proceeds:—

6. "But one in a certain place testified, saying, What is man, that thou," &c. One in a certain place, *i.e.*, David in the eighth Psalm, the Psalm which the Lord quoted when the Pharisees would have Him reprove the children for crying Hosanna to Him in the temple.

"What is man, that thou art mindful of him and the Son of man," &c. The Apostolic writer only quotes what is necessary for his purpose. The exclamation, "what is man that thou art mindful of him," is really called forth by the thought of the vast host of the heavenly bodies which in their immensity reduce this world to a mere speck, and its inhabitants seem beneath Divine notice.

7. "Thou madest him a little lower than the angels." This is the Septuagint translation of a place in the Hebrew, the strict rendering of which is, "Thou madest him to want but little of God," but inasmuch as it cannot be predicated of any finite creature that he "wants but little of God" when the infinite distance of the finite from the infinite is realized, the Hebrew word God (Elohim) is translated both in our authorized and in the Septuagint and the Targum by "angels," following the necessary lower rendering of Exod. xxi. 6, where "his master shall bring him before the judges,"

angels; thou crownedst him with glory and honour, and didst set him over the works of thy hands:

8 ᵐ Thou hast put all things in subjection under his feet. For in that he put all in subjection under him, he left nothing *that is* not put

ᵐ Matt. xxviii. 18. 1 Cor. xv. 27. Eph. i. 22. ch. i. 13.

---

is the translation of "shall bring him before the Elohim (or God)."

Man is in his origin lower than the angels, for he has a gross corporeal frame, whereas the angels have an ethereal one. He is more subject to the conditions of space than the angels, for he can with difficulty move from one place to another, whereas the angels can fly with the speed of lightning. He is at present under the dominion of sexual desires, whereas Christ promises that the children of the Resurrection shall neither marry nor be given in marriage, but be equal to the angels.

"Thou crownedst him with glory and honour." This seems to refer not to man considered as in the first Adam, but to man considered as in the Second.

The words "Thou madest him a little lower than the angels," may be taken as indicating the very exalted nature of man or the contrary. When said with reference to the Son of God, as they are here, they set forth His humiliation—the King of heaven and of angels submits to take an inferior nature, lower than the angels.

"And didst set him over the works of thy hands." This is not found in the Hebrew of the Eighth Psalm, but nevertheless it is true, for at the creation of man God said to him, "Have dominion over the fish of the sea, and over the fowl of the air, and over every living thing that moveth," &c. (Gen. i. 28.)

8. "Thou hast put all things in subjection under his feet." Thou hast set man, in the Person of Jesus, at thy right hand, not only over the creatures of earth, but "far above all principality and power and might and dominion," &c. (Ephes. . 21.)

"For in that he put all in subjection under him, he left," &c. The reasoning of the Apostolic writer requires the fullest sense to be given to this "all." St. Peter, in preaching to Cornelius, speaks of Jesus Christ as Lord of all, evidently in the most absolute sense.

under him. But now ⁿ we see not yet all things put under him.

9 But we see Jesus, ᵒ who was made a little lower than the angels ‖ for the suffering of death, ᵖ crowned with glory and honour; that he by the grace of God should taste death ᑫ for every man.

ⁿ 1 Cor. xv. 25.
ᵒ Phil. ii. 7, 8, 9.
‖ Or, *by.*
ᵖ Acts ii. 33.
ᑫ John iii. 16. & xii. 32. Rom. v. 18. & viii. 32. 2 Cor. v. 15. 1 Tim. ii. 6. 1 John ii. 2. Rev. v. 9.

9. For the difference in rendering the latter part see below.

"But now we see not yet all things put under him." We see not yet all things put under man. His dominion over the greater part of the creatures is but imperfect and partial. Some escape him, others resist or defy him. Out of immense numbers he can tame very few to his purposes. The dominion assured to the race is not theirs. But there is a pledge that it will be theirs in due time, for the writer proceeds:

9. "But we see Jesus, who was made a little lower than the angels." By assuming our lower nature He became as we are for a time, a little lower than the angels. A difference is made by some (as Bishop Wordsworth) between the "we see" (ὁρῶμεν) as signifying the seeing with the outward eye, and "we see" (βλέπομεν), the seeing by faith.

"For the suffering of death, crowned with glory and honour." The first clause, "for the suffering of death," may be taken either with the preceding, "made a little lower than the angels," or with the succeeding, "crowned with glory and honour." If with the preceding, then it means that he was made of a nature which, being subject to death, was lower than that of the angels who are immortal; or if with the latter, then He was crowned with glory and honour because of, or in reward of, His suffering of death. Both are perfectly true. The latter accords best with Phil. ii. 8. "Being found in fashion as a man, he humbled himself, and became obedient unto death, even the Death of the Cross, wherefore God also hath highly exalted him," &c.

"That he by the grace of God should." The "that" (ὅπως) cannot depend upon "crowned with glory and honour" because his exaltation was subsequent to His tasting death, and was the reward of it. He tasted death for every man at His Crucifixion; but there is a sense in which His subsequent exaltation was inseparable from His tasting death for every man, for by His exaltation alone He began

10 ʳFor it became him, ˢfor whom *are* all things, and by whom *are* all things, in bringing

ʳ Luke xxiv. 46.
ˢ Rom. xi. 36.

---

10. " In bringing; " or, " having brought."
to apply the merits of His Death and the power of His Resurrection to every man who would receive it; and inasmuch as the Atonement was on behalf of every man, every man had an interest in it. As St. John says, " He is the propitiation for our sins, and not for ours only, but for the sins of the whole world " (1 John ii. 2).

10. "For it became him, for whom are all things and by whom are," &c. "Him for whom and by whom," &c. God the Father, by Whose council and decree every part of the redeeming work of God the Son was brought about. " By whom are all things." The "by" (δἰ ὄν), denoting instrumentality, is usually said of God the Son, "by Whom also He made the worlds; " but the Fathers notice that being here said of God the Father, no idea of inferiority can be attached to it as if the Son was a mere subordinate agent.

" In bringing many sons unto glory." This may be rendered in "having brought," and if so, it seems to refer to the saints of the old dispensation, all of whom were perfected more or less through suffering.

Thus in this Epistle again, vi. 12, " Followers of them who through faith and patience inherit the promises," evidently alluding to the worthies of the old covenant; and if thus taken, its meaning is in remarkable accordance with the words, " it became him," it was fitting for him if He perfected the elder saints through sufferings, to make the captain of their salvation perfect also through the same. To this, however, it is objected, as by Alford, that it could not well be said of the saints of the older covenant, that they were brought to glory, seeing that it is said in this very epistle, that they without us should not be made perfect, and it can scarcely be said that Christ was the captain of their salvation—seeing that he was not yet revealed. Alford considers that it refers to the whole process of bringing sons to glory, and suggests as the nearest rendering, " It became him .... bringing as he did many sons unto glory, to make the captain," &c. But the difficulty is not removed by this. It is inherent in the past form of ἀγαγόντα. The remarks of Cornelius à Lapide seem most satisfactory, " Loquitur autem Apostolus maxime de Sanctis qui ante Christum vixerunt, jamque defuncti erant in statu salutis, et

many sons unto glory, to make ᵗ the captain of their salvation ᵘ perfect through sufferings.

11 For ˣ both he that sanctifieth and they who

ᵗ Acts iii. 15. & v. 31. ch. xii. 2.
ᵘ Luke xiii. 32. ch. v. 9.
ˣ ch. x. 10, 14.

---

certa spe gloriæ; tantum enim expectabant qui morte sua cœlum et aditum ad gloriam aperiret: hi enim jam quasi adducti ad gloriam, unumque pedem in cœlo habere videbantur." But it may be asked, how could One Who was the express image of the Person of God be made perfect? Simply, we answer, in His human nature. In the nature which He had assumed, He required to be perfected as a Mediator, and this could only be through His partaking of the temptations and trials, the sorrows and sufferings, even unto death, of those on whose behalf He came to mediate.

"The captain of their salvation." The same word which in Acts iii. 11 is translated "the Prince of Life." "The leader," perhaps, would suit best if we could intimately associate with it the idea of "author" and of "sovereign prince" combined. "Captain" has rather to do with the leading of those saved, and does not sufficiently embrace the authorship or beginning. The idea seems to be that the Author or Beginner of salvation by His Incarnation is perfected by His sufferings to be the Mediator Who applies It.

11. "For both he that sanctifieth and they who are sanctified are all of one." The work of sanctification is generally assigned to the Holy Spirit, as in the Catechism. But inasmuch as the Holy Spirit sanctifies in Christ, and by the application of His life, and we are sanctified by being members of Christ, Christ is here said to be "He who sanctifieth." In 1 Cor. i. 30, Christ is said to be made unto us, "Wisdom, and righteousness, and sanctification, and redemption."

"They who are sanctified." That is, the members of the mystical Body are all of one—"of," in the sense of "from," out of." Not, of course, after the same manner of derivation. "The Son is of the Father alone, not made, nor created, but begotten," and men, His brethren, are from the Father, as all creatures are. "To us there is one God the Father, of whom are all things, and we in (or for) Him" (1 Cor. viii. 6), but it is most probable that the phrase "all of one" is not applied to the members of the Church as having the same derivation from God, but as deriving from him their true spiritual nature by Regeneration, as it is written in

| CHAP. II.] | ALL OF ONE. | 69 |

are sanctified ʸ *are* all of one: for which cause ᵃ he is not ashamed to call them brethren,

12 Saying, ᵃ I will declare thy name unto my

ʸ Acts xvii. 26.
ᶻ Matt. xxviii. 10. John xx. 17. Rom. viii. 29.
ᵃ Ps. xxii. 22, 25.

11. "Of one." "From one."

John i. 13, "Born, not of blood, nor of the will of the flesh, nor of man, but of God."

"For which cause he is not ashamed to call them brethren." The most remarkable instance of this is when the Lord said to Mary Magdalene, "Go to my brethren, and say unto them, I ascend unto my Father and your Father, and to my God and your God" (John xx. 17).

"He is not ashamed." Notwithstanding the infinite difference between His origin and theirs, He being the Son of God by nature, they being the sons of God by creation. Notwithstanding also the amazing difference between His human generation and theirs—He being conceived by the Holy Ghost, and so without sin; they being by nature born in sin, yet "He is not ashamed to call them brethren."

12. "Saying, I will declare thy name unto my brethren, in the midst," &c. This is a quotation from the 22nd Psalm, which is allowed by both Jews, *i.e.*, the ancient ones, and Christians to be the utterance of Christ on the Cross. It is ascribed in the title to David; but there are many expression in it which it seems impossible to apply to David, as particularly verses 16 and 17: "They pierced my hands and my feet, I may tell all my bones. They look and stare upon me. They part my garments among them, and cast lots upon my vesture." No sufferings of David which we read of at all correspond to this. Bishop Westcott writes: "The Psalm itself, which probably dates from the time of David's persecution by Saul, describes the course by which the anointed of the Lord made his way to the throne, or more generally, the establishment of the righteous kingdom of God through suffering." But surely it is very difficult to treat the sufferings in the cave of Adullam as in any way typifying the Sufferings Which redeemed the world. We must apply to David in composing this Psalm the words of St. Peter, "Searching what, or what manner of time the Spirit of Christ which was in them did signify, when it testified beforehand the sufferings of Christ, and the glory that should follow.

brethren, in the midst of the church will I sing praise unto thee.

<sup>b</sup> Ps. xviii. 2.
Isa. xii. 2.
<sup>c</sup> Isa. viii. 18.
<sup>d</sup> John x. 29.
& xvii. 6, 9, 11, 12.

13 And again, <sup>b</sup> I will put my trust in him. And again, <sup>c</sup> Behold I and the children <sup>d</sup> which God hath given me.

---

Unto whom it was revealed, that not unto themselves but unto us they did minister the things which are now reported unto you by them that have preached the Gospel," &c. (1 Pet. i. 11). Alford has some admirable remarks on this Psalm, as cited by the Apostolic writer. "No word prompted by the Holy Ghost had reference to the utterer only. All Israel was a type; all spiritual Israel set forth the coming Man, the quickening Spirit: all the groanings of God's suffering people prefigured, and found their fullest meaning in His groans Who was the chief in suffering. The maxim cannot be too firmly held, nor too widely applied, that all the Old Testament utterances of the Spirit anticipate Christ; just as all His new Testament utterances set forth and expand Christ: that Christ is everywhere involved in the Old Testament as He is everywhere evolved in the New." We must put the highest possible meaning upon this verse. Christ makes known the Name of God as Father. He manifested it in all His preaching. He manifested it particularly to His chosen ones, inasmuch as He said to His Father, 'I have manifested Thy Name unto the men which thou gavest me out of the world' (John xiii. 6). He manifested it, we may be sure, when He preached in the unseen world, and He now manifests it in His Church by His Spirit.

"In the midst of the Church will I sing praise unto thee." It is true, literally true, that He leads the praises of His Church. He is the Priest in every Eucharist—the Church's great act of thanksgiving. "Where two or three are gathered together in His name there is He in the midst of them" as the receiver of their prayers and the Inspirer of their devotions.

13. "And again, I will put my trust in him." These words are to be found in Isaiah viii. 17, Sept., also in Psalm xviii. 3, verbatim as they are to be found in 2 Sam. xxii. 3. Here the Messiah is represented as having the same trust in God as His Father as all God's children have. The words are those of David, but He speaks them typically as the utterance of His Antitype and Descendant.

14 Forasmuch then as the children are partakers of flesh and blood, he ᵉ also himself likewise took part of the same; ᶠ that through death he might destroy him that had the power of death, that is, the devil;

ᵈ John i. 14.
Rom. viii. 3.
Phil. ii. 7.
ᶠ 1 Cor. xv. 54,
55. Col. ii. 15.
2 Tim. i. 10.

"And again, Behold I and the children which God hath given me." The Apostolic writer here uses a part of a passage in Isaiah taken out of its context, but he has a right, if one may say it, so to do, for the whole verse is, in its fullest signification, peculiarly appropriate to the Lord, and those made the children of God by the power of His word. Isaiah had two sons given to him which were intended by God, though we cannot say how, to be signs of prophetic import to the Jews of his day. But much more were the spiritual children of Christ, the Apostles and others, "for signs and for wonders in Israel from the Lord of Hosts." The Apostles, and those whom they converted on the day of Pentecost, were as men raised from the dead. The Apostles, in their message, their miraculous powers, and in the character of goodness and holiness and self-denial which they formed in their converts were "for signs and wonders in Israel from the Lord of Hosts." It is true that the Apostle only uses that part of the prophetic utterance in verse 18 which serves his purpose of shewing that the Lord claims those who believe in Him to be His brethren, but as the whole prophecy is in its fulness applicable to Christ alone, he is quite entitled to use any part of it which sets forth any truth concerning Christ.

14. "Forasmuch then as the children are partakers of flesh and blood," &c. Partaking of flesh and blood, no doubt, here includes the idea of mortality. Flesh and blood cannot inherit the kingdom of God. Before this can take place they must pass through death, and so the Lord took our mortal nature, and in it became obedient unto death.

"He also himself likewise took part of the same." "Likewise," *i.e.*, "in like manner." He was born like other men, of the blessed Virgin—of her substance, though through His Divine conception He took it without sin.

"That through death he might destroy him that had the power," &c. Through death He won immortality.

"Him that had the power of death." Inasmuch as Satan

g Luke i. 74.
Rom. viii. 15.
2 Tim. i. 7.

15 And deliver them who <sup>g</sup> through fear of death were all their lifetime subject to bondage.

brought sin into the world, he brought death by sin. He does not wield the power to kill whom he pleases. Death comes upon men in what is called the natural course, but Satan has power to make use of it, as the next verse tells us, to keep men in bondage. Death, and the uncertainty of things after death, the dread of extinction, or the dread of punishment on account of sin for which they knew no real atonement, was a hard bondage. Men might brave it, and conceal it, but it was, nevertheless, a terrible bondage. Even a very good man, like Hezekiah, could say, "I said in the cutting off of my days, I shall go to the gates of the grave: I am deprived of the residue of my years. . . . Like a crane or a swallow, so did I chatter, I did mourn as a dove. . . . The grave cannot praise thee, death cannot celebrate thee . . . the living, the living, he shall praise thee as I do this day."

"Destroy him that had the power of death." "Destroy" is rather "bring to nought him that had the power," &c.; but how can this be said, seeing that Satan yet exists? This word, "destroy him that had the power of death," refers to the power which the devil had over men through death as the consequence of sin. Death was once the king of terrors. Death instead of being annihilation or destruction, is now the gate of life. The Apostle, and all who believe in the same Christ as the Apostle, can say, "O Death, where is thy sting? O grave, where is thy victory?" We can now look upon the grave as the gate of a joyful resurrection. For Christ hath abolished death, and brought life and immortality to light by the Gospel. If we truly believe, death can never be used by Satan as a means of keeping us alienated from God; it is rather the call of God to free us from a state in which it is possible to fall from God to a state in which we cannot fall from God, but shall be for ever with the Lord.

15. "And deliver them who through fear of death were all their lifetime," &c. This cannot mean that we Christians are forbidden to have a certain awe of death. For what is death? It is to pass out of the visible world into the invisible—out of a world with which we are familiar, into one of which we know nothing—out of a state which has become natural to us, into one of which we can form no conception as to how we shall exist in it. Above all, it is

16 For verily † he took not on *him the nature of* angels; but he took on *him* the seed of Abraham.

17 Wherefore in all things it behoved him ʰ to be made like unto *his* brethren, that he might be ⁱ a

† Gr. *he taketh not hold of angels, but of the seed of Abraham he taketh hold.*
ʰ Phil. ii. 7.
ⁱ ch. iv. 15. & v. 1, 2.

---

to pass through a judgment—not the judgment of the Great Day, but one in which we shall be sealed to the award to be passed upon us at that Day. It is, as one has well said, "To close our eyes upon weeping friends, and to open them upon the angels of God." How did the Lord Himself regard it? "Father, if it be possible, let this cup pass from me; nevertheless, not my will, but thine be done." We are delivered then from the bondage of its fear. It has lost its sting, but it has not lost its mystery. It is said of those who have been brought to its very gates, and have been respited for a season, that their whole life with all its circumstances, has been brought before them as in a moment. Is this nothing?

16. "For verily he took not on him the nature of angels; but he took on him the seed of Abraham." "He took not on him." Properly, he doth not lay hold of angels, *i.e.*, to lift them up; but he lays hold on the seed of Abraham, that through it He might lift up mankind. In order to lay hold of us He must become incarnate, and in becoming incarnate He must take hold of some race, and He took hold of that which God at the first had "planted a noble vine, wholly a right seed."

It is objected that ἐπιλαμβάνεται is a present and the Incarnation is past, and so it cannot refer to It; but surely this cannot be urged, because Christ took the nature of man that He might continuously assist us. Every act by which He now applies His grace is a laying hold of some sinner or other in the way of helping him, but He helps them through His human Nature, which He could not have done unless He had assumed it. The beginning of help was the Incarnation, and the continuance of help is through the same (John vi.).

17. "Wherefore in all things it behoved him to be made like unto his brethren." The stress is to be laid on the words "in all things." It was not enough that He should partake of the flesh and blood of which the children partook—it was not enough that He should simply lay hold of the seed of Abraham. He

merciful and faithful high priest in things *pertaining* to God, to make reconciliation for the sins of the people.

---

is to raise up His brethren, by acting on their behalf as a merciful and faithful High Priest, and on this account He must be in all things likened unto His brethren; for His action as High Priest is not a mere external action on behalf of a nation or people taken in the mass, as it were, but it is on behalf of each and every individual, and is of such a sort that He must know their whole internal state, if there is to be a perfect reconciliation of their whole soul and spirit; in fact, of all that is within them, to God. To this end He must be able to enter into all their difficulties—to know and take account of their most secret sins; or else the reconciliation would be like that of the Jewish High Priest—superficial and external only. In this respect human priests, as ministers of reconciliation, are faint types of Him. In order that they may fulfil their mission judiciously in the matter of the application of the reconciling word to consciences, they must have great powers of sympathy, as well as impartiality. And so must, and so has, He Who is the Priest of priests: Who is with every faithful priest in His ministrations; so that the inferior and merely human priest in dealing with souls is strictly and merely His instrument. To this end amongst these "all things" must above all be reckoned sufferings and temptations. He must have sounded the profoundest depths of our sufferings; and so He has. No one of His brethren can say that he has suffered more than the Son of God.

"That he might be a merciful and faithful high priest." "Merciful." This seems to mean one who is not hard or unsympathizing, but the contrary. "Faithful." This seems to mean dealing faithfully—not salving over a wound which ought to be probed, but dealing faithfully with the sinner, faithfully both in respect of keeping promises, and faithfully in the matter of needful reproof and correction.

"To make reconciliation for the sins of the people." The context seems to bid us look not so much to the one act of reconciliation upon the Cross, as the continued application of that act in the reconciling of individual consciences to God.

18. "For in that he himself hath suffered being tempted, he is able," &c. This seems the best translation. If in *all* things He was made like unto His brethren, He must have been made like

CHAP. III.]    HE IS ABLE TO SUCCOUR.    75

18 ᵏ For in that he himself hath suffered being tempted, he is able to succour them that are tempted.   <sup>k</sup> ch. iv. 15, 16. &. v. 2. & vii. 25.

unto them in enduring temptation; for that is the universal lot of mankind. In enduring temptation His holy Soul must have suffered intensely, far more than we suffer when we endure temptation, so that He has sounded all the depths of temptation or trial, and from His knowledge of it is able to succour us, no matter how severe and seemingly overwhelming the assault of the tempter.[1]

And how does He apply His help? In many ways. He infuses strength into us. He renews our wills, so that we will the things of God far more than we will the things of the world and the flesh. He provides the way of escape, and gives us grace to avail ourselves of it. He reminds us of His love in dying for us. He brings to bear upon us that part of the word of God which is the sword of the Spirit most fitting to drive back the particular enemy which assaults us.

## CHAP. III.

WHEREFORE, holy brethren, partakers of ᵃthe hea-

<sup>a</sup> Rom. i. 7.
1 Cor. i. 2.
Eph. iv. 1.
Phil. iii. 14.
2 Thess. i. 11.
2 Tim. i. 9.
2 Pet. i. 10.

1. "Wherefore, holy brethren, partakers of the heavenly calling, consider," &c. "Wherefore," from all that I have said before of God having spoken to us by His Son, the shining forth of His Glory, the express image of His Essence; Whom the angels are to worship—to Whom God says, "Thy throne, O God, is for ever and ever," under Whose feet God has put all things—Who, notwithstanding these infinitely great things said of Him was yet as the archegos of our Salvation, made perfect through sufferings, Who to this intent partook

---

[1] It is impossible to suppose that that meaning can be true which would limit the assisting power of the Great High Priest; as, for instance, if we should render this place, "in that which" or "in the things which" he suffered being tempted, he is able to succour them that are similarly tempted; He must be able to succour all the tempted. His experience must cover the whole region of temptation.

venly calling, consider [b]the Apostle and High Priest of our profession, Christ Jesus;

[b] Rom. xv. 8. ch. ii. 17. & iv. 14. & v. 5. & vi. 20. & viii. 1. & ix. 11. & x. 21.

---

of our flesh and blood—Who took not hold of angels to assist them, but took hold of the seed of Abraham, Who was in all things made like unto us that He might be a merciful and faithful high priest —because of all this, " consider Him."

"Holy brethren." Holy, because dedicated to God, and partakers of His Spirit. All professing Christians are, in the view of the Apostle, ἅγιοι. Bishop Wordsworth, however, thinks that the expression looks to the holiness of the Jewish people as an holy nation, as well as to the Christian standing of the converts. The bulk of them were not holy in the modern use of the term.

"Partakers of the heavenly calling." There is no article before calling, but it must mean the calling, for they were not partakers of one calling out of many. "The called according to God's purpose." "Whom he did predestinate, them he also called." The calling is heavenly, because it comes from heaven, and calls us to lead the life of heaven, and at last to attain to the kingdom of heaven.

"Consider the Apostle and High Priest of our profession." The term Apostle is not usually applied to the Lord, but it underlies every place in which God is said to send (ἀποστέλλειν) His Son. Thus, John iii. 17: "God sent not His Son into the world to condemn the world." He whom God hath sent speaketh the words of God. "As my Father sent me, so send I you" (John iii. 17, 34; xx. 21). The words Apostle and High Priest are here combined because of the mention of Moses in the following verses, Moses being especially the Apostle of God, because He was sent by God to the children of Israel ("I AM hath sent me unto you"), and because he was the priest of God to consecrate Aaron himself to the Priesthood.

"Consider . . . who was faithful." Attention is first directed to the faithfulness of Christ to His Father; but then the Apostolic writer proceeds to the glory of Christ as the Son being greater than that of Moses the Servant.

"Of our profession." Notice that He is not the Apostle and High Priest of our religion, but of our profession—or, rather, of our confession—that which we in common, or as one man, hold

## FAITHFUL IN ALL HIS HOUSE.

2 Who was faithful to him that †appointed him, as also ᶜ Moses *was faithful* in all his house.

† Gr. *made*, 1 Sam. xii. 6.
ᶜ Num. xii. 7. ver. 5.

---

2. "In all his house." So ℵ, A., C., D., E., K., L., M., P., all Cursives, &c.; but B., Copt., and Sah. omit "all."

and acknowledge to be our belief. The joining together of Christians in one common profession or confession was not an accident, but of the very essence of Christianity. As there is one Lord, so there is one faith—the faith of Christ Incarnate, Crucified, Risen, and Ascended. He would especially remind the Hebrew Christians of their profession of Christ, because it was their bond of union as co-religionists. The unbelieving part of their nation held to the unity—the being and attributes of God; but *their* confession was the Divine Nature and Redeeming work of the Son of God.

2. "Who was faithful to him that appointed him, as also Moses was faithful." Christ always set Himself forth as under His Father in the dispensation which He inaugurated. "I came not to do mine own will, but the will of Him that sent me" (John v. 30; vi. 38). "Not my will, but thine be done" (Matth. xxvi. 39).

"To Him that appointed Him"—*i.e.*, made Him to be Apostle and High Priest, by sending Him and consecrating Him. "All things are of God" (2 Cor. v. 18).

"As also Moses was faithful in all his house."

"Faithful," &c. This is a quotation from Numb. xii. 6. The Lord in reproving Aaron and Miriam for their rebellion against Moses places Moses far above all other prophets. "If there be a prophet among you, I the Lord will make myself known unto him in a vision, and will speak unto him in a dream. My servant Moses is not so, who is faithful in all mine house," &c.

"His house"—that is, God's house. This, as we shall see, is important. Both the Jewish and the Christian dispensations are called houses of God. Thus, respecting the Jewish, God said, "I the Lord dwell among the children of Israel" (Deut. xxxv. 34). "Here will I dwell, for I have a delight therein" (Ps. cxxxii. 11, 14); and, respecting the Christian, the Holy Ghost said, "Ye are builded together for an habitation of God through the Spirit" (Ephes. ii. 22).

But the union of Christ with His Church is far closer than the

3 For this *man* was counted worthy of more glory than Moses, inasmuch as ᵈ he who hath builded the house hath more honour than the house.

4 For every house is builded by some *man;* but ᵉ he that built all things *is* God.

ᵈ Zech. vi. 12. Matt. xvi. 18.
ᵉ Eph. ii. 10. & iii. 9. ch. i. 2.

---

head of the house to the house or household. The Church and Christ form parts of one great Divine organization, for Christ is the Head of the Church in the sense that the whole body, through its connection with Him, receives life from Him (Coloss. ii. 19).

3. "For this man was counted worthy of more glory than Moses," &c. Moses was held in the highest honour by the ancient people of God; but when Christ came, He was not only honoured, but worshipped. He received worship. He was constantly addressed in terms which of right can be only applied to the supreme God; and He did not reprove those who so honoured Him, but received it as His due. He suffered Himself to be called "Lord" and "God," and praised the man who did so as one who believed, and this for the simple reason that He was the Builder, the Constitutor, the Ruler of the house of God.

"He who builded the house hath more honour than the house." Moses, great though he was, was but a part of the house or household; and so the Eternal Son, Who built Moses into the house, and constituted him for a time the head of the household, was of infinitely greater account than the stone which He took and set in its place in the house, or the servant whom He put over His other domestics.

The Builder or Constitutor of the house has, of course, more honour than all the house put together: much more is He more honourable than any part of it.

4. "For every house is builded by some man; but he that built all things is God." This is a very unequivocal declaration of the Godhead of the Son: for the Son is He that built and constituted the house in question. It did not come into being of itself—no house can; but He that built it is God—not the Father, but the Son, by Whom (i. 2) God made the worlds, the ages, and so important a creation in these ages as the older dispensation cannot have come into being without Him.

CHAP. III.]   CHRIST AS A SON.   79

5 ᶠAnd Moses verily *was* faithful in all his house, as ᵍa servant, ʰfor a testimony of those things which were to be spoken after;
6 But Christ as ⁱa son over his own house; ᵏwhose house are we, ˡif we hold fast the confidence and the rejoicing of the hope firm unto the end.

f ver. 2.
g Ex. xiv. 31. Num. xii. 7. Deut. iii. 24. Josh. i. 2. & viii. 31.
h Deut. xviii. 15. 18, 19. 1 ch. i. 2.
k 1 Cor. iii. 16. & vi. 19. 2 Cor. vi. 16. Eph. ii. 21, 22. 1 Tim. iii. 15. 1 Pet. ii. 5.
l ver. 14. Matt. x. 22. & xxiv. 13. Rom. v. 2. Col. i. 23. ch. vi. 11. & x. 35.

6. "Firm unto the end" omitted by B. only.

5. "And Moses verily was faithful in all his house, as a servant, for a testimony." He was faithful over that part of the great family of God over whom he was set; but his faithfulness to God was especially manifested in this, that he did not set forth his own dispensation as final; on the contrary, he proclaimed its temporary character when he said, "The Lord thy God will raise up unto thee a Prophet from the midst of thee—of thy brethren, like unto me: unto him shall ye hearken." In this he was a testimony "of those things which were to be spoken after" by the Lord Himself. Respecting this his testimony, the Lord Jesus witnesses, "Had ye believed Moses ye would have believed me, for he wrote of me" (John v. 46).

6. "But Christ as a son over his own house; whose house are we," &c. How is it said that He is faithful as a Son over His own house? Is not the house the house of God His Father? Yes; but He is appointed the heir of all things (i. 2). "All things are delivered unto him of His Father." "All power is given to him in heaven and in earth." "God hath put all things under his feet" (Matth. xi. 27; xxviii. 18; Ephes. i. 22).

"Whose house are we, if we hold fast the confidence and the rejoicing," &c. Here our continuing in the house of God is made to depend, not only on Christ's faithfulness, but upon ours. We have to hold fast the confidence—rather, "the boldness." How will this be shown? By our boldness in coming to the throne of grace in prayer. We are to hold fast "the rejoicing of the hope." How will this be shown? By having within us as a constant abiding principle the evidence of things not seen (xi. 1).[1]

---

[1] Bishop Westcott translates "the boast of our hope," and writes, "This exultation is here regarded in its definite concrete form (καυχήμα, boast), and not as finding personal expression (καυχήσις, boasting)."

7 Wherefore (as ᵐ the Holy Ghost saith, ⁿ To day if ye will hear his voice,

8 Harden not your hearts, as in the provocation, in the day of temptation in the wilderness:

<small>ᵐ 2 Sam. xxiii. 2. Acts i. 16.
ⁿ ver. 15. Ps. xcv. 7.</small>

---

"Firm unto the end." The Hebrews to whom this was written were under persecution which put them in daily jeopardy of their lives. The end with them would be the end of life, or, perhaps, the end when the Son of Man should come.

7. "Wherefore, as the Holy Ghost saith, To-day if ye will hear his voice." He now applies the warnings with which the 95th Psalm closes to the Hebrew Christians. The place is parallel to 1 Cor. x. 6, &c., where the Israelites are taken to be a type of Christians in the Apostle's day. And the things which happened to them, the punishments inflicted on them, are said to be written for " our admonition."

"As the Holy Ghost saith." Here the Book of Psalms is appealed to as the words of the Holy Ghost. Thus the Lord had asked respecting the words of Ps. cx., Why doth David in Spirit—*i.e.*, by inspiration of the Spirit—call him Lord?

" To day if ye will hear his voice." The Psalm was written long after the sojourn in the Wilderness, and yet the Psalmist makes it of ever present application.

"His voice." If we take into full account chap. ii. verses 2, 3, we shall acknowledge that this is the voice of the Son.

8. "Harden not your hearts, as in the provocation, in the day of temptation." The provocation alluded to is described in Exod. xvii., where the people, when they came to Rephidim, murmured because there was no water; the Lord was there daily showering down upon them the manna and the quails, and yet they had so little confidence, so little hope of the ultimate possession of the land of Canaan—so little affected by the wonders of the passage of the Red Sea—that they said to Moses, "Wherefore is this, that thou hast brought us out of the land of Egypt to kill us and our children and our cattle with thirst." And it is said that Moses called the name of the place Massah and Meribah, because of the chiding of the children of Israel, and because they tempted the Lord, saying, " Is the Lord amongst us or not?"

Now this was the very temptation to which the Hebrew Chris-

9 When your fathers tempted me, proved me, and saw my works forty years.

10 Wherefore I was grieved with that generation, and said, They do alway err in *their* heart; and they have not known my ways.

---

tians were exposed. Is the Lord amongst us in very deed, are we his house? Does He dwell in us His Church, or does He make no difference between ourselves and our unconverted or unbelieving brethren? If such thoughts found lodgment in their minds they would assuredly not hold fast their confidence and rejoicing, and the firmer they believed in the presence of Christ amongst them, the more confidence they would have in a glorious issue. In the Hebrew, the names which Moses gave to the scene of the temptation form part of the text, "As Meribah, as the day of Massah in the desert?" It was the first great trial which overtook the Israelites, and its point was, Is the Lord present with us in any peculiar special supernatural mode of presence or not?

9. "When your fathers tempted me, proved me, and saw my works forty years." In the Hebrew text, and in the Septuagint, the words, "forty years," seem to be taken with the next verse, "Forty years long was I grieved with this generation, and said." By the Apostolic writer they are rather connected with the Israelites seeing the marvellous works for forty years, and the bulk of the nation not converted by them. Almost all commentators draw attention to the fact that as the Israelites saw the works of God forty years, so the Jewish nation saw the works wrought by the Apostles for about the same time, and yet were finally rejected because of unbelief.

10. "Wherefore I was grieved with that generation, and said, They do always," &c. "I was grieved," the word expresses more than being grieved; it rather expresses loathing and abhorrence.

"They have not known my ways." If any generation that ever lived on the face of the earth knew God's ways they did: and yet in the better and deeper sense they saw them not. They did not recognize or realize either the mercies or the judgments of God. Their stupidity and unbelief seems more marvellous than the wonders by which they were sustained, or the miraculous judgments by which they perished.

11 So I sware in my wrath, † They shall not enter into my rest.)

† Gr. *If they shall enter.*

12 Take heed, brethren, lest there be in any of you an evil heart of unbelief, in departing from the living God.

---

11. "So I sware in my wrath, They shall not enter into my rest." The writer has occasion afterwards to draw attention to God's confirming His promise by an oath. If He confirmed His threatening by an oath, much more His promise.

"They shall not enter into my rest." Literally, "if they shall enter into my rest,"—the Hebrew form of an oath. The full form is given in such a place as 1 Kings xix. 2, "So let the gods do to me, and more also, if I make not thy life as the life of one of them." The full form when God takes such an oath as this would be, "I am not God, I am not the God of Abraham, if they shall enter," &c. What is the rest? No doubt the land of Canaan. Thus Deut. iii. 20 and Joshua i. 13.

But the land of Canaan is typical of the full and perfect kingdom of God, which will be given to the faithful at the coming of the Lord. When in their glorified bodies they will be safe from the assaults of sin, and they will have a place and sphere fitted to be the habitation of such renewed and glorified frames.

12. "Take heed, brethren, lest there be in any of you an evil heart of unbelief," &c. Reference seems to be made to the complaint of Almighty God in Deut. v. 29: "O that there were such an heart in them that they would fear me, and keep all my commandments always," &c.

Notice how the Apostle says, "Lest there be in any of you." Rebellions such as these of the children of Israel must have their origin in some particular heart or other. Some leader will put himself forward and speak out, and when this is done the evil will be contagious, and the little leaven will leaven the whole lump.

"In departing from the living God," literally in apostatizing from, in standing away from Him, in taking the side contrary to His side.

"From the living God." The cause of Christ is that of the living God. "He is the Son of the living God" (Matth. xvi. 16); "He has in Himself life from the living God" (John v. 26); "I

13 But exhort one another daily, while it is called To day; lest any of you be hardened through the deceitfulness of sin.

14 For we are made partakers of Christ, ᵒ if we  ᵒ ver. 6.
hold the beginning of our confidence stedfast unto the end;

---

am he that liveth and was dead, and behold I am alive for evermore" (Rev. i. 18).

13. "But exhort one another daily, while it is called To day." It is incumbent upon Christians not to leave the duty of exhortation to ministers, but each one to remind his neighbour of his duty. There is a special blessing pronounced by the Lord upon such Christian intercourse; thus Malachi iii. 16: "Then they that feared the Lord spake often one to another, and the Lord hearkened and heard it, and a book of remembrance was written before him for them that feared the Lord," &c.

"To day" practically means the day of grace of each person, the day or time of his continuance in life, in the Church, within reach of the sound of exhortation and reproof.

Such an application of the word "To-day" could not have been unless the day of grace was NOW. ("Now is the accepted time, now is the day of salvation.")

"Lest any of you be hardened through the deceitfulness of sin." This has been explained in the case of the Hebrew Christians, Lest any of you be led away by the specious sophisms and plausible reasonings of the unbelieving Jews; but it must not be narrowed in this way. All sin is deceitful, because it hardens that within us which is our great defence against all moral and spiritual deceit, the conscience.

14. "For we are made partakers of Christ, if we hold the beginning of our confidence," &c. The Israelites might be said to be partakers of the rest of Canaan as soon as they passed the Red Sea, and were safe in the wilderness. In God's intention they were already in possession, for He by inspiration taught them to sing (Exod. xv. 17), "Thou shalt bring them in and plant them in the mountain of thine inheritance, in the place, O Lord, which thou hast made for thee to dwell in, in the sanctuary, O Lord, which thy hands have established." And so every baptised Christian has assigned to him, by virtue of his Sacramental Death and Resur-

15 While it is said, ᵖTo day if ye will hear his voice, harden not your hearts, as in the provocation. 16 ᑫFor some, when they had heard, did provoke: howbeit not all that came out of Egypt by Moses.

ᵖ ver. 7.
ᑫ Num. xiv. 2, 4, 11, 24, 30. Deut. i. 34, 36, 38.

---

rection with Christ, typified by the passage of the Red Sea, a part in Christ's eternal kingdom, but he has to make his calling and election sure, he has to work out his salvation, he has to "endure to the end," he has to "continue in God's goodness." Just, then, as the Israelites were sure of the possession of Canaan, so far as God was concerned, so we are assured of life everlasting; but as God did not annihilate the free will of the Israelites, which will, because it was evil, prevented them from attaining to their rest, so He has not annihilated our free-will; we have to hold the beginning of our confidence steadfast unto the end. If the Israelites had continued in the confidence which the song of Moses expressed, they would have quickly been in possession of their inheritance; but they did not, and the Apostolic writer cites their case as an example (1 Cor. x. 1-10). Such a place as this should teach us to pray to God very earnestly that He would make us to will and to do of His good pleasure; that He would renew our wills, that He would make us "willing in this day of His power."

15. "While it is said, To-day if ye will hear his voice, harden not your hearts." There is a difficulty as to what preceding verse this is to be connected with. Very probably it must follow "Exhort one another . . . lest any of you," &c., and would then signify, "since it is said," or "in that it is said."

"To-day if ye will hear his voice, harden not." The emphasis may be laid on the words, ἐν τῷ λέγεσθαι, as denoting the present time. In its being now said by God, To-day if ye will hear. The Psalm was not written for the Jews only, but for us. It is, in fact, written for all who have a day of grace. "To-day, whilst your day of grace lasts, if ye will hear his voice." Heb. xii. 25 is an exactly parallel exhortation.

16. "For some, when they had heard, did provoke: howbeit not all." Almost all expositors seem agreed in taking these two sentences interrogatively, "Who then when they had heard, did provoke?" "Was it not all that came out of Egypt by Moses?"

CHAP. III.]   THEM THAT BELIEVED NOT?   85

17 But with whom was he grieved forty years? *was it not with them that had sinned,* ʳ *whose carcases fell in the wilderness?*

18 And ˢ *to whom sware he that they should not enter into his rest, but to them that believed not?*

ʳ Num. xiv. 22, 29, &c. & xxvi. 65. Ps. cvi. 26. 1 Cor. x. 5. Jude 5.
ˢ Num. xiv. 30. Deut. i. 34, 35.

---

This removes the difficulty which is felt in applying the words, "not all," to Caleb and Joshua only; but it is to be remembered that all who were under age, all the young men, women, and children who were under twenty, who must have been in number far more than those above that age, did not perish with the rebels in the rebellions in the wilderness.

17. "But with whom was he grieved forty years?" Was it not with them that murmured, not believing that God was among them? With them that rebelled in the matter of Korah, not believing that God had instituted the priesthood and would uphold what He had ordained? With them that joined in the idolatrous rites of the Moabites, not believing that God was a jealous God, and would not be worshipped as if He was one of "Gods many and Lords many"?

18. "And to whom sware he that they should not enter into his rest, but," &c. The provocation on account of which God swore that that evil generation should not enter into His rest, was not a sin of idolatry, or of fornication, or of lust, but of sheer unbelief. We have the account very fully related in Num. xiii. and xiv.: Twelve spies were sent out, ten of whom brought an evil report that the people were giants, the cities great, and walled up to heaven, and that they were unable to go up against the people of the land. The children of Israel listened to the cowardly spies, and forgot the passage of the Red Sea, and the manna, and the water out of the rock; and said, "Let us make us a captain, and let us return into Egypt." Then it was that the Lord sware in his wrath "that they should not enter into his rest." They had faith when they came out of Egypt, for the Psalmist witnesses, "Then believed they his word, and sang praises unto him," but this did not last. "They thought scorn of that pleasant land, and gave no credence unto his word." The root, then, of their sin was unbelief, and its fruit was disobedience. They sinned because they believed

19 ᵇSo we see that they could not enter in because of unbelief.

ᵇ ch. iv. 6.

not. And so it would be with the Hebrew Christians. They had the clearest prophecies from the lips of Christ Himself, that the city and nation to which they belonged would perish through its unbelief. They had had forty years of the preaching of the Apostles themselves, forty years of miracles, not only of miracles wrought by the Apostles, but power to perform miracles given by the Apostles. They had the Spirit of God, as St. Stephen witnessed, remonstrating with them, and yet they would not believe, and so "the wrath was come upon them to the uttermost."

## CHAP. IV.

LET ᵃus therefore fear, lest, a promise being left *us* of entering into his rest, any of you should seem to come short of it.

ᵃ ch. xii. 15.

19, iv. 1. "So we see that they could not enter in because of unbelief. Let us therefore fear, lest, a promise being left us of entering into his rest, any of you," &c. This is the conclusion of what has gone before. They perished singly and individually through various sins, but they were excluded from entering into rest because of unbelief. Let us therefore fear, for they are our types, our ensamples, "lest a promise being left us of entering into his rest. . . ." The promise is not limited to the Israelites. All men whom God has called to join in the spiritual warfare have a promise that, if they will endure in the faith and love of God, they shall enter into rest. We then have a promise of rest—of a better rest than that which was promised to them. But this promise is not absolute, just as theirs was not absolute. It is conditional, and the condition is that we abide in the faith—in the faith which, while it is realized, purifies the heart, and makes our will one with God's will.

"Should seem to come short of it." Why "seem"? Should

2 For unto us was the gospel preached, as well as unto them: but †the word preached did not profit them, ‖ not being mixed with faith in them that heard *it*.

† Gr. *the word of hearing.*
‖ Or, *because they were not united by faith to.*

2. "Not being mixed." See below.

we not have expected simply " come short of it " ? The answer is twofold. First, we can never pronounce respecting any individual believer, that he has actually come short, because we cannot read the heart, and God may see some faith where we in our rashness pronounce that there is none. And, secondly, it is a bad thing even to seem to come short. To seem to come short is to set a bad example of holding slackly or loosely that which we should hold firmly, and adorn with our lives.

2. "For unto us was the gospel preached, as well as unto them." "Unto us was the gospel preached." This is a very misleading translation, for it implies that the same Gospel was preached to them as to us—*i.e.*, the Gospel of the Incarnation, of the Life, of the Death, and of the Resurrection of the Son of God; but it was not. Their Gospel—that is, their good tidings, for that is the meaning of the term Gospel—was the possession of the land of Canaan, and prosperity in it if they were obedient: our Gospel is the promise of forgiveness of sins and eternal life of body and soul in the heavenly Jerusalem. The best translation is that of the Revisers: "For indeed we have had good tidings preached unto us even as they also had."

" But the word preached did not profit them, not being mixed with faith," &c. The particular reading of the word " being mixed" ($\sigma\upsilon\gamma\kappa\epsilon\kappa\rho\alpha\mu\acute{\epsilon}\nu\sigma\varsigma$) which we adopt will considerably modify the meaning. If we adopt that of the Received Text (participle in the nominative), then it means that the word which they heard was not in them mixed with faith. The bare hearing was not sufficient, it must be received and amalgamated, as it were, by faith. And this they did not furnish.

But a very large number of authorities take "being mixed" in the accusative plural, $\sigma\upsilon\gamma\kappa\epsilon\kappa\rho\alpha\mu\acute{\epsilon}\nu\sigma\upsilon\varsigma$, agreeing with "them," and understand it as signifying "the word did not profit them since they were not mixed or united by faith with them that effectually heard it—*i.e.*, with Joshua, Caleb, and others who had true faith."

3 ᵇFor we which have believed do enter into rest, as he said, ᶜAs I have sworn in my wrath,

ᵇ ch. iii. 14.
ᶜ Ps. xcv. 11.
ch. iii. 11.

---

Bishop Wordsworth has some admirable remarks: "They ought all to have been tempered together by faith and charity, into one harmonious body, but only a few hearkened to the word—emphatically the word of *hearing*, because all were bound to hearken to it. The others were not *tempered* with them, but rebelled against Moses and Aaron, and were ready to stone Caleb and Joshua, who did hearken unto the word (Numb. xiv. 10), 'Therefore the word spoken did not profit them.'"

"No more will the word now spoken by Christ profit you, unless you comply with the conditions He requires of you. He has said, 'He that hath ears to hear let him hear' (Matth. xi. 15), and 'Take heed how ye hear' (Luke viii. 18). His word will not be profitable to you unless you are blended together in faith with those who *have* hearkened to Christ's word, and who believe on Him, and have been incorporated into His Church, and who dwell together as fellow-members in unity in His mystical Body, of which He has tempered all the members together as one man in Himself."

3. "For we which have believed do enter into rest, as he said, As I have sworn," &c. In order fully to enter into the meaning of this and the following verses we must consider that the argument leads up to verse 9: "There remaineth therefore a rest for the people of God." There are four or five "rests" spoken of in the Bible:

(1.) There was first the rest of God after the works of creation (Gen. ii. 2), "God rested on the seventh day from all his work which he had made."

(2.) There was the rest which God promised to the children of Israel after their bondage in Egypt, and after their wanderings in the wilderness. They—*i.e.*, those that believed, and those who were under twenty years old when they came out of Egypt—were put into possession of this rest (the rest of the land of Canaan) by Joshua.

(3.) But four hundred years after Joshua had put them in possession of the rest of Canaan David was inspired to write a Psalm which treated the "rest" as yet future, and capable of being forfeited, if they did not keep their hearts tender towards God, and loyal to Him. Now it will be needful to consider the question

if they shall enter into my rest: although the works were finished from the foundation of the world.

4 For he spake in a certain place of the seventh *day* on

---

whether David (or the Psalmist who wrote Ps. xcv.) meant eternal blessedness alone when he applied the words, "So I sware in my wrath they shall not enter," &c. I scarcely think so, for the times which succeeded those of Joshua—the times of the Judges, of Barak, Gideon, Jephtha, Samson, Eli, Saul—could scarcely be called times of rest. They were during the greater part of these times by no means in quiet possession of their own land; and when the Ninevites carried away the ten tribes, they ceased to enjoy the rest of Canaan; and when the king of Babylon carried away Judah and Jerusalem captive, he certainly for the time put an end to the rest of the remainder of the people of God in Canaan.

(4.) But another rest is proclaimed, and by the voice of God Himself. "Come unto me all ye that labour and are heavy laden, and I will give you rest. Take my yoke upon you, and learn of me . . . and ye shall find rest unto your souls." This rest must be insisted upon, for it is not only the earnest, but the beginning of the rest of heaven. Without having something of this rest, we cannot hope to enjoy the rest of heaven.

(5.) And, lastly, the writer of this Epistle asserts that the rest is yet future, when he says, "There remaineth therefore"—at this time—"a rest for the people of God." We shall now examine singly verses 3 to 9.

3. "For we which have believed do enter into rest, as he said, As I have sworn in my wrath, if they shall enter into my rest: although the works were finished from the foundation of the world." This must be understood thus. We who have believed do enter into rest: we now enter into a present rest, which is plain from the fact that after the works of God in creation were finished, and He had rested on the seventh day, He yet swore centuries after this that unbelievers should not enter into His rest, which most assuredly implies that believers do enter into God's rest, whatever that rest be.

4, 5. "For he spake in a certain place of the seventh day on this wise, And God did rest . . . "And in this place also, If they shall enter," &c. Here we have the idea repeated. In Gen. ii. 2, God

this wise, <sup>d</sup> And God did rest the seventh day from all his works.

<sup>d</sup> Gen. ii. 2.
Exod. xx. 11,
& xxxi. 17.

5 And in this *place* again, If they shall enter into my rest.

6 Seeing therefore it remaineth that some must enter therein, <sup>e</sup> and they to whom ‖ it was first preached entered not in because of unbelief:

<sup>e</sup> ch. iii. 19.
‖ Or, *the gospel was first preached.*

7 Again, he limiteth a certain day, saying in David, To day, after so long a time; as it is said,

<sup>f</sup> To day if ye will hear his voice, harden not your hearts.

<sup>f</sup> Ps. xcv. 7.
ch. iii. 7.

8 For if ‖ Jesus had given them rest, then would he not afterward have spoken of another day.

‖ That is, Joshua.

---

is said to have rested; and, in Psalm xcv., to have sworn that unbelievers should not enter into His rest. What, then, is the rest?

6. "Seeing therefore it remaineth that some must enter therein, and they to whom it was first preached entered not in because of unbelief." From this it seems that the rest must be the possession of Canaan, from which the people who disbelieved were excluded, and into which the people who obeyed were led by Joshua after all the rebels had been weeded out. But this is not so. The conclusion is not yet reached, for—

7. "Again, he limiteth" (rather, "defineth a certain day" Revisers), "saying, To-day, after so long a time." This was said "in David"—that is, by one who lived some centuries after the time of Joshua; so that the conclusion mentioned in the next verse but one is absolutely certain.

8. "For if Joshua had given them rest, then would he not afterward" (after Joshua's time) "have spoken of another day"—in which if they believed they might enter into rest, and in which if they believed not they would be excluded from God's rest.

Now the times—the centuries which succeeded that of Joshua—reached to the times of the Messiah, and afterwards.

During this time they had scarcely for two centuries quiet possession of their own land, and this because of their unbelief. The

9 There remaineth therefore a ‖ rest to the people of God.

‖ Or, *keeping of a sabbath.*

Lord during this long period was constantly excluding first one generation and then another from His rest. And so the inspired writer, but a short time before the final catastrophe, says in the Holy Ghost,—
9. "There remaineth therefore a rest for the people of God." Now this was said in view of the fact that a very short time after the Apostolic author writes this verse God would take away from the whole nation the place of earthly rest which He had given to their fathers. For eighteen hundred years and more they would be in a state of unrest, because they resisted the Holy Ghost when He witnessed to them that the Man Whom they had crucified was the Messiah. There would be no rest remaining to them till they turned to the Lord, and looked on Him Whom they had pierced, and this they have not done yet.

Was there, then, a rest remaining to them? Yes, certainly—the rest of redemption, which the Lord assured to all who would come to Him when He said, "Come unto me, all ye that labour and are heavy laden, and I will give you rest." This rest was the deep, calm, unutterable peace—"the peace of God which passeth all understanding;" and this was the assurance and foretaste of that eternal rest which they should enjoy for ever in the presence of God in that place—if place it can be called—of which the land of Canaan was a very feeble type.

It is to be remarked that the word for "rest" is not the same as in the previous verses. There it is Katapausis, here it is Sabbatismos, which signifies a "Sabbath rest"—the cessation from work peculiar to the Sabbath. This difference is made, no doubt, to distinguish the spiritual rest into which the people of God, whether Jews or Gentiles, now enter, from the temporal or earthly rest, into which they were introduced by Joshua. The rest, so far as it is entered into in this world, is spiritual and unworldly.

Bishop Wordsworth argues from this verse, which asserts that there yet remains a Sabbath-keeping to the people of God, that Christians are bound to have one day in seven as a day of rest; but it seems dangerous to base it on such an inference as this; rather the words of the Lord, "the Sabbath was made for man," seem authoritatively to assign him a weekly cessation from toil—a

10 For he that is entered into his rest, he also hath ceased from his own works, as God *did* from his.

---

weekly portion of time in which to recruit his strength, whereas " the rest that remaineth " is that which Christ gives to be enjoyed every day in this world, and to have its completion in the eternal world.

10. " For he that is entered into his rest, he also hath ceased," &c. This follows up the idea that the rest which remains is not such as Joshua gave, but is Sabbatical. It is a rest in which he who enjoys it hath ceased from his own works. Now what can these works be from which a man ceases when he enters into Christ's rest? If we take Heb. vi., " repentance from dead works," as our guide, we should think that they must be sinful works, but this seems contrary to the spirit of the whole passage.

But again, "own " works may be the same as own righteousness when a man ceases to rely upon them for purposes of justification. But this also seems foreign to the purpose of the Epistle, in which there is no contention against legality as in other epistles where Gentile converts are warned against Judaizing. It has, therefore, been supposed that the verse refers to the completion of the rest in the future state. Thus in Rev. xiv. 13, "Blessed are the dead which die in the Lord from henceforth. Yea, saith the Spirit, that they may rest from their labours, and their works do follow them." Thus Theodoret, " For as the God of the universe, when on the sixth day he had completed the whole creation, on the seventh day ceased to create; so also they who have departed this life and have passed into that beyond the grave, are freed from their present labours."

Alford, however, and some others, interpret "he that is entered into his rest," of Christ. He rested from His work of redemption as did God from His own proper works of creation, and therefore from the fact of our forerunner having entered into this Sabbatism, it is reserved for us, the people of God, to enter into it with, and because of, Him. Thus as Ebrard says, " Jesus is placed in the liveliest contrast to Joshua who had not brought God's people to their (true and final) rest, and is designated as, ' That one who entered into God's rest.'"

11. "Let us labour therefore to enter into that rest, lest any

11 Let us labour therefore to enter into that rest, lest any man fall ᵏ after the same example of ∥ un-belief.

12 For the word of God *is* ʰ quick, and powerful,

ᵍ ch. iii. 12, 18, 19.
∥ Or, *disobedience.*
ʰ Isa. xlix. 2. Jer. xxiii. 29. 2 Cor. x. 4, 5. 1 Pet. i. 23.

man," &c. That rest is not given once for all the moment a man believes—believes that he is saved, or that Christ died for him in particular—but it has to be diligently sought ($\sigma\pi o\upsilon\delta\acute{a}\sigma\omega\mu\epsilon\nu$), and has to be worked out (Phil. ii. 12). We have rather to give diligence to make our calling and election sure (2 Peter i. 10).

"Lest any man fall after the same example of unbelief." 1 Corinth. x. 11, is so exactly parallel that the two places might be quoted to show that if the Epistles have not the same author, yet that the same mind made itself felt in both.

Unbelief may be rendered "disobedience," but in the case cited the unbelief and disobedience were inseparable.

12. "For the word of God is quick, and powerful, and sharper than," &c. Is this Word which is living and powerful, the Word —the Logos—Who became Incarnate, or is it the word spoken by Moses or David, or even by our Lord?

I cannot resist the reasons which lead us to believe that it is the Personal Logos, for personal attributes are ascribed to It which cannot be ascribed to a thing.

In the first place, the two verses 12 and 13 evidently refer to one Being, which is "Him with Whom we have to do," particularly Him with Whom we have to do in the way of judgment, for He is *criticos—criticos* of the thoughts and intents of the heart, and this because he is "piercing even to the dividing asunder of soul and spirit," so that there is one reference, and only one, all through the passage, and the last clause ("Him with Whom we have to do") teaches us that this Entity is personal. The word of God considered as the preached or written word is not living and powerful *in itself.* It is the instrument of a Personality Who is living and powerful. It is nothing without Him Who inspires it and works by it. This is one of the first truths which the true child of God learns. He has heard the word numberless times, and it has not evinced itself living and powerful, but rather a dead letter, but at last it comes with life and power, because He Who is Life and Power comes with it and works by it.

<sup>i</sup> Prov. v. 4.
<sup>k</sup> Eph. vi. 17.
Rev. i. 16. &
ii. 16.

and <sup>i</sup> sharper than any <sup>k</sup> two-edged sword, piercing

They who refuse to see a reference to the Second Person of the Trinity, bring forward such arguments as, "The first obvious objection is that this mode of expression is confined to St. John among the New Testament writers;" but this is begging the question, for here is a writer whose name the objectors to whom we allude—Alford and others—profess not to know, who applies it to the Son. Why should it be held to be the sole property of St. John? If there had been overwhelming evidence that this Epistle was written by St. Paul, then it might have been urged with some degree of likelihood that as St. Paul constantly speaks of the Divine relations of Christ to His Father on the one side and to Christians on the other,[1] and never uses the term Logos, it is unlikely that he would use it in this single place. But these objectors urge that St. Paul was not the author of this Epistle in the same sense in which he was the author of other epistles, and as undoubtedly the Epistle or treatise now before us was written for the benefit of Hebrews, it was only likely that he should allude to that remarkable development of Jewish doctrine in which God is said to have a Word, a Meymera whom He constantly commissions to act as Mediator between Himself and His people. I give several instances from Targums and Jewish writers in a note.[2] There is a very remarkable passage in Philo which it is very difficult to suppose could have been absent from the mind of the author of this Epistle when he wrote this place. Commenting on Gen. xv. 10, "And he took unto him all these, and divided them in the midst and laid each piece one against another," Philo says, "He does not add *who* did it in order that you may understand that it is the

---

[1] See Excursus on Christology of St. Paul at the end of my volume on Romans.

[2] Thus Onkelos on Gen. iii. 8, "And they heard the voice of the Word (מֵימְרָא) of the Lord God." Also Exod. xiv. 31, "And they believed the Word of the Lord" (מֵימְרָא). Deut. xviii. 16, "I will not proceed further, the voice of the Word of the Lord my God." Also Jonathan ben Uzziel on Judges vi. 12, "The Word (מֵימְרָא) of the Lord be to thy help." And on Isaiah ix. 7, "By the Word" (מֵימְרָא). Again on Joel ii. 23, "And exult, ye sons of Zion, and rejoice in the Word of the Lord your God" (מֵימְרָא). Many other instances are to be found in Schaaf's "Opus Aramæum," page 10 of Lexicon at the end, from which I have selected the above.

even to the dividing asunder of soul and spirit, and of the

---

undemonstrable God Who cuts asunder the constituent parts of all bodies and objects that appear to be coherent and united, by the Word that penetrates all things. Which being whetted to the keenest possible edge, never ceases to pierce all things that can be appreciated by the senses. But because it reaches even to the minutest particles, even to those which are termed indivisible, the above-mentioned penetrating Word suffices to divide things which can be appreciated by reason alone, into untold and indescribable portions. . . . For the Divine Word has pierced and divided all things in nature. Even our own mind never ceases to divide what objects or bodies it may have apprehended into an infinite and unappreciable number of particles. But this happens on account of the resemblance to the Father and Maker of all things." Quoted in Rev. J. B. McCaul's " Commentary on the Hebrews," p. 45.

It seems impossible, then, from internal considerations, and from the known opinions of the Jews, both of the Rabbinical and Alexandrian schools, to resist the conclusion that the Word here is the Personal Word.

So it was understood by the fathers. Theodoret, " Nothing can be hid from that incorruptible Judge. For He knows all things perfectly, even the motions of their thoughts." And Athanasius, " And again, saying all things are naked and open to the eyes of Him with Whom is our account, he signifies that He is other than all of them. From hence it is that He judges, but each of all things generate is bound to give account to Him." " Discourse II. Against the Arians," Oxford translation, p. 383.

" The word of God is living and powerful." " I am he that liveth and was dead, and behold I am alive for evermore, and have the keys of hell and of death " (Rev. i. 18).

" And sharper than any two-edged sword." " All the Churches shall know that I am he which searcheth the reins and hearts; and I will give unto everyone of you according to your works " (Rev. ii. 23).

" Piercing even to the dividing asunder of soul and spirit." He searches us through and through, and sees in a moment whether any thought in our mind proceeds from the animal soul which is earthly and sensual, because of the body of flesh with which it is

joints and marrow, and *is* ¹a discerner of the thoughts and intents of the heart.

13 ᵐ Neither is there any creature that is not manifest in his sight: but all things *are* naked ⁿ and opened unto the eyes of him with whom we have to do.

¹ 1 Cor. xiv. 24, 25.
ᵐ Ps. xxxiii. 13, 14. & xc. 8. & cxxxix. 11, 12.
ⁿ Job xxvi. 6. & xxxiv. 21. Prov. xv. 11.

---

in concert, or from the spirit which is in communion with the Spirit of God.

"And of the joints and marrow." The whole body, as well as the soul or spirit, is known by Him as to its every particle. If He is to be a perfect Saviour, He must discern how the body acts on and is reacted upon by the soul; for many sins, or at least temptations, arise from the connection between the soul and the body. "I keep under my body, and bring it into subjection, lest when I have preached to others, I myself should be unapproved (ἀδόκιμος)." (1 Cor. ix.)

Some, however, consider that "piercing, even to the dividing asunder ... of the joints and marrow," is to be taken spiritually; but the difficulty of this seems to be that it would be no addition to the piercing power of the Divine Word that it should divide the joints and marrow after it had divided between soul and spirit; the piercing to the dividing of soul and spirit being so infinitely greater.

"And is a discerner of the thoughts and intents of the heart." This seems to imply the discernment of a person, not that of a speech or book merely.

13. "Neither is there any creature that is not manifest in his sight." Not only man, but every creature of God is manifest in His sight, showing that the meaning of λόγος is far beyond a revelation. It is the Revealer in the Revelation, Who discriminates and judges by means of the Revelation, whatsoever form it takes, whether of a written or a spoken word.

"But all things are naked and opened before the eyes of him with whom we have to do." Almost all commentators seem to be agreed in giving to the very difficult word "opened" (τετραχηλισμένα) the sense of "laid open;" so Westcott, Alford (lying open), and the Revisers; "opened even to the back-bone," Wordsworth: "with whom we have to do, to whom we have to give account," Westcott; "with whom is our reckoning," Wordsworth.

14 Seeing then that we have °a great high priest, ᴾthat is passed into the heavens, Jesus the Son of God, ᑫlet us hold fast *our* profession.

15 For ʳwe have not an high priest which cannot be touched with the feeling of our infirmities;

° ch. iii. 1.
ᴾ ch. vii. 26. & ix. 12, 24.
ᑫ ch. x. 23.
ʳ Isa. liii. 3.
ch. ii. 18.

---

14. "Seeing then that we have a great high priest, that is passed," &c. The writer had been speaking of a heart-searching judge, not of a sympathising priest; how is it that he passes so rapidly to the idea of the priest? I think because in the high priest the functions of scrutinizer and priest, *i.e.*, sympathizing priest, were united. Thus Ezekiel, whose directions respecting the priest evidently contain much that had been held and taught long before his time, says, "And they shall teach my people the difference between the holy and profane, and cause them to discern between the unclean and the clean" (xliv. 23). Thus Wordsworth: "This mention of the high priesthood of Christ seems to have been suggested to the writer by the metaphor just employed by him concerning the judicial inquisition of victims to be offered to God ... Christ is our High Priest and offers us. But as our priest He also examines us, He anatomizes us as victims; He proves our hearts and reins; He scrutinizes our inward parts, our joints, and marrow, our thoughts, affections, motives, and designs."

"That is passed into the heavens," rather, that is passed through the heaven, "far above all principality and power, and might and dominion, and every name that is named, not only in this world, but also in that which is to come" (Ephes. i. 21).

"Jesus the Son of God," infinitely greater in person and functions than Jesus the son of Nun.

"Let us hold fast our profession." Because He is the Apostle and high Priest of our profession (iii. 1). "Let us hold fast our profession," for it is by holding fast our profession, clinging to it, realizing it, adorning it, that we hold fast to Him.

15. "For we have not an high priest which cannot be touched," &c. The Apostolic writer here drops any explicit reference to the Lord as an Apostle, or Captain of salvation, as Joshua, and during the remainder of the Epistle confines himself to the priesthood of the Lord. He is henceforth not so much the prophet or the king, but the "Priest on the Throne" (Zech. vi. 13).

H

> <sup>s</sup> Luke xxii. 28.
> <sup>t</sup> 2 Cor. v. 21.
> ch. vii. 26.
> 1 Pet. ii. 22.
> 1 John iii. 5.
> <sup>u</sup> Eph. ii. 18.
> & iii. 12. ch. x. 19, 21, 22.

but <sup>s</sup> was in all points tempted like as *we are*, <sup>t</sup> *yet without sin.*

16 <sup>u</sup> Let us therefore come boldly unto the

---

The Epistle is written to the Hebrews, and so the idea of the kingdom of Christ is not so much the headship over a body, as it is in the Epistles written to the Gentiles, but rather the old theocracy restored, the ruler and priest in one: but the Priest not a common priest, not even a common high priest, but One Whose priestly functions are mainly exercised through sympathy—entering into the sins and follies, and temptations and trials, and sorrows and perplexities, and dangers of each one with a perfectness to which the Hebrew high priest, in the execution of his office, presents scarcely any parallel—at least no account of such a marvellous individualizing of his functions has come down to us.

"But was in all points tempted like as we are, yet without sin." This is a great wonder, an unspeakable mystery that He should be in all points tempted like as we are, yet without sin. For our temptations are accompanied with sin, in that our secret will yields long before the overt act. We allow the thoughts to dwell in our minds. We take a pleasure in them, and we have often to confess with shame that there has been some sin in the suffering of temptation. We have not resisted manfully. We have not fought a good fight, but a half-hearted one. Now we have to lay hold on the Lord's sinlessness in temptations under which we have succumbed, or half-succumbed, and we have to lay hold at the same time of His sympathy, for the two go together. It is His sinlessness which perfects His sympathy. If He had yielded in the least it would have destroyed His power of sympathy, but He is a perfectly sympathising Mediator because He is a perfectly sinless One. This I have more fully entered into in the note on ch. ii. 17, 18.

16. "Let us therefore come boldly unto the throne of grace, that we may," &c. Boldly, of course, does not mean irreverently, or familiarly, not remembering the difference between God and ourselves, but it means with the utmost confidence, remembering that in the matter of the removal of sin God is far more willing to deliver us than we are to be delivered.

For what is redemption in all its parts appointed and ordained by

throne of grace, that we may obtain mercy, and find grace to help in time of need.

---

God but for the destruction of sin? so what can give us more confidence in coming to God than the thought that we come to Him for the completion in *our* case of that for which He gave us His Son to be at once our Victim and our Priest?

"And find grace to help in time of need." That we may find strength to resist, that we may be enabled resolutely to turn our heads another way, that when the way of escape is shown us we may instantly avail ourselves of it and be delivered, that we may without a moment's delay remember and plead the promises of Divine help.

## CHAP. V.

FOR every high priest taken from among men ᵃ is ordained for men ᵇ in things *pertaining*   ᵃ ch. viii. 3.
ᵇ ch. ii. 17.

---

1. "For every high priest taken from among men is ordained for men." "Every high priest taken from among men." The high priest of the Jews, the highest functionary of the only true religion then existing in the world, was taken not from the angelic host, but *from men*. In some respects the discharge of his duties might have been more dignified and perfect if he had been taken from amongst angels, but it would have lacked the all-important element of sympathy.

"Taken from among men" signifies "being taken from among men." It was the first condition that he should be always taken from among his brethren.

"Is ordained for men in things pertaining to God." "Ordained" or "appointed." If the choice is by the Will of God and by His special sanction, then he is ordained, and any outward form of setting apart will follow in due course. It is a question whether Caiaphas, being the son-in-law and not the son of the high priest, could have been the strictly legal high priest, seeing that the office was by God's appointment hereditary.

to God, <sup>c</sup> that he may offer both gifts and sacrifices for sins:

2 <sup>d</sup> Who ‖ can have compassion on the ignorant, and on them that are out of the way; for that <sup>e</sup> he himself also is compassed with infirmity.

<sup>c</sup> ch. viii. 3, 4. & ix. 9. & x. 11. & xi. 4.
<sup>d</sup> ch. ii. 18. & iv. 15.
‖ Or, can reasonably bear with.
<sup>e</sup> ch. vii. 28.

---

2. "On them that are out of the way"—the erring—wanderers.

"In things pertaining to God," *i.e.*, "To offer both gifts and sacrifices for sins." Gifts and sacrifices were not only to be offered by man, but to be received by God. Remission or atonement comes from God, the priest merely dispenses it: so that the priest is in no sense ordained by man, but for men, in such matters as worship through atoning sacrifice.

"That he may offer both gifts and sacrifices for sins." Westcott says that when gifts and sacrifices are distinguished, the former marks the mincha, or meat-offering, and the latter, as their names express, the bloody offerings, that is, the slain sacrifices. But why was it in the mind of the writer to mention both these, and particularly why should he mention the mincha first? No doubt because it was prophesied by the last of the prophets, viz., Malachi, that the mincha should supersede all others. In every place "incense shall be offered unto my name, and a pure mincha (offering)," and this mincha is universally understood by the Fathers as signifying one element of the Eucharist.

2. "Who can have compassion on the ignorant, and on them that are out of the way." "Have compassion on" is translated by Revisers, "Who can bear gently with the ignorant and erring."

Here, again, we have to notice that the functions of the priests among the Jews were of such a mechanical character that there seems no room for the exercise of discrimination and of sympathy as here mentioned; but though not specifically mentioned, there must have been some place for judging whether the state of mind of the offerer was such that his sacrifice could be properly offered to a holy God. "It is obvious," as Mr. Blunt says, "that the priests could not be forced to offer, without any inquiry, the gifts and sacrifices which were brought to them, and that especially in the case of sin offerings and trespass offerings (Levit. iv. v.), they must have exercised their discretion respecting the spiritual

3 And ᶠ by reason hereof he ought, as for the people, so also for himself, to offer for sins.
4 ᵍ And no man taketh this honour unto himself, but he that is called of God, as ʰ *was* Aaron.

ᶠ Lev. iv. 3. & ix. 7. & xvi. 6, 15, 16, 17. ch. vii. 27. & ix. 7.
ᵍ 2 Chron. xxvi. 18. John iii. 27.
ʰ Exod. xxviii. 1. Num. xvi. 5, 40. 1 Chron. xxiii. 13.

condition of the offerer in some such manner as they did respecting the bodily condition of the leper (Levit. xiii.). St. Paul implies that such discretion was to be exercised with a judicious and considerate allowance for human weakness, not with severe strictness, and that this compassion was to be influenced by the priest's personal experience of his own infirmity."

3. "And by reason hereof he ought, as for the people, so also for himself." By reason of his infirmities, which in the natural course of things would generate sins, he must offer sacrifices for himself and for his brother priests. On the great day of atonement especially he was required to offer particular sacrifices for the expiation of the sins of the priests (Levit. xvi. 6-11).

In reminding the Hebrew believers that the high priest offered special sacrifices to atone for his own sins, he no doubt intended to remind them that the Divine High Priest had no sins to atone for, and so was infinitely above the Jewish High Priest, who was one with his brethren in their sin.

4. "And no man taketh this honour unto himself, but he that is called," &c. No one assumes of himself this honour, but being called of God (he assumes it). Korah assumed the priesthood without a call, or, in fact, in opposition to the call of God, and perished. And I believe it is true of all priesthoods whatsoever, and certainly those of ancient religions, that no man can merely of himself assume the priesthood, but must go through some form of ratification, or choice, or consecration.¹ In our ordination service there is a twofold call recognized: the inward call, which can be only really known by the candidate himself, "Do you think in your heart that you be truly called, according to the will of our

---

¹ It seems to me a mistake to quote this place against teachers belonging to all religious bodies external to the Church. The principal of these bodies, Presbyterians and Wesleyans, have quite as strict examinations of their candidates for their ministry as we have, and admit them to their ministry with some form which is not at the choice of the person made a minister, but imposed upon him by those in authority.

5 ¹So also Christ glorified not himself to be made an high priest; but he that said unto him, ᵏThou art my Son, to day have I begotten thee.

6 As he saith also in another *place,* ¹Thou art a priest for ever after the order of Melchisedec.

<sup>j</sup> John viii. 54.
<sup>k</sup> Ps. ii. 7. ch. i. 5.
<sup>l</sup> Ps. cx. 4. ch. vii. 17, 21.

---

Lord Jesus Christ?" and when this question has been first answered, then comes the call of the Church in the laying on of hands, "Receive the Holy Ghost, for the office and work of a priest in the Church of God."

Aaron's call is to be found in Exod. xxviii. 1 : "And take thou unto thee Aaron thy brother, and his sons with him, from among the children of Israel, that he may minister unto me in the priest's office."

5. "So also Christ glorified not himself to be made an high priest," &c. In all that Christ did He was careful to assert that He did it by the will and direct appointment of the Father. Thus John vi. 38: "I came down from heaven, not to do mine own will, but the will of him that sent me."

"But he that said unto him, Thou art my Son, to day have I," &c. This is said by St. Paul to have been fulfilled at the Lord's Resurrection, for He then received that new and exalted Life in and by which He discharges the functions of His Mediating High Priesthood. A Priest on behalf of men must be a living man, and He received on His Resurrection His Life again, that He might live to God and for us.

6. "As he saith also in another place, Thou art a priest for ever after," &c. The 110th Psalm is claimed by our Lord as referring to Himself rather than to David. In fact, of its seven verses, four cannot by any possibility be referred to anything in the life of David. Applied to the temporal David, it is rhetorical exaggeration; applied to the spiritual David, it is true to the letter.

It is necessary to consider the meaning, so far as we can ascertain it, of the word "order"—"after the order of Melchisedec." It is often taken to mean after the order, in the sense of "after the succession of Melchisedec;" but this can scarcely be, for Melchisedec had no successors in the priesthood, and if he had, Our Lord was in no way ordained into or inserted into such an order. It has consequently been rendered as "after the manner of Mel-

7 Who in the days of his flesh, when he had ᵐ offered up prayers and supplications ⁿ with

<sup>m</sup> Matt. xxvi. 39, 42, 44. Mark xiv. 36, 39. John xvii. 1.
<sup>n</sup> Ps. xxii. 1. Matt. xxvii. 46, 50. Mark xv. 34, 37.

chisedec." Primasius, cited by Westcott, gives three main points in which the High Priesthood of Christ was like that of Melchisedec:

(1.) It was not for the fulfilment of legal sacrifices of bulls and goats, but for the offering of bread and wine, answering to Christ's Body and Blood. Animal Sacrifices have ceased; these remain.

(2.) Melchisedec combined the kingly with the priestly dignity.

(3.) Melchisedec appeared once as Christ appeared once.

But there are other points of resemblance. Melchisedec's priesthood was especially one of blessing; and so he blessed Abraham and all his spiritual descendants in him. And so Christ blesses all the people of God, all the children of Abraham by faith. But other points we shall have to consider further on, as this resemblance between the Priesthoods is several times drawn out in this Epistle.

The 110th Psalm must have been acknowledged by the converted Jews, to whom this Epistle was sent, to have been written of Christ. The Lord's citation of it, to confute the Pharisees, was undoubtedly a part of the original tradition of the Lord's teaching. We have it in full in each one of the three Synoptics, and from each account it appears that His adversaries were not able to answer it.

7. "Who in the days of his flesh, when he had offered up prayers and supplications." The Apostolic writer returns to verse 4. There and in the two following verses he asserts that Christ was not a self-chosen, but a Divinely appointed Priest; now he resumes what he had just touched upon in ii. 17 and iv. 15—that in all things it behoved Him to be made like unto His brethren; that in all points He was tempted like as we are, yet without sin; and so He has been able to learn, not by precept, but by experience, that spiritual function of a true priest which consists in the exercise of sympathy with those whom He is absolving.

"Who in the days of his flesh"—that is, when He experienced the sinless infirmities of our flesh, whilst His Body was yet a natural Body, and not raised a spiritual Body.

strong crying and tears unto him ᵒ that was able to save him from death, and was heard ‖ ᵖ in that he feared;

ᵒ Matt. xxvi. 53. Mark xiv. 36.
‖ Or, *for his piety*.
ᵖ Matt. xxvi. 37. Mark xiv. 34. Luke xxii. 43. John xii. 27.

---

"When he had offered up prayers and supplications with strong crying," &c. This no doubt refers to His Agony: prayers means verbal entreaties, supplications; ἱκετηρίας seems a stronger term, and is derived from a verb, ἵκομαι, signifying "to come." One of the forms of suppliant entreaty was to come with an olive branch bound with white wool.

"With strong crying and tears." We are not told particularly of the crying in the Garden, but there can be little doubt that if His Agony was such as to make Him sweat blood, His voice would be raised, and His tears flow abundantly. He cried twice with a loud voice when on the cross—when He exclaimed, "My God, my God, why hast thou forsaken me?" (Matth. xxvii. 46), and when He commended His Spirit into the hands of His Father (Luke xxiii. 46); but the Agony in Gethsemane seems to be more particularly in the writer's mind.

"Unto him that was able to save him from death"—*i.e.*, to the Father. God, Who can do all things, could have saved Him from death; but all the providences of the world seem to have been ordained so that He should die on the cross. Almost all the prophecies pointed to a suffering and dying Messiah. All the types typified suffering. And what is more, His reward depended upon His suffering. "He shall see of the travail of his soul, and shall be satisfied." "Therefore will I divide him a portion with the great, and he shall divide the spoil with the strong, because he hath poured out his soul unto death." "He became obedient unto death, even the death on the cross; *therefore* God hath highly exalted him" (Phil. ii. 8).

"And was heard in that he feared." There are two significations given of this—(1) was heard so as to be delivered from His fear; (2) was heard from, or on account of, His reverence, His godly fear, His piety and submission to God, as especially shewn in the words, "Nevertheless, not my will, but thine be done." He was heard, not that the cup should pass from Him, but that He should drink, and redeem mankind by the draught, and win, in the

## BEING MADE PERFECT.

8 ᵠThough he were a Son, yet learned he ʳobedience by the things which he suffered;  
9 And ˢbeing made perfect, he became the author of eternal salvation unto all them that obey him;

ᵠ ch. iii. 6.
ʳ Phil. ii. 8
ˢ ch. ii. 10. & xi. 40.

---

nature which suffered and submitted, the highest place in the universe. He was heard, so that the most righteous and most merciful Will of God should be glorified by His Sufferings and Death. He was heard, so that His Death should be terminated by His most glorious Resurrection and His Ascension, and by His having all things put under His feet, and made Head over all things to the Church.

8. "Though he were a Son, yet learned he obedience," &c. Though He were Son—the Eternal Word, the pre-existent Wisdom —"yet learned He obedience." The Son of God, if one may so say, became perfectly Incarnate. He took all the sinless conditions of our nature. Both His Body and Soul passed through various stages till they were perfected. He passed through one stage of partial knowledge or wisdom to another and a higher. As we do, He learnt wisdom by experience; and above all He learnt the wisdom most important for Him in the exercise of His function of Mediating High Priest by experience, and the last and perfecting lesson was His Passion and Death.

He had in numberless ways to mediate for His brethren in matters both of life and death. He learnt life, and at last He learnt death. He learnt not only its pains, and its fears, but He learnt what His brethren have to submit to in the prospect of it, as well as in the suffering of it.

9. "And being made perfect, he became the author of eternal salvation." And being, or having been, made perfect, perfected in sympathy, and therefore "through sufferings" (ii. 10), "He became the author of eternal salvation to all that obey him." Not to those who believe in Him merely, but to those whose faith lives by works. (James ii. 17.)

He is not only the captain or ἀρχηγὸς to a multitude or army, but by His mediatorial action He works salvation in each one—in each one who yields himself to be worked upon by Him. There can be no salvation except by obedience. The faith by which we

10 Called of God an High Priest ᵗafter the order of Melchisedec.

ᵗ ver. 6. ch. vi. 20.

11 Of whom ᵘwe have many things to say, and hard to be uttered, seeing ye are ˣdull of hearing.

ᵘ John xvi. 12. 2 Pet. iii. 16.
ˣ Matt. xiii. 15.

---

come to Christ is a belief in Him as a Saviour from the power as well as the consequences of sin. Faith exacts obedience, or how can there be such a thing as the obedience of faith? So that in a very wide and deep sense faith is obedience, and faith is consummated by obedience, for the purpose of all God's relations to us, is that we should submit to God, which is obedience.

10. "Called of God an High Priest of the order of Melchisedec." The word "called" is not the same as that in verse 4, but rather means "addressed by God." The address of God to His Son "Thou art a priest for ever" rather ratifies a previous call.

11. "Of whom we have many things to say, and hard to be uttered, seeing ye are dull of hearing." "Of whom." This relative may refer either to Melchisedec, or to Christ, a priest of the order of Melchisedec. In all probability the latter, because the writer blames the Hebrews for their want of spiritual perception. There would have been little need of spiritual perception to understand the two or three brief notices of Melchisedec to be found in the Old Testament, but the relation of Christ to His people as their eternal priest after the order of Melchisedec requires the highest powers of apprehension of heavenly truths.

"We have many things to say." Rather "much discourse." The whole of the seventh chapter is occupied with this unique priesthood of Christ, and the contrast between the priesthoods of Aaron and of Melchisedec.

"Hard to be uttered." Properly, "hard to be understood—hard of interpretation," Revisers.

"Seeing ye are dull of hearing." "Seeing ye are become dull of hearing." They were not originally dull, but became so by want of interest in the wonderful revelations of God. "In saying, 'Seeing ye are become dull of hearing,' he shows plainly that formerly they were sound in health, and were strong and fervent in zeal, which he also afterwards testifies respecting them." (Chrysostom.)

CHAP. V.]  THE FIRST PRINCIPLES.  107

12 For when for the time ye ought to be teachers, ye have need that one teach you again which be ʸ the first principles of the oracles of God; and are become such as have need of ᶻ milk, and not of strong meat.

ʸ ch. vi. 1.
ᶻ 1 Cor. iii. 1, 2, 3.

12. "Strong meat;" rather, "solid food."

12. " For when for the time ye ought to be teachers, ye have need that one," &c. " For the time," considering the time ye have have been under instruction, ye ought to be teachers. " Ye ought to be able to teach others," whereas ye have need that one teach you—that is—remind you of first principles, even the elements, the A B C of the oracles of God. What are these elements or first principles of the oracles of God? In Rom. x. the oracles of God signify the Old Testament revelation, but this can hardly be the meaning here, for by the revelation of the Son of God, and the instruction, first by His own words, then by those that heard Him (ii. 3), a knowledge of God and of His Will had been communicated to these Hebrew Christians, compared to which the revelations of God in the Old Testament, great though they were, were insignificant.

" And are become such as have need of milk, and not of strong meat." The milk signifies the first principles, the meat denotes the higher teaching of the deeper mysteries. With regard to the teaching of this Epistle, the milk—the first principles—is only cursorily referred to in vi. 3; the meat denotes the doctrine of the eternal priesthood of Christ as a priest after a very different order to that of Aaron.

" The strong meat" should rather be rendered " solid food."

It has been supposed and asserted that the milk was the teaching respecting the Lord's humanity, and the meat that which had to do with His Divine Nature; but this is scarcely possible. The simplest teaching respecting the Lord was that He was the Son of God in a very different way to which other good and holy men were sons of God. The first teaching never could have been Humanitarianism, for it would suggest such enormous difficulties as how a mere man was to be the object of trust, and belief, and Divine worship? The simplest questions which the neophyte

13 For every one that useth milk † *is* unskilful in the word of righteousness: for he is ᵃ a babe.

14 But strong meat belongeth to them that are ‖ of full age, *even* those who by reason ‖ of use

† Gr. *hath no experience.*
ᵃ 1 Cor. xiii. 11. & xiv. 20.
Eph. iv. 14.
1 Pet. ii. 2.
‖ Or, *perfect.*
1 Cor. ii. 6.
Eph. iv. 13.
Phil. iii. 15.
‖ Or, *of an habit*, or, *perfection.*

could ask could only be intelligently answered on the assumption of His full participation in the Divine Nature.

13. "For every one that useth milk is unskilful the word of righteousness: for he is a babe." "Every one that useth milk," *i.e.*, every one that confines himself to mere rudiments, and declines to proceed further, on the plea that if he does, he will have to face mysteries, and consider matters which are beyond his natural understanding—such an one is (as the Revisers render it) "without experience" in the word of righteousness. He ought to have some experience of its depth, whereas he confines himself to paddling amongst its shallows. The word of Christ, whether uttered by Himself or by His inspired servants, was all of righteousness, all tended to righteousness, all was designed to make men holier and better than they could be made by the law.

"For he is a babe." "Thou seest that there is another infancy. Thou seest that there is another full age. Let us become of full age in this sense. It is in the power even of those that are children and young persons to arrive at that *full age*. For it is not of nature, but of virtue (John vii. 17)." Chrysostom.

14. "But strong meat belongeth unto them that are of full age," &c. By far the best exposition of this view seems to me to be that of Chrysostom: "He is not speaking now concerning life (*i.e.*, ordinary human life) when he says, to discern good and evil, for this is possible and easy for every man to know, but concerning doctrines that are wholesome and sublime, and those that are corrupted and low. The babe knows not how to distinguish the bad and the good food. Oftentimes, at least, it puts even dirt into its mouth, and takes what is hurtful; and it does all things without discernment: but not so that which is of 'full age.' Such (babes) are they who listen to all things without distinction, and give up their ears indiscriminately, which seems to me to imply blame on these (Hebrews) also, as being lightly carried about

have their senses exercised ᵇ to discern both good and evil.  ᵇ Isa. vii. 15.
1 Cor. ii. 14, 15.

(Ephes. iv. 14), and now giving themselves up to these, now to those. Which he also hinted at near the end of the Epistle saying, 'Be not carried aside by diverse and strange doctrines.' This is the meaning of 'To discern good and evil.' 'For the mouth tasteth food, but the soul trieth words' (Job xxxiv. 3)."

"By reason of use." By reason of using them properly, by reason of habit.

## CHAP. VI.

THEREFORE, ᵃ leaving ‖ the principles of the doctrine of Christ, let us go on unto perfection; not laying again the foundation of  ᵃ Phil. iii. 12, 13, 14. ch. v. 12.
‖ Or, *the word of the beginning of Christ.*

1. "Therefore, leaving the principles of the doctrine of Christ." Revisers translate this, "Wherefore let us cease to speak of the first principles of Christ." Margin, "The word of the beginning of Christ." What does he allude to? Some think that it is the application of the prophecies of the Old Testament to Christ, but it seems better to take it of the six foundations which he enumerates in the latter part of this verse, and in the next. "Let us for the present leave the consideration of these and proceed to the higher doctrines, which are the superstructure."

"Not laying again the foundation of repentance from dead works," &c. It is very remarkable that this is the only list which we have in the New Testament of the fundamental or initial doctrines of Christ which were taught to the converts when they first believed and were baptized. I mean the doctrines of Christianity as distinguished from its creed. Constantly in the Epistles of St. Paul have we allusions to the creed, as in Rom. i. 1-4, 1 Cor. xv. 1, 10, but nowhere except in this place to the fundamental doctrines which are the outcome of the creed. On this account it will be well to examine them in full.

"Repentance from dead works." Repentance is a change of

repentance [b] from dead works, and of faith towards God,

---

mind or heart with respect to sin and to God. It is of necessity the first principle, the first step in the Christian life. It was the first thing which our Lord's forerunner preached in order to prepare the way for Him. It was the first thing which the Lord Himself preached (Mark i. 15). It was the first thing which St. Peter preached on the day of Pentecost (Acts ii. 38). It was the first thing which St. Paul preached (Acts xxvi. 20).

But what is repentance from dead works? What are dead works? We should have thought that there could have been but one opinion. Repentance from evil works; from deadly sins; from enmity to God, and such things.

Many orthodox divines, however, as Bishop Wordsworth, explain these dead works as works done before justification. But is this possible? Suppose that a heathen or a Jew before Baptism keeps himself from adultery or fornication, and when tempted to lie tells the truth, or when tempted to defraud continues honest, is he to repent of this? We should say certainly not. But are not such things as these done before the inspiration of God's Spirit? We cannot say with any certainty in any one single case that they are. For that Holy Spirit "bloweth where he listeth." If all good comes from God, then those heathen of whom the Apostle speaks as shewing the works of the law written in their hearts, do what is pleasing to God through His Spirit, though they have never heard of Christ. There can be no doubt then but that the dead works are the works of the flesh, adultery, fornication, uncleanness, lasciviousness, and the remainder of the black list of evil things enumerated by the Apostle (Gal. v. 19), of which he says they that do such things "shall not inherit the Kingdom of God."

"And of faith towards God." Inasmuch as the principles here enumerated are the principles of the doctrine of Christ, this faith cannot be a faith in God apart from Christ, which a Jew might have before he was converted. It must be faith in God as the Father of Christ, and the Sender of His Son into the world to save us. All Christian faith must ultimately rest on God the Father as the Fountain of Deity; thus the Lord says, "He that heareth my word and believeth on him that sent me, hath everlasting life" (John v. 24).

2 <sup>c</sup> Of the doctrine of baptisms, <sup>d</sup> and of laying   <sup>c</sup> Acts xix. 4, 5.
                                                                                    <sup>d</sup> Acts viii. 14,
                                                                                   15, 16, 17. &
                                                                                   xix. 6.

In Titus iii. also, belief in God is assumed to be Christian faith, though Christ is not mentioned. "He that cometh to God must believe that He is," and he that cometh to the God of the Gospel must believe that He is the God revealed in the Gospel, the Father of One only Son, Who is His proper Son (ἴδιος); and on account of His having this Son He is essentially the Father. This second of the "first principles" of course includes all which is naturally and inseparably joined with faith, as trust and hope and confession with the lips and prayer and belief in the Scriptures.

2. "Of the doctrine of Baptisms." This also must be Christian, for there was no doctrine that we know of connected with Jewish lustrations, and the Baptism of John had long ceased, whereas with Christian Baptism the highest doctrine was associated, as that it was a new birth of water and of the Spirit unto the kingdom of God (John iii. 5), that it was the means by which the Holy Spirit grafted men into the Body of Christ, and that it was a Sacramental Death, Burial and Resurrection with Christ. There is a question, however, how it was that the Apostolic writer used the plural, "the doctrine of baptisms" for surely there is but one Baptism—"One Lord, one Faith, one Baptism" (Ephes. iv. 5)? Various reasons have been given for this: one that he spoke of Baptisms because each administration of the Sacrament was a separate Baptism—another that he included the Jewish Baptism of Proselytes and John's Baptism. But may not the reason be something of this sort: The value of Christian Baptism is brought out and intensified by comparing it with those of the Jews, and that of John. John the Baptist in particular lays much stress upon the difference between His Baptism and that of the Lord. "I indeed baptize you with water, but he shall baptize you with the Holy Ghost and with fire (Matth. iii. 11.) The practical doctrine of Baptism is that at the very outset of our Christian career, when we are made members of Christ we are gifted with all grace sufficient to enable us to fulfil our place in the mystical body, but this grace has constantly to be realized by an act of faith, to be stirred up and to be continued in. (See notes on Rom. vi. 1-12; Coloss. ii. 12; and Titus iii. 5).

"And of laying on of hands." There are two "layings on of

e Acts xvii. 31, 32.
f Acts xxiv. 25. Rom. ii. 16.

on of hands, <sup>e</sup> and of resurrection of the dead, <sup>f</sup> and of eternal judgment.

---

hands" mentioned in the New Testament. One for what we call confirmation (Acts viii. 17 ; xix. 6). In each of these cases it is expressly said that through it God gave the Holy Ghost. The other "Laying on of hands" is at Ordination, for we read, "I put thee in remembrance that thou stir up the gift of God which is in thee by the laying on of my hands. For God hath not given us the spirit of fear, but of power, and of love and of a sound mind" (2 Tim. i. 6, 7 ; also 1 Tim. iv. 14, v. 22 ; Acts vi. 6, xiii. 2, 3, 4).

The doctrine of the laying on of hands is this, that God has sent the Holy Spirit once for all on the day of Pentecost, and that He has left a power in His Church of transmitting the Spirit of God by laying on of hands. Many sincere Christians object to this. They have persuaded themselves that the only means of grace which God accompanies with His Spirit is the listening to preaching, and the reading of Scripture: but the word of God gives us no warrant so to restrict His power. St. Timothy had from a child known the Scriptures, but St. Paul twice reminded him that he had received that gift of the Spirit which had made him a minister of Christ, through the "Laying on of hands." The Samaritans had believed the word of the Gospel through preaching, but the Apostles did not judge this to be sufficient, but sent two of their number to lay hands on those converts, that they might receive the Holy Ghost.

The doctrine of the laying on of hands carries with it the whole Church system, which is this: the same God Who for certain purposes of grace, accompanies the preaching of the Gospel with the enlightening and comforting influences of His Spirit, for certain other and kindred purposes of grace is pleased to accompany the "Laying on of hands" with gifts of the same Spirit. It is God's will that His people should not be merely instructed as if they were so many separate units, but that they should be knit together in a Body, which Body or Organization is that fellowship of the Apostles which took its beginning on the day of Pentecost itself, and which in so far as it is an outward and visible fellowship has been transmitted to us by the "Laying on of hands," and by that alone; which "laying on of hands" was ordained that men should have through it such gifts of the Holy Spirit as are necessary for the right exercise of the Christian ministry. But this "laying on of hands" is not only conferred in Ordination on ministers, but in Confirmation on all Christians who have received Holy Baptism, in order to strengthen the whole number of the Baptized who receive it worthily with the ordinary gifts of the Holy Spirit.

"And of resurrection of the dead." The fifth principle or foundation is the Resurrection of the dead. That the Resurrection is a primary truth is abundantly clear from Scripture; Jesus calls Himself the Resurrection and the Life. The Apostle's preaching was described as the preaching of "Jesus and the Resurrection" (Acts xvii. 18). When St. Paul preached the Gospel at Athens, no motives of worldly prudence hindered him from preaching the Resurrection of the body, though he must have foreseen that of all Christian truths, it was most likely to excite the ridicule of the sceptical Athenians.

Again, the Resurrection of our bodies is so intimately connected with that of Christ's Body, that "if the dead rise not, then Christ Himself is not raised." So the truth of our Religion stands or falls with the truth of the Resurrection, for the Apostle says, "If Christ be not raised, your faith is vain: ye are yet in your sins" (1 Cor. xv. 17). Now why should the Resurrection of the Body be of such importance as to be accounted a first principle in a spiritual system? I answer, because without it there is no full redemption—no redemption of the whole man. The whole man, body, soul, and spirit, is redeemed, that the whole man may be renewed in the likeness of our Redeemer. Our souls are now renewed after the likeness of His Holy Soul, and our bodies are hereafter to be renewed after the likeness of His glorious Body. So that unless the body be redeemed from corruption, Redemption itself is maimed and incomplete; and so, in the view of the Apostle, they who say that the Resurrection is past, overthrow the faith (2 Tim. ii. 18), and contrariwise "they who have the firstfruits of the Spirit wait for the adoption, that is, the Redemption of their bodies" (Rom. viii. 23). The Redemption and consequent Resurrection of the body is the Christian form of the future state. As in this life, so in the next we shall not be ghosts or unembodied spirits, not unclothed, but clothed upon: mortality, the mortality of these corruptible bodies, being swallowed up of life.

"And of eternal judgment." Rather, perhaps, of an eternal

⁶ Acts xviii. 21.
1 Cor. iv. 19.     3 And this will we do, ᵍ if God permit.

---

3. "And this will we do." So ℵ, B., K., L., most Cursives, d, e, f, Vulg.; but A., C., D., L., P., thirty-five Cursives, &c., read, "And this let us do."

award, the result of the Judgment. The last of these six principles is "eternal judgment," that is, that the Son of God will, on a particular day appointed by God, Himself proceed to judge all men for the deeds done in their bodies. He will then finally separate between the righteous and the wicked. The reward which He will assign to those who have done good will be in exact proportion to what they have done (Luke xix. 16-19; 2 Cor. v. 10; Gal. vi. 7-11). And the punishment of the wicked will also be in exact proportion to the evil which they have done, or the good which they have neglected to do.¹ This sentence will be most divinely just, and so the Judge will take into account every circumstance which can possibly modify it. Every degree of light, whether of nature or of grace, every influence of education, or example: all opportunities improved or wasted: strength of temptation, national character, hereditary prejudices or influence, even disease of mind or body influencing the will—all will be taken into full account; for God is a righteous Judge. This judgment will embrace the whole universe of intelligent creatures—men, angels, devils: none will be exempt. The Apostle who laboured more abundantly than all, and the sinner saved so as by fire alike will stand before the judgment-seat of Christ.

But not from this place only (Heb. vi. 2), do we infer that eternal judgment is a principle or foundation. The judgment is set forth in every part of God's Word. It is so universally set forth as taking account of all persons, and all events; as taking cognizance of all thoughts, all words, all works; that no matter how few the first principles or foundations of our religion may be reduced to, eternal judgment must be one of them.

3. "And this will we do, if God permit." That is, if God permit, we will leave the enforcement of these lower truths and proceed to consider "perfection," the highest truth which the Christian religion reveals—in the case of this Epistle, the High Priesthood of our Lord.

---

¹ Luke xii. 47, 48; xix. 16, 17; Rom. ii. 6, 7, 8; 1 Cor. iii. 8; xv. 58; 2 Cor. ix. 6; Gal. vi. 7; Eph. vi. 8; Phil. iv. 17; Col. iii. 24, 25; Rev. xx. 13; and very many more.

4 For ᵇ *it is* impossible for those ⁱ who were once enlightened, and have tasted of ᵏ the hea-

ᵇ Matt. xii. 31, 32. ch. x. 26.
² Pet. ii. 20, 21. 1 John v. 16.
ⁱ ch. x. 32.
ᵏ John iv. 10. & vi. 32. Eph. ii. 8.

4. "For it is impossible for those who were once enlightened," &c. The sequence is difficult. What is the significance of the "for"? Upon the whole the best statement of the connection seems to be this: "Let us go on to perfection, not laying again the foundation of repentance, for if you have apostatized, or fallen from Christ, and now deny Him, after having practically learned repentance and faith, and been enlightened, and been made partakers of the heavenly gift, &c., then the preaching of first principles is thrown away upon you. We must not lose time with dealing with you. We must rather lay ourselves out to teach those who are willing to progress in divine knowledge. In your present state the inculcation of repentance as a first principle and faith as following on it, would be mere empty words. We must leave you in God's hands, and teach those who desire to grow in the Divine Life. If you had never learnt these principles, then it would be our duty to evangelize you in them as we should the heathen; but you have known them, and known them practically, and rejected them, so we must pass you by, and give to others the exalted truths for which you have made yourselves unfit."

We now must consider, by itself, each clause of this fearful place.

"Those who were once enlightened." The Fathers almost universally understand this of Baptism, which they called the Illumination: and no doubt, in the early Church, Baptism was accompanied with an accession of light and knowledge such as vindicated the application of such a term to it.¹ The candidates

---

¹ There is a well-known passage in Cyprian describing the change wrought in him at the time of his own baptism, which is worth transcribing: "For as I myself was held in bonds by the innumerable errors of my previous life, from which I did not believe that I could by possibility be delivered. So I was disposed to acquiesce in my clinging vices; and because I despaired of better things, I used to indulge my sins as if they were actual parts of me, and indigenous to me. But after that, by the help of the water of new birth, the stains of former years had been washed away, and a light from above serene and pure had been infused into my reconciled heart—after that, by the agency of the Spirit breathed from heaven, a second birth had restored me to a new man—then in a wondrous manner doubtful things began at once to assure themselves to me, hidden things to be revealed, dark things to be enlightened; what before had seemed difficult

venly gift, and ¹ were made partakers of the Holy Ghost,

5 And have tasted the good word of God, and the powers of ᵐ the world to come,

¹ Gal. iii. 2, 5. ch. ii. 4.
ᵐ ch. ii. 5.

were not, as far as we can gather, instructed in high truths, but only in mere rudiments. They only learnt the creed on the very eve of their Baptism. They were not allowed to use the Lord's Prayer till they received Baptism. So that, on the comparatively low ground of human instruction, it might well be called an enlightenment. But when we add to this the universal faith of those ages in the supernatural agency of God in the Sacraments, we may well believe that, " according to their faith," it was done to them, and a miracle of enlightening and sanctifying grace accompanied the administration.

"And have tasted of the heavenly gift." Chrysostom explains this of forgiveness.

"And were made partakers of the Holy Ghost." Either through the laying on of hands, or by a direct act of God. They partook of the Holy Ghost, not merely so as to be endued with supernatural gifts, but so as to be purified and sanctified by His indwelling.

5. "And have tasted the good word of God." That is, have tasted its sweetness and its excellence; as the Psalmist sings, "More to be desired are they than gold, yea, than much fine gold; sweeter also than honey and the honeycomb." This is an advance upon what has gone before. It is one of the highest works of the Spirit to bring the Scriptures, which He Himself has inspired, to bear upon the heart, to unfold to the spirit the wonders which they contain, so that reading or hearing which, if performed at all, was an irksome duty, is now a delight.

"And the powers of the world to come." There are those in whom heaven is begun upon earth. "How powerful in it will be redemption and freedom from all evil and misery, what joy and happiness, what power God will manifest in His blessed ones, in

---

began to suggest a means of accomplishment; what had before been thought impossible, to be capable of being achieved; so that I was enabled to acknowledge that what previously having been born of the flesh had been living in the practice of sin, and was of the earth, earthly, had now begun to be born of God, and was animated by the Spirit of holiness."

6 If they shall fall away, to renew them again unto repentance; ⁿ seeing they crucify to themselves the    ⁿ ch. x. 29. Son of God afresh, and put *him* to an open shame.

---

6. "If they shall fall away." "And having fallen away."

their glory, honour. and immortality, in their eternal life, in their vision and fruition of God." (Cornelius à Lapide.)

6. "If they shall fall away, to renew them again unto repentance." Revisers translate thus: "And then (after these blessed experiences), fell away, to renew them again unto repentance." The all-important question is, what is this falling away? The word does not occur elsewhere in the New Testament. It must mean one of two things—falling into, or committing some sin, as fornication or theft, or it must mean utter apostasy. It cannot mean the former, for the grossest sins are supposed to be pardonable if men repent, and submit to the discipline of the Church.

A grosser case of sin cannot well be imagined than that of the incestuous Corinthian, and yet the Apostle not only absolves him (2 Cor. ii. 10), but earnestly asks his brother Christians to "comfort him, lest, perhaps, such an one should be swallowed up with overmuch sorrow" (7). And at the end of the same Epistle (xii. 21), "Lest, when I come again, my God will humble me among you, and that I shall bewail many which have sinned already, and have not repented of the uncleanness and fornication and lasciviousness which they have committed." Both St. James and St. John also assume that baptized or enlightened Christians will commit sins which need forgiveness. (James v. 14-16; 1 John i. 8-10; ii. 1.)

The Apostolic writer must, then, of necessity, have in his mind utter apostasy, and this is evident from the parallel expression in x. 29: hath "trodden underfoot the Son of God, and hath counted the blood of the covenant, wherewith he was sanctified, an unholy thing." The case of the apostate Jew was far worse than that of the apostate heathen, because a middle course was, by the nature of things, not possible to him. An apostate Jew, by the very fact of his apostasy, must have acknowledged that our Lord was an impostor, Who worked His miracles by the power of Satan, and that He was justly condemned and justly crucified. Now, when a Jew

7 For the earth which drinketh in the rain that cometh oft upon it, and bringeth forth herbs meet for them ‖ by whom it is dressed, ° receiveth blessing from God: 8 ᵖ But that which beareth thorns and briers is

[ Or, *for*.
º Ps. lxv. 10.
ᵖ Isa. v. 6.

---

thus fell away, there seems to have been, humanly speaking, no possibility of repentance. He had knowingly and willingly cut away from under himself the only ground which made repentance available. I say, humanly speaking, because all things are possible to God, and this raises the question whether the writer of the Epistle is speaking absolutely, as if, under no circumstances, could such an apostate be reclaimed, or that his repentance was a case of such difficulty that it must be regarded as practically impossible. I dare not say which. One thing is certain, that the writer did not consider those to whom he wrote as absolutely free from all danger of such a fall. Their faith, their Christianity, was in a declining state, and we know not to what depths a soul on the decline will sink. The Apostolic writer bids us have a wholesome fear of the lowest.

The Jew, then, by his apostasy, as far as man could do, crucified the Son of God afresh, for after acknowledging Him to be the Messiah, he turned round and proclaimed Him an impostor.

This place, of course, cuts at the roots of the necessary final perseverance of a soul once in grace, as held by Calvinists.

7, 8. "For the earth which drinketh in the rain which cometh oft upon it, &c. . . . . . nigh unto cursing; whose end is to be burned." In this illustration the reception by the land of the rain which cometh upon it, is the leading feature, and the action of the husbandmen (" meet for them by whom it is dressed "), is in the background. By this the Apostolic writer would emphasize the fact that those whom he so solemnly warns had not only received labour from the spiritual husbandmen, but grace from heaven. The same grace descends alike on the ground which produces useful produce, and that which produces what is noxious. Notice also that the ground is supposed to have received what descends from heaven with some degree of avidity ("the earth which drinketh in the rain"), receiveth blessing from God. (Compare Matth. xiii. 20.)

God blessed the ground and all which lived upon it after He had made it, and it was after Adam had sinned that He pronounced the

rejected, and *is* nigh unto cursing; whose end *is* to be burned.

9 But, beloved, we are persuaded better things of you, and things that accompany salvation, though we thus speak.

---

curse. ("Cursed is the ground for thy sake; thorns also and thistles shall it bring forth to thee.")

The earth is the soil, the rain is heavenly grace; especially, if not altogether, the grace of the Holy Spirit; the "oft" coming of the rain is the abundance of grace ("which he shed on us abundantly," Titus iii. 6); the dressing is the labour of the ministers and stewards of God's mysteries; the herbs "meet for them by whom it is dressed," are the good fruit which true Christians bear to the glory of God, and the benefit of their fellow-creatures; the briars and thorns are evil deeds, or neglect of grace to produce good works; the blessing includes all good gifts from God, particularly greater fruitfulness in good works; the rejection is the final rejection.

"Nigh unto cursing," why does the apostolic writer say "nigh" unto cursing, instead of cursed? Does he mean to imply that the curse is not yet pronounced, but is on the point of being pronounced, but there is space left for repentance? We hope so. Chrysostom says, "Oh! how great consolation is there in this word! For he said 'nigh unto a curse,' not a 'curse.' Now he that hath not yet fallen into a curse, but is come to be near thereto, may also come to be afar off from it (by repentance)."

"Whose end is to be burned." "If a man abide not in me" (and all grace is given to us that we may abide in Him) "if a man abide not in me, he is cast forth as a brand and is withered, and they gather them, and cast them into the fire, and they are burned." (John xv. 6.)

9. "But, beloved, we are persuaded better things of you, and things," &c.; "better" than that they should fall away into apostasy.

"Things that accompany salvation." Joined to, laying hold of salvation. They who are in the way of attaining salvation are those who are advancing instead of declining in the Divine Life, they receive the rain of the heavenly grace and receive it not in vain, but bear fruit to God.

10 ⁹For ʳGod *is* not unrighteous to forget ˢyour work and labour of love, which ye have shewed toward his name, in that ye have ᵗministered to the saints, and do minister.

q Prov. xiv. 31.
Matt. x. 42.
& xxv. 40.
John xiii. 20.
r Rom. iii. 4.
2 Thess. i. 6, 7.
s 1 Thess. i. 3.
t Rom. xv. 25.
2 Cor. viii. 4.
& ix. 1, 12.
2 Tim. i. 18.

10. "And labour of love." "Labour" omitted by ℵ, A, B., C., D., E., P., nine or ten Cursives, d, e, f, Vulg., Syriac, &c.; but retained by K., L., most Cursives, Copt.

---

"Though we thus speak." We speak thus because we would be on the safe side, with respect to you. There is a spirit of declension among many of our countrymen, and you may be drawn into it.

10. "For God is not unrighteous to forget your work and (labour of) love." God has very distinctly promised to reward all good works of benevolence and self-denial. Our Lord Himself goes as far as possible in this way when he says, "Whosoever shall give to drink to one of these little ones a cup of cold water only, in the name of a disciple, verily I say unto you, he shall in no wise lose his reward" (Matth. x. 42). And our Lord in Matth. xxv. makes the final judgment itself turn upon the doing of deeds of benevolence or the doing them not. "Come ye blessed, I was an hungered and ye gave me meat." God exhibits His righteousness, not only in taking vengeance, as some seem to think, but in rewarding that which he has promised to reward, and there is nothing which he has so unreservedly promised to reward as benevolence and kindly deeds.

"Which ye have shewed towards His Name, in that ye have ministered," &c. What they did must have been because they believed in the Name of God as set forth in His Son Jesus Christ "I have declared unto them Thy Name, and will declare it," (John xvii. 26), and for this reason, that their love and kindliness was especially manifested to the saints in those parts, ministering to their wants and persevering in doing so. These saints, of course, were Christians, and on that account were worked for and loved by the Hebrew believers.

It has been thought by some that these Hebrew Christians thus commended were converted Jews of Rome, who had, along with the Gentiles, sent contributions to the poor saints in Judea, and there

## CHAP. VI.   THAT YE BE NOT SLOTHFUL.

11 And we desire that ᵘ every one of you do shew the same diligence ˣ to the full assurance of hope unto the end: ᵘ ch. iii. 6, 11. ˣ Col. ii. 2.

12 That ye be not slothful, but followers of them who through faith and patience ʸ inherit the promises. ʸ ch. x. 36.

---

is a certain likeness in language and thought to Rom. xv. 15, but there is very great difficulty in pronouncing to what Jews this Epistle was written.

11. "And we desire that every one of you do shew the same," &c. "We desire." It is our personal wish and desire, because we know what more abundant happiness ye will enjoy in eternity.

"Every one of you do shew." The Apostles and Apostolic writers never lose sight of the fact that though the Church is One Body, it is made up of individuals; and that on the holiness and goodness of individuals depends the welfare of the whole mystical body. The love and services of each are necessary to the perfect well-being of the whole.

"To the full assurance of hope." In the word rendered full assurance (πληροφορία) there is not, as far as I can see, any thing of the modern idea of assurance. It is rather the "fulness of hope," but, of course, the fuller the hope is, the more confidence a soul has of fruition.

"Unto the end." "He that endureth unto the end, the same shall be saved" (Matth. x. 22, xxiv. 13).

"'Hope,' he means, carries us through: it recovers us again. Be not wearied out, do not despair, lest your hope should be in vain. For he that worketh that which is good hopeth also that which is good, and never at any time despairs of himself." (Chrysostom.)

12. "That ye be not slothful, but followers of them who through faith," &c. "Slothful," that is, "sluggish," "supine."

"But followers of them who through faith," &c. In a short time he will give them the examples of many of the chief of their forefathers who through faith inherited the promises, and a faith which shewed its reality and strength by its endurance. So Rom. ii. 7: "To them who by patient continuance in well doing look for glory, honour, and immortality."

13. "For when God made promise to Abraham, because he

13 For when God made promise to Abraham, because he could swear by no greater, *he sware by himself,

*Gen. xxii. 16, 17. Ps. cv. 9, Luke i. 75.

14 Saying, Surely blessing I will bless thee, and multiplying I will multiply thee.

---

could," &c. God sware to Abraham, not when He first called him, but when he had in intention offered up Isaac. The oath was not that he should have a seed, that was given him long before—but that in that son He would most surely bless Abraham, and most surely multiply his seed—and in his seed should all the nations of the earth be blessed, *i.e.*, in the Messiah. It was in this very juncture in all probability that Abraham was enabled in prophetic vision to see Christ's day—to see it and be glad. But this would not be a sufficient fulfilment. Abraham never really died. God was the God of Abraham—after his body was buried—and God is the God of the living. In his place in Paradise God made him to know the Incarnation and Birth of Christ. In some way unknown to us God made him to see it, and he saw it, and was glad. (See my note on John viii. 56.)

There is a remarkable Rabbinical commentary on this oath of God. In Exod. xxxii. 13, we have Moses pleading with God, "Remember Abraham, Isaac and Israel thy servants, to whom thou hast sworn (בּי) by thine own self." What does בּי denote? Rabbi Eleazer answered, Moses spake thus to the Holy One, "Blessed be the Lord of the world, if thou hadst sworn by the very heavens and the earth, then I should have said: as the heavens and the earth shall perish, so also thy oath. But now thou hast sworn to them by Thy great Name which lives and endures for ever, so also shall thy oath endure for ever, and evermore." (Berachoth, fol. 32, i. quoted in McCaul on Hebrews, p. 64.)

14. "Saying, surely blessing I will bless thee, and multiplying I will multiply thee." This could not be fulfilled in the few remaining prosperous years of Abraham's life. It must look to the eternal fulfilment beginning in paradise, continued in the ages when God shewed him the development of His designs respecting His Son, and accomplished when Abraham saw the Lord exalted, and all things put under His feet.

15. "And so, after he had patiently endured, he obtained the promise." He had patiently to endure both to obtain the fulfilment

15 And so, after he had patiently endured, he obtained the promise.

16 For men verily swear by the greater: and ᵃ an oath for confirmation *is* to them an end of all strife.

17 Wherein God, willing more abundantly to shew unto ᵇ the heirs of promise ᶜ the immutability of his counsel, † confirmed *it* by an oath:

ᵃ Ex. xxii. 11.
ᵇ ch. xi. 9.
ᶜ Rom. xi. 29.
† Gr. *interposed himself by an oath.*

---

16. "For men verily." "Verily" (μὲν) omitted by ℵ, A., B., D., E., P; retained by C., K., L., most Cursives, Copt., Æth.

of God's promise of a son, and also that through him in that son the human race should be blessed. What years of patient waiting are embodied in his complaint, "Lord God, what wilt thou give me seeing I go childless and the steward (or heir) of my house is this Eliezer of Damascus," and what intensity of patience must have been his during the three days journey to the Land of Moriah, to the mount of sacrifice.

16. "For men verily swear by the greater." Thus Joseph swore by the life of Pharaoh, Gen. xlii. 16.

"And an oath for confirmation is to them an end of all strife." Rather, perhaps, as Revisers render it, "and in every dispute of theirs the oath is final for confirmation." Here is very probably an allusion to the law respecting disputes which is laid down in Exod. xxii. 7-11: "If a man deliver unto his neighbour an ass or an ox, and it die or be hurt, no man seeing it: Then shall an oath of the Lord be between them both, that he hath not put his hand unto his neighbour's goods: and the owner of it shall accept thereof, and he shall not make it good."

17. "Wherein God, willing more abundantly to shew unto the heirs," &c. "Wherein," in which respect of oaths for confirmation.

"Willing more abundantly to shew unto the heirs of promise," &c. Almighty God, therefore, condescending to Abraham, and conforming Himself to human usage with regard to oaths, called as it were Himself to witness, and so came between Abraham and Himself with an oath for greater assurance to Abraham. But it was not for Abraham's sake alone, but for all who should inherit his faith—for such were the heirs of promise. The word "confirm"

18 That by two immutable things, in which *it was* impossible for God to lie, we might have a strong consolation, who have fled for refuge to lay hold upon the hope ᵈ set before us:

19 Which *hope* we have as an anchor of the soul, both sure and stedfast, ᵉ and which entereth into that within the veil:

ᵈ ch. xii. 1.

ᵉ Lev. xvi. 15. ch. ix. 7.

---

is strictly " mediated, interposed an oath." It was a promise, the fulfilment of which they would have to expect or wait for during long centuries, and so God, compassionating human infirmity, interposed with this oath in addition to his promise.

18. "That by two immutable things, in which it was impossible for God," &c. "Two immutable things," the promise and the oath. The promise was such in form as what God constantly gives. The oath was superadded because, as I said, of the long centuries in which the heirs of promise had to wait for its perfect fulfilment.

"We might have a strong consolation who have fled for refuge," &c. "Strong consolation," translated by Revisers, by Westcott and by Alford, "strong encouragement."

"Who have fled for refuge to lay hold upon the hope set before us." The "hope set before us" is the Lord Jesus Christ, the Son of God, in whom all the promises of God are assured to us. We have, however, to lay hold of Him, and this can only be by a continuous act of faith in His Incarnation, Death, Resurrection, and Real Abiding Presence in His Church; so that, though apparently absent, He is really present according to His promise, "Lo, I am with you alway, even unto the end of the world."

This Jesus, Who is our Hope when He is laid hold of, communicates hope to us, and the firmer we lay hold of Him, the firmer our hope.

19. "Which hope we have as an anchor of the soul." The hope which each Christian has within him is the anchor, but instead of being cast below into the depths of the sea, as the anchor of earth is, it is cast above—into heaven, where Jesus is, and lays firm hold upon Him. The point of the simile or allusion is that, as the anchor of the storm-tossed mariner enters into the unseen depths, and finding a ground on which it can fasten holds the ship firm,

## CHAP. VII.] THE FORERUNNER.

20 ᶠ Whither the forerunner is for us entered, even Jesus, ᵍ made an high priest for ever after the order of Melchisedec.

ᶠ ch. iv. 14. & viii. 1. & ix. 24.
ᵍ ch. iii. 1. & v. 6, 10. & vii. 17.

so the Christian's anchor of hope enters into the unseen place—a place hid by the veil, or rather, typified by that Holy of Holies which was hid from the eyes of all worshippers by the veil, and there it finds that on which it can securely fasten, even Jesus, the true mercy-seat of God.

The figure which the Apostolic writer uses is a very bold one; as we should say, somewhat strained, but it teaches us three things—

1. That we must ourselves cast out the anchor of hope.
2. That there is sure and certain ground on which it may always fasten and hold us safe.
3. And that this sure ground is in the heaven of heavens, where is the true Mercy-seat of God.

20. "Whither the forerunner is for us entered, even Jesus." "The forerunner." "I go to prepare a place for you, and if I go away I will come again and receive you unto myself, that where I am, there," &c. (John xiv. 2). Perhaps he speaks with reference to the High Priest entering the Holy of Holies, but not as a forerunner. As long as the old state of things lasted none of the children of Israel could follow, but now the Lord in this new dispensation has entered into the Holiest that He may be followed.

## CHAP. VII.

FOR this ᵃ Melchisedec, king of Salem, priest of the most high God, who met Abraham

ᵃ Gen. xiv. 18, &c.

1. "For this Melchisedec, king of Salem, priest of the most high God." Three times has the writer declared that the Lord was a "priest after the order of Melchizedec" (v. 6, 10, v. 20).

And now he proceeds to set forth the Priesthood of Melchisedec, and its contrast with that of Aaron.

returning from the slaughter of the kings, and blessed him;

All that is known of Melchisedec is to be found in three verses of the book of Genesis which run thus: " And Melchisedec, king of Salem, brought forth bread and wine ; and he was the priest of the Most High God. And he blessed him and said, Blessed be Abram of the Most High God, Possessor of heaven and earth. And blessed be the Most High God, which hath delivered thine enemies into thine hands. And he gave him tithes of all " (Gen. xiv. 17, 20). This is the most mysterious passage in the Book of Genesis. Here Abraham comes across one of whose parentage not a word is said, and yet he is called the priest of the Most High. Now all the ideas of the Israelites respecting priests were connected with their parentage or genealogy, and their consecration. But from whom did this man receive his priesthood ? To what succession did he belong ? Who consecrated him? And to the service of what Deity was he consecrated ? and how did he exercise his priesthood? What was its manner? It may be well to endeavour to answer these questions seriatim.

To what succession did he belong ? There are some intimations, few it is true, but such as cannot be set aside, that an ancient worship of the true God existed in Palestine, of which Melchisedec was the last interpreter.[1] If the extreme wickedness of the Pales-

---

[1] The reader will find a most interesting examination of this matter in " The Journal of Sacred Literature," No. xxi., for April, 1860, vol. xi. The essay is entitled, " A Critical Inquiry into the Route of the Exodus." The first argument is derived from the pre-Exodus name of Horeb as "the Mount of God." " Now Moses kept the flock of Jethro . . . came to the Mount of God, even to Horeb." It appears that in the immediate vicinity of the mountain there was a tribe of Midianites who worshipped the true God. This was the tribe of which Jethro was the chieftain, for it is said of him that Jethro "rejoiced for all the goodness which the Lord had done to Israel, whom he had delivered out of the hand of the Egyptians" (Exod. xviii. 5-12).

The next argument is from a prophecy of Ezekiel respecting Tyre (Ezek. xxviii. 11-19), extremely difficult to interpret of the Tyre of Jewish history at any period, but quite in accordance with the fact that in the beginning of the Tyrian nation, when they inhabited the desert to the south of Palestine, they were in the favour of God, and had a worship and ritual acceptable to Him, from which they declined through the luxury and consequent wickedness brought upon them by their traffic. This worship had its chief seat in the Mount of God (verse 14). It had symbolic cherubim and stones like those on the breastplate of Aaron. The following is an extract giving the pith of the argument : " It has been usually supposed that this prophecy was addressed to some actual king of Tyre. This we believe to be perfectly impossible. Tyre, from its first foundation on the Syrian coast, was always so pre-eminently idolatrous, that no kings of this Baal and

tinian tribes be urged against this, we reply that it is only likely their degradation was not original barbarism, but a fall from the true God, which made their case infinitely worse.

That he belonged to some sort of succession of King-Priests is evident from this, that five hundred years after Abraham's time the king of Jerusalem, who fought against Joshua, and who must have been his successor, had a name of exactly the same character, Adonizedec, the Lord of Righteousness; but by this time the witness for Truth and Righteousness had become extinct, for Adonizedec was arrayed with certain heathen kings against one whose ancestor his own forefather had blessed in the name of the

---

Astarte worshipping city could have merited the praises here bestowed by Ezekiel upon the primitive orthodoxy of the object of the prophecy. Nor could there have ever been a period when the Syrian Tyre could have deserved the title of the 'guardian cherub of the Holy Hill of God.' The worship of Baal was contemporary with the foundation of the city. The temple of this Deity was as old as the city itself. The fervour of idolatrous bigotry and superstition never seems to have been intermitted. Ithobal, the 'manservant' of Baal, was a favourite name of the kings. Nor would it be easy to understand to what territory ever possessed by the Syrian Tyre the name of 'the Holy Hill of God' could be applied. But assume that the Tyrian *people* is here singled under the figure of its king, and that the first stanza relates to the innocent youth of the Phœnician nation when they inhabited the Negeb (south desert), and when Mount Sinai was the great gathering place of their religious assemblies, and the whole prophecy becomes clear and intelligible.

"The concurrent testimony of sacred and profane history proves the Phœnicians to have been a Cushite colony from Chavilah, on the Persian Gulf, who first settled in the Negeb, and were afterwards transferred by the Assyrians to the Mediterranean coast, south of Lebanon. Thus Herodotus, i. 1, 'the Persian historian states that the Phœnicians emigrated from the Erythræan to the Mediterranean;' again from vii. 8, 9, 'the Phœnicians anciently came from the Erythræan and settled in Syria by the sea-border.' In the early days of their settlements in the Negeb, they cultivated the pure worship of Jehovah (Elion?) which they had brought from the yet uncorrupted parent nation of Chavilah. Afterwards, enriched by a lucrative commerce, they 'waxed fat and kicked,' and began to prefer the idols of Egypt or Canaan to the eternal Creator. Then their power was broken. They were cast as profane from the Mount of God, and transplanted by the Assyrians out of the Negeb, a situation unrivalled in the world for a maritime people."

It is to be remembered that the verbs of the 16th and 17th verses should be rendered in the past tense rather than in the future. "I will cast thee out as profane," "I will destroy thee," should rather be rendered, "I cast thee out," "I destroyed thee."

It is clear, then, that if there was a very ancient revelation of the Supreme God in Palestine, that Melchisedec derived his knowledge of God Most High from it, and that he was probably its last priest or representative, for it is beyond measure improbable that in the time of Abraham God should raise up this greatest of priests, and allow his priesthood to expire after he had had a momentary interview with Abraham. If he was the representative of the old state of things which was passing away, and Abraham of the new, then all is consistent. The witness of the faith of Elion passes by blessing to the new faith of Jehovah and His Christ.

2 To whom also Abraham gave a tenth part of all; first

most High God. That there was a succession of witnesses for the truth of God in Salem or Jerusalem seems certain, for it is not likely that God would raise up one contemporaneously with Abraham to testify to his truth. It would be far more significant that the last witness for a purer and more ancient faith should solemnly bless the wandering stranger from the God of Whom he was the priest, and so make over to this man and his descendants his own witness for the true God.

Of what deity was Melchisedec the priest? Of El Elion. Now these two words are of totally different derivations: El from a root signifying power, and Elion from a root signifying exaltation. The initial letter in each is totally different. The word Elion is not commonly used in the Old Testament to designate the Supreme Being; only in this place, and twice in the Psalms, but these are sufficient to shew that it is lawful to give Him this name. According to Gesenius it was the original Divine name among the Phœnicians, and so presumably among the Canaanitish nations; but the worship of the true God under this name soon gave way to names indicating the powers of nature.

The designation of Melchisedec as the priest of Elion seems to imply that he was the acknowledged priest of the Supreme under this name, and probably that he was the only one, the original pure worship fast dying out. We shall consider the exercise or manner of his priesthood a little further on.

" King of Salem." This was either Jerusalem, or a place called Salem, not far from Sychem, the great preponderance of both authority and probability being in favour of the former.

" Priest of the most High God." This, we repeat, implies that among the Canaanitish nations he was the acknowledged priest, though not a word is said about his call or consecration. If he had been in the least degree connected with idolatrous worship it would have been impossible for Abraham to have received his blessing.

" Who met Abraham returning from the slaughter of the kings." This connects Melchisedec with the history as being a real personage, and not in any sense a mythical one.

2. " To whom also Abraham gave a tenth part of all." Thus acknowledging him as a true priest of God.

being by interpretation King of righteousness, and after that also King of Salem, which is, King of peace;

3 Without father, without mother, † without descent, having neither beginning of days, nor

† Gr. *without pedigree.*

---

"First being by interpretation King of righteousness, and after that also King," &c. This must indicate the true character of Melchisedec, for a wicked, or even a warlike prince, would not have had such names preserved to us by the inspiration of the Spirit of God.

"King of Salem, which is King of peace." Jerusalem (יְרוּשָׁלִַם) signifies either possession of peace, or foundation of peace. The significance of the two names points to the Lord as the King who shall reign and prosper and execute judgment and justice in the earth, and Whose name shall be "the Lord our righteousness," and "the Lord our peace." "He is our peace who hath made both one" (Ephes. ii. 14).

3. "Without father, without mother, without descent, having neither beginning," &c. The figure is not a strained one if we can but transport ourselves back to the times of the Law. It answers fully the objections which the Jew would make to the priesthood of Christ on the score of His descent. The Jew would ask, how can the Lord be a priest since He is not of the tribe of Levi? As far as we can gather, though it seems a bold thing to say, the qualification of the Aaronic priest was not character but descent—an unimpeachable pedigree having no flaw on either side.[1] Thus it is recorded in Ezra ii. 62, that a certain family "sought their register among those that were reckoned by genealogy, but they were not found: therefore were they, as polluted, put from the Priesthood." When, then, the Jew asked "how could Jesus of the tribe of Judah be a priest?" the answer is that the most venerable and honoured of all earthly priests had no pedigree—not a word recorded respecting his descent or successors; so far as the sacred record is concerned, he had neither beginning of days nor end of life. He comes for a moment on the stage of sacred history as if he were the denizen of another world, and then disappears, and

---

[1] On the mother's side as well, though it is not certain that she must be of the Levitical tribe, yet she must be an Israelite.

end of life; but made like unto the Son of God; abideth a priest continually.

---

yet he leaves the type of so exalted a priesthood that, centuries afterwards, the Christ, the Eternal Son, is pronounced a High Priest for ever after his order. Bishop Wordsworth on this place very finely says:—"The Apostle expressly declares here that there was a Divine meaning in the silence of scripture, not recording the birth, parentage, or death of Melchisedec, as compared with the priests of the line of Aaron, and that this silence prophecies of Christ."

"But made like unto the Son of God." "Made like unto the Son," *i.e.*, in the pages of Scripture. He is made like unto the Son, both in what is written of him and in what is not written.

It is written of him that he was the greatest of all merely human priests, for the father of the faithful, the friend of God, the inheritor of the promises of Salvation, receives his blessing. He is made like unto the Son of God in that his priesthood is in some way connected with the exhibition of bread and wine; he did not bring forward a sacrifice which he slew and whose blood he presented, but he brought forth that which his great Antitype consecrated as the perpetual memorial and means of application of His own sacrifice.

It is not written of him that he had predecessors or successors—that he was of a priestly race or family, and that at his departure from this world others were invested with his priestly robes, as Eliezer was with the robes of Aaron (Num. xx. 26).

What, in a word, was the characteristic of his priesthood? It was no other than its absolute uniqueness. He was one—none going before him, none succeeding him; and so he was the fitting type of One Whose priesthood is unique and unapproachable, a King as well as Priest; as a King dispensing righteousness, as a Priest dispensing peace.

"Abideth a priest continually." Where? There can be but one answer. In his great Antitype : the Priesthood of Aaron has passed away, but not so that of Melchisedec. That abideth. If Christ be a priest for ever after the order of Melchisedec, then the priesthood of Melchisedec has not and never will pass away. If it be replied the priesthood abides, but the priest has passed away, we

4 Now consider how great this man *was*, ᵇ unto whom even the patriarch Abraham gave the tenth of the spoils.  ᵇ Gen. xiv. 20.

5 And verily ᶜ they that are of the sons of Levi, who receive the office of the priesthood, have a commandment to take tithes of the people accord-  ᶜ Numb. xviii. 21, 26.

---

answer that Melchisedec is now in the unseen world as truly living as when he met Abraham, and what his function there is it is not for us to inquire. (Ps. cxxxi.)

4. "Now consider how great this man was unto whom even the patriarch," &c. Great in the estimation of God. This could not have been unless he was worthy of it, so far as a creature can be worthy. In all probability, as the priest of the One True and Holy God amongst a reprobate race, his holy soul was vexed with the dishonour done to God by the iniquity of his countrymen. If he was made like unto the Son of God we may be sure that suffering constituted a great part of that likeness.

"Unto whom the patriarch Abraham gave a tenth part," &c. This tenth could not have been mere gifts or presents, for as Cornelius à Lapide says, "mere gifts are not only given to lay people, but also to equals and, indeed, generally to inferiors; but he gave to Melchisedec the sacerdotal tenths as priest and pontifex."

The "spoils" signifies properly the best part of the spoils. Commentators notice how much more emphasis is laid upon the greatness of Abraham, and by consequence that of Melchisedec, by the order of the words in the Greek; "how great this man was to whom Abraham gave a tithe of the chief spoils, even the Patriarch."

5. "And verily they that are of the sons of Levi who receive," &c. Not all the sons of Levi were priests. If the Levites received any part of the tithes it was in virtue of their doing quasi-priestly offices in the service of the priests.

"Have a commandment to take tithes of the people according," &c. The commandment to take tithes was both to them and to the people—to them to enforce their collection both in regard of what was due to the service of God and to their posterity. The people were in no sense wronged in this, because Levi had no inheritance among his brethren. If Levi had had his portion of the

ing to the law, that is, of their brethren, though they come out of the loins of Abraham:

‖ Or, *pedigree*.
d Gen. xiv. 19.
e Rom. iv. 13.
Gal. iii. 16.

6 But he whose ‖ descent is not counted from them received tithes of Abraham, ᵈ and blessed ᵉ him that had the promises.

7 And without all contradiction the less is blessed of the better.

---

promised land assigned to him each of the other tribes would have had a tenth less.

"That is, of their brethren, though they come out of the loins of Abraham." The priestly tribe received tithes of those who were equally descendants of Abraham, and so were civilly their equals in virtue of their descent from the same patriarch.

6. "But he whose descent is not counted from them received tithes," &c. Received tithes, *i.e.*, received acknowledgment of his priesthood; and so of his superiority over him who paid the tithes in things pertaining to religious order or ceremonial or even outward access to God.

"And blessed him that had the promises."

7. "And without all contradiction the less is blessed of the greater." Abraham was great as being honoured of God to be the recipient of His best and greatest promises to the race. In fact, so far as his relations to God were concerned, no man, except the God-Man, could be esteemed greater. But in the matter of religion, in so far as it involves united approach to God, Abraham, taught by God Himself, acknowledged the superiority of Melchisedec in that he not only paid tithes to him as God's priest, but submitted to receive his blessing.

In the latter point, especially, Abraham acknowledged that Melchisedec was greater than himself.

In this seventh verse is contained the whole question of Sacerdotalism as setting forth assumptions which are not allowed by the world. The Apostolic writer asserts that "without all contradiction the less is blessed of the better." And a very little thought will convince us that it must be so. All the different forms of religion, whether in Christianity or out of it, which have a settled or permanent ministry, delegate to that ministry certain offices—particularly these three—teaching, administration of sacraments,

8 And here men that die receive tithes; but there he *receiveth them*, ᶠof whom it is witnessed that he liveth.

ᶠ ch. v. 6. & vi. 20.

---

and blessing. If any Christian whatsoever attends a place of worship he, by so doing, puts himself into the place of a disciple, and takes the place of the learner, or of the man who needs exhortation, not of him who gives it. And I believe, that without exception, all bodies or congregations of Christians depute to their ministers the function of blessing. Now they who submit to be blessed by their fellow man must acknowledge that in the matter of conveying or pronouncing blessing from God, he is the better or greater. They cannot submit to receive his blessing as a mere fellow creature. They must believe that there must be something sacred in his office, or why should he be ordained, or set apart, or even recognized. His blessing, if it be not the merest farce, must be assumed to come from God, and, if so, he is so far between them and God, and so far he is the better. They can only get rid of this by forbidding him to bless.

8. "But here men that die receive tithes; but there he receiveth," &c. Successive generations of priests, from Aaron to Caiaphas, died, having performed priestly functions and received priestly dues. Provision was made in the law for the succession of priests on the assumption that those offices would be terminated by death.

"But there," that is, in the page of holy writ, "he receiveth them, of whom it is witnessed that he liveth." Does this "of whom it is witnessed that he liveth" mean that there is no record of his death? From the analogy of the necessary interpretation of verse 3, "without father, without mother," &c., it would seem so, but I scarcely think that the mystery is so easily solved. We must take into account what our Lord says respecting the absolute existence of Abraham in the unseen world, when He says, respecting God being the God of Abraham, Isaac, and Jacob, that He is not the God of the dead but of the living. If Abraham is now living in the Paradisaical state, so living that our Lord represents him as having the faithful departed in his bosom, and living so as to speak and to rejoice at the Day of Christ, must not that better one, who blessed him, be living also with as true, as active, as blessed a life?

9 And as I may so say, Levi also, who receiveth tithes, payed tithes in Abraham.

10 For he was yet in the loins of his father, when Melchisedec met him.

<sup>g</sup> Gal. ii. 21. ver. 18, 19. ch. viii. 7.

11 <sup>g</sup> If therefore perfection were by the Levitical priesthood, (for under it the people received the law), what further need *was there* that another priest

---

This may not solve the mystery, but it may assure us that if we were not in such profound ignorance of the conditions of saints in the unseen world it might be solved.

9, 10. "And as I may so say, Levi also, who receiveth tithes, payed tithes in Abraham. For he was yet in the loins," &c. "As I may so say." This phrase is introduced when something which the speaker enumerates is a matter of difficulty to be received, *i.e.*, a paradox.

"Levi also, who receiveth tithes." This is introduced to show the greatness of Melchisedec over all the race of priests which sprung from Abraham as the father of Levi, the ancestor of the Levitical line. The Jew might have alleged that it was in the power of God to raise up a greater priest than Melchisedec, and that He did so when He constituted Aaron His High Priest. To this the Apostolic writer answers by bringing forward the principle so often insisted on in the Old Testament, that a whole race is often included in their first ancestor. The descendants of the three sons of Noah, and of the two sons of Isaac, and the twelve sons of Jacob, were all blessed in their ancestors. So that, if Levi was blessed in Abraham, *i.e.*, whilst he was in the loins of Abraham, he might well be accounted to receive the blessing of Melchisedec in Abraham, and to acknowledge in Abraham the greatness of the Priest-King's blessing, by paying him tithes in his great ancestor.

11. "If therefore perfection were by the Levitical priesthood, for under," &c. What is this perfection? According to the analogy of the rest of the Epistle it is twofold, perfect reconciliation with God, and complete conformity to the image of God. If the Levitical law had put men in possession of these blessings through the action of its priesthood, then,—

should rise after the order of Melchisedec, and not be called after the order of Aaron?

12 For the priesthood being changed, there is made of necessity a change also of the law.

13 For he of whom these things are spoken pertaineth to another tribe, of which no man gave attendance at the altar.

14 For *it is* evident that [h] our Lord sprang out of Juda; of which tribe Moses spake nothing concerning priesthood.

[h] Isa. xi. 1.
Matt. i. 3.
Luke iii. 33.
Rom. i. 3.
Rev. v. 5.

---

11. "And not be called." Rather, "be reckoned."

"What further need was there that another priest should rise?" &c. The writer alludes to the fact that during the time of the law, in which time the 110th Psalm was written, the Messiah is addressed as a Priest of the Order of Melchisedec, and not of Aaron. The whole Psalm is addressed to one of superhuman power and greatness. God says to him, "Sit thou on my right hand." The centre of his dominion is the Holy City itself. "His people, in the day of his power, offer him free-will offerings with a holy worship." If he be a priest, then, after what order or pattern is he? Not of that of Aaron, but of that of Melchisedec. It is plain, then, that the Priesthood of Aaron is not the highest of priesthoods, neither is it final, nor eternal, and the priesthood which is assigned to the Son of God is for ever and ever.

12. "For the priesthood being changed, there is made of necessity a change," &c. The Priesthood of the Eternal Son is a Priesthood of grace. He pardons through the grace of His Atonement. He pours forth His Spirit, the Spirit of grace; consequently, the rites which He ordains are not mere outward signs, but sacraments —things totally unknown under the Law—outward visible signs of inward spiritual grace. Old things under Him pass away—all things become new.

13, 14. "For he of whom these things are spoken .... nothing concerning priesthood." The Messiah spoken of in prophecy was to be of the tribe of Judah, for He was to be the Son of David, and of this tribe nothing was spoken concerning Priesthood, and when

15 And it is yet far more evident: for that after the similitude of Melchisedec there ariseth another priest,

16 Who is made, not after the law of a carnal commandment, but after the power of an endless life.

---

one of the good kings of this line ventured to perform a priestly office he was struck with leprosy, and till the day of his death lived as an excommunicated person.

15, 16. "And it is yet far more evident: for that after the similitude of Melchisedec." It is far more evident even than the fact that our Lord traces His descent from Judah, that another priest ariseth after the order of Melchisedec. This I take to mean that though we are certain of the descent of Christ from Judah, because of the accuracy of the genealogies, yet there is a very direct word of God in Psalm 110, that Messiah is a priest after the order of Melchisedec.

16. "Who is made, not after the law of a carnal commandment." The law of a carnal commandment is supposed to be the law or rule of a fleshly descent, for that was the law after which the sons of Levi obtained the priesthood. Others refer it to the whole legal dispensation, which, though St. Paul calls it spiritual (Rom vii.), was, compared to the Gospel, carnal.

"But after the power of an endless (indissoluble) life." Westcott well says, "Other priests were made priests in virtue of a special ordinance. He was made priest in virtue of His inherent nature." And so also, apparently, Chrysostom. "Because he lives by his own power."

But there is a remarkable analogy, not sufficiently noticed, between the idea here and that in Gal. iii. 21 : "For if a law had been given which could have given life, verily righteousness should have been by the law." And Rom. viii. 3, "What the law could not do, in that it was weak through the flesh, God sending his own Son in the likeness of sinful flesh . . . that the righteousness of the law might be fulfilled in us," &c. Christ now exercises His Priesthood through His Life, by imparting to those who sincerely avail themselves of His priesthood His very Life, the Life which is inherent, not only in His Spirit, but in His glorified Flesh. He exercises, at God's right hand, the power of an endless life, not merely exercising that power externally to Himself, as it were, but communicating

## A PRIEST FOR EVER.

17 For he testifieth, <sup>l</sup>Thou *art* a priest for ever after the order of Melchisedec.

18 For there is verily a disannulling of the commandment going before for <sup>k</sup> the weakness and unprofitableness thereof.

<sup>l</sup> Ps. cx. 4. ch. v. 6, 10. & vi. 20.
<sup>k</sup> Rom. viii. 3. Gal. iv. 9.

---

17. "He testifieth." "It is testified," א, A., B., D., F., P., five or six Cursives, Sah., Copt., Syriac; but C., K., L., most Cursives, Arm., Æth., read, "he testifieth."

His Life to us so that the power of His Life should be within us, because His Life itself is within us.

17. "For he testifieth, Thou art a priest for ever after the order of Melchisedec." Rather, "it is testified of Him." The emphasis in the quotation is to be laid on the "for ever." He is made after the power of a life which endures for ever.

18. "For there is verily a disannulling of the commandment going before for the weakness and unprofitableness thereof." When was this "disannulling of the commandment going before?" No doubt when Christ completed His Sacrifice, and its acceptance on God's part was shown by His Resurrection from the dead. After that God, for a short time, suffered the continuance of the Jewish sacrifices in condescension to the infirmities of His people among the Jews, but when this Epistle was written it was on the eve of vanishing away.

"For the weakness and unprofitableness thereof." It was weak "through the fles' " (Rom. viii. 3). It was unprofitable because it did not produce the fruits which it seemed from its holy nature calculated to produce: and this because, being mere unassisted command, it brought no life with it. (Gal. iii. 21). This place (verses 15-18) is of extreme importance, because here the doctrine of the Epistles to the Romans and Galatians meet and coalesce. According to Galatians iii. 21, the law could not produce righteousness because it could give no life, and according to Rom. viii. 1-4, it was weak through the flesh, and so One must come Who could give life and therefore strength to counteract its weakness, and here the weakness and unprofitableness is done away with because of the power of the Endless life of the Priest after the order of Melchisedec.

19. "For the law made nothing perfect, but the bringing in of

[margin notes:
l Acts xiii. 39. Rom. iii. 20, 21, 28. & viii. 3. Gal. ii. 16. ch. ix. 9.
ǁ Or, *but it was the bringing in,* Gal. iii. 21.
m ch. vi. 18. & viii. 6.
n Rom. v. 2. Eph. ii. 18. & iii. 12. ch. iv. 16. & x. 19.
ǁ Or, *without swearing of an oath.*]

19 For ¹ the law made nothing perfect, ǁ but the bringing in of ᵐ a better hope *did*; by the which ⁿ we draw nigh unto God.

20 And inasmuch as not without an oath he *was made priest:*

21 (For those priests were made ǁ without an oath; but this with an oath by him that said

19. For translation of this see below. The Revisers translate, "There is a disannulling of a foregoing commandment because of its weakness and unprofitableness (for the law made nothing perfect), and a bringing in thereupon of a better hope."

a better hope." This, and the latter part of the last verse should be rendered thus: "There is a disannulling of the commandment going before, for the law made nothing perfect, and there is also the bringing in of a better hope." These two things are side by side, as it were: the disannulling of the law, and the bringing in of a better hope.

"Bringing in," a bringing in therefore ("super-introduction," Wordsworth,) of a better hope. The law was not abolished till a new and better thing, containing far greater hopeful promise, had taken its place.

"By which we draw nigh unto God." The Law made nothing perfect. Something else was required to perfect the worshipper, and this was the bringing of the better Hope. Must not this hope (as Mr. Blunt suggests) be understood of the Personal Hope, the Lord Jesus Christ Who is our hope (1 Tim. i. 1)? "For the hope of Israel I am bound with this chain" (Acts xxviii. 20). By this hope, by Him, we are made perfect. We get as near to God spiritually and sacramentally as creatures can come. (Heb. x. 20).

20. "And inasmuch as not without an oath he was made priest." A clause has to be supplied here. It may be as in the Authorized, "He was made priest," or "inasmuch as not without an oath it was done," *i.e.*, the better hope was brought in. Both in the end are the same. For the bringing in of a better hope entirely depends upon the infinite greatness of the Priesthood.

21. "For those priests were made without an oath; but this with an oath." The Aaronic priests were constituted priests by

unto him, ºThe Lord sware and will not repent, Thou *art* a priest for ever after the order of Melchisedec:)  º Ps. cx. 4.

22 By so much ᵖ was Jesus made a surety of a better testament.  p ch. viii. 6. & ix. 15. & xii. 24.

23 And they truly were many priests, because they were not suffered to continue by reason of death:

24 But this *man*, because he continueth ever, hath ‖ an unchangeable priesthood.  ‖ Or, *which passeth not from one to another.*

---

21. "After the order of Melchisedec." So A., D., E., K., L., P., most Cursives, d, e, Copt., Syriac; but omitted by ℵ, B., C., Vulg., &c.

God indirectly through the Mediatorship of Moses, but the High Priest of our profession by God himself with an oath in the words, "The Lord swear and will not repent, Thou art a priest for ever."

22. "By so much was Jesus made a surety of a better testament." "Testament" should here be rendered "covenant;" for it is the same word, and evidently stands for the same thing as in viii. 6, "The mediator of a better covenant."

"By so much," by the fact that He was constituted by God Himself priest with an oath which the Aaronic priests were not.

"Better," inasmuch as it made perfect those who availed themselves of it, which the Aaronic covenant did not (verse 19).

23. "And they truly were many priests, because they were not suffered," &c. "And they too were constituted priests many in numbers" (Revisers). That is, not only were there more priests than one at a time, for the sons of Aaron, though they did not exercise the one great characteristic function of the High Priesthood on the great day of atonement, assisted their father in the highest ministration: but there was a perpetual succession of high priests, for as each one soon passed away in death another had to be consecrated to supply his place. Now this constant succession of high priests must have interfered with the faith with which the Jews regarded the functions of their office. Where the reconciling person was so often changed, there could not well be faith in the permanency of the reconciliation.

24. "But this man, because he continueth ever, hath an unchangeable priesthood." Not so much an unchangeable priesthood

| Or, *evermore*.
q Rom. viii. 34.
1 Tim. ii. 5.
ch. ix. 24.
1 John ii. 1.
r ch. iv. 15.

25 Wherefore he is able also to save them ‖ to the uttermost that come unto God by him, seeing he ever liveth ⁹ to make intercession for them.

26 For such an high priest became us, ʳ *who is*

---

as a priesthood that doth not pass away, *i.e.*, to another. I have noticed before (p. 58) how throughout this Epistle the idea of fixity and permanence attaches to Christ and His work.

25. "Wherefore he is able also to save them to the uttermost that come." "To the uttermost." This may mean that no matter to what length sin goes he is able to subdue it and destroy it: or it may have regard to time, and is contrasted with the transient function of the Aaronic priest. Perhaps both ideas are combined.

"That come unto God through him." They come to God pleading His Intercession. They come unto God through prayer and especially through the Eucharist in which they in an especial manner plead His Death—setting it forth till He comes.

"Seeing he ever liveth to make intercession for them." It is quite supposable that if a Jew in the old times came to God through some particular high priest, that high priest might be cut off by death, before the spiritual work was accomplished, but it cannot be so with the Great High Priest. Owing to His perpetuity, His endless Life, He can bring the particular salvation of each soul to perfection. This place teaches us that the salvation of a soul is the work of God the Father through Christ, just as the creation of the world was the work of God through Christ. No Person in the Godhead does anything by Himself apart from the Others. "I can do nothing by myself." "He (the Holy Spirit) shall not speak of Himself." The work in each soul depends on the intercession of Christ working (humanly speaking) on the will of the Father.

26. "For such an high priest became us, who is holy, harmless," &c. "Became us," was fitting for us, answers our deepest needs. We are unholy, malicious, defiled, we participate with oui fellow-sinners in their sin, we are of the earth, earthy. The Highpriest that befits our state must be holy, because we have to be made holy. Any sympathy, even the least which He might have with sin, would prevent Him cleansing us from it. He must be harmless (ἄκακος) because we are full of malice and envy, and

holy, harmless, undefiled, separate from sinners, <sup>s</sup> and made higher than the heavens;

27 Who needeth not daily, as those high priests, to offer up sacrifice, <sup>t</sup> first for his own sins, <sup>u</sup> and

<sup>s</sup> Eph. i. 20. & iv. 10. ch. viii. 1.
<sup>t</sup> Lev. ix. 7. & xvi 6, 11. ch. v. 3. & ix. 7.
<sup>u</sup> Lev. xv. 15.

He must put out all His power to fill us with His own loving Spirit. He is undefiled, in order that whilst He loves us He may abhor our defilement and assist us to the uttermost in cleansing us from it. He must be separate from sinners, because we are involved not only in our own sins, but more or less in the sin of those around us. Christ asserted most strongly His separation from sinners when He asked, "Which of you convinceth me of sin?" And though He was tempted like as we are, yet it was without sin.

"And made higher than the heavens." In this He is in contrast with the highest human priest who entered into the holy places made with hands, whereas He, our Mediator, enters into heaven itself; and so we have "an Advocate with the Father," as near to Him as possible—on His Throne—on His right Hand.

27. "Who needeth not daily, as those high priests, to offer up sacrifice, first for his own sins," &c. A very considerable difficulty has been made respecting the reconciliation of this place with Levit. vi. 20. From this latter place it has been gathered that the sin offering for the high priest was made only once in his life, on the day when he was anointed; but the writer of the Epistle certainly implies that it was a daily offering; and there seems to be no doubt of it if we take into consideration the word perpetual, (תָּמִיד), generally rendered continually, "This is the offering of Aaron and of his sons, which they shall offer unto the Lord in the day when he is anointed, the tenth part of an ephah of fine flour for a meat-offering perpetually (or continually), half of it in the morning, and half of it thereof at night." It is on the face of it exceedingly unlikely that so important a matter of atonement as the perpetual cleansing of the high priest should be confined to the presentation of the least and cheapest of all the offerings once in his life. No doubt the daily mincha was a memorial of the more important sacrifice mentioned in Levit. ix. 7, and xvi. 6.

"First for his own sins, and then for the people's." In Levit. xvi.

then for the people's: for ˣthis he did once, when he offered up himself.

28 For the law maketh ʸmen high priests which have infirmity; but the word of the oath, which was since the law, *maketh* the Son, ᶻwho is †consecrated for evermore.

ˣ Rom. vi. 10.
ch. ix. 12, 28.
& x. 12.
ʸ ch. v. 1, 2.
ᶻ ch. ii. 10. & v. 9.
† Gr. *perfected*.

---

containing the account of the ceremonies of the great day of atonement, peculiar stress is laid upon the fact that the high priest must first cleanse himself by sacrifice before he offered for the people (xvi. 6).

"For this he did once (*i.e.*, once for all), when he offered up himself." Because Christ is both God and Man His Sacrifice is all available with God for all men. He is both Priest and Victim in one. From all eternity in the Divine Counsels He was the Priest. Particularly He was the Priest when He parted with all power over His own Body, when He said at the Institution, "This is my Body; this is my Blood." It is necessary to remind the reader that though the repetition of this Sacrifice cannot be so much as imagined, the representation or sacrificial memorial of it should be perpetual.

28. "For the law maketh men high priests which have infirmity." The law ordained that there should be a succession of priests of the line of Aaron, springing from his loins, and by consequence inheriting his infirmities.

"But the word of the oath, which was since the law." Whilst the priesthood of Aaron was in its vigour as the greatest institution among the chosen people, a Psalm was written which recognized that there existed in the counsel and foreknowledge of God a greater priesthood, which was to appertain to the Son of God, and to which He was consecrated (or perfected) by the oath of God Himself, and this for evermore. The Aaronic priests had no abiding priesthood, because each one in his time was removed by death, but the Son had an abiding priesthood, because the word of the oath was, "Thou art a priest for ever."

"Consecrated," *i.e.*, perfected, τετελειωμένον. The high priests were consecrated, *i.e.*, perfected to their office by ceremonies such as investing them with holy garments by their fellow men, but the Son is consecrated, is perfected for His office by the oath of God.

## CHAP. VIII.

NOW of the things which we have spoken *this is* the sum: We have such an High Priest, <sup>a</sup> who is set on the right hand of the throne of the Majesty in the heavens;

2 A minister ‖ of <sup>b</sup> the sanctuary, and of <sup>c</sup> the true tabernacle, which the Lord pitched, and not man.

<sup>a</sup> Eph. i. 20. Col. iii. 1. ch. i. 3. & x. 12. & xii. 2.

‖ Or, *of holy things.*

<sup>b</sup> ch. ix. 8, 12, 24.

<sup>c</sup> ch. ix. 11.

---

1. "Now of the things which we have spoken," &c. "Now on the things which we are saying the chief point is this."

1. "Now of the things which we have spoken this is the sum." Rather, this is the principal. This passage does not contain the summing up of all that precedes, but its chief point. We have such an High Priest: so transcendentally great a One as sat down on the right Hand of the Majesty on high. This refers to Psalm cx., "Sit thou on my right hand." The human high priest stood trembling once a year in the presence of the Schechinah. The Divine Priest is on His Throne at the right Hand of God. "A priest on his throne" (Zech. vi. 13).

2. "A minister of the sanctuary." A minister (leitourgos), *i.e.*, a minister who performs a liturgy or public service in some respects answering to that performed by the priests, His types.

"Of the sanctuary," *i.e.*, following the meaning of the word in ix. 8. "The holiest of all, the holy of holies." Christ is the minister of that heavenly thing or place, which answers in sacredness and dignity to that of the earthly holy of holies.

"And of the true tabernacle." "True" here is in opposition not to false, but to typical. The true tabernacle is the reality, of which the earthly tabernacle is the representation.

"Which the Lord pitched, and not man." We shall have to examine a little further on whether this tabernacle be the "pattern" showed to Moses on the Mount, or whether it be a higher and more transcendental thing, nearer to the divine reality.

3 For <sup>d</sup>every High Priest is ordained to offer gifts and sacrifices: wherefore <sup>e</sup>*it is* of necessity that this man have somewhat also to offer.

4 For if he were on earth, he should not be a Priest, seeing that ||there are Priests that offer gifts according to the law:

<sup>d</sup> ch. v. 1.
<sup>e</sup> Eph. v. 2. ch. ix. 14.
|| Or, *they are Priests.*

---

4. "For if." א, A., B., D., 17, 73, 80, 13, d, e, f, Vulg., read, "Nay if." E., K., L., most Cursives, "for if."

"There are Priests." So K., L., most Cursives, Syriac; but א, A., B., D., E., P., d, e, f, Vulg., Copt., read, "there are those that offer."

Whether the one or the other, it was the direct creation of God, not made with hands, but pitched, or set up by God Himself.

3. "For every High Priest is ordained to offer gifts and sacrifices." This is the essence of the priestly office, and by consequence that of the High Priest, not to preach, or teach, or govern, or even to lead the devotions of his fellow-worshippers, but to offer gifts and sacrifices; gifts, *i.e.*, unbloody sacrifices, as the mincha—sacrifices, *i.e.*, slain animals.

"Wherefore it is of necessity that this man have somewhat also to offer." What has He to offer? Evidently Himself, but in Himself His Church, His people, with all their prayers, their offerings, their good deeds, their self-denials.

4. "For if he were on earth, he should not be a Priest, seeing that there," &c. The succession of Aaronic priests and their sacrifices were by God's own appointment, and He did not supersede and abolish them till He had raised up an infinitely better one to fill their place, or rather, to do what they could not do, to make perfect reconciliation. In this He respected not the priests, but His own appointment. He must be served by Priests. The cessation of the Levitical priesthood seems to me to be most emphatically illustrated by the rending of the veil at the moment of the completion of the all-sufficient sacrifice. Then the entrance into the holiest was made manifest. Then, when the symbol of exclusion was done away with, there was no need of a priest to enter in as the representative of his brethren; all, if they understood the significance of what God then accomplished, could enter. But of this more hereafter.

Of course, as Bishop Wordsworth says, He would not have been

CHAP. VIII.] ACCORDING TO THE PATTERN. 145

5 Who serve unto the example and ᶠ shadow of heavenly things, as Moses was admonished of God when he was about to make the tabernacle : ᵍ for, See, saith he, *that* thou make all things according to the pattern shewed to thee in the mount.

ᶠ Col. ii. 17. ch. ix. 23. & x. 1.
ᵍ Exod. xxv. 40. & xxvi. 30. & xxvii. 8. Num. viii. 4. Acts vii. 44.

---

5. "Who serve unto the example and shadow of heavenly things." "Who serve that which is the copy and shadow," &c.

a priest in the Jewish sense of the word, for they could only imagine priests who were to be the sacrificers of victims.

"The Apostle says this by way of self-defence, in order that he may show to the Hebrews that he does not disparage the Levitical Law, but rather regards it with veneration, as being a figure of heavenly things. Hence he admits that it would have been superfluous to call Christ a priest if He were on earth, inasmuch as there are still priests who discharge the priestly functions according to the Levitical Law." (Theodoret.)

5. "Who serve unto the example and shadow of heavenly things." Serve, *i.e.*, serve after the manner of divine service, "serve liturgically."

"After the example." Sketch, dim outline, shadow.

"Of heavenly things, as Moses was admonished of God ... shewed thee in the mount." A question of some importance must be shortly considered. We find that Moses was oracularly warned (κεχρημάτισται) twice that he should make all according to the pattern shewed to him in the mount. On both these occasions the warning was given, not respecting the general outlines of the tabernacle, but respecting its details, even to the minutest particulars. Thus in Exod. xxv. 40: "Thou shalt make the tongs thereof, and the snuff dishes thereof shall be of pure gold. And look that thou make them after their pattern which was shewed thee in the mount," and in chap. xxvi. 30: "And the middle bar in the midst of the boards shall reach from end to end. And thou shalt overlay the boards with gold, and make their rings of gold for places for the bars ... according to the fashion thereof which was shewed thee in the mount."

Now was this pattern, which Moses was bid to copy so exactly, the heavenly things themselves, the greater and more perfect tabernacle which some, following Plato, call the ideal tabernacle,

L

6 But now ʰ hath he obtained a more excellent ministry, by how much also he is the mediator of a better ‖ covenant, which was established upon better promises.

ʰ 2 Cor. iii. 6, 8, 9. ch. vii. 22.
‖ Or, *testament*.

7 ⁱ For if that first *covenant* had been faultless, then should no place have been sought for the second.

ⁱ ch. vii. 11, 18.

---

the true tabernacle, which the Lord pitched and not men, or was it this transcendental tabernacle translated, as it were, into a shape capable of being minutely copied, and so brought within reach of the intellects of the poor semi-barbarous people just emancipated from the Egyptian brick-kilns? I think it must have been the latter. The heavenly tabernacle, parts of which St. John saw in his Apocalyptic visions, whether real or ideal, must have been infinitely beyond the power of the Israelites to copy, or to conceive of even in any worthy adequate way; and a small outline, as it were, an ὑπόδειγμα, was placed before Moses, of whose details he could easily retain the memory.

That which was shewed to Moses must have been as true a representation as the mind of man could take in of the eternal and transcendental realities; and it taught him how these eternal things could be represented in the forms of time and sense.

6. "But now hath he obtained a more excellent ministry, by how much," &c. The ministry which was superseded was good for the time before the Incarnation, for every thing ordained by God for the service of man is good; though in the fulness of time it may be succeeded by a better.

"By how much also he is the Mediator of a better covenant." "A better covenant," that is a covenant of grace rather than of works.

"Established upon better promises." These better promises will be found in the words of Jeremiah prophesying of it, which immediately succeed.

7. "For if that first covenant had been faultless, then should no place," &c. It was faulty, not on the score of unholiness or unworthiness, but on the score of deficiency. It could not give life, for, as the apostle says (Gal. iii. 21), "If there had been a law given which could have given life, verily righteousness should have been by the law"—*i.e.*, by that law.

8 For finding fault with them, he saith, ᵏ Behold, the days come, saith the Lord, when I will make a new covenant with the house of Israel and with the house of Judah:

ᵏ Jer. xxxi. 31, 32, 33, 34.

9 Not according to the covenant that I made with their fathers in the day when I took them by the hand to lead them out of the land of Egypt; because they continued not in my covenant, and I regarded them not, saith the Lord.

---

8. "For finding fault with them, he saith, Behold the days come," &c. With the people who disobeyed the law, not with the law itself.

"The days come," &c. This is taken from the Septuagint of Jeremiah xxxi. 31, 34, which chapter is numbered xxxviii. in the Septuagint.

The Lord speaks by the prophet to reassure the people of Israel who should return from the captivity of His continued blessing and protection, but the fulfilment of the promise was in the far future. The new life—the law written not on tables of stone, but on the heart—could not be given till the new Nature was given in the Person of the Second Adam, the New Man.

"With the house of Israel and with the house of Judah." This looks to the time prophecied of in Ezekiel: "I will make them one nation in the land upon the mountain of Israel: and one king shall be king to them all: and they shall be no more two nations, neither shall they be divided into two kingdoms any more" (Ezek. xxxvii. 21, 22).

9. "Not according to the covenant . . . in the day when I took them." "In the day" must not be pressed literally, but signifies "the time." The covenant was made on the 50th day after the Exodus. The ratification is described in Exod. xxiv. 6₂: "And Moses wrote all the words of the Lord . . . and he took the book of the covenant, and read in the audience of the people, and they said, All that the Lord hath said we will do," &c.

"And I regarded them not," in the Hebrew "I was married to them." The Hebrew seems to agree best with the sense, when the people of Israel declined from God, God did not apparently disre-

10 For ¹this *is* the covenant that I will make with the house of Israel after those days, saith the Lord; I will †put my laws into their mind, and write ‖ them in their hearts: and ᵐ I will be to them a God, and they shall be to me a people: 11 And ⁿ they shall not teach every man his neighbour, and every man his brother, saying,

¹ ch. x. 16.
† Or *give*.
‖ Or, *upon*.
ᵐ Zech. viii. 8.
ⁿ Isa. liv. 13.
John vi. 45.
1 John ii. 27.

---

11. "His neighbour." Rather, "his fellow citizen" (τὴν πολίτην). So ℵ, A., B., D., E., K., L., most Cursives; but P. only among Uncials, and Vulg. and some Cursives read "neighbour."

---

gard them, but punished them till he brought them to repentance. No way of reconciling the two versions seems satisfactory.

10. "For this is the covenant that I will make ... I will put my laws into their mind, and write them in their hearts," &c. This is not strictly a covenant so much as a bestowal of grace without the least word respecting any requirement on the part of those who came under the covenant. No stipulation whatsoever is spoken of. It is simply "receive and live." He who comes to partake of this covenant has simply to believe in the promises of God, and is then admitted into the covenant, and at his admission has grace given to him to enable him to live hereafter as a member of Christ. If he fails to do so it is because he fails to live to, to realize, to continue in, to stir up, the grace of his initiation.

"I will be to them a God." I will be to them all that can be comprehended under the Name "God"—I will be their Father, their Protector, their Instructor, their Leader and Guide, their Redeemer, their Sanctifier, and their Life-Giver.

"They shall be to me a people." They shall be my chosen, my children, my heirs, my Church.

11. "And they shall not teach every man his neighbour, and every man his brother," &c. This does not mean that under the New Covenant there shall be no teaching or instruction, for respecting the times of this New Covenant Isaiah prophecies: "Thy teachers shall not be removed into a corner any more, but thine eyes shall see thy teachers" (xxx. 20), but it means that the knowledge of God in the Christian faith shall be readily received and acted upon in the life.

Some questions suggest themselves on the above prophecy. We

Know the Lord: for all shall know me, from the least to the greatest.

---

are now living, or suppose that we are living, under this new Covenant. We believe that it commenced at Pentecost, and has continued unto this time. Is it true of Christendom, of baptized and professing Christendom, at this day? Has it been true or, to any great extent, true, of any period in any Christian country of which we have any knowledge? Under the idea that this beautiful picture has never had any real existence, some have thought that it has only been true of a very select few—a Church consisting only of the true elect, an invisible Church composed altogether of true Christians and none else.

But the terms of the prophecy altogether forbid any such a mode of explanation. It points to a general state of things. "I will make a new covenant with the house of Israel, and with the house of Judah; I will put my laws in their mind, they shall all know me from the least to the greatest"—to limit this to one man in, say, ten or twenty in the visible Church seems on the face of it, in utter disregard of the express language of the prophecy.

Some, consequently, have explained it as if the fulfilment was yet future, that it principally refers to the ingathering of the whole Jewish people, but undoubtedly the Apostolic writer treats it as if it referred to the Covenant then administered by the Son of God.

It may help us to the true understanding of all this to remember that the Church of Christ in the day of Pentecost actually commenced with the state of goodness and holiness here described. Acts ii. 40 pictures a state of things exactly answering to the establishment in the whole Christian body of this new and better covenant. The Epistles to the Thessalonians seem to describe a similar diffusion of the Spirit in the Church. So do the Epistles to the Ephesians and Philippians. If we take knowledge into account, so does the beginning of the Epistle to the Corinthians: "In every thing ye are enriched by him in all knowledge and in all utterance." The Epistle of St. John assures those who received it that "they have an unction from the Holy One, and they know all things."

The possession of the New Covenant—the writing of the law in the heart—does not imply sinlessness. It does not make declension from God impossible. It does not mean that the old nature is eradicated, or that the flesh is wholly subdued to the spirit: but

12 For I will be merciful to their unrighteousness, °and their sins and their iniquities will I remember no more.

° Rom. xi. 27. ch. x. 17.

13 ᵖ In that he saith, A new *covenant*, he hath made the first old. Now that which decayeth and waxeth old *is* ready to vanish away.

ᵖ 2 Cor. v. 17.

---

12. "And their iniquities" omitted by א, B., f, Vulg., Copt., Syriac, Æth.; but retained by A., D., E., K., L., P., and most Cursives.

if we are to do what may be unlawful, *i.e.*, to judge of the state of Churches or bodies of men, it seems to demand an immense difference between professing Christians and unconverted heathen or unbelievers, and those who have been able to compare Christian and heathen society tell us that there is this difference. A man of great piety and intelligence assured me that between Christians attached to what he conceived to be a superstitious form of worship and the heathen around them there seemed an impassable gulf.

I have heard from Bishop Horden of the great lone land of whole tribes of Red Indians, once the most degraded and murderous of mankind, living as close to the teaching of the Gospel as seems possible on this side of eternity. I have read of whole tribes of Australian savages being made saints of God.

The literal meaning of this prophecy is to be held to, and it is in our power to revive it by prayer and faith, but this faith must be faith in the presence of Christ in His Church.

12. "For I will be merciful to their unrighteousness, and their sins," &c. Let the reader note that in this prophecy the Sanctification, *i.e.*, the writing of the law on the heart, is put first; and the Justification, or what answers to it, afterwards.

13. "In that he saith, A new covenant, he hath made the first old." When God pronounces anything of man or thing, it takes place.

The Revisers, with singular awkwardness, translate "that which decayeth and waxeth old" by "that which becometh old and waxeth aged." Surely "the old is better."

## CHAP. IX.

**T**HEN verily the first *covenant* had also ‖ ordinances of divine service, and ᵃ a worldly sanctuary.   Or, *ceremonies*.
2 ᵇ For there was a tabernacle made; the first,   ᵃ Exod. xxv. 8.
ᵇ Exod. xxvi. 1.

---

1. "A worldly sanctuary." "The worldly sanctuary" (its).

Having in the last chapter demonstrated the greatness of the priesthood of Christ above that of Aaron, and the superiority of the New Covenant compared to the old, he now proceeds to speak of the infinitely higher nature of the offering which He presented to God and the perfection of the cleansing by which the people of God were purified from sin.

1. "Then verily the first covenant had also ordinances of divine service." "Then verily," translated by Revisers "now even."

"The first covenant." Covenant is not expressed; so we have to choose between covenant and tabernacle.

"Ordinances of divine service." That is, things ordered by God as right and fitting for His service or worship.

"And a worldly sanctuary," *i.e.*, a sanctuary made of materials found in this world, and having its place amongst the things of time and sense—in contrast with the sanctuary above.

2. "For there was a tabernacle made; the first, wherein was the candlestick." It may be well here to notice that it is not the temple, but the tabernacle whose arrangement and furniture the apostolic writer contrasts with those of the heavenly One. Why should this be? Was it because the ordering of the tabernacle was more directly from God? But surely Solomon himself was inspired with wisdom for the accomplishment of this work. May it not rather be explained thus: the tabernacle was ordered by God as to its minutest details, but the temple was only permitted? The terms on which it was permitted were very reserved, as if God gave the permission somewhat reluctantly. Solomon was suffered to build the temple, but God significantly reminded his father that during the time of the existence of the tabernacle, nearly 500 years, He had not said a word to any of the judges or rulers respecting

c Exod. xxvi. 35, & xl. 4.
d Exod. xxv. 31.
e Exod. xxv. 23, 30. Lev. xxiv. 5, 6.
∥ Or, *holy.*
f Exod. xxvi. 31, 33, & xl. 3, 21. ch. vi. 19.

c wherein *was* d the candlestick, and e the table, and the shewbread; which is called ∥ the sanctuary.

3 f And after the second veil, the tabernacle which is called the Holiest of all;

---

the erection of a more permanent habitation: " In all the places wherein I have walked with all the children of Israel spake I a word with any of the tribes of Israel, whom I commanded to feed my people Israel, saying, Why build ye not me an house of cedar ? " (2 Saml. vii. 7.)

One of the chief significances of the tabernacle was its want of fixity. It betokened a presence which was not permanent, which depended upon the loyalty of the people to the one true God, and on this account, as well as because in its details it was more true to the original idea, the apostolic writer chose it as the text of his remarks.

" The first." That is, the outer one.

" Wherein was the candlestick." This was the seven-branched lamp stand described in Exod. xxv. 31. It may signify the seven-fold, *i.e.*, the most perfect light of God's presence. In Revel. iv. 5, the seven lamps of fire burning before the throne are the seven Spirits of God, *i.e.*, the Spirit of God in His seven-fold illuminating energy.

" And the table and the shewbread." This must have been the table on which the two rows of the loaves of the shewbread were placed. This seems to betoken that God would feed His people who came near to Him. The bread, *i.e.*, the twelve loaves, were considered to be the offering of the people. They were brought near to God, and by this nearness they became hallowed. The shewbread in the Hebrew means " bread of the presence," because it was exhibited on the table just in front of the veil which concealed the mercy seat.

" Which is called the Sanctuary," *i.e.*, the Holy Place, literally " holies " (ἅγια).

3. " And after the second veil, the tabernacle which is called the Holiest of all." The first veil was that between the Holy Place and the court where the altar was situated. It is described, Exod.

4 Which had the golden censer, and ᵍ the ark of the covenant overlaid round about with gold, wherein was ʰ the golden pot that had manna, and ⁱ Aaron's rod that budded, and ᵏ the tables of the covenant:

g Exod. xxv. 10, & xxvi. 33.
a xl. 3, 21.
h Exod. xvi. 33, 34.
i Num. xvii. 10.
k Exod. xxv. 16, 21 & xxxiv. 29, & xl. 20. Deut. x. 2, 5. 1 Kin. viii. 9, 21. 2 Chron. v. 10.

xxxvi. 37. The second veil, which was more costly and ornamented with the figures of cherubim, was between the Holy Place and the Holy of Holies. This was the veil which was rent at the moment when the Lord expired.

4. " Which had the golden censer, and the ark of the covenant." There is very considerable difficulty here. Some suppose that it was the altar of incense which was before the inner veil alongside of the candlestick and the table of shewbread; but it seems impossible to suppose that not even by mistake or inadvertence could this altar of incense be said to be in the Holy of Holies, for the most Holy Place could only be entered on one day in the year, and this altar of incense was used twice a day. It is very probable that there was a censer of pure gold which was kept in the Holy of Holies and only used there when the High Priest entered. The reader will find in McCaul on the Epistle to the Hebrews, pages 111-112, ample evidence from Rabbinical writers that they recognized that there was a golden censer for incense devoted exclusively to the ceremonial of the great day of atonement, a censer of silver being used on all other occasions.

" And the ark of the covenant overlaid round about with gold." Whether there was any ark in the temple of Herod is more than doubtful. It is mentioned by Josephus that when Pompey intruded into the Holy of Holies, he found it quite empty. He saw without the candlestick, and the table, and the pouring vessels, but not a word about that which was incomparably the most sacred thing of all.

" Wherein was the golden pot that had manna, and Aaron's rod," &c. It is expressly said that at the dedication of Solomon's temple " there was nothing in the ark save the two tables of stone, which Moses put there at Horeb when the Lord made a covenant with the children of Israel, when they came out of the land of Egypt" (1 Kings, viii. 9).

" And the tables of the covenant." Such were the glories of the

5 And ¹over it the cherubims of glory shadowing the mercyseat; of which we cannot now speak particularly.

¹ Exod. xxv. 18, 22. Lev. xvi. 2. 1 Kin. viii. 6, 7.

6 Now when these things were thus ordained,

---

first covenant at its first establishment. They had all disappeared ages before the Epistle was written, and yet the Apostolic writer recounts them, for it is his desire to describe the circumstantials of the first covenant when it was at its best, in its pristine glory, not when it was in a decaying state.

It may enter into the minds of some, how was it that these relics of a glorious past were not preserved by the providence of God? but if it had been so, they would have been mere antiquities—mere curiosities. For what would the pot of manna have signified when the Living Bread was given at the altar of the Church—what the rod of Aaron's succession after the Lord had said respecting the Apostles, "As my Father sent me, so send I you"—what the tables written on stone when the spiritual law was written by the Holy Ghost Himself on the fleshly tables of every Christian's heart?

5. "And over it the cherubims of glory shadowing the mercy seat." In all the visions of the manifestation of the presence of God these winged creatures are represented as very near to Him. Thus, in Isaiah vi. (where, however, they are called the seraphim), and in Ezekiel i. and in Revel. iv. If then the presence of God was supposed to be manifested in any local sanctuary, representations of these, his immediate attendants, were very fitting. Prideaux quotes a Rabbinical book which says, "the author of the book Cozri justly says that the ark, with the mercy seat and cherubims, were the foundation, root, heart and marrow of the whole temple and all the Levitical worship therein performed." (Quoted in McCaul, p. 119.)

"Of which we cannot now speak particularly." That is, we cannot describe them minutely. Some suppose that he means that he cannot speak at any length respecting their typical meaning. So Chrysostom, "In these words he hints that there was not merely what was seen, but that they were also a sort of figures with hidden meaning."

6. "Now when these things were thus ordained, the Priests went always," &c. The priests entered every day into the Holy

ᵐ the Priests went always into the first tabernacle, accomplishing the service *of God*.

7 But into the second *went* the High Priest alone ⁿ once every year, not without blood, ᵒ which he offered for himself, and *for* the errors of the people:

m Num. xxviii. 3. Dan. viii. 11.
n Exod. xxx. 10. Lev. xvi. 2, 11, 12, 15, 34. ver. 25.
o ch. v. 3. & vii. 27.

---

Place to trim the seven-branched candlestick, to offer incense on the altar of incense, and once a week to put new loaves on the table of shewbread.

7. "But into the second went the High Priest alone once every year." Into the second, *i.e.* the Holy of Holies.

"The High Priest alone." Not only did he enter into the Holy of Holies by himself, but it was expressly ordained that "no one was to be in the tabernacle of the congregation when he goeth in to make atonement" (Levit. xvi. 17).

"Once every year." This more properly means on one day in the year, for on that day the High Priest went into the Holy of Holies twice at least; later Rabbinical traditions say four times in all.

"Not without blood." First he had to offer the blood of a bullock for himself (Levit. xvi. 14), and then that of a goat, the blood of each of which he had to bring with the veil, "and sprinkle it on the mercy seat and before the mercy seat."

"Which he offered for himself, and for the errors of the people." "Errors," apparently sins of ignorance. But the words of Levit. xvi. are not confined to these. "He shall make atonement for the Holy Place, because of the uncleanness of the children of Israel, and because of their transgressions in all their sins."

It is remarkable, however, that in the accounts of the sin-offerings and trespass-offerings in Levit. iv. and v., only sins of ignorance, or committed in ignorance, seem to be recognized as within the scope of such offerings. There seems to be no atonement by sacrifice contemplated for idolatry, or breaches of the sixth and seventh commandments. This is alluded to by St. Paul in Acts xiii. 39.

Calvin has a good remark: "No sin is free from error or ignorance; for however knowingly or ignorantly any one may sin, yet it must be that he is blinded by his lust, so that he does not judge

8 ᵖThe Holy Ghost this signifying, that ᑫthe way into the holiest of all was not yet made manifest, while as the first tabernacle was yet standing:

9 Which *was* a figure for the time then present, in which were offered both gifts and sacrifices, ʳthat could not make him that did the service perfect, as pertaining to the conscience:

p ch. x. 19, 20.
q John xiv. 6.

r Gal iii. 21. ch. vii. 18, 19. & x. 1, 11.

---

rightly, or rather he forgets himself and God; for men never deliberately rush headlong into ruin, but being entangled in the deception of Satan, they lose the power of judging rightly."

8. "The Holy Ghost this signifying, that the way into the holiest of all," &c. "The holiest of all" signifies or typifies the very presence of God Himself—God perfectly reconciled. A description of this "holiest" is given us in images taken from outward and visible things in Rev. iv. The entrance into its earthly type was made manifest by the rending of the veil at the moment of the Lord's Death. The fact that the Holiest of all was concealed behind a veil, signified that there was a something between God and His chosen people which hindered their free access to Him, which thing was not removed till the Son of God had completed His Sacrifice.

"The first tabernacle was yet standing." Literally, "had standing," or as Bishop Westcott paraphrases, "Whilst the first tabernacle still has an appointed place, answering to a Divine Order." The first tabernacle here signifies not the mere tent, but the whole Levitical system of which it was the sphere.

9. "Which was a figure for the time then present, in which were offered," &c. "Figure," literally "parable." "For the time then present," rather, "for the time now present." Though the new state of things was already revealed, and had been for some time, yet God at this time had not altogether set aside the old dispensation, but permitted its continuance among the converted Jews.

The Jew when he worshipped God in the temple according to the Mosaic ritual, worshipped in a place the very structure of which betokened imperfection in the relations of the worshippers to the God Whom they worshipped. If the veil which hid the

10 *Which stood* only in ˢmeats and drinks, and ᵗdivers washings, ᵘand carnal ‖ ordinances, imposed *on them* until the time of reformation.

s Lev. xi. 2. Col. ii. 16.
t Num. xix. 7, &c.
u Eph. ii. 15. Col. ii. 20. ch. vii. 16.
‖ Or, *rites*, or, *ceremonies*.

10. "And carnal ordinances." "And" omitted by ℵ, A., D., P., eight Cursives, d, e, Sah., Copt., Syr., Arm., Æth.; but retained by B., E., K., L., almost all Cursives, f, Vulg., &c.

place of God's immediate presence from the worshippers had any meaning, it betokened that God was not yet perfectly reconciled, because sin was not perfectly atoned for, or done away.

"In which were offered both gifts and sacrifices, that could not," &c. It is impossible that the sacrifice of animals, the blood of bulls and goats, should take away sin. Sin could not be expiated by such sacrifices, and therefore sin must remain to a certain extent on the consciences of the offerers. How far the offerers were enabled by faith to look upon these sacrifices as typical of an all-sufficient Sacrifice we are never told, and there is no evidence that even the most select spirits ever did so. What they were intended to do, and what they did, was to restore the worshipper to the courts of the Lord, to enable him in communion with his brother Israelites to continue in a fellowship with God, which, though a lower one, compared to that which we enjoy, was infinitely greater than any thing out of heaven itself.

10. "Which stood only in meats and drinks, and divers washings," &c. This is translated by revisers, "being only (with meats and drinks, and divers washings), carnal ordinances." All the sacrificial ordinances of the law, with their distinctions of meats and abstinence from drinks (as from wine in the case of the Nazarites), and divers washings, were carnal, and had only to do with the purification of the outer man. None of these ordinances, for instance, were sacraments, outward visible signs of inward spiritual grace given to men. The Jews had no idea of such a thing.

"Imposed on them until the time of reformation." Which reformation, of course, was the Coming of Christ, Who brought in a spiritual worship, spiritual sacrifice, and sacraments replete with grace.

11. "But Christ being come an High Priest of good things to

11 But Christ being come ˣan High Priest ʸof good things to come, ᶻby a greater and more perfect tabernacle, not made with hands, that is to say, not of this building;

ˣ ch. iii. 1.
ʸ ch. x. 1.
ᶻ ch. viii. 2.

---

11. "To come" (μελλόντων). So ℵ, A., E., K., L., P., most Cursives, f, Vulg., Copt.; but B., D., d, e, Syr., &c., read, "that have come" (γενομένων).

come." Of the good things to come—of the good things which were future in the days of the old dispensation, but are now present to us who live after His Ascension.

"By a greater and more perfect tabernacle, not made with hands." Properly " by *the* greater and more perfect tabernacle." What is this tabernacle? The fathers (Chrysostom, Theodoret, and others,) say that it is the Body or Flesh of Christ. They appeal to such passages as, "The Word was made flesh, and 'tabernacled' amongst us." "Destroy this temple (or tabernacle) and I will raise it up in three days" (John i. 14; ii. 19). But in the next verse there is mention of the Holy Place into which Christ entered. This Holy Place, or Holy of Holies, is a part of the heavenly tabernacle whose figure or shadow was the Holy of Holies on earth in "the tabernacle made with hands." This heavenly Holy Place cannot be a part of Christ Himself, for He entered into it. I cannot help thinking, then, but that this was the greater and more perfect tabernacle of which St. John saw the vision described in Revelations iv. and v. In it was the throne, or mercy seat of God. In it were the four living ones or Cherubim. In it the Lamb stood as slain. In it was an altar under which were the souls of the martyrs. In it was the offering of incense. What the actual realities of these things were, we cannot inquire. God has not given to us the key to unlock such mysteries; but it is quite clear that the Body of the Eternal Son passed into the highest place of this heavenly tabernacle, for He was seen by the Apostle in its most sacred part (Rev. v. 6) as the Lamb standing as slain.

"Not made with hands, that is to say, not of this building." The earthly tabernacle was made with hands; it was "of this building," or rather creation. The heavenly is not made even with the hands of angels. It does not belong to the material order of things, but to the Immaterial, the Spiritual, the Eternal.

12 Neither <sup>a</sup> by the blood of goats and calves, but <sup>b</sup> by his own blood he entered in <sup>c</sup> once into

<sup>a</sup> ch. x. 4.
<sup>b</sup> Acts xx. 23.
Eph. i. 7.
Col. i. 14.
1 Pet. i. 19.
Rev. i. 5 &
v. 9.
<sup>c</sup> Zech. iii. 9.
ver. 26, 28.
ch., x. 10.

12. "Once." "Once for all."

12. "Neither by the blood of goats and calves, but by his own blood." "By the blood," *i.e.*, by the efficacy of the blood, &c. The offering of the bullock and of the goat was ordained by God. The one as an expiation for the High Priest's own sins, and the other for the sins of the people, and so had efficacy for the purposes for which God had appointed it.

"But by his own blood." This must mean by the efficacy of His own Blood, as representing His Death. The Sacrifice of the Death of Christ was not a sacrifice in the natural world, as the sacrifices of the goats and calves were, but it was in the moral and spiritual world. It involved a preparation lasting through ages. It was before the Son of God all through His Life. It was the purpose of His Coming. The Son of man "came not to be ministered unto, but to minister, and to give His Life a ransom for many." His Blood, *i.e.*, His Blood shed in death, was the outcome of the most stupendous act of self-sacrifice which the Universe ever had seen or ever can see. It was an act done in obedience to duty; it was done in devotion to His Father's will. It was the fruit of His witness to God, to His character, and to His love to His creatures. Because His obedience was to Death, even the death of the Cross, He entered on our behalf into the heaven of heavens, as the Apostle says: "He became obedient unto death, even the Death of the Cross, wherefore God also hath highly exalted Him." He entered, then, into the heaven of heavens through His Blood, not "*with* His Blood," as Bishop Wordsworth remarks, but "through it," as the only efficacious condition of entrance.

And yet, knowing so little of the heavenly state as we do, we dare not absolutely deny that there was in some sort a material presentation. Whether the Lord entered with His own Blood in some way, after the manner of the high priest, we know not, but we do know that He appears in heaven with the marks of Death—"The Lamb standing as slain." His Blood, as His Body, is incorruptible: where it exists, and under what condition, we know not.

the holy place, <sup>d</sup>having obtained eternal redemption *for us.*

13 For if <sup>e</sup> the blood of bulls and of goats, and

<sup>d</sup> Dan. ix. 24.
<sup>e</sup> Lev. xvi. 14, 16.

---

We shall, God willing, allude to this deep and mysterious subject in our remarks on xii. 24.

"He entered in once into the holy place." "Once" should be translated "once for all." He did not enter in and come out again as the high priest of the Jews did, but He entered in, and continues there, making unceasing Intercession for us.

"Having obtained eternal redemption for us." Eternal, as distinguished from the temporary cleansing, or redemption of the people of Israel, who worshipped in the tabernacle "of this building."

"Redemption" (Λύτρωσις). To whom was this redemption paid? Many of the Fathers say to Satan, to whom we had sold ourselves by committing sin. But it seems impossible to suppose that God would permit Satan to have such a place in His providential dealings as to be able to exact or require a ransom. The most natural way of explaining the ransom is to take it to be the payment of what is due to the Divine Justice. It is impossible to suppose that God could pass over the sins of such a race as the human race without exacting atonement, and this was by the Life and Death of His Incarnate Son. "The Redemption which is in Christ Jesus, Whom God hath set forth to be a propitiation." Rom. viii. 24, 25. There may be great difficulty in explaining the mode in which the offering of the Divine Son affects the mind of God the Father, but that it is a propitiation made for sin, and by consequence a ransom paid for sinners, is most certain, and under these figures God has required us to regard it.

13. For if the blood of bulls and of goats, and the ashes of an heifer." "The ashes of an heifer." This is the red heifer of Numb. xix., which was sacrificed and burnt, and its ashes gathered and put into water, with which those who were unclean from touching a dead body were purified from the ceremonial uncleanness which they had contracted.

"Sanctifieth to the purifying," (*i.e.*, from ceremonial pollution) "of the flesh." The law of Christ, which He enunciated so clearly in Mark vii. 18-20, has so wholly emancipated His Church from all

CHAP. IX.]  THE PURIFYING OF THE FLESH.  161

*the ashes of an heifer sprinkling the unclean, sanctifieth to the purifying of the flesh:      f Num. xix. 2, 17, &c.

ideas of ceremonial uncleanness that it is difficult for us to understand how there ever could have been such a thing. It may be illustrated thus: A man might be perfectly clean so far as the outward condition of his body was concerned. He might not have a speck of dust or an atom of dirt upon him, and yet, because he had accidentally touched a dead body, or even the bone of one which was lying in the field, he was considered ceremonially unclean. He could not enter into the tabernacle or temple that day till he had washed himself, and till the evening was come. And, on the contrary, a man might, owing to his occupation, be begrimed and covered with dust, and yet if he had touched nothing which made him ceremonially unclean, he might worship in the tabernacle or temple, no matter how offensive his company would be to his fellow-worshippers.

Such was ceremonial uncleanness. It was neither natural nor yet moral uncleanness.

Why God should so peremptorily insist upon the exclusion from worship of those thus polluted we cannot tell. It is hidden from us. It is not difficult to see how it was that God insisted upon abstinence from the flesh of certain animals, which were eaten freely by the heathen. It was to prevent His people from having social intercourse, as far as possible, with the heathen, lest they should fall into the same state of moral pollution; but this does not account for the laws respecting ceremonial uncleanness. With respect to uncleanness from the touching of a dead body, it may have been in order to connect pollution with death, as being the penalty of sin; or it may have been that these laws of ceremonial uncleanness were ordained to impress upon the people of Israel that they were dedicated to God in body as well as in spirit. The constant daily watchfulness against the contraction of ceremonial uncleanness may have tended to impress upon the whole people that they were a separate, a consecrated, and a holy people to the Lord their God. All this has passed away utterly from the Christian Church, because an infinitely higher consideration, tending to the holiness of the body, has been revealed in the Incarnation of the Eternal Son. Now we are to realize that our bodies are the Members of Christ. And from considerations arising from this

**14** How much more ᵍ shall the blood of Christ, ʰ who through the eternal Spirit ⁱ offered himself

<small>ᵍ 1 Pet. i. 19. 1 John i. 7. Rev. i. 5.
ʰ Rom. i. 4. 1 Pet. iii. 18.
ⁱ Eph. v. 2. Tit. ii. 14. ch. vii. 27.</small>

we are to "glorify God in our bodies and in our spirits, which are God's" (1 Cor. vi. 20).

However, no matter what the secret mystery of this ceremonial pollution, it is evident that God would have them look upon it as a real defilement, and would have His people very careful about it, lest they polluted His sanctuary; and moreover, any carelessness on their part in applying the easy means of purification which He had appointed, was treated as a presumptuous sin, which would cut them off from His worship and the fellowship of His people.

This sanctifying to the purifying of the flesh, then, was not an unimportant matter, if it impressed upon the Israelites that their bodies were holy, and that in all the acts of daily life they must be exceedingly careful, lest they rendered themselves unfit for Divine worship and the fellowship of God's people; and the due consideration of it is most important, as it teaches us the purification of all human nature by the Sacrifice of the Son of God.

14. "How much more shall the blood of Christ, who through the eternal Spirit," &c. The Blood of Christ, which was separated from His Flesh in Death. The shedding of a man's blood presumes his death by the hands of his fellow man.

"Who through the eternal Spirit offered Himself without spot." The Eternal Spirit is to be connected with the Lord's being in His human Nature without spot. As the creatures sacrificed to God were to be without blemish, so the Lord was to be wholly sanctified by that Divine Spirit by Which His people—those who share with Him in His human nature—are sanctified. Some, however, suppose from the absence of the article that this refers to His human spirit, which along with His Body and human Soul, was a creation of God, but it seems better to take it as signifying the Holy Spirit, the third Person of the Trinity. All the Three Persons co-operate in the work of Redemption. The Father by giving the Son, the Son by offering Himself, and the Holy Spirit by, so far as His human nature was concerned, sanctifying and preparing the Sacrifice.[1]

---

<small>[1] The term Holy Spirit without the article is constantly used where it can only refer to the Holy Spirit, the third Person; as, for instance, in the two first instances of its use</small>

without ‖ spot to God, ᵏ purge your conscience from ˡ dead works ᵐ to serve the living God?

15 ⁿ And for this cause ᵒ he is the mediator of the new testament, ᵖ that by means of death, for the redemption of the transgressions *that were*

‖ Or, *fault*.
ᵏ ch. i. 3.
& x. 22.
ˡ ch. vi. 1.
ᵐ Luke i. 74.
Rom. vi. 13, 22.
1 Pet. iv. 2.
ⁿ 1 Tim. ii. 5.
ᵒ ch. vii. 22.
& viii. 6. &
xii. 24.
ᵖ Rom. iii. 25.
& v. 6. 1 Pet.
iii. 18.

14. "Your conscience." So ℵ, F., L., most Cursives, Vulg. (Amiat.), Arm., Æth.; but A., D., K., P., and a few Cursives, read, "our."

Chrysostom says: "This is (the meaning of) through the Holy Spirit, not by means of fire, or by any other things."

"Purge your conscience from dead works." Cleanse not your flesh, but your conscience. The conscience of sin hinders your prayers as well as defiles all your religious acts; but the Blood of Christ, *i.e.*, His all-atoning Death, when realized by faith, quiets the conscience, assuring it that all its sins in past time are fully propitiated. The mind of the Christian is enabled to lay fast hold of such a promise as: "If any man sin we have an advocate with the Father, Jesus Christ the Righteous, and He is the propitiation for our sins" (1 John ii. 1).

"From dead works to serve the living God." From dead, *i.e.*, from evil works, as I showed in notes on chap. vi. 1.

"To serve the living God." The word "dead" seems to have suggested to the writer's mind the living God: living not merely in Himself but as the source of all life, natural and spiritual, to His creatures.

15. "And for this cause he is the mediator of the New Testament." For this cause—that is, because His Blood cleanses, not the flesh, but the conscience, He is the mediator of the New Testament. Is this word διαθήκη to be translated Testament or Covenant?

The New Testament is a book, or rather a number of books, collected in one volume. It signifies, in the case of all English-speaking people, the book itself, not its contents. The moment we have to abstract the contents from the book we have to render it

---

in the New Testament, "She was found with child of the Holy Ghost" (ἐκ Πνεύματος Ἁγίου), "that which is conceived in her is of the Holy Ghost" (without article); "He shall baptize you with the Holy Ghost and with fire" (also without article), Matt. iii. 12.

under the first testament, ⁹ they which are called might receive the promise of eternal inheritance.

⁹ ch. iii. 1.

16 For where a testament *is*, there must also of necessity ‖ be the death of the testator.

‖ Or, *be brought in.*

---

" covenant." For the leading feature of the book, that which makes it of the deepest possible value to us, as compared with the Old Covenant, is the New Covenant which it contains. The Old Covenant, the leading feature of the Old Testament, is, "Do this and live." The New Covenant, on the contrary, is, "I will put my law in their hearts." Now this Covenant, more than the Old, requires a Mediator Who shall act between God and the people, One Who having made atonement for their sins ("their sins and their iniquities will I remember no more") now communicates His New Nature to them so that they may be new creatures in Him.

"That by means of death for the redemption of the transgressions which were under the Old Testament"—not by means of death, but rather "a death having taken place."

Why are we told that there was a death for the redemption of the transgressions which were under the *old* Covenant? It may be that in the wise counsels of God the New Covenant could not be introduced till the sins under the old had been fully atoned for. The outstanding arrears of guilt must be first wiped away.

"They that are called might receive the promise." "They that are called" means all that are called by God, whether they be Jews or Greeks, exactly parallel to 1 Cor. i. 24.

"Eternal inheritance," as distinguished from the temporal inheritance of the land of Canaan.

16. "For where a testament is, there must also of necessity be the death of the testator." We are told that it is imperative here to give to the word "diatheke" the meaning of a will or testamentary disposition of property. But it is scarcely possible to do so, for neither before this in the previous part of the Epistle, nor during the remainder of the chapter is there any place for any idea of a bequeathing of property in either a temporal or a spiritual sense. And another matter also of great difficulty to this interpretation presents itself, which is, that in almost every instance the death of a testator is a quiet death in his bed, after which his will becomes

## A TESTAMENT IS OF FORCE.

17 For ᵣa testament *is* of force after men are    r Gal. iii. 15.

available for the disposition of his property: but here the Apostolic writer most certainly contemplates a bloody death, in which the blood shed in death can be sprinkled upon the contracting parties (verses 19, 20, 21).

The fact is, that in the ancient covenants, particularly those which are contemplated under the old dispensation, the death of the contracting parties is brought in vicariously; an animal, or animals, being slaughtered for the ratification of the covenant. Thus, in the first account of the ceremonies which ratify a covenant in Gen. xv. 9, we have Abraham by God's direction taking certain creatures and dividing them, and the lamp of fire, which betokened the presence of God, passing between the sections, or sundered parts of the creatures. And it is a circumstance which I do not see has been noticed by any commentators, that the Hebrew phrase for making a covenant is invariably "to cut a covenant," alluding to the original dividing of the carcasses. Now the animal slaughtered was representative. It was taken to represent the death of the covenanting parties—that they should die rather than break the covenant.

Verse 16 then means, where there is a covenant, there must of necessity be brought in (or offered, or set forth, $\phi\acute{\epsilon}\rho\epsilon\sigma\theta\alpha\iota$) the death of the contracting person—not of the person who makes a will, but of the principal person who contracts by covenant, ritual, or ceremony, to confer some benefit. In the case of the New Covenant it is our Blessed Lord Himself Who is both Priest and Victim, or rather, He represents God, Who covenants to bring in the New Covenant, and He is Himself the Victim Whose Blood is to be sprinkled. Now inasmuch as He is God His Death may be taken ($\phi\acute{\epsilon}\rho\epsilon\sigma\theta\alpha\iota$) as God's (Acts. xx. 28), and inasmuch as He is man—the Second Adam, the representative man—His Death is man's death, it is literally equivalent to the death of all men.

17. "For a testament is of force after men are dead." This place is translated as it is in the Authorized solely with a view to agree with the idea of a will, but it is, when translated with a view to the idea of a covenant, much more in accordance with the context and with the use of "diatheke" all through the Epistle. A covenant is of force upon dead things ($\dot{\epsilon}\pi\grave{\iota}\ \nu\epsilon\kappa\rho\circ\widetilde{\iota}\varsigma$), otherwise (seeing that) it is of no avail at all till the creature is slain which repre-

dead: otherwise it is of no strength at all while the testator liveth.

<sup>s</sup> Ex. xxiv. 6, &c.
‖ Or, *purified.*

18 <sup>s</sup> Whereupon neither the first *testament* was ‖ dedicated without blood.

<sup>t</sup> Ex. xxiv. 5, 6, 8. Lev. xvi. 14, 15, 18.
<sup>u</sup> Lev. xiv. 4, 6, 7, 49, 51, 52.
‖ Or, *purple.*

19 For when Moses had spoken every precept to all the people according to the law, <sup>t</sup> he took the blood of calves and of goats, <sup>u</sup> with water, and ‖ scarlet wool, and hyssop, and sprinkled both the book, and all the people,

---

17. "It is of no strength at all" (μήποτε). So A., E., K., L., P., almost all Cursives; but ℵ, D. read, μήποτε, "it is not then of strength."

sents the contracting party (or parties). In the case of the New Covenant, that covenant does not come into force till the Death of Him Who represents both parties, *i.e.*, in Whom they both contract.

"While the testator liveth." The covenant only comes into force when the representative creature is slain whose death constitutes the ratification of the covenant.

18. "Whereupon neither the first testament (covenant) was dedicated (or consecrated or consummated) without blood." This is as if he meant to say, "You or your countrymen or co-religionists object to the idea of the Messiah shedding His Blood in a violent death, but your own original covenant was not consecrated without blood, as you will see if you turn to your law as written in Exodus xxiv. 5-9."

19. "For when Moses had spoken every precept to all the people," &c. . . . "sprinkled both the book, and all the people." The account of the inauguration of this first covenant is not taken verbatim from the book of Exodus, but probably from some tradition. No mention is made in Exodus of the particular creatures, calves and goats, nor of the scarlet wool, nor of the hyssop, but if blood was sprinkled there must be some instrumental medium in taking it up, other than the hand.

"And sprinkled both the book, and all the people." There is no mention of the sprinkling of the "book" with blood in Exodus. From the way in which it is introduced here the book, being the record of His will, may be taken to represent God.

"And all the people." It is very probable that in order that *all*

20 Saying, *This *is* the blood of the testament which God hath enjoined unto you.

21 Moreover ʸ he sprinkled with blood both the tabernacle, and all the vessels of the ministry.

22 And almost all things are by the law purged with blood; and ᶻ without shedding of blood is no remission.

x Ex. xxiv. 8.
Mat. xxvi. 28.
y Ex. xxix. 12, 36. Lev. viii. 15, 19, & xvi. 14, 15, 16, 18, 19.
z Lev. xvii. 11.

---

the people might participate in the sprinkling they all passed before him in order.

20. "Saying, This is the blood of the testament which God hath enjoined unto you." Literally, "This is the blood of the covenant which God hath cut with you." It is to be noted that Moses on this occasion, and I think only on this occasion, divided the blood, half to be sprinkled on the altar and half on the people.

21. "Moreover he sprinkled with blood both the tabernacle, and all the vessels," &c. Here, of course, he alludes to what was done some time after this ratification of the covenant, for when its ratification, as described in Exod. xxiv., took place, the tabernacle was not in existence.

There is no word of the tabernacle being sprinkled with blood in the Scripture, but singular enough, there is in Josephus, "And when Moses had sprinkled Aaron's vestments, himself, and his sons with the blood of the beasts that were slain, and had purified them with spring water and ointment, they became God's priests. . . . The same he did to the tabernacle and the vessels thereto belonging, both with oil first incensed, as I said, and with the blood of bulls and rams," &c.—Josephus, "Antiquities," book iii. ch. i. sec. 36.

22. "And almost all things are by the law purged with blood." In accordance with the position of "almost" ($\sigma\chi\epsilon\delta\dot{o}\nu$), this sentence is rendered by the Revisers, "and according to the law, I may almost say all things are cleansed with blood."

"And without shedding of blood there is no remission." This seems laid down as an universal axiom, and it is so if we consider the universal application of the Blood of Christ, "Having made peace through the blood of his cross, by him to reconcile all things to himself; by him, I say, whether they be things in earth, or things in heaven" (Colos. i. 20).

23 *It was* therefore necessary that ᵃ the patterns of things in the heavens should be purified with these; but the heavenly things themselves with better sacrifices than these.

ᵃ ch. viii. 5.

Bishop Westcott writes as if the blood purified because it was the representation of a pure life; but the blood was the life only when it was in the veins. The blood when separated from the body implied death, and the death which was the penalty of sin expiated. The writer alludes to Levit. xvii. 11, "For the life of the flesh is in the blood: and I have given it to you upon the altar to make an atonement for your souls, for it is the blood that maketh an atonement for the soul." The antithesis here is between "purification" and "remission." In certain cases simple washing (*e.g.*, of clothes, Levit. xvi. 26, 28), or the passing of metal vessels through the fire (Numb. xxxi. 23) was permitted to remove the ceremonial taint. But expiation and atonement for sin could only be obtained by the shedding of blood (for "the blood is the life") which was offered in vicarious symbolism representing at once the life of the sinner forfeited by disobedience, and the life of the Perfect Sacrifice once for all offered when the fulness of time came, for the sins of the whole world. The familiar proverbial saying of the Rabbis, "There is no expiation except by blood alone," is illustrated by the following Talmudical comment on Levit. i. 4, "And he shall put his hand upon the head of the burnt-offering, and it shall be accepted for him to make atonement for him." What then, does the laying on of the hands make expiation? Certainly not; expiation is made by nothing else than blood, because it is said (Levit. xvii. 11), "For it is the blood which maketh an atonement for the soul." (From McCaul "On Hebrews," p. 135.)

23. "It was therefore necessary that the patterns of things in the heavens should be purified with these; but the heavenly things themselves with better sacrifices," &c. "The patterns," *i.e.*, figures or copies. These patterns, or figures, were of course the earthly tabernacle, which was made after a pattern showed to Moses, but there is great difference of opinion as to what the "heavenly things themselves" are. It is clear that St. John saw in his vision of heaven many things corresponding to the things in the earthly tabernacle, as for instance the four living

24 For ᵇChrist is not entered into the holy places made with hands, *which are* the figures of ᶜthe true; but into heaven itself, now ᵈto appear in the presence of God for us:

ᵇ ch. vi. 20.
ᶜ ch. viii. 2.
ᵈ Rom. viii. 34.
ch. vii. 25.
1 John ii. 1.

---

creatures: the lamb standing as slain, the sea or laver, above all an altar and the offering of incense and the ark of the covenant. These things might, for anything we know, require a purification answering to their transcendental nature and uses. We are told expressly that even things in heaven require reconciliation (Colos. i. 20). And it may be that the services even of unfallen creatures require allowances to be made for them, and perhaps even compassion to be extended to them on God's part. If the blessed spirits have any free will, or require any discipline or education, there may be room for something answering to atonement in the place where they minister.

Chrysostom and Theodoret among the ancients explain these heavenly things themselves of the Church, which, being the body of Christ, has its Head in the highest heaven, and whose high Priest of its worship is in heaven, and whose sacraments being above this order, are heavenly, and the citizenship of its citizens is in heaven (Phil. iii. 20); but taking it thus is scarcely consistent with the next verse, "Christ is not entered into the holy places made with hands, but into heaven itself," &c. And yet the words of ch. xii. 22, seem to teach us that there is no local distance between us and heaven, that in a sense we are come to it and are in it; but the whole subject is so transcendental, so mysterious, that it must be left to God, and to the time when we shall not know in part but shall with open face behold the glory of the Lord.

24. "For Christ is not entered into the holy places made with hands," &c. The Hebrew high priest entered once a year into that part of the earthly tabernacle which signified the heaven where dwells the peculiar presence of God, but Christ never entered into this, though the veil which shut it out was rent at the moment of His Death, but on His Ascension He entered into that which was signified by the most holy place, even into the heaven of heavens; and there in the midst of the throne He appears, the Lamb standing as slain, and there we have an advocate *with* the Father, Jesus Christ the Righteous.

25 Nor yet that he should offer himself often, as ᵉ the high priest entereth into the holy place every year with blood of others;

26 For then must he often have suffered since the foundation of the world: but now ᶠ once ᵍ in the end of the world hath he appeared to put away sin by the sacrifice of himself.

ᵉ ver. 7.
ᶠ ver. 12. ch. vii. 27. & x. 10.
ᵍ 1 Pet. iii. 18. 1 Cor. x. 11. Gal. iv. 4. Eph. i. 10.

---

25. "Nor yet that he should offer himself often, as the high priest," &c. The high priest's offering was repeated every year; every year he entered into the Holy of Holies with blood of others, *i.e.*, not his own, but that of creatures having each a separate life; but the offering of Christ is not of this kind. It is a continuous offering. It is His presence in the heaven of heavens which presents His Sacrifice. The Intercession of Christ is thus declared to be a continuous act, in which His human Nature having once for all entered into the Divine Presence abides there for ever, and by its abiding intercedes.

26. "For then must he often have suffered since the foundation of the world." The argument here is remarkable. If His priestly function had taken the form of a series of separate or successive acts, then each act would require its sacrifice, as each entrance of the high priest into the Holy of Holies required its particular antecedent sacrifice, but the sacrifice of Christ being infinite in its atoning efficacy could only take place once. For how could there be another if His was infinite? Now being infinite, for it was the sacrifice of the God-man, it must be retrospective as well as prospective. It must make atonement for the past sins of the race as well as for the future ones. And so He could only suffer once, just as He could only become incarnate once, or ascend into heaven once.

"But now once in the end of the world (or of the ages) hath he appeared." He appeared or has been manifested. The purpose of His manifestation was mainly this, that in the human nature which He had assumed He might incur death, the penalty of sin; thus He says, "The Son of man came not to be ministered unto but to minister, and to give His life a ransom for the many."

"To put away sin." That is, so far as God was concerned. God has no more price of propitiation or satisfaction to exact, but so

27 ʰ And as it is appointed unto men once to die, ⁱ but after this the judgment:

28 So ᵏ Christ was once ˡ offered to bear the sins ᵐ of many; and unto them that ⁿ look for

ʰ Gen. iii. 19.
Eccles. iii. 20.
ⁱ 2 Cor. v. 10.
Rev. xx. 12, 13
ᵏ Rom. vi. 10.
l Pet. iii. 18.
l 1 Pet. ii. 24.
1 John iii. 5.
ᵐ Matt. xxvi. 28. Rom. v. 15.
ⁿ Tit. ii. 13.
2 Pet. iii. 12.

28. "So Christ." ℵ, A., C., D., E., K., L., P., most Cursives, d, e, f, g, Vulg., Syr., &c., read, "So also Christ." "Also" (καὶ) omitted only by a few Cursives.

far as we are concerned, we must be in a condition to accept and benefit by this atonement, which is by our repentance and faith.

27. "And inasmuch as it is appointed unto men once to die, and," &c. It was appointed unto men once to die when God said to Adam, "Dust thou art, and unto dust shalt thou return."

"After this the judgment," *i.e.*, the judgment of the deeds done in the body—done before each man had suffered the death pronounced upon the race.

28. "So Christ was once offered to bear the sins of many." He suffered once, as all his brethren suffered, the common lot of all men, but when He did thus suffer God appointed that His Death should be no common death, but an all-atoning one. God then laid on Him the iniquity of us all. God then "made Him Who knew no sin to be sin for us, that we might be made the righteousness of God in him " (2 Cor. v. 21).

"Was once offered." Who offered Him? Himself. " I lay down my life for the sheep. On this account doth my Father love me, because I (ἐγώ, emphatic,) lay down my life that I might take it again." (John x. 15, 17). " He gave himself for us that he might redeem us from all iniquity " (Titus ii. 14).

" To bear the sins of many." To bear them in sacrifice, and also to bear them in sympathy, as we learn from Matth. viii. 17. This He did before He offered His Sacrifice, but it is well for us to remind ourselves that He did bear them in this sense.

"And unto them that look for him shall he appear the second time without sin unto salvation." "Unto them that look for him." Why is this introduced? It seems a reference to the coming of the high priest out of the Holy of Holies while the people were waiting for him, to see if he came out alive and in safety, for that proved that his atonement had been accepted. " The Mishna

him shall he appear the second time without sin unto salvation.

informs us that after he had deposited the incense before the ark, and the Holy of Holies was filled with the fumes, he came back into the outer house and offered up a short prayer, making it very short, in order that the congregation might not be unduly apprehensive on his account." (From McCaul's "Hebrews," p. 138). "When he came out he came χωρὶς ἁμαρτίας, having left their sins behind, and cancelled by the blood of expiation."

But how does the "appearing without sin" apply to Christ? It is much more than without a sin offering. It seems to imply the excess of glory. As long as He was upon earth, He was in humiliation, the Man of Sorrows, because our Sin-bearer. But when He comes again He will be in all the glory which God and the universe can heap upon Him: "In his own glory, in the glory of his Father and of the holy angels."

"Unto salvation." Unto the full salvation of the whole man, body and soul. Redemption in its fulness is not complete till the second coming. Jesus Christ made unto us wisdom and righteousness, and sanctification, and redemption—redemption coming last. "Our citizenship is in heaven, from whence also we look for the Saviour, the Lord Jesus Christ who shall change the body of our humiliation in order that it may be made like unto the body of His glory" (Phil. iii. 21).

## CHAP. X.

<sup>a</sup> Col. ii. 17.
ch. viii. 5, &
ix. 23.
<sup>b</sup> ch. ix. 11.

FOR the law having <sup>a</sup> a shadow <sup>b</sup> of good things to come, *and* not the very image of the

1. "For the law having a shadow of good things to come, and not the very image," &c. Shadow (umbra), a dim outline, like a shadow cast on the ground "—of good things to come," in this case the perfect Atonement made by the Son of God on the Cross.

"And not the very image of the things." This cannot mean

## CHAP. X.] NO MORE CONSCIENCE OF SINS. 173.

things, <sup>c</sup> can never with those sacrifices which they offered year by year continually make the comers thereunto <sup>d</sup> perfect.

2 For then ‖ would they not have ceased to be offered? because that the worshippers once purged should have had no more conscience of sins.

<sup>c</sup> ch. ix. 9.
<sup>d</sup> ver. 14.

‖ Or, *they would have ceased to be offered, because, &c.*

---

1. " It " (the law) " can never " (δύναται). So D., E., H., K., L., many Cursives, d, e, f, Vulg.; but א, A., C., P., between thirty and forty Cursives, read, "they can " (δύνανται).

that if there had been any perfect image of the Lord's Sacrifice, it would have made the worshippers perfect; it must be taken as signifying that the law was a mere shadow, not even a perfect resemblance or image. Thus we have in Colos. ii. 17, that the ordinances of Judaism are " a shadow of things to come, but the body is of Christ." As applied to the Son of God in Coloss. i. 15, Heb. i. 3, it denotes the most perfect resemblance conceivable, even that of identity of nature.

" Can never with those sacrifices which they offered year by year continually." " Which they offered year by year continually," *i.e.*, each recurring day of atonement; some, however, take it to mean all regularly recurring sacrifices, as the two lambs daily.

" Make the comers thereunto perfect." " Perfect," *i.e.*, partakers of a perfect atonement and reconciliation.

" The comers." Those who drew near to God through the sacrifice. It does not mean worshippers only, but those who approach God in the way of His appointment, whatever it be.

2. " For then would they not have ceased to be offered ? " (*i.e.*, they would have ceased to be offered) " because that the worshippers once purged," &c. Supposing, for instance, the initial or inaugurating sacrifice of the dispensation, that recorded in Exod. xxiv. (and no sacrifice could exceed or even equal this in importance) made an all-sufficient atonement, then there need have been no subsequent sacrifice.

" Because the worshippers once purged would have no more," &c. That is, of course, if they fully believed in the all-sufficiency of the atonement. It is also plain that we must understand, if they sinned no more, for if they sinned wilfully again they would require repentance and confession. " Conscience of sin" means sin lying

3 *But in those *sacrifices there is* a remembrance again made of sins every year.

* Lev. xvi. 21.
ch. ix. 7.

---

heavy on the conscience, and it is of great importance that if a man has sinned his conscience should accuse him and give him no rest till he has obtained forgiveness, or he may go on to the end of his days saying to himself that he has no sin, and so deceiving himself, and having no truth in him (1 John i. 8).

3. "But in those sacrifices there is a remembrance again made of sins." "In those sacrifices," evidently those made on the Great Day of Atonement, for we read at the end of the verse "made of sins *every year.*"

"A remembrance." This word (ἀνάμνησις) is a most important one, for it is the word used by the Lord when He instituted the Eucharist, as recorded by St. Paul and St. Luke. The whole significance of the Eucharist in its memorial aspect depends upon it. The use of it in this place requires an examination of this question, before whom was the anamnesis, or remembrance, or memorial, or commemoration made? Was it made, or intended to be made, primarily, before God or before men? Now this question seems to be capable of but one answer, for the anamnesis in this case was a sacrifice or an offering, and surely a sacrifice is sacrificed to God, and an offering offered to God. But of all the sacrifices of the Jewish year this of the great day of atonement was most exclusively done to God: for the blood had to be brought into the Holy of Holies corresponding to the heaven where God's peculiar presence is manifested, and into which most holy place no man but the high priest was permitted to enter, and there was a special ordinance of God that no man was to be in the tabernacle of the congregation "when he goeth in to make an atonement." So that the anamnesis is wholly before God (Levit. xvi. 17).

But Bishop Westcott writes, "It is a calling to mind of sin whereby men are put in remembrance of them by a public institution." Now the calling to mind of sin must precede the offering of the sacrifice for sin. There must be some conscience of sin, or else a man of intelligence would not offer (or assist in offering) a sacrifice for sin. If the sacrifice teaches anything, it teaches atonement to the man previously convinced of sin. To the Jew it was the sacrifice of something out of himself to make atonement. Thus God says "The life of the flesh is in the blood, and I

4 For *it is* not possible that the blood of bulls and of goats should take away sins. <sup>f</sup> Mic. vi. 6, 7. ch. ix. 13. ver. 11.

have given it to you upon the altar to make an atonement for your souls: for it is the blood that maketh an atonement" (Levit. xvii. 11).

It is exceedingly important to remember that the bloody sacrifices of the Jews were not preaching or teaching ordinances. They were pleading ordinances—pleading with God for atonement, and they were also absolving ordinances, conveying absolution within the limits which God had assigned to their efficacy. But they presumed some knowledge of sin in the conscience of the man who brought them, before he brought them. Such is the anamnesis of this verse.

And the Church has always taken the use of the word by Our Lord in the Institution of the Eucharist (1 Cor. xi. 24; Luke xxii. 19) as if He ordained a memorial or anamnesis of Himself before His Father, for she has from the very first embodied the words of Institution in a prayer to God; and in one respect this is more emphasized in our Communion Office than in any other, for with us the breaking of the bread takes place not in an address to the people, but in a prayer to God. It is on this view of the Eucharistic action as a memorial before God that its sacrificial aspect depends.

And it is well to remember that Calvin, in instituting a service for Holy Communion from which he of set purpose desired to exclude all ideas of sacrifice, abolished all prayer of consecration, that is, all that prayer by which from the first ages our heavenly Father has had brought before Him the anamnesis of His Son's Atoning Sacrifice, and he (Calvin) substituted in its stead an exposition to the people of his view of the nature of the Lord's Supper.

So that instead of the Eucharist being ordained "to bring to men's minds the recollection of the Redemption which He had accomplished," it was ordained that those who previously remembered it should have a means of pleading it, which pleading necessarily became the one great Act of the Church's united worship.

4. "For it is not possible that the blood of bulls and of goats should," &c. It is not possible that any outward thing whatsoever parted with or surrendered to death, or in any way devoted

to God, can make amends for wrong-doing. This is recognized by Isaiah in the first page of his prophecy, "To what purpose is the multitude of your sacrifices unto me? saith the Lord: I am full of the burnt-offerings of rams, and the fat of fed beasts; and I delight not in the blood of bullocks, or of lambs, or of he-goats" (i. 11), and yet the same prophet foretells that the sin which no blood of such creatures could expiate should in due time be laid upon a human being. And who could this be? Evidently One who was able to be Sponsor for the race, and this must be One Who could stand outside of the race, and yet be One of the race. He must be a Son of Adam, and yet be an Adam.

The next few verses answer this question, as, I think, it is nowhere else answered in the whole range of Scripture. The only atonement for human beings which God can accept must be the outcome of a will—of a will which submits to God under circumstances of such intense devotion, that it can be accepted on behalf of the race. And this the Son of God alone could accomplish. For the Sacrifice which He was destined in God's counsel to make, with all its horrors, its pains, its humiliations, its extreme distress, was before Him during the past eternity. He was the Lamb ordained to be slain before the foundation of the world in the counsels of God (1 Pet. i. 20), and He was the Lamb slain from the foundation of the world in sacrificial type. This He had before Him in His worship all through. Whenever He worshipped in the temple, He saw before Him the image of His own Sacrifice. Whenever in synagogue worship be repeated the Psalms (as the twenty-second), he rehearsed the awful circumstances of His own Sacrifice. So He knew what the Will was to which He had to yield obedience, and yet the circumstances which led to His sufferings were natural—they were all the development of extreme human wickedness. The hatred of the chief priests, the disappointment of the Jews, the treachery of Judas, the desertion by His chosen ones, the cowardice of Pilate, the fury of the mob, the torture of the crucifixion, all were natural; they were all called out and intensified by His own goodness and meekness. And to all this must be added His sinlessness and His Divine greatness; and so we can see, faintly it is true, but yet with much certainty, how the submission of the God-Man—because He witnessed to goodness, and truth, and love, and trust in God—was sufficient to be accepted on behalf of the race.

[Chap. X.] A BODY HAST THOU PREPARED ME. 177

5 Wherefore when he cometh into the world, he saith,
<sup>g</sup> Sacrifice and offering thou wouldest not, but a
body ‖ hast thou prepared me:
6 In burnt offerings and *sacrifices* for sin thou
hast had no pleasure.

<sup>g</sup> Ps. xl. 6, &c. & l. 8, &c. Isa. i. 11. Jer. vi. 20. Amos v. 21, 22.
‖ Or, *thou hast fitted me.*

---

We now come to the revelation of the efficacy of this "will" in the words of the Psalmist.

5, 6. "Wherefore when he cometh into the world, he saith, Sacrifice ... thou wouldest not. In burnt offerings, &c. ... no pleasure." And yet God ordained them. How then could He have no pleasure in that which He ordained? Evidently in this way: they were ordained as mere figures or foreshadowings to set forth the all-atoning Sacrifice; it was as if a schoolmaster, or tutor, or governor ordained a discipline or exercise which had no value in itself, except as a preparation for something better.

"But a body hast thou prepared me." There is an extraordinary difference between this as read in the Septuagint and in the Hebrew. The Hebrew reads "mine ears hast thou opened," or rather cut, or digged, or bored. As read in the Hebrew, there seems a manifest allusion to the surrender of the servant to his master, so that he should belong to him for ever, as we read in Exod. xxi. 6. But in the Septuagint there is an equally manifest allusion to our Blessed Lord's Incarnation, "A body hast thou prepared me." Now in comparing these places, it is clear that the Septuagint gives us the underlying truth, without which in the case of our Blessed Lord there could have been no such thing as the opening or boring of the ears. Whatever the digging or opening of the ear is, there must be one which can be surrendered, or which can be opened to receive the command embodying the will of God.

The obedience of the Eternal Son was not to be rendered whilst He received the worship of the hosts of Heaven, but upon earth, in the flesh, as the Son of Man. And for this a Body was prepared for Him— He "was conceived by the Holy Ghost, and born of the Virgin Mary "He was made man." So that the Septuagint paraphrases the Hebrew with a most necessary gloss—a gloss which explains how

7 Then said I, Lo, I come (in the volume of the book it is written of me,) to do thy will, O God.

---

7. "Lo, I come."  "Lo, I am come."

it was possible that the Messiah should render all reconciling and atoning obedience.[1]

7. "Then said I, Lo I come (in the volume of the book it is written of me,) to do thy will, O God." In the Hebrew this runs "in the roll of the book," alluding to the ancient form of books which were rolled round a stick. The Greek word used in the Septuagint, κεφαλίς, is supposed to mean the horn or end of the roller round which the parchment was rolled, and so comes to be put for the whole book, but some have taken it to refer to the commencement of the book, in which case it is very difficult indeed to explain it of anything written in our present Scriptures.

There is no passage in our present Scriptures in which the words, "Then said I, Lo, I come (in the volume of the book it is written of me,) to do thy will, O God," are spoken prophetically of the Messiah. So that, if this passage is, or was to be, found in any Sacred Book of the Hebrews, that book is now lost. This is not impossible, for perhaps the chief feature of the book in question may have been this very prophecy which is preserved to us in this 40th Psalm. Or it may be that this passage refers not to any particular words found in any place, but to the fact that the Old Testament throughout leads the people to expect One Who shall reconcile man to God by perfectly submitting to God's will. Bishop Wordsworth expresses this exceedingly well where he writes: "The decree of God that Christ should come to do His will is not declared in this or that part only, but in the volume itself taken as a whole and rolled up together, but to be afterwards unfolded in Christ."

"I am come to do thy will" is the especial characteristic of the words of Christ in that Gospel which reveals to us His more intimate relations to His Father. "My meat is to do the will of him that sent me and to finish his work" (iv. 34); "I seek not mine

---

[1] The way of reconciling the Hebrew with the Septuagint which has been suggested is to suppose that originally the Hebrew read אז גויה, "then a body hast thou," &c., and that some careless copyist altered this into אזוים (ears), but there is no authority whatsoever for this reading in any existing Hebrew manuscript, nor is it supported by either the Syriac or Chaldee.

8 Above when he said, Sacrifice and offering and burnt offerings and *offering* for sin thou wouldest not, neither hadst pleasure *therein;* which are offered by the law;

9 Then said he, Lo, I come to do thy will, O God. He taketh away the first, that he may establish the second.

10 ʰ By the which will we are sanctified ⁱ through the offering of the body of Jesus Christ once *for all.*

ʰ John xvii. 19. ch. xiii. 12.
ⁱ ch. ix. 12.

---

9. "O God" omitted by א. A., C., D., E., K., L., P., a few Cursives, d, e, Sah., Copt.; but retained by L., most Cursives, Vulg., Syriac, &c.

own will, but the will of the Father which sent me" (v. 30); "I came down from heaven, not to do mine own will, but the will of him that sent me" (vi. 38); and the seventeenth chapter throughout. To this may be added, "Not my will but thine be done," and "The Son of man came not to be ministered unto but to minister, and to give his life a ransom for many."

In this connection, however, the will is in contrast with the sacrifices and burnt-offerings, as we read in the next two verses.

8, 9. "Above when he said, Sacrifice and offering and burnt offerings . . . which are offered by the law. Then said he, Lo, I come . . . He taketh away the first, that he may establish the second." "He taketh away the first," the sacrifices, and burnt-offerings, that He may establish the eternal efficacy of the surrender of the obedient Will of the Son of God. The Will is primarily that of the Father, "I am come to do thy Will, O God," but the Son, by accepting it and surrendering His Will to it, makes it His own perfectly and completely.

10. "By the which will we are sanctified through the offering of the body," &c. Through the offering or surrender of the Will of Christ we are sanctified, but not whilst it rested in His Bosom, but when it became effective even to the immolation of His Body. The Will was the inward and spiritual emotion which was manifested in its intensity by the outward submission of the body to the most cruel and shameful of deaths. "He became obedient unto death even the death of the cross" (Phil. ii. 8).

"We are sanctified." This "sanctified" does not mean sanctified as used in modern evangelical language as opposed to justified,

11 And every priest standeth [k] daily ministering and offering oftentimes the same sacrifices, [l] which can never take away sins:

12 [m] But this man, after he had offered one sacrifice for sins for ever, sat down on the right hand of God;

13 From henceforth expecting [n] till his enemies be made his footstool.

[k] Num. xxviii. 3. ch. vii. 27.
[l] ver. 4.
[m] Col. iii. 1. ch. i. 3.
[n] Ps. cx. 1. Acts ii. 35. 1 Cor. xv. 25. ch. i. 13.

---

11. "Every priest standeth." So ℵ, D., E., K., L., 17, 47, most Cursives, d, e, f, Vulg. Copt.; but A., C., P., a few Cursives, Syriac, Arm., Æth., read, "high-priest."

but it means cleansed from sin and dedicated (or re-dedicated) to God. It means that *that* is done to us in the spiritual and eternal world which is figured by cleansing by the blood of immolated creatures in the earthly sanctuary. This is done by Christ offering Himself once for all (ἐφάπαξ), and so this offering, partaking of His Infinity, is perfect for all time to cleanse from all sin.

11. "And every priest standeth daily ministering and offering," &c. Some MSS. read "High Priest," but the difference is of no real consequence. The High Priest's offerings were constantly reiterated as well as those of the rest of the priests, and neither the one nor the other was able to cleanse the conscience.

12. "But this man, after he had offered one sacrifice for sins for ever," &c. It is somewhat uncertain whether the "for ever" (εἰς τὸ διηνεκὲς) is to be taken with the former clause of the verse, "after he had offered one sacrifice for sin," or with the latter, "sat down at the right hand of God." Most probably with the former, if we compare the usage with three other places in this Epistle" (viii. 3; x. 1, and x. 14). If so, the place should be paraphrazed: "This man, after he had offered one sacrifice of eternal validity." Bishop Wordsworth quotes Theodoret: "Christ offered one Sacrifice for our sins, namely, His own Body, a Sacrifice which is sufficient for us for ever."

"Sat down on the right hand of God."

13. "From henceforth expecting till his enemies be made his footstool." This is another reason why we should connect the "for ever" with the offering. Christ does not *sit* for ever: at the signal given by the Father He will rise up for judgment.

14 For by one offering °he hath perfected for ever them that are sanctified. ° ver. 1.

---

14. "That are sanctified." More properly, "that are being sanctified," as in Acts ii. 47, "such as are being saved."

"His enemies." All who say either aloud, or in their hearts, "we will not have this man to reign over us."
" But perhaps some one might say: Wherefore did he not at once put [them under his feet] ? For the sake of the faithful who should afterwards be brought forth and born. Whence then (does it appear) that they shall be put under ? By the saying ' he sat down.' He called to mind again that testimony which saith, *until I put his enemies under his feet*. But his enemies are the Jews. Then inasmuch as He said, ' Till his enemies be put under his feet,' and they to whom He wrote were vehemently urgent (that they should at once be subdued in order that Christians might no longer be persecuted) for this cause he introduces all that follows after this; all his discourse concerning faith. But who are the enemies ? All unbelievers, the dæmons. And intimating the greatness of their subjection, he said not ' are subjected,' but *are put under his feet*."
14. "For by one offering he hath perfected for ever them that are sanctified." This, of course, means He hath accomplished perfectly all that is required for their reconciliation to God. This, we have been repeatedly told, the Levitical High Priests, or Priests, could not do, because of the insufficient value or power of their sacrifices. What they by their sacrifices could not accomplish He by His One Sacrifice accomplished, and that for ever. It is well expressed by Wesley in his note on this verse: "He hath perfected them for ever, that is, has done all that was needful in order to their full reconciliation with God." It is quite clear that we must put out of the question here the modern idea of perfecting, as signifying the making of a man internally holy by having his heart filled with holy thoughts, or his outer life full of holy actions. This perfection is by its very nature progressive, it can only be by our growing in grace, and by our constantly putting off the old man, and putting on the new.
Thus Delitzsch: " It is perfect, requiring no addition ; but at the

**15** *Whereof* the Holy Ghost also is a witness to us: for after that he had said before,

*p Jer. xxxi. 33, 31. ch. viii. 10, 12.*

**16** ᵖ This *is* the covenant that I will make with them after those days, saith the Lord, I will put my laws into their hearts, and in their minds will I write them;

† *Some copies have, Then he said, And their.*

**17** † And their sins and iniquities will I remember no more.

---

15. "Said before." "Before" omitted by ℵ, A., C., D., E., P., a few Cursives, Ital., Vulg., Syriac, &c.; but retained by K., L., V., most Cursives.

same time it is not as to its effects a past work, but one perpetually realized in those who accept it, and are, thereby, being sanctified." Bishop Westcott: "Those who are being sanctified," "All who from time to time realize progressively in fact that which has been potentially obtained for them."

15. "Whereof the Holy Ghost also is a witness to us: for after," &c. "Whereof," *i.e.*, of the fact that by one offering He hath so perfected them that are being sanctified that no other offering is needed. For after that he had said this, he again reverts to the prophecy of Jeremiah respecting the New Covenant, taking, however, only the first and last clauses of it.

16, 17. "This is the covenant that I will make ... remember no more."

"I will put my laws in their minds," &c. This really means, "I will give them repentance unto salvation." For when a man grieves for past sin and hates it, and turns from sin and turns to God, it is because God has written (or at least begun to write) His law in that man's heart.

Before the words, "And their sins and their iniquities," we must supply the words, "then he said," "and their sins and their iniquities," &c., or there will be nothing to correspond to "after that he had said."

It is to be noticed that the Apostolic writer cites the words very shortly, giving their gist rather than the quotation in full. And yet they are the words of the Holy Ghost. So Delitzsch says: "The sacred writer regards the words which he is citing as an utterance of the Holy Spirit, and yet deals so freely with them; but this very freedom with regard to the mere letter of Scripture is also a work of the Holy Spirit.'

18 Now where remission of these *is, there is* no more offering for sin.

19 Having therefore, brethren, ⁋ ‖ boldness to enter ʳ into the holiest by the blood of Jesus,

20 By ˢ a new and living way, which he hath

⁋ Rom. v. 2.
Eph. ii. 18.
& iii. 12.
‖ Or, *liberty.*
ʳ ch. ix. 8, 12.
ˢ John x. 9. &
xiv. 6. ch.
ix. 8.

20. "By a new and living way," &c., translated by Revisers, "By the way which he dedicated for us, a new and living way, through the veil, that is to say, his flesh."

18. "Now where remission of these is, there is no more offering for sin." Because the purpose of offering for sin is remission; and if there be remission, the object of sacrifice is attained, and to offer anything further is unbelief—unbelief in the eternal and supreme efficacy of the Sacrifice of the Son of God.

19. "Having therefore, brethren, boldness to enter into the holiest by the blood of Jesus." So the Apostolic writer in iv. 16, "Seeing therefore that we have a great High Priest, let us therefore come boldly to the throne of grace."

Does this mean that we enter *in* Him, as included in Him, or through Him? I think here the latter. The place seems parallel to "through Him we both have an access by one Spirit unto the Father" (Ephes. ii. 18).

"Through the blood of Jesus." Calvin says: "Because the door of the sanctuary was not opened for the periodical entrance of the High Priest, except through the Intervention of Blood." But he afterwards marks the difference between this blood and that of beasts: "for the blood of beasts, as it soon turns to corruption, could not long retain its efficacy, but the Blood of Christ, which is subject to no corruption, but flows ever as a pure stream, is sufficient for us even to the end of the world. It is no wonder that beasts slain in sacrifice had no power to quicken, as they were dead, but Christ, Who arose from the dead to bestow life on us, communicates His own life to us."

20. "By a new and living way, which he hath consecrated for us through the veil," &c. Here the entrance seems to be through the Flesh (the veil, that is to say, His Flesh), and yet He has just said that our entrance is through the Blood—but the reconciliation of the two is clear. The Flesh is only the "new and living way" after it has been separated from its Blood in death. There

|| Or, *new made.*
† h. ix. 3.

|| consecrated for us, † through the veil, that is to say, his flesh;

---

is first the virtue of the Will which determines to endure death in its extremity of pain and shame—then there is the pouring out of the Blood in death, and this shedding of the Blood, *i.e.* this Death, reconciles to God and consecrates the means of approach through the veil, the rent Flesh.

Much difficulty has been made about this place, because it is asked, how can the flesh be at once a veil—a thing which hides, and a mode of access into the Holiest? We answer that it was so at the moment of the Lord's Death. The veil which to that moment had hid the Holy of Holies from all worshippers but one, now became a way of approach to the Holiest through that very rent which betokened the all-sufficiency of the reconciliation, and so of welcome to God. For if one who was thus worshipping in the temple had been suddenly enlightened as to the true significance of the rending of the veil, and had been emboldened by faith to enter into the Holiest, through what would he have entered? Through the veil which betokened the Body or Flesh of Christ, and through the rent in the veil which betokened that the Body of Christ was broken or rent for sinners. He would not have pushed aside the end of the veil, but stepped boldly and yet reverently through the very middle of it.

But was not the body of Christ at that moment deprived of life? Yes; but it was within a few hours to resume its life, and be able to impart that life to us.

But what was the new and living way which He hath *consecrated?* This word consecrated (ἐγκαινίζειν) can scarcely be applied to an approach through private prayer, but seems to demand some outward means of approach, if such be possible, and such a mode of approach He inaugurated at the time of His Sacrificial Death, when He instituted the Eucharist.

The Eucharist was a new way; as to its design and scope unknown to the Jews. It is also a living way, "I am the living bread which came down from heaven." It is "through the veil," that is, through the Flesh or Body of Christ which was given for us. From the times of the New Testament till the sixteenth century it was the great Church Act of Worship. Nobody dreamt of approaching God

21 And *having* ᵘan high priest over ˣthe house of God;

22 ʸLet us draw near with a true heart ᶻin full assurance of faith, having our hearts sprinkled

ᵘ ch. iv. 14.
ˣ 1 Tim. iii. 15.
ʸ ch. iv. 16.
ᶻ Eph. iii. 12. James i. 6.
1 John iii. 21.

---

21. "High priest." Literally, "great priest."

in the Church, in communion with its members, except through it, or at least never apart from it.

21. "And having an high priest over the house of God." Christ yet performs priestly functions, not the functions of an Aaronic Priest nor such as He performed when He laid down His Life for us on the Cross, but such as becomes a priest of intercession, Who by His very Presence in the Heaven of Heavens, as "the Lamb standing as slain," represents His past Sacrificial Death and pleads it with God.

"Over the house of God." That is, the Church of God, so in 1 Tim. iii. 15, "The house of God, which is the Church of the living God, the pillar and ground of the truth." A "high priest" is literally a "great priest."

22. "Let us draw near with a true heart in full assurance of faith." To what are we to draw near? To God. And by what way of access? By the new and living way. The Fathers naturally understood this of the Eucharist. Thus Chrysostom: "To what should we draw near? To the holy things (*i.e.*, the mysteries), to the faith, to the spiritual service." And Theodoret, "For as the high priest of the law was wont to enter the Holy of Holies through the veil, nor was there any other means of entrance, so they who have believed in the Lord through participation of His most holy Body, obtain an entrance into the heavenly city."

"With a true heart." That is, a heart true to God and sincere in approaching Him in the way which He has appointed.

"In full assurance of faith." Nothing requires more fully persuaded faith than sacramental access to God, for as Chrysostom and Theodoret say, "The high priest is unseen, the altar is unseen, the victim is unseen, the true benefit, *i.e.*, the reception of the inward part is undiscernible by the senses, but discernible by faith."

"Having our hearts sprinkled from an evil conscience, and our

<sup>a</sup> ch. ix. 14.
<sup>b</sup> Ezek. xxxvi. 25. 2 Cor. vii. 1.
<sup>c</sup> ch. iv. 14.
<sup>d</sup> 1 Cor. i. 9. & x 13. 1 Thess. v. 24. 2 Thess. iii. 3. ch. xi. 11.

<sup>a</sup> from an evil conscience, and <sup>b</sup> our bodies washed with pure water.

23 <sup>c</sup> Let us hold fast the profession of *our* faith without wavering; (for <sup>d</sup> he *is* faithful that promised;)

---

23. "Faith." Really, "hope."
"Without wavering." Literally, "that it waver not," but after all the words in which hope is embodied cannot waver. It is we that waver.

bodies washed with pure water." "An evil conscience." Here is a reference to the inability of the Levitical sacrifices to cleanse the conscience. "Offerings, both gifts and sacrifices, that could not make him that did the service perfect, as pertaining to the conscience," and to the power of the Blood of Christ to cleanse the conscience, "much more shall the blood of Christ ... purge your conscience from dead works to serve the living God."

"Our hearts sprinkled, our bodies washed." The sprinkling seems to have tacit reference to the sprinkling with blood (ix. 21), and the "bodies washed," to the cleansing of the priests or washing of the sacrifices in the laver.

The two must refer to two different things in the Christian system, for the sprinkling of the heart is set against the washing or bathing of the body. The latter seems to carry a reference to Holy Baptism. But it may be asked why should there be a reference to outward baptism, when its inward grace is also seemingly referred to under the sprinkling of the heart? To which we answer, that in the Christian state of things the body is redeemed by Christ and has immortality assured to it, and the pledge of this immortality is the baptism ordained by the Lord, as we read in Rom. vi. "If we have been planted together in the likeness of His death, we shall be also in (the likeness) of His resurrection." If the Christian's baptism is his union with his Lord in His Death and Resurrection, it is indeed worthy of being mentioned in connection with the cleansing of his soul.

23. "Let us hold fast the profession of our faith without wavering." It seems that there is a mistake in our Authorized Version, by the substitution of "faith" for "hope." No authority whatsoever reads "faith." But the profession or confession of the Christian faith is a confession, in a great measure, of "things hoped

24 And let us consider one another to provoke unto love and to good works:

25 ᵉ Not forsaking the assembling of ourselves ᵉ Acts ii. 42. Jude 19.

---

for" as the second coming of Christ, and the Resurrection of the Body, and the life everlasting. We firmly hope that Christ will continue to act as our high priest to the end, and that we shall ever be the objects of His gracious Intercession.

"He is faithful that promised." To what particular promise does the writer refer? Is it to that in which the New Covenant is embodied, "I will put my law in their minds, and write it in their hearts ... and their sins and iniquities will I remember no more"? Or taking into account their then persecuted state, is it the substance of such promises as "God is faithful, who will not suffer you to be tempted above that ye are able; but will with the temptation also make a way of escape, that ye may be able to bear it" (1 Cor. x. 13)?

24. "Let us consider one another to provoke unto love and to good works." If one member suffer (*i.e.*, in the matter of the maintenance of the life of God within him), all the members suffer with it. Again, "Look not every man on his own things, but every man also at the things of others" (Phil. ii. 4). If Christians are not mere isolated units, but knit together in the Church, each one must have an eye to the spiritual good of all around him. Not only in what pertains to purity and honesty, but in what pertains to charity and mutual help, must there be a sincere attempt to stimulate our fellow-Christians. It is not an easy matter, for we have to act in the spirit of Christ's words, "Let not thy left hand know what thy right hand doeth," and in the spirit of His other words, "Let your light so shine before men that they may see your good works and glorify your Father which is in heaven."

25. "Not forsaking the assembling of ourselves together, as the manner," &c. This, no doubt, refers to meeting together for the great Church act of worship, the celebration of the Eucharist, but it also includes, of course, all meetings for prayer and instruction. Why did those who required this reproof absent themselves from the Christian assemblies? Perhaps through fear of persecution, perhaps through indifference, or both. Wesley says, "Or through a vain imagination that they were above external ordinances."

together, as the manner of some *is;* but exhorting *one another:* and ᶠ so much the more, as ye see ᵍ the day approaching. 26 For ʰ if we sin wilfully ⁱ after that we have

ᶠ Rom. xiii. 11.
ᵍ Phil. iv. 5.
2 Pet. iii. 9, 11, 14.
ʰ Num. xv. 30. ch. vi. 4.
ⁱ 2 Pet. ii. 20, 21.

It should be remarked that this is the only direct exhortation throughout the New Testament to attend public worship. Is this because such attendance was a matter of little consequence? Quite the contrary. It was so universally practised that there was absolutely no need of exhortation. The exhortation most needed was that in these assemblies they should not display their spiritual gifts or their personal consequence (1 Corinth. xiv.; James ii. 2).

"Exhorting,"—rather, perhaps, "comforting."

"As ye see the day approaching." All Christians were bound always to look for the coming of the day of God. "What I say unto you, I say unto all, Watch." "Watch ye therefore and pray always that ye may be accounted worthy to escape those things which shall come to pass, and to stand before the Son of man." But here allusion may be made to the signs immediately preceding the destruction of Jerusalem, and of the Temple—the only authorized seat of Jewish worship.

26. "For if we sin wilfully after that we have received the knowledge of the truth, there remaineth no more sacrifice for sins." Almost all, if not all commentators explain this "sinning wilfully" as falling into apostasy; and in fact the words of the whole passage require some such explanation. They require to be understood as if the sinner who so sinned cut himself off deliberately and determinedly from all further part in the Sacrifice of Christ, and demanded for himself some other sacrifice, rejecting the Lord's Sacrifice as insufficient. This place must, of course, be explained in accordance with other plain statements of the Holy Spirit, as particularly with the words of St. John: "If we say that we have no sin, we deceive ourselves, and the truth is not in us. But if we confess our sins, He is faithful and just to forgive us our sins, and to cleanse us from all unrighteousness." "If any man sin, we have an advocate with the Father, Jesus Christ the righteous, and He is the propitiation for our sins" (1 John i. 9; ii. 1, 2); and, again, St. James writes: "Is any sick among you, let him call for the elders

received the knowledge of the truth, there remaineth no more sacrifice for sins,

---

of the Church .... and the prayer of faith shall save the sick .... if he have committed sins, they shall be forgiven him" (James v. 15); and again, St. Paul writes respecting the incestuous Corinthians: "If I forgave anything .... for your sakes forgave I it in the person of Christ" (2 Cor. ii. 10).

It is clear, then, that in these fearful words the Apostolic writer cannot contemplate a fall into some common sin, as fornication, or uncleanness, or theft. It must be some special sin by which a man shuts the door of salvation in his own face. And what can this be but the sin against the Holy Ghost, which an apostate to Judaism must of necessity commit. For if such an one, after having believed in the Divine mission of Christ, of set purpose rejected Him, it must have been because he rejected the evidence of the miracles of Christ to the truth of His mission from God; and the miracles of Jesus being to one living at that time beyond all doubt, the evidence for them being overwhelming, he could only account for them by ascribing them to the author of evil. He would say respecting our blessed Lord, "He casteth out devils through Beelzebub, the chief of the devils." Such a man, and only such a man, would count the Blood of the Covenant wherewith he had been sanctified an unholy thing, because he would count it to be the blood of a malefactor; he would do despite to the Spirit of Grace because he would ascribe the works of the Holy Ghost to the enemy of God.

Such, I think, must be the meaning of this fearful place, but we must not take it as if its denunciation was confined to the apostasy of Jews; on the contrary, its terms are such as to teach us that all wilful sin is of the nature of apostasy, it is always revolting from God. Sins of uncleanness are defilings of the body of Christ: ("Shall I take the members of Christ and make them the members of an harlot? God forbid" (1 Cor. vi. 15). Sins of division and party spirit rend the body of Christ (1 Cor. iv. 16-23). Sins of the tongue are like the kindling of a destructive fire, and defiling also, for "it defileth the whole body, and setteth on fire the course of nature, and it is set on fire of hell" (James iii. 6-8). Sins of covetousness are sins of idolatry, so that we are warranted in saying that all sin has in it the nature of apostasy.

27 But a certain fearful looking for of judgment and ᵏ fiery indignation, which shall devour the adversaries.

28 ˡ He that despised Moses' law died without mercy ᵐ under two or three witnesses:

29 ⁿ Of how much sorer punishment, suppose ye, shall he be thought worthy, who hath trodden

ᵏ Ezek. xxxvi. 5. Zeph. i. 18. & iii. 8. 2 Thess. i. 8. ch. xii. 29.
ˡ ch. ii. 2.
ᵐ Deu. xvii. 2, 6, & xix. 15. Matt. xviii. 16. John viii. 17. 2 Cor. xiii. 1.
ⁿ ch. ii. 3. & xii. 25.

---

27. "But a certain fearful looking for of judgment and fiery indignation (rather, a jealousy of fire), which," &c. Does the Apostolic writer here allude to the judgment of the last day, or to that which in its terrific nature was a type of it, the fearful horrors of the siege and destruction of Jerusalem? Perhaps both. Continuance in infidelity and sin must end at the coming of Christ in vengeance on them that know not God, and obey not the Gospel.

It is confidently stated by historians that no Christian perished at the destruction of Jerusalem; but what became of the apostates? It was probably in the mind of the Spirit who spake by this Apostolic writer to warn, and so save them from the wrath which then overwhelmed the enemies of Christ to the uttermost (1 Thess. ii. 16).

28. "He that despised Moses' law died without mercy under," &c. When we turn to the passage referred to in Deut. xvii. 2-6, we find that it was not the breach of an ordinary or inferior law which was thus punished, but an act of apostasy from God Himself by deliberate idolatry. It is important that this should be taken into full account in interpreting this passage, since twice in his Epistles does St. Paul refer to this rule respecting witnesses (2 Cor. xiii. 1, and 1 Tim. v. 19). This is one of those many indications which connect this Epistle with St. Paul, though they do not amount to any decided proof that he wrote it.

29. "Of how much sorer punishment, suppose ye, shall he be thought worthy who hath trodden under foot the Son of God," &c. The treading under foot of the Son of God seems to refer not only to apostasy, but to contempt and enmity of the most determined character. There is no parallel expression in the New Testament. That which comes nearest to it is "the enemies of the cross of Christ" in Phil. iii. 18.

under foot the Son of God, and °hath counted the blood of the covenant, wherewith he was sanctified, an unholy thing, ᵖ and hath done despite unto the Spirit of grace?

° 1 Cor. xi. 29. ch. xiii. 20.
ᵖ Matt. xii. 31, 32. Eph. iv. 30.

---

"Counted the blood of the covenant, wherewith he was sanctified," &c. Unless Christ was the God-appointed Redeemer, he came under the ban of Deut. xxi. 23: "Cursed is every one that hangeth on a tree." His blood, being that of a malefactor, was unholy, and so in the view of the deliberate apostate He deserved the death which He died. Chrysostom (too harshly) applies all this to sinful partakers of the Eucharist. "How does a man tread under foot the Son of God? Why (he would say) when partaking of Him in the mysteries he has wrought sin, has he not trodden Him under foot, has he not despised Him? For just as we make no account of those who are trodden under foot, so also they who sin have made no account of Christ; and so they have sinned. Thou art become the body of Christ, and thou givest thyself to the devil, so that he treads thee under foot."

"Wherewith he was sanctified." When? No doubt in Baptism, in which he was dedicated to God, by being therein made a member of Christ. The higher we put the grace of internal sanctification, the more difficult it is to account for so utter an apostasy as is here described.

"And hath done despite unto the Spirit of grace." It is constantly said of the Spirit in the Scriptures that He can be resisted, grieved, vexed, so that He will depart from hearts which determinedly disobey His godly motions. Thus of the Israelites: "They rebelled and vexed His holy Spirit" (Isaiah lxiii. 10); of the Jews (Acts vii. 51); of the Ephesian Christians (iv. 30): "Grieve not the holy Spirit of God;" of the Thessalonian converts: "Quench not the Spirit" (v. 19). Those who thus resist the Spirit, though their resistance may not by any means have reached open apostasy, yet assuredly are in the way of it.

The words "done despite" here signify to reject with injury and insult, and is the worst and most wilful form of opposition to the Spirit.

30. "For we know him that hath said." We know how He adheres to His word. We know not only how merciful, but how

30 For we know him that hath said, <sup>q</sup> Vengeance *belongeth* unto me, I will recompense, saith the Lord. And again, <sup>r</sup> The Lord shall judge his people. 31 <sup>s</sup> *It is* a fearful thing to fall into the hands of the living God.

32 But <sup>t</sup> call to remembrance the former days,

<sup>q</sup> Deut. xxxii. 35. Rom. xii. 19.
<sup>r</sup> Deut. xxxii. 36. Ps. l. 4.
<sup>s</sup> cxxxv. 14. Luke xii. 5.
<sup>t</sup> Gal. iii. 4. 2 John 8.

---

30. "Saith the Lord." So A., E., K., L., most Cursives, Arm.; but ℵ, D., P., d, e, f, Vulg., Copt., Syriac, omit.

---

just and truthful He is. The quotation is from Deut. xxxii. 35, where it is said of the persecutors of God's people, "Their foot shall slide in due time: for the day of their calamity is at hand."

"The Lord shall judge his people." This probably means "the Lord shall avenge his people;" but He is inflexibly just, and if they need retribution He will assuredly award it to them. Let all remember that the Lord will not only pardon, justify, sanctify, comfort, guide His people, but the Lord will also judge His people. "Judgment," as the Apostle says, "must begin at the house of God" (1 Pet. iv. 17).

31. "It is a fearful thing to fall into the hands of the living God." That is, to fall into His hands as His enemies, when we are at open war with Him, and are making naught of the offers of His mercy. Some suppose that the word "living" refers to the gods of the heathen, wood and stone, who cannot feel; whereas the true God is all life, and lives for ever; so that nothing which can occur in time or eternity can rescue us out of His Hands. Compare the words of the Lord, solemnly warning, not His enemies, but His friends, "I say unto you, my friends, be not afraid of them that kill the body, and after that have no more that they can do. But I will forewarn you whom ye shall fear: fear Him which after He hath killed hath power to cast into hell: yea, I say unto you, fear Him" (Matt. x. 28).

32. "But call to remembrance the former days, in which, after ye were," &c. That is, the days immediately succeeding their conversion. From the tone of the passage it would seem that he referred to days long past.

"After ye were illuminated." See particularly note on verse vi. 4.

in which, <sup>u</sup> "after ye were illuminated, ye endured <sup>x</sup> a great fight of afflictions;

33 Partly, whilst ye were made <sup>y</sup> a gazingstock both by reproaches and afflictions; and partly, whilst <sup>z</sup> ye became companions of them that were so used.

<sup>u</sup> ch. vi. 4.
<sup>x</sup> Phil. i. 29, 30. Col. ii. 1.
<sup>y</sup> 1 Cor. iv. 9.
<sup>z</sup> Phil. i. 7. & iv. 14. 1 Thess. ii. 14.

---

"Ye endured a great fight of afflictions." If the Epistle was addressed to Jews at or near Jerusalem, it seems needless to inquire respecting the date. The first great persecution was that at the time of the death of Stephen, and that must have been thirty years before. Then there were the subsequent persecutions under Saul, and that under Herod, in which the Apostle James, the son of Zebedee, was beheaded. Delitzsch mentions a later one of the Sanhedrim appointed by the Sadducean high-priest Ananus between the death of the Roman governor Festus and the arrival of his successor Albinus, which culminated (Jos. Ant. xx. 9, 1) in the martyrdom of James the Just.

33. "Partly, whilst ye were made a gazingstock both by reproaches," &c. "Made a gazingstock" (θεατριζόμενοι) means rather "were exposed," as in a theatre, so that all eyes were fastened on them. This added to the contumely. A similar expression (referring to the Apostles) is in 1 Cor. iv. 9, "We are made a spectacle (θέατρον) unto the world, and to angels, and to men."

"And partly, while ye became companions of them that were so used." Chrysostom says that he brings forward here the very Apostles themselves; and this is probable if he had in his mind the last cited passage. Notice that to become willing companions of those in afflictions for the truth's sake, is to endure a great fight of afflictions ourselves. The contrast in the tenses of the participles θεατριζόμενοι, γενηθέντες ... suggests that upon some special occasion the persons addressed had in a signal manner identified themselves with their fellow Christians in an outbreak of persecution (συνεπαθήσατε, προσεδέξασθε) while they were habitually exposed to public reproach. (Bishop Westcott.)

34. "For ye had compassion of me in my bonds, and took joyfully the spoiling," &c. There is an important difference of reading affecting the sense of the former part of the verse. The

34 For ye had compassion of me [a] in my bonds, and [b] took joyfully the spoiling of your goods, knowing ‖ in yourselves that [c] ye have in heaven a better and an enduring substance.

[a] Phil. i. 7. 2 Tim. i. 16.
[b] Matt. v. 12. Acts v. 41. James i. 2.
‖ Or, *that ye have in yourselves, or, for yourselves.*
[c] Matt. vi. 20. & xix. 21. Luke xii. 33. 1 Tim. vi. 19.

34. "Compassion of me in my bonds." "Of them that were in bonds" (δεσμίοις). So A., D., seven or eight Cursives, f, Vulg., Syr., Copt., Arm.; but τοῖς δεσμοῖς μου by א, F., H., K., L., P., most Cursives, d, e.

"In heaven." So E., K., L., P., most Cursives, Syr., Arm.; but א, A., D., H., d, e, f, Vulg., omit.

Alexandrian and Codex Bezæ reading, "Ye had compassion on prisoners," *i.e.*, those in bonds, and the Sinaiticus, with some other Cursives, reading "of my bonds," *i.e.*, "of me in my bonds," as our Authorized translation. If the latter is the true one it tells very much in favour of the Pauline authorship of the Epistle; if the former it is more in accordance with the plural in the last clause of the preceding verse, "Ye became companions of them that were so used." Bishop Wordsworth, who holds strongly the Pauline authorship, believes that δεσμίοις (those in bonds), is the true reading, but yet that the Apostle alludes to their assistance of himself. " It is very likely that in commemorating their affection and succour to those who were in bonds for Christ, the Apostle intends to include a grateful tribute of acknowledgment for their kindness to *himself*, who had lately been a bondsman for Christ for four years, two at Cæsarea, and two at Rome."

"And took joyfully the spoiling of your goods." They had received that which entitled them to the Lord's beatitude. "Blessed are ye when men shall revile you, and persecute you . . . for my sake" (Matth. v. 11).

"Knowing that ye have in yourselves (or yourselves) a better and an enduring substance." The words "in heaven" are doubtful, as shown in the critical note. If the reading "yourselves," "ye have yourselves" is preferred, there is but one parallel place to it in the New Testament, which is in St. Paul's Epistle to Philemon, where he writes, "Thou owest unto me even thine own self besides." Knowing that ye have your own selves for a better possession, and an abiding one. The Christian having Christ within him is in the highest sense of the term self-sufficient. He has in himself a well-spring of happiness, which all the world besides,

35 Cast not away therefore your confidence, ᵈ which hath great recompence of reward.

36 ᵉ For ye have need of patience, that, after ye have done the will of God, ᶠ ye might receive the promise.

37 For ᵍ yet a little while, and ʰ he that shall come will come, and will not tarry.

ᵈ Matt. v. 12. & x. 32.
ᵉ Luke xxi. 19. Gal. vi. 9. ch. xii. 1.
ᶠ Col. iii. 24. ch. ix. 15.
ᵍ 1 Pet. i. 9. Luke xviii. 8. 2 Pet. iii. 9.
ʰ Hab. ii. 3, 4.

---

apart from God, could not afford him, and "enduring" for ever and ever.

35. "Cast not away therefore your confidence." Fling it not away as a thing of no value. Such is the value of the hopes of eternal life through the Gospel that there seems no medium between casting them away as worthless, and retaining them as our very life. It is this confidence, that is, the confident, even bold trust, that God will fulfil His promises, which has the recompence of reward. God rewards trust in Him with the greatest possible reward, because it is this trust which inspires the deepest love and self surrender.

This and the following verses are an introduction to the grand eulogium of the power of Faith in the next chapter.

36. "For ye have need of patience, that after that ye have done," &c. "After that ye have done the will of God." The will of God here seems primarily that having suffered persecution for the sake of Christ, "ye should receive," &c. It is possible that these Christians thought that having endured their first persecution they would be free afterwards, but it was not to be so. There was further need of patience. It is to be remarked that in the message which the Lord sent to the Church of Ephesus (Rev. ii. 2, 4), there is mention twice made of patience or endurance (ὑπομενή), as if there was a first and a second, a subsequent endurance.

"Ye might receive the promise." That is, the fulfilment of the promise.

37. "For yet a little while, and he that shall come will come," &c. Again we have waiting and watching for the day of Christ pressed upon the Church. "He that shall come," the coming One, no matter how His coming is delayed, will come. The latter part taken from Habakkuk, ii. 3.

"And will not tarry." The hour of his advent comes on apace

¹ Rom. i. 17.
Gal. iii. 11.

38 Now ¹the just shall live by faith; but if

38. "Now the just shall live." So D., E., K., L., P., nearly all Cursives, d, e, Syr., Copt., Æth.; but ℵ, A., H., f, Vulg., Arm., read, "my just man."

as regards the will of God, nothing delays it. It may seem slow, but it is sure. Is this the coming of the Lord for the destruction of the old state of things, or for the day of judgment? The first was then at hand, advancing with fearful rapidity; and as to the last it is the duty of Christians to be always in an attitude of expectation.

"The day of Jehovah (the Lord) becomes in the New Testament the day of Christ, the Judge. He is here called ὁ ἐρχόμενος, not ὁ ἐλευσόμενος, because since His Ascension He has been always coming. His return is a matter of constant expectation. Whenever he comes it will be suddenly, οὐ χρονιεῖ: there will be no delay beyond the final term fixed by the Divine wisdom, long-suffering, and mercy" (Delitzsch).

38. "Now the just shall live by faith, but if any man draw back, my soul shall have no pleasure in him." Three times is this passage cited in the New Testament, as proving the paramount place of faith in the salvation of each individual soul (Rom. i. 17; Gal. iii. 11). The Hebrew runs, "Behold his soul which is lifted up is not upright within him, but the just shall live by his faith." The Septuagint translates, "If he should draw back, my soul has no pleasure in him, but the just shall live by my faith." The Prophet foretells in this place and in its context the invasion of Judæa by the Chaldees, and the destruction, in God's time, of the invading nation. The people of God were to trust in God under the invasion of the Chaldees, and to wait in true faith for the end, *i.e.*, the end of the Chaldees in their destruction. But how were their spirits to be sustained during this calamitous time? The Prophet, or rather God by the Prophet, says, "By faith," either by his faith, *i.e.*, the faith of the just, or as the Septuagint has it, "by my faith," a faith resting on Me, and looking for the fulfilment of My promises. The Apostolic writer, desiring the encouragement of believers, puts the encouraging clause first, "The just shall live by faith," and the warning one last, because he intends to soften the severity of the warning by the words of the next verse, which he makes to follow on them at once, "We are not of them who draw back unto

any man draw back, my soul shall have no pleasure in him.

---

perdition." The difference between the Hebrew, "By his faith," and of the Septuagint, "by my faith," or "the faith of me," is not material. The only faith which can truly uphold the soul is faith in God, but this faith is the gift of God, and is given to each soul to be a part, as it were, of that soul, and so becomes the faith of the individual man, as the Hebrew has it, "The just shall live by his faith."

Taken in the Christian sense we must understand "the just shall live by faith" as meaning the just—the justified man shall live the life of God by his constant trust in God, and by his reliance on the atoning work of the Son of God, and by his constantly coming to God through the intercession of the Great High Priest. Thus he will live to God, having within him the Resurrection Life of the Son of God.

"But if he (any man) draw back, my soul shall have no pleasure in him." This undoubtedly refers to the δίκαιος of the Septuagint. It can refer to nothing else, because if any one draws back, he must draw back from some state of security in which he was before his apostasy, and this is evidently intended to be emphasized by the writer of this Epistle by his inversion of the two clauses, *i.e.*, putting the "just shall live by faith" first, and "if he draw back" second. Whatever the meaning of the Hebrew or Septuagint is, the inspired writer undoubtedly appends to it *his* meaning, which, if he was as much the organ of God's Spirit as Habakkuk, he had a right to do, and indeed was the instrument of God in fixing the true meaning. "The just man," the man accepted before God, lives by faith; but if he loses his faith, and draws back from the right path, his acceptance is forfeited. That such apostasy is possible, even for those who have been truly justified, that is, for Christians who have had more than a superficial experience of Divine grace, is one of the main points of instruction in this Epistle. To teach this lesson the two clauses of the prophetic utterance are inverted. The second as it stands here is a warning to the readers of their own danger, a warning as from the mouth of God Himself, a warning in a high prophetic tone. But the writer, as twice before, resumes the language of comfort and encouragement after words of the saddest foreboding. He proceeds, therefore, with

39 But we are not of them [k] who draw back unto perdition; but of them that [l] believe to the saving of the soul.

[k] 2 Pet. ii. 20, 21.
[l] Acts xvi. 30, 31. 1 Thess. v. 9. 2 Thess. ii. 14.

pastoral gentleness and wisdom to encourage the faint hearted, and establish the wavering, by rousing their Christian confidence, and associating himself with them, as exposed to the same dangers, and courageously defying them.

39. "We are not of them who draw back unto perdition, but of them," &c. Precisely similar is the spirit of vi. 9. "But, beloved, we are persuaded better things of you, and things that accompany salvation, though we thus speak. For God is not unrighteous to forget your work and labour of love," &c.

The exact literal translation is somewhat more forcible: "We are not of shrinking back into perdition, but of faith unto the full possession of the soul."

"Of believing to the salvation," *i.e.*, of persevering faith, faith enduring to the end, faith overcoming the world.

## CHAP. XI.

NOW faith is the || substance of things hoped for, the evidence [a] of things not seen.

|| Or, *ground*, or, *confidence*.
[a] Rom. viii. 24, 25. 2 Cor. iv. 18. & v. 7.

1. "Now faith is the substance of things hoped for, the evidence," &c. Substance (ὑπόστασις) is rendered by many (as Revisers) "the assurance," or by others "confidence;" but it gives a far better sense to keep to our version, and paraphrase it "now faith gives substance; it gives a substantial reality to things hoped for; the things hoped for are, without faith, unrealities, airy nothings, mere conjectures, surmizes. Faith makes them so real to us, that we act upon them in the most momentous concerns of our lives."

It may be well to say a word or two respecting faith considered as a function of the human soul or mind. Faith is a faculty given to us by our Maker to enable us to carry on this present life, as

2 For ᵇ by it the elders obtained a good report. ᵇ ver. 39.

---

well as to enable us to look forward to a future, and prepare for it. All commercial transactions, for instance, require faith. They require us to believe in countries and societies which we have never seen, and to trust in persons whose honesty, as well as all their interior motives and dispositions, we cannot absolutely see. We must take very much concerning them on trust.

Faith, as well as reason or will, is absolutely natural to us as human beings. The most wicked men constantly exercise it as well as the most righteous. In all the affairs of human life, the atheist exercises it as often as the Christian. The man who plans some scheme for his own purposes, and acts upon it, has faith just as much as the Christian has when he acts upon some plan for advancing the salvation of his own soul or that of others. What is the difference, then, between the faith (considered as a faculty) of the bad and the good man? The difference is in themselves—the self, the *ego*, the central personality in each makes the difference. According to the Lord's words, "He that is of God heareth God's words." He hears them with the ear of faith, and, as we say, appropriates them, lays them to heart, realizes them.

It is very needful to insist on this, for faith is nothing in itself. It is the function of the soul which is in the soul as a faculty, and goes out of it, as it were, to lay hold of something unseen, which it enables the soul to make its own.

So it is the substance of things hoped for, because it gives substance, it gives reality to, the things hoped for.

And the second clause, "the evidence of things not seen," expresses the same idea. Faith evidences things not seen to us—so evidences them that we act on their reality.

The Revisers render it "proving," but though this cannot be called wrong, it is somewhat misleading, for the evidence of faith is rather intuition than proof. There is no proof of unseen things as there is proof of a problem. We intuitively perceive them, and it is the state of our interior, our innermost souls, our self, or *ego*, which enables us thus to use the faculty of faith.

2. "For by it the elders obtained a good report." For through it the men of ancient days had a good witness borne to them. Some of those men of old time he proceeds to enumerate, and to

3 Through faith we understand that ᶜthe worlds were framed by the word of God, so that things which are seen were not made of things which do appear.

ᶜ Gen. i. 1.
Ps. xxxiii. 6.
John i. 3.
ch. i. 2.
2 Pet. iii. 5.

---

3. "Things which are seen." So K., L., most Cursives, f, Vulg., Syriac; but ℵ, A., D., E., P, d, e, Copt., Æth., read, " that which is seen."

tell us how to them faith was so much the substance of things hoped for, that their godly lives are now our consolation and example.

3. " Through faith we understand that the worlds were framed by the word of God, so that things which are seen were not made of things which do appear." "In other words, the conception of God pre-existent to matter, and by His fiat calling it into being is beyond the domain of reason or demonstration. It is simply accepted by an act of faith " (McCaul, 172).

All nature, *i.e.*, mere nature, apart from Revelation, seems to teach that all new forms of matter, as, for instance, a new tree or animal, is formed out of pre-existent matter. All the parts of the tree, trunk, branches, leaves, fruit, come out of the ground by means of the roots, but it is by faith that we realize that the original matter of the worlds was not in existence from eternity, but was created out of nothing by God.

By faith, then, we believe that whatever place Natural Selection or Evolution may have had in God's providential action upon His creatures, yet that God called into existence the matter out of which they were created, and if there be Evolution or Development the direction in which it was to act, and the mode of its action, were at the first assigned to it by God.

This verse, then, means that by faith we believe in the existence of a creating and all-sustaining God, and though the preservation of all things is not mentioned specifically, yet it is absurd to suppose that the Being Who created such an universe of creatures should leave it to itself: and so, though we are fully aware of all difficulties which may be urged from such considerations as the origin of evil, the seeming ability for such things as natural selection to account for certain differences, the mystery of an infinite Being so conducting Himself towards each one of us as if He was finite—notwithstanding all this, we believe that the absurdity of all absurdities is to disbelieve in the existence of an intelligent Creator

4 By faith <sup>d</sup> Abel offered unto God a more excellent sacrifice than Cain, by which he obtained

<sup>d</sup> Gen. iv. 4.
1 John iii. 12.

---

when the least part of the material universe requires an intelligence far above the human to understand it.

"The worlds were framed," literally, "the ages," æons. These æons contain invisible beings as well as visible. "Framed," that is, not only brought into being, but joined together in one whole. There is, for instance, no world in any part of space which is not united to the rest by the law of gravitation.

4. "By faith Abel offered unto God a more excellent sacrifice than Cain." There have been differences of opinion respecting the sacrifice of Abel in comparison with that of Cain. In what did its greater excellency consist? Some suppose that it was a more abundant sacrifice, *i.e.*, greater in quantity (so apparently Bishop Westcott). He says, quite unwarrantably, that " Abel did not, like Cain, offer at the end of time." But the narrative certainly implies that they offered their respective offerings simultaneously. " Abel was a keeper of sheep, but Cain was a tiller of the ground. And in process of time (at the end of days) it came to pass that Cain brought of the fruit of the ground an offering unto the Lord. And Abel he also brought of the firstlings of the flock, and of the fat thereof." The "process of time" evidently refers to both offerings.

The difference evidently was that the one offering was with blood, and the other not. The one was life itself, and the other the product of life, and of a very inferior life.

It appears from the narration that God had given directions to the first family respecting sacrifice, and if He did this He would have respect to the axiom which was afterwards illustrated by the whole God-ordained Mosaic code that without shedding of blood there was no remission. Now the sin of Cain apparently was this, he would not come to Abel to obtain from him the material for the perfect sacrifice, but chose to take his own independent way. He said to himself, Why should God be appeased with blood? If I offer of my own—of the fruit of the tillage of my land—is it not enough? It ought to be acceptable to the author of life, for it necessitates no death. This apparently was his sin— independence, unsubmissiveness, and so unbelief. There must

witness that he was righteous, God testifying of his gifts: and by it he being dead ᵉ ‖ yet speaketh.

ᵉ Gen. iv. 10.
Matt. xxiii. 35.
ch. xii. 24.
‖ Or, *is yet spoken of*.

4. "Yet speaketh." So ℵ, A., P., a few Cursives, f, Vulg., Syr., Copt., Arm.; but D. E., K., L., most Cursives, d, e, Æth., read, "is yet spoken of."

have been a previous revelation of the necessity of approaching God through sacrifice, for it is scarcely to be supposed that they would both together at this time have struck out, as it were, such a mode of worship.

But this does not exclude the fact that Abel's sacrifice was more acceptable because his life was purer. It was his religion, *i.e.*, his faith, which made him more simple-minded Godward, which made him offer the better sacrifice.

"By which he obtained witness that he was righteous, God testifying of his gifts." In what way did God testify of his gifts? It must have been in some open way which was visible to Cain, and this way must (it can hardly be doubted) have been by God causing fire to descend to consume the sacrifice of Abel, and withholding this token of His approval from that of Cain. There are numerous instances of this in pre-Christian times. Thus that of Moses and Aaron (Levit. ix. 24), "and there came a fire out from the Lord and consumed upon the altar the burnt-offering," &c. Thus especially the fire that consumed the sacrifice of Elijah, and not that of the priests of Baal (1 Kings xviii. 29 and 38); then that of Gideon (Judges vi. 21), and of Manoah (xiii. 20), and of David (1 Chron. xxi. 26), and Solomon (2 Chron. vii. 1).

"God testifying of his gifts." By his manifest and open acceptance of his gifts, God bore witness to the integrity of his life. 'If I regard iniquity in my heart the Lord will not hear me" (Ps. lxvi. 18). "Whatsoever we ask we receive of God because we keep his commandments, and do those things which are pleasing in His sight" (1 John i. 22).

"And by it he, being dead, yet speaketh." "By it;" this is true whether we take it of his faith or of his sacrifice; "by it" taken as his faith, he has the foremost place amongst the witnesses for God, for the Lord, in speaking of the death of the martyrs which should be visited on Jerusalem, speaks of "the blood of righteous Abel." And it is true also of his sacrifice. It speaks to

5 By faith 'Enoch was translated that he should not see death; and was not found, because God had translated him: for before his translation he had this testimony, that he pleased God.  [f Gen. v. 22, 24.]

6 But without faith *it is* impossible to please *him:* for he

---

the fact that God in the order of sacrifice which He gave to the first family ordained it in blood, so that it is absolutely true of the human race, " without shedding of blood there is no remission."

5. "By faith Enoch was translated that he should not see death, and was not found," &c. "By faith," because of his faith, because of the life of faith which he led, " Was translated so as not to see death."

" Was not found." God took him away in a mysterious manner so that his body could not be found. Thus it was with Elijah, the only other man thus honoured by God. Even the sons of the prophets importuned Elisha that they might seek for him. In the case of each of these the Resurrection of the body was anticipated. They slept not, but they were changed.

" For before his translation he had this testimony, that he pleased God." It is remarkable that it is not said of Enoch, that he lived, but that he " walked with God." (" Enoch walked with God after he begat Methuselah three hundred years.") The Septuagint renders this by " he pleased God," εὐαρεστηκέναι. Walking with God implies a sustained effort to keep close to Him. It implies that the person so walking believes God to be ever at his side, and so as God leads him on he keeps up with Him. It implies not only a simple reliance upon God, but a constant endeavour to be in communion with Him.

6. " But without faith it is impossible to please him, for he that cometh," &c. Here the Apostolic writer, instead of adducing, as in most succeeding cases, a single instance of faith, refers the whole life of one who could be said to " walk with God," to faith as its root.

" Without faith it is impossible to please God." Now this faith must be a bonâ fide acceptance of any revelation which God may have given. If a man has every reason to believe that the Christian religion is true, it will not do for him virtually to fall back upon some more imperfect revelation, and say, this is enough for me. He must believe that " God is " in accordance with that manifesta-

that cometh to God must believe that he is, and *that* he is a rewarder of them that diligently seek him.

<sup>g</sup> Gen. vi. 13, 22.
‖ Or, *being wary.*
<sup>h</sup> 1 Pet. iii. 20.
<sup>i</sup> Rom. iii. 22. & iv. 13. Phil. iii. 9.

7 By faith <sup>g</sup> Noah, being warned of God of things not seen as yet, ‖ moved with fear, <sup>h</sup> prepared an ark to the saving of his house; by the which he condemned the world, and became heir of <sup>i</sup> the righteousness which is by faith.

---

tion of God which His providence has put within his reach, and brought home to him.

" He that cometh to God must believe that he is." " Cometh." This implies that walking with God is a constant, indeed incessant coming to God.

" That he is "—that He exists as He has revealed Himself to us; in Patriarchal times the Creator and Supreme Ruler (Elion), in Jewish times the God of Abraham, in Christian times the Father of the Son.

" And that he is a rewarder of them that diligently seek him." From what did the belief in this arise? Did God then manifestly take the side of the righteous who sought Him, and reward them that seek him? Probably more manifestly than He does now; but perhaps from this, that believing God to be the Supreme Ruler they judged that He would rule as other righteous monarchs ruled, by encouraging the good and punishing the wicked.

7. " By faith Noah, being warned of God of things not seen as yet." This is narrated in Gen. vi. 13, " And God said unto Noah, " the end of all flesh is come before me; for the earth is filled with violence through them . . . Make thee an ark,'" &c.

" Of things not seen as yet," *i.e.*, of the coming Deluge.

" Moved with fear." Various expositors endeavour to soften this, and discard the word "fear," as being, we suppose, inconsistent with the righteousness which is by faith; but surely the persevering in the building of the ark through one hundred years, showed his fear of being drowned with the ungodly world. Probably when God threatened the world, at first He said nothing of the way of escape, and revealed it to the inquiries of Noah.

" By the which he condemned the world." The lives of the children of God, living according to His Word, condemn the

8 By faith ᵏAbraham, when he was called to go out into a place which he should after receive for an inheritance, obeyed; and he went out, not knowing whither he went.  ᵏ Gen. xii. 1, 4. Acts vii. 2, 3, 4.

---

world. They are witnesses to a power of righteousness above the world, just as the building of the ark, through long years of ridicule and perhaps persecution, was witness to the fact that Noah had received a revelation from the Supreme God. The event proved that Noah's work did not proceed from some deceitful vision, or some groundless imagination. All the world was on one side, and he on the other, yet he persevered in faith, and the event condemned those who would not listen to his preaching of righteousness.

"And became heir of the righteousness which is by faith." What is "to be heir of righteousness?" It seems to mean that the person who is thus "heir" comes into the righteousness of those who went before him, of Abel, for instance, and Melchisedek, but we must lay stress upon the words "of faith." He inherited not only natural righteousness, but that especially which springs from the belief "that God is and that he is the Rewarder of them that diligently seek him."

"By faith Abraham, when he was called to go out into a place," &c. . . . obeyed." The call of Abraham was "Get thee out of thy country and from thy kindred, and from thy father's house unto a land that I will shew thee . . . and in thee shall all the families of the earth be blessed." The faith of Abraham was shown in his obeying God, but it was also shown conspicuously in his breaking through all the ties of country and family, and the religious traditions which he had inherited (Joshua xxiv. 2, 3).

"He went out not knowing whither he went," seems to be a certain inference from the words of God, "unto a land which I will shew thee of," God not naming the country.[1]

9. "By faith he sojourned in the land of promise as in a strange

---

[1] A difficulty has been made respecting this that in Genesis xi. it is said, "They went forth with them from Ur of the Chaldees to go into the land of Canaan, and they came into Haran and dwelt there." But the matter seems simply this. The command of God came to Abraham whilst he was in Ur, and by God's direction he halted at Haran, as that was on the way to his destination. Nothing in the narrative shows that Abraham knew all God's plan respecting him.

## DWELLING IN TABERNACLES. [HEBREWS.

9 By faith he sojourned in the land of promise, as *in* a strange country, ¹dwelling in tabernacles with Isaac and Jacob, ᵐ the heirs with him of the same promise:

10 For he looked for ⁿ a city which hath foundations, ᵒ whose builder and maker *is* God.

<small>ˡ Gen. xii. 8.
& xiii. 3, 18. &
xviii. 1, 9.
ᵐ ch. vi. 17.
ⁿ ch. xii. 22.
& xiii. 14.
ᵒ ch. iii. 4.
Rev. xxi. 2, 10.</small>

country." His faith is thus brought out by St. Stephen, "And he (God) gave him none inheritance in it, so much as to set his foot on ; yet he promised that he would give it to him for a possession, and to his seed after him when as yet he had no child."

By faith he dwelt not in houses, but in tents. He could easily have built houses. Men in those days were not long in building a walled city, but he chose to dwell in tents signifying that the fulfilment of the promise was yet in the future, and that when his posterity entered into possession it would be not piecemeal, as it were, but at once.

"With Isaac and Jacob, the heirs with him," &c. This expresses that the period of faith was a long period, so that Isaac lived to a great age, and Jacob too was advanced in years when he quitted Palestine for Egypt.

10. "For he looked for a city which hath foundations, whose builder and maker," &c. Literally it reads " he looked for the city which hath the foundations." This means the city which hath the only foundations worthy of the name, the true and immovable foundations. Time has shown that Nineveh, Babylon, even Jerusalem have had no permanent foundations. They became in the time of their visitation as unstable as the tents of the Patriarchs, but we have in the Apocalyptic visions a city described whose foundations are of the most precious and the most incorruptible things to be found on earth. Did Abraham look for such a city ? No doubt his regenerated spirit told him that nothing on earth can have permanence, for heaven and earth shall pass away. No doubt he realized that there remaineth a rest for the people of God. If he had faith in the eternal and unseen God he must have believed that His promises were not restricted to the few years of man's mortal life, but must be carried forward through that Eternity which He Himself inhabits. If God be Abraham's friend, Abraham cannot perish, Abraham will rise again, Abraham

11 Through faith also ᵖSara herself received strength to conceive seed, and ᵠwas delivered of a child when she was past age, because she judged him ʳfaithful who had promised.

12 Therefore sprang there even of one, and ˢhim as good as dead, ᵗ*so many* as the stars of the sky in multitude, and as the sand which is by the sea shore innumerable.

p Gen. xvii. 19.
& xviii. 11, 14.
& xxi. 2.
q See Luke i. 36.
r Rom. iv. 21.
ch. x. 23.
s Rom. iv. 19.
t Gen. xxii. 17.
Rom. iv. 18.

---

11. "And was delivered of a child" (ἔτεκεν) omitted by א, A., D., d, e, f, Vulg., Sah., Copt.; retained by E., K., L., P., almost all Cursives, Syriac, Arm.

will have an abiding place in God's presence worthy of the greatness of God.

11 "Through faith also Sara herself received strength to conceive seed." Both Abraham and Sara received the promise of the birth of Isaac with some degree of incredulity. It seemed so contrary to the whole course of nature, perhaps it seemed too good to be true.

But the omniscience displayed by Him Who was outside the tent talking with Abraham of all that was going on within seems to have brought her to her senses. She then seems to have perceived that it was either God Himself or some special messenger of His who was talking with Abraham. Like Nathaniel, who was convinced that one who could tell him the secret passages of his life was the Christ, so Sara seems instantly to have accepted the words of the Divine Stranger as those of God, and by the exercise of faith received "strength to conceive seed." It does not appear that it was by the example of Abraham (who himself also had laughed at the idea, Gen. xvii. 17), but by the display of supernatural knowledge on the part of the visitors, that she was enabled to receive the promise in faith. The words "even herself" (καὶ αὐτή) seem to tell us that it was an independent exercise of faith on her part, and not merely inspired by the example of her husband.

12. "Therefore sprang there even of one, and him as good as dead." "Of one," *i.e.*, of Abraham.

"And him as good as dead." "As good as dead," that is, when he received the promise that Sara should have a son.

13 These all died † in faith, ᵘ not having received the promises, but ˣ having seen them afar off, and were persuaded of *them*, and embraced *them*, and ʸ confessed that they were strangers and pilgrims on the earth.

14 For they that say such things ᶻ declare plainly that they seek a country.

15 And truly, if they had been mindful of that *country* from whence they came out, they might have had opportunity to have returned.

† Gr. *according to faith.*
ᵘ ver. 39.
ˣ ver. 27. John viii. 56.
ʸ Gen. xxiii. 4. & xlvii. 9.
1 Chron. xxix. 15. Ps. xxxix. 12. & cxix. 19. 1 Pet. i. 17. & ii. 11.
ᶻ ch. xiii. 14.

---

13. "And were persuaded of them" omitted by ℵ, A., D., E., K., L., P., most Cursives, d, e, f, Vulg., Sah., Copt., Syriac, Arm., Æth.; but retained by only a very few Cursives.

"As many as the stars." This is the whole Jewish nation which sprang from his loins. It is mentioned here because it was the fulfilment of the promise in Gen. xxii. 17.

13. "These all died in faith."

These "all" were the three patriarchs and Sara. The faith of Jacob, the last of the three, is evidenced by the words with which he blessed his twelve sons, especially Judah. He believed that God would bring them up out of Egypt, and he confessed to Pharaoh that he was a mere sojourner in the land of promise when he said, "The days of the years of my pilgrimage are one hundred and thirty years; few and evil have the days of the years of my life been, and have not attained unto the days of the years of the life of my fathers in the days of their pilgrimage" (Gen. xlvii. 9).

14. "For they that say such things declare plainly that they seek a country." They do this because they acknowledge themselves strangers in this world. All men naturally look for an abiding-place, a home which they can call their own, and of which they cannot be dispossessed. By some this is translated "fatherland," but this gives a wrong idea to English ears, for Palestine was not their fatherland, but a land given to them, of which the aboriginal inhabitants were dispossessed. They sought, then, not Canaan, but heaven.

15. "And truly, if they had been mindful of that country from whence," &c. We learn from Genesis xiv. 14, that Abraham could bring above three hundred men into the field. With these he

16 But now they desire a better *country*, that is, an heavenly: wherefore God is not ashamed ᵃ to be

ᵃ Exod. iii. 6, 15. Matt. xxii. 32. Acts vii. 32.

could easily have fought his way back to his original home. But he chose rather to live upon the hopes of a promise to be fulfilled in the far future than to dwell again amongst his idolatrous kindred.

16. " But now they desire a better country, that is, an heavenly." Abraham was promised the land of Canaan, but his descendants would not begin to take possession of it till after 400 years had passed.

Had he no desire, then, for what God had promised? Yes, he had faith to look beyond the promise of Canaan, to a better country, and that must be one not of this world, but one into which he must enter through the grave and gate of death. Delitzsch has a remarkable comment: "Must we not say, then, that here again the Apostolic writer of our Epistle imports New Testament ideas into the histories of the Old? In a certain way this is true. He does explain and illustrate the promises and wishes of the Patriarchs by New Testament light, and gives to both an evangelical expression. But in doing so he discloses their true inward meaning. The promise given to the Patriarchs was a divine assurance of a future rest: that rest was connected, in the first instance, with the future possession of an earthly home; but their desire for that home was, at the same time, a longing and a seeking after Him Who had given the promise of it, Whose presence and blessing alone made it for them an object of desire, and Whose presence and blessing, wherever vouchsafed, makes the place of its manifestation to be indeed a heaven. The shell of their longing might thus be of earth, its kernel was heavenly and divine, and as such God Himself vouchsafed to honour and reward it."

"Wherefore God is not ashamed to be called their God." God is not only not ashamed to be called the God of Abraham, Isaac, and Jacob, but He asserts it, as it were, when he reveals himself to Moses in the bush (Exod. iii. 6). The question arises, has this name, as the name of God, passed away. The Lord says: "I have declared unto them thy name, and will declare it," which cannot be the name by which God was familarly known to the Jews, and must have been the Name of the Father. St. Paul says,

P

210　　　　　WHEN HE WAS TRIED.　　　　[HEBREWS.

<sup>b</sup> Phil. iii. 20.
ch. xiii. 14.

<sup>c</sup> Gen. xxii.
1, 9.

<sup>d</sup> James ii. 21.
‖ Or, *To.*
<sup>e</sup> Gen. xxi. 12.
Rom. ix. 7.

called their God: for <sup>b</sup> he hath prepared for them a city.

17 By faith <sup>c</sup> Abraham, when he was tried, offered up Isaac: and he that had received the promises <sup>d</sup> offered up his only begotten *son*,

18 ‖ Of whom it was said, <sup>e</sup> That in Isaac shall thy seed be called:

---

not the God of Abraham, but " the God and Father of our Lord Jesus Christ."

" He hath prepared for them a city." Why is this given as a reason ? If he has prepared for them a city, He will be their God after death. If He is the God of Abraham He is the God of the living, for " all live to him." In speaking thus to Moses He calls Himself the God of Abraham, for Abraham was then as much living in His sight as when he was a stranger and sojourner in Canaan. He could not be called their God if they had perished at death, but He can well be called their God if he has prepared for them an eternal mansion.

17. " By faith Abraham, when he was tried, offered up Isaac," &c. Offered up—literally, hath offered up Isaac. As if the Holy Spirit here takes the intention for the deed: and counts that he actually offered him: and rightly so, for Abraham had taken the knife to consummate the sacrifice.

" When he was tried." " It came to pass after these things that God did tempt Abraham," that is, tried him. For whose sake did he try Abraham ? not for himself, for He knew well the strength of his faith, but for our sakes, that we should see what true and living faith will surrender to God.

"And he that had received the promises offered up his only-begotten son."

18. " Of whom it was said, That in Isaac shall thy seed be called." If he had had many sons it would have been the sorest of trials, but being the one on whose life all the future of redemption depended, it was, as Chrysostom says, " What was of God seemed to be at variance with what was of God. He saith (to Abraham) 'in Isaac shall thy seed be called,' and he believed: and again He saith, ' Sacrifice to me this child who was to fill all the world from his seed.' Thou seest the opposition between the command

19 Accounting that God *was* able to raise *him* up, even from the dead; from whence also he received him in a figure.   *f* Rom. iv. 17, 19, 21.

---

and the promise; He enjoined things that were in contradiction to the promise, and yet not even so was the righteous man staggered, nor did he say that he had been deceived."

This was for our sakes. We have not to sacrifice our child, but we have in will to surrender him. And they who can say, with respect to the dearest objects of their love, " Thy will be done— the Lord gave and the Lord hath taken away—blessed be the Name of the Lord," they inherit something of the faith of Abraham.

Now this command of God came not to one unprepared. It came to one who had believed in and experienced a similar resuscitation. He had believed in and had experienced a restoration to life in the matter of the functions of his own body and that of Sarah, and so he now believed in a similar exercise of Resurrection Power. He had received Isaac from a dead womb, and he fully believed that he should receive Isaac from the unseen world—the world of the dead. His faith reversed the saying of David, "I shall not go to him, but he shall come back to me."

"Of whom it was said," rather, "to whom it was said," *i.e.*, to Abraham. God said this to Abraham when it seemed grievous to him to cast out his son Ishmael. "Let it not be grievous in thy sight because of the lad and because of thy bondwoman, for "in Isaac shall thy seed be called." The Hebrew barely translated is, "in Isaac shall a seed be called to thee," *i.e.*, "shall be reckoned to thee."

19. "Accounting that God was able to raise him up, even from the dead." The original is not that he accounted that God was able to raise up Isaac, but to raise all from the dead.

"From whence also he received him in a figure." A "figure" in the sense of "parable" in ch. ix. 9. " Isaac was dead in the intention and thought of Abraham, so when the ram was substituted for him it was, in a figure, life from the dead; but another and a much deeper sense has been given to these words. They have been taken to signify that Abraham received in the rescue of Isaac a figure or type of the Lord's Death and Resurrection—that at this time especially Abraham 'rejoiced to see Christ's day.' Isaac was

20 By faith ᵍIsaac blessed Jacob and Esau concerning things to come.

ᵍ Gen. xxvii. 27, 39.

21 By faith Jacob, when he was a dying, ʰblessed both the sons of Joseph; and ⁱworshipped, *leaning* upon the top of his staff.

ʰ Gen. xlviii. 5, 16, 20.
ⁱ Gen. xlvii. 31.

20. "Even concerning things to come." A., D., d, e, f, Vulg., read, "even" concerning, &c.

sacrificed, and yet lived to show that Christ should truly die and truly rise again. In Abraham's intention Isaac died: indeed, the Apostle does not hesitate to say that Abraham offered him up. In his expectation he was to rise from the dead; and therefore, being spared, Isaac was received by Abraham as from the dead. And all this was transacted in order to presignify that the only Son of God was really and truly to be sacrificed and die, and after death to be raised in life." (Wordsworth.)

20. "By faith Isaac blessed Jacob and Esau concerning things to come." In what way was Isaac's faith shewn in this bestowal of his blessing? Evidently in this, in that he believed himself to be the instrument or medium of conveying blessing from God. When he blessed he knew that he prophesied, and that the prophecy was not his own but came direct from God and could not be reversed, even though it was uttered by him not only unconsciously, but against his will. Thus he said, "Who? where is he that hath taken venison, and brought it me, and I have eaten of all before thou camest, and have blessed him? yea, and he shall be blessed" (Gen. xxvii. 33).

21. "By faith Jacob, when he was a dying, blessed both the sons of Joseph." The blessing was prophetical, and Jacob believed that in making the difference between the two sons of Joseph he was declaring the will of God. He blessed both the sons of Joseph, making each of them the head of a tribe (xlviii. 5, 6,) though he assigned preeminence to the younger.

"And worshipped, leaning upon the top of his staff." The Hebrew reads, in xlvii. 31, "And Israel bowed himself upon the bed's head." The writer of our Epistle changes this word "bed" into "staff," by alteration of the masoretic points מִטָּה into מַטֶּה. In the Hebrew it means he gathered up himself into a position

CHAP. XI.] BY FAITH JOSEPH, WHEN HE DIED. 213

22 By faith ᵏ Joseph, when he died, ‖ made mention of the departing of the children of Israel; and gave commandment concerning his bones.

ᵏ Gen. l. 24, 25. Exod. xiii. 19.
‖ Or, *remembered.*

---

of lowliest devotion. He prostrated himself upon the bed's head. In the Septuagint, which is adopted by the Apostolic writer, "He inclined towards the top of his staff."

Very remarkable interpretations have been given to this incident. One is, that it was Joseph's staff, or had a figure of Joseph at the top of it, and that by Jacob's bowing himself towards it the prophecy was fulfilled, that he himself as well as his wife and sons should bow down to Joseph (Gen. xxxvii. 10).

Another is, that it was intended to afford a vindication of image worship—there being some figure on the top of the staff, to which Jacob bowed himself, but of what we are not told. Delitzsch's explanation is good. "The $\pi\rho o\sigma\kappa\acute{u}\nu\eta\sigma\iota\varsigma$ of the latter (Jacob) was also in combination with the calm unhesitating manner in which Jacob arranged for his own burial in the distant land of Canaan, an eminent act of faith; his earnest entreaty that Joseph would solemnly promise this shewed how firm his reliance was upon the Divine promise, and when Joseph had given the promise he further shewed the energy of his faith by the energy and attitude of his thankful prayer. Notwithstanding the infirmities of old age and the exhaustion of approaching death he summoned all his bodily powers, and placed his aged limbs as well as he could in the posture of profoundest adoration."

If we read according to the Septuagint, then the patriarch put himself into a kneeling posture leaning on his staff.

22. "By faith Joseph, when he died, made mention . . . . and gave commandment respecting his bones." Unless he had believed that God would bring them out of Egypt and give them possession of the promised land, he would have given no direction respecting the removal of his body as he did, as related in Gen. l. 24. An important question arises, which is this: Joseph's whole life was a life of faith, especially was his faith shewn when he replied to his mistress, How shall I do this great wickedness and sin against God? Why, then, is this one instance singled out? Because it sharply defined his faith, that it was not a general faith in a supreme moral ruler and judge, but that it was a faith in the God of Abraham, the

23 By faith ¹Moses, when he was born, was hid three months of his parents, because they saw *he was a proper child*; and they were not afraid of the king's ᵐ commandment.

24 By faith ⁿ Moses, when he was come to years, refused to be called the son of Pharaoh's daughter:

25 º Choosing rather to suffer affliction with the

<small>
ˡ Exod. ii. 2. Acts vii. 20.
ᵐ Exod. i. 16, 22.
ⁿ Exod. ii. 10, 11.
º Ps. lxxxiv. 10.
</small>

---

God who had given special promises to Abraham that his seed should inherit the land.

23. "By faith Moses, when he was born, was hid three months," &c. Josephus mentions a tradition respecting the extraordinary beauty of Moses when a child. It is probable that his parents had a secret intimation from God that through him a great deliverance would be wrought for Israel. The parents, it is to be remembered, saved his life at the risk of their own, because they saw he was a "proper" child—the same word as is used by St. Stephen in Acts vii. 20. Bishop Wordsworth gathers from this that the writer of this epistle knew Stephen's speech: but is it not more likely that both Josephus and St. Stephen held some Hebrew tradition?

24, 25. "By faith Moses, when he was come to years . . . pleasures of sin for a season." There is no account of this refusal in Exodus, only this: "It came to pass in those days when Moses was grown, that he went out unto his brethren, and looked on their burdens: and he spied an Egyptian smiting an Hebrew," &c. (Exod. ii. 11). But we have in Josephus ("Antiquities," book ii. chap. ix.), the account of the daughter of Pharaoh, called Themuthis, bringing Moses to her father, and praying that she might adopt him as her son, so that he should be the heir of the kingdom, and the king took him into his arms and placed his royal diadem on his head, but Moses threw it on the ground, and trod it under his feet, which seem to bode ill to the kingdom of Egypt. It seems probable that there was some foundation of truth in this traditionary legend, for the passage in Exodus gives little ground for the statement of the Apostolic writer respecting Moses rejecting the honours of the Egyptian Court.

25. "Choosing rather to suffer affliction with the people of God, than to enjoy," &c. His faith enabled him to discern in the poor

people of God, than to enjoy the pleasures of sin for a season;

26 Esteeming ᵖ the reproach ‖ of Christ greater riches than the treasures in Egypt: for he had respect unto ᑫ the recompence of the reward.

ᵖ ch. xiii. 13.
‖ Or, *for Christ.*
ᑫ ch. x. 35.

---

26. "Treasures in Egypt." So a few Cursives; "of Egypt," א, D., E., K., L., P., &c.

slaves working in the brick kilns the people of God, and his faith enabled him to see in the Court of Pharaoh, with all its grandeur and sensual enjoyments, the kingdom opposed to that of God, which must come to naught, and make those who chose their part in it unable to take part in the joys of the heavenly and eternal kingdom.

26. "Esteeming the reproach of Christ greater riches than," &c. In what sense could taking side with the people of Israel be called "preferring the reproach of Christ?" Some have said that his prophetic spirit looked to Christ's coming in God's good time amongst them, and so that he literally looked for the Advent and Crucifixion of Christ; others have said that the whole people were separated to God, and so anointed, according to the words of the Psalmist, "touch not mine anointed" (in the Septuagint, "my Christs"), "and do my prophets no harm." But may it not be in somewhat of this way: he looked for deliverance for the seed of Abraham, and without examining narrowly into the amount of light God had vouchsafed to him respecting the Messiah, he regarded the whole nation as the seed whom the Lord had blessed. It was enough for him that they were the people of God, and that a future of blessing to the whole world was in store for them. As Christ accounts the murder of the children at Bethlehem to be a sharing of His Cross, so would He account the sufferings of the bondmen of Pharaoh to be a partaking with Him in His reproach.

"He had respect unto the recompence of the reward." This cannot be regarded as a reward in the land of Canaan, but in a future state of blessedness; because Moses when he went out unto his brethren, and espied their burdens, and took active part with one, at least, who was oppressed, had not as yet the vision of God vouchsafed to him, in which God promised to bring them into the land of Canaan (Exod. iii. 17).

27 By faith ʳ he forsook Egypt, not fearing the wrath of the king: for he endured, as ˢ seeing him who is invisible. 28 Through faith ᵗ he kept the passover, and the sprinkling of blood, lest he that destroyed the firstborn should touch them.

ʳ Exod. x. 28, 29. & xii. 37. & xiii. 17, 18.
ˢ ver. 13.
ᵗ Exod. xii. 21, &c.

---

27. "By faith he forsook Egypt, not fearing the wrath of the king." There is a great difficulty about this place as to its position in the narrative of the Exodus. It seems to refer to the first flight of Moses to the land of Midian; but how can this be the meaning, seeing that Moses fled from the face of Pharaoh because he sought to slay him? It has been explained somewhat in this way: He feared lest Pharaoh should take away his life. He feared not that Pharaoh should deprive him of the throne, or, at least, of the honour of his court. But this is most unsatisfactory. Others have interpreted it as meaning, he left Egypt through faith, though he feared not the wrath of the king. It would naturally seem to refer to the Exodus, in which Moses, strong in the faith of God, feared not the pursuit of the army of Pharaoh; but the proper place of that would come after, not before, the keeping of the Passover. Notwithstanding, however, the want of chronological accuracy, it seems most probable that it refers to the Exodus.

"For he endured, as seeing him who is invisible." This is the never failing characteristic of faith. Faith evidences to the soul the presence, the protection, the favour, and the judgment of the unseen God.

28. "Through faith he kept the passover, and the sprinkling of blood." "He kept," *i.e.*, he sacrificed the Passover. The original Passover must have been kept in very earnest faith in the promise of God that when the destroying angel saw the blood on the door-posts, he would pass over that house and not destroy the firstborn therein. All succeeding Passovers were but memorials of that one, for by that one only did God accomplish their deliverance." If, then, the blood of a lamb preserved the Jews unhurt in the midst of the Egyptians, and under so great a destruction, much more will the Blood of Christ save us, who have had it sprinkled, not on our door-posts, but in our souls." (Chrysostom.)

"Christ, our Passover is sacrificed for us" (1 Cor. v. 7).

29 By faith ᵘ they passed through the Red sea as by dry land: which the Egyptians assaying to do were drowned.   ᵘ Exod. xiv 22, 29.

30 By faith ˣ the walls of Jericho fell down, after they were compassed about seven days.   ˣ Josh. vi. 20.

31 By faith ʸ the harlot Rahab perished not with them ‖ that believed not, when ᶻ she had received the spies with peace.   ʸ Josh. vi. 23. Jam. ii. 25. ‖ Or, *that were disobedient*. ᶻ Josh. ii. 1.

---

29. "By faith they passed through the Red Sea as by dry land." It must have demanded considerable faith on the part of the people to pass between the two walls of water: but did the Egyptians who essayed to pass through share this faith? No; the Israelites passed through in faith, seeing the finger of God; but the Egyptians, in blind presumption, attributing the dividing of the sea to the east wind, or to some unusually low tide, or to some other natural cause.

30. "By faith the walls of Jericho fell down," &c. In this case the faith of the whole multitude of Israel took part, in that they obeyed the command of Joshua, and marched round the city seven days. The power by which the walls were levelled with the ground was wholly that of God, but He made it to depend upon the obedience of the Israelites in a matter which especially called forth faith. They were to compass the city seven days. They were to do nothing which could in any way whatsoever contribute to its overthrow. They were merely to show their simple faith in God, and shout.

31. "By faith the harlot Rahab perished not with them," &c. Why did she receive the spies in peace? What occasioned it? Let the answer be given in Rahab's own words, "I know that the Lord hath given you the land, and that your terror is fallen upon us, and that all the inhabitants of the land faint because of you. For we have heard how the Lord dried up the water of the Red Sea for you, and what ye did unto the two kings of the Amorites ... The Lord your God, He is God in heaven above, and in the earth beneath." Her faith, then, was that the God of Israel was the one true God, and acting on this, she believed that He had rightly, on account of their extreme wickedness, taken the land from the

32 And what shall I more say? for the time would fail me to tell of ᵃGedeon, and *of* ᵇBarak, and *of*

ᵃ Judg. vi. 11.
ᵇ Judg. iv. 6.

---

seven nations, and given it to Israel. Her allegiance was at once transferred from the King of Jericho to the King of all the earth. In this she acted not treacherously in concealing the spies, but according to her better moral nature which made her side with holiness rather than with degrading wickedness.

"Perished not with them that believed not." We are assured by this verse that if any of her countrymen had believed and turned to God, they would have been similarly saved. It was not their heathenism or idolatry, but their unbelief when the truth respecting the God of Israel was presented to them, which destroyed them.

32. "And what shall I more say? for the time would fail me," &c. What, or why should I say more? I have only time to mention great names, and not particularize their deeds of faith.

"Gedeon, and of Barak, and of Samson, and of Jephthae." It is to be remarked that the names of these heroes are arranged in pairs, and in each pair the second is really the first in chronological order, Barak being anterior to Gedeon, Jephthae to Samson, and Samuel preceding David.

Respecting this arrangement in pairs, Bishop Wordsworth writes: "In each of these pairs there is, as it were, an act of retrogression from the principal person mentioned to another person who resembled him, or was connected with him, and ought not to be forgotten. Such a mode of speech is peculiarly natural to persons who are compelled to hurry forward, and yet look back wistfully on those objects which they are obliged to leave behind." And also Mr. Blunt: "It is also perhaps an evidence in the same direction (that St. Paul was speaking and not writing) that the three couplets of names are each of them put in a reversed order, the latter name occurring first as the most conspicuous and first remembered, and the earlier name being then also mentioned as it arose in the memory.

It may be well to dwell for a moment on some particular in the case of each name, as showing the person's faith in God. Thus Gedeon (Judges vi. 12), "The Lord is with thee, thou mighty man of valour.... And Gideon said to him, Oh, my Lord, if the Lord

ᶜ Samson, and of ᵈ Jephthae; of ᵉ David also, and ᶠ Samuel, and of the prophets:

33 Who through faith subdued kingdoms, wrought righteousness, ᵍ obtained promises, ʰ stopped the mouths of lions,

c Judg. xiii. 24.
d Judg. xi. 1. & xii. 7.
e 1 Sam. xvi. 1, 13. & xvii. 45.
f 1 Sam. i. 20 & xii. 20.
g 2 Sam. vii. 11, &c.
h Judg. xiv. 5, 6. 1 Sam. xvii. 34, 35. Dan. vi. 22.

be with us, why then is all this befallen us? and where be all his miracles which our fathers told us of, saying, Did not the Lord bring us up out of Egypt? . . . And the Lord looked upon him and said, "Go in this thy might, and thou shalt save Israel from the hand of the Midianites."

Thus Barak said to the prophetess of God, "If thou wilt go up with me then I will go up, but if thou wilt not go with me then I will not go" (Judges iv. 8).

Thus Samson, "O Lord God, remember me, I pray thee, and strengthen me, I pray thee, only this once, that I may be avenged of the Philistines for my two eyes" (Judges xvi. 28).

Thus Jephthah (Judges xi. 23), "So now the Lord God of Israel hath dispossessed the Amorites from before his people Israel, and shouldest thou possess it?"

Thus David, "The Lord that delivered me out of the paw of the lion, and out of the paw of the bear, he will deliver me out of the hand of this Philistine" (1 Sam. xvii. 37).

Thus Samuel, "And Samuel grew, and the Lord was with him, and did let none of his words fall to the ground" (1 Sam. iii. 19).

33. "Who through faith subdued kingdoms, wrought righteousness." These, Gedeon, Jephthae, and David, subdued the heathen with forces far inferior, relying on God's promise, "one of you shall chase a thousand" (Deut. xxxii. 30).

"Wrought righteousness." This seems to refer to their righteous government of Israel.

"Obtained promises." This seems particularly to refer to David, who obtained the promises that his seed should sit on his throne, and when this seemed to fail, it was renewed in the promises respecting the greater than David, the greater than Solomon, even the "Lord our Righteousness."

"Stopped the mouths of lions." Thus Samson (Judges xiv.

34 ¹ Quenched the violence of fire, ᵏ escaped the edge of the sword, ˡ out of weakness were made strong, waxed valiant in fight, ᵐ turned to flight the armies of the aliens.

---

5, 6). Thus David (1 Sam. xvii. 37). Thus Samson (Judges xiv. 6). Thus Daniel, vi. 22.

34. "Quenched the violence of fire." Quenched not the fire itself, but its burning and slaying power. No doubt there is allusion to Daniel iii. 25, "Lo, I see four men loose walking in the midst of the fire, and they have no hurt, and the form of the fourth is like the Son of God."

"Escaped the edge of the sword, out of weakness were made strong." Dilitzsch, the German Protestant commentator, finds the fulfilment of these four last clauses of this verse in the time of the Maccabees. Their position in the narrative seems to demand it. "The sacred writer, without excluding older deeds of faith, had more especially the Maccabean times in view, and may be particularly alluding to the happy escape of Mattathias and his sons into the mountains (1 Mac. ii. 28), the growing strength of their little troop, which at first seemed in its weakness so insignificant; the valiant deeds of Judas Maccabeus in conflict with Appollonius, Seron, and others, and finally the victorious wars waged by the Asmonean heroes with the Syrian monarchy and the neighbouring nationalities. . . . The book of Daniel, in its prophetic pictures of that very time, portrays a holy people of the Most High at war with godless Antichristian powers. . . . I therefore hold that these last relative clauses carry on the review of the ancestral achievements of Israel's faith beyond the times of the prophets and the book of Daniel into those of the first book of Maccabees, which in the Septuagint follows it; and this indeed is generally conceded with regard to the two last clauses, being rendered the more certain by the fact that παρεμβολή in the double sense of camp and army is a favourite word with the writer of the first of Maccabees, and that ἀλλότριοι (with ἀλλόφυλοι) repeatedly occurs there as the rendering of זָרִים or נָכְרִים (i. 38; ii. 7; Comp. xv. 33).

"Escaped the edge of the sword," has been referred to the wonderful deliverance of the Jews in Ahasuerus's time.

35 ⁿ Women received their dead raised to life again: and others were ᵒ tortured, not accepting deliverance; that they might obtain a better resurrection: 36 And others had trial of *cruel* mockings and scourgings, yea, moreover ᵠ of bonds and imprisonment: 37 ʳ They were stoned, they were sawn asunder,

ⁿ 1 Kings xvii. 22. 2 Kings iv. 35.
ᵒ Acts xxii. 25.
ᵠ Gen. xxxix. 20. Jer. xx. 2. & xxxvii. 15.
ʳ 1 Kings xxi. 13. 2 Chron. xxiv. 21. Acts vii. 58. & xiv. 19.

37. "They were sawn asunder, were tempted." So A., E., K., most Cursives, d, e, f, Vulg., Cop,, Arm.; but ℵ, D., L., P., reverse the order, "they were tempted, were sawn asunder."

35. "Women received their dead raised to life again: and others were tortured," &c. Thus the woman of Zarephath (or Sarepta) in 1 Kings xvii. 22; and the woman in Shunem (2 Kings iv.).

In apparent contrast to this is the next clause, where allusion is without all doubt made to the heroic mother and her seven sons mentioned in 2 Maccabees, chap. vii., each one of whom in succession was cruelly tortured, but refused to disobey the law of God by eating swines' flesh.

"That they might obtain a better resurrection." Thus the fourth son confessed the Resurrection to life in the words, "It is good being put to death by man, to look for hope from God, to be raised up again by him" (vii. 14).

36. "And others had trial of cruel mockings and scourgings, yea, moreover of bonds and imprisonment." The allusion probably is to the insults which the seven sons endured, all of whom were cruelly mocked before they were put to death. Ἐμπαιγμοί are not mere mockings, but cruel, sportive forms of ill-treatment of all kinds." Thus the second son had the skin of his head and hair pulled off before he was tortured to death.

Bonds and imprisonment were the common lot of the persecuted in all ages. The writer may have in his mind the imprisonment of Jeremiah.

37. "They were stoned, they were sawn asunder, were tempted." "They were stoned," so Naboth (1 Kings xxi. 13); so Zechariah, the son of Jehoiada (2 Chron. xxiv. 21): Our Lord denounced Jerusalem as "Thou that stonest them that are sent unto thee" (Matt. xxiii. 37).

were tempted, were slain with the sword: *they wandered about ᵗ in sheepskins and goatskins; being destitute, afflicted, tormented;

38 (Of whom the world was not worthy:) they wandered in deserts, and *in* mountains, and ᵘ *in* dens and caves of the earth.

* 2 Kings i. 8. Matt. iii. 4.
ᵗ Zech. xiii. 4.
ᵘ 1 Kings xviii. 4. & xix. 9.

---

"They were sawn asunder." It is related in Jewish tradition that Isaiah suffered this horrible form of death under Manasseh.

"Were tempted." There is considerable difficulty respecting the interpretation of this "tempted." It comes in amongst bodily tortures, and is altogether out of place if it refers to spiritual trials. It has been supposed that the word is a repetition by mistake of "were sawn asunder" (ἐπρίσθησαν) the word for "were tempted" (ἐπειράσθησαν) having a similar sound. May it not allude to some horrible form of temptation in which the martyrs were tied to women, or exposed to a death of hunger unless they eat swines' flesh?

"Were slain with the sword." This also seems a mild punishment compared to some enumerated. There seems a reference to the complaint of Elijah, "The children of Israel have forsaken thy covenant, thrown down thine altars, and slain thy prophets with the sword" (1 Kings xix. 10).

"They wandered about in sheepskins and goatskins." Commentators usually refer to the rough garments worn by the prophets. Thus Zechariah xiii. 4, "Neither shall they (the prophets) wear a rough garment to deceive;" but may it not refer to some plan of concealing themselves in the skins of these animals to deceive their pursuers?

"Being destitute," *i.e.*, of the barest necessaries of life, as Elijah was when he was fed by the ravens.

38. "Of whom the world was not worthy." How different the judgment of God from that of the world! In the sight of men they were, like the Apostles, "The filth of the earth, the off-scouring of all things" (1 Cor. iv. 13). In the sight of God they were the salt of the earth, the ten righteous on whose intercession He suspended His judgment, and gave a little respite to the condemned kingdoms.

So it has ever been with the saints of God. The world is not

39 And these all, [x] having obtained a good report through faith, received not the promise :   [x] ver. 2, 13.

39. "The promise." So ℵ, D., E., K., L., P., most Cursives, d, e, f, Vulg.; but A. reads "the promises."

worthy of such, and God takes them away, perhaps before their time, cutting them off in the midst of their witness, as He did John the Baptist, and James the brother of John, and they pass away and take their place under the altar, and cry, "How long, O Lord?"

This clause may be taken parenthetically, but some connect it with the next words, " of them the world was not worthy," and so God withdrew them from its society and made them " wanderers in deserts, and in mountains, and in dens, and in caves of the earth," but the former interpretation, that which makes the sentence parenthetical, or interjected, as it were, seems the best.

39. " And these all, having obtained a good report through faith, received not," &c. Here the Apostolic writer resumes what he had said in verse 2. By it (faith) the elders, Abel, Enoch, Noah, Abraham, and the rest whose deeds of faith he has just finished recording—these all obtained a good report through faith, but received not the promise. Thus Abraham, during all the time of his sojourn, looked for and received not the city which hath the foundations. What, then, is this promise? There can be no doubt but that it is the final consummation at the Second Coming of the Lord. We must make the needful distinction between receiving the promise in its being given to us in the words of God, and receiving the promise in its fulfilment in the final consummation. All these elders accomplished these glorious deeds of faith because they believed in the words of God that He would fulfil His promise.

And yet "they received not the promise." And why? Because it is the will of God that the whole congregation of his saints, from righteous Abel to the very last received into Paradise, should be perfected in their glorified bodies at the same time.

40. " God having provided some better things for us, that they

| Or, *foreseen*.
y ch. vii. 22.
 & viii. 6.
z ch. v. 9. &
xii. 23. Rev.
vi. 11.

40 God having || provided ʸ some better thing for us, that they without us should not be ᶻ made perfect.

without us." What is this better thing? It cannot be the consummation, because that is yet future. St. Paul says that he shall receive the crown of righteousness which the Lord, the righteous judge, shall give him *at that day;* and yet it must be something better than that which the elders, who died in faith, received. What is it? It can only be the dispensation of Christ, the revelation in the flesh of the Eternal Son, the words and deeds by which He instructed us in the perfect will of God (Matth. xiii. 17), His atoning Death, His life-giving Resurrection, our being gathered into His Church, our being made members of His mystical Body, our eating His Flesh and drinking His Blood that we may have eternal life, and that we may dwell in Him and He in us. It can be only this, for this is the better thing which the elders had not and which we have.

"That they without us." They await not only the Consummation of the last day, but the better thing which God has foreseen or provided for us. The dispensation of Christ is the preparation for being made perfect at the last. It is because we have the full knowledge of Christ as Incarnate, Crucified, Risen and Ascended, and are members of His mystical Body, and continue so to the end, that we attain the promise.

They await this revelation of Christ and have it revealed to them in their present state. Thus the Lord Himself preached it to those in the unseen state. How God makes up to them the want of union with His mystical Body we know not, but we are sure that He does.

The souls of the departed "elders," having received the knowledge of the Person and work of Christ, are in the same condition as the Christian souls now in Paradise.

## CHAP. XII.

WHEREFORE seeing we also are compassed about with so great a cloud of witnesses, [a] let us lay aside every weight, and the sin which doth so

[a] Col. iii. 8.
1 Pet. ii. 1.

---

1. "Wherefore seeing we also are compassed about with so great," &c. The Hebrew Christians under severe persecution and trial are contending in the arena for the prize. The spectators in the vast amphitheatre, rising rank upon rank above one another are the elders whose names have been mentioned with honour as having obtained a good report, and these are but representatives of a vastly greater number, so as to be compared to an overhanging or encircling cloud, and the judge or distributor of the crowns is the Lord Himself.

"Let us lay aside every weight." Let us do what those have to do who contend for the prize of running. Let us lay aside every weight, every hindrance, every impediment which prevents us using our limbs to the uttermost. Chrysostom says "all what" that is all slumber, indifference, mean reasonings, all human things. There can be little doubt that the image is taken from the immediate preparations for the decisive effort, and it is hardly possible that ἀποθέσθαι ὄγκον could be used of the effects of training. The wr.ter seems to have had in mind the manifold encumbrances of society and business which would be likely to hinder a Christian convert (compare the Lord's parable of the great supper, Luke xiv. 16, &c.).

"And the sin which doth so easily beset us." The meaning assigned to εὐπερίστατον as readily besetting sin seems the most in accordance with the derivation of the word, and what is most surely required by the circumstances. Everyone has his peculiarly besetting sin, which must be got under and conquered if the Christian's conflict is to issue in victory. So it was with such a saint as St. Paul (1 Cor. ix. 27), "I keep under my body and bring it into subjection lest that, by any means, having preached to others I myself should be unapproved." It is to this besetting sin that

Q

easily beset *us*, and [b] let us run [c] with patience the race that is set before us,

2 Looking unto Jesus the || author and finisher of *our* faith; [d] who for the joy that was set before

[h] 1 Cor. ix. 24. Phil. iii. 13, 14.
[c] Rom. xii. 12. ch. x. 36.
|| Or, *beginner*.
[d] Luke xxiv. 26. Phil. ii. 8, &c. 1 Pet. i. 11.

---

the Lord alludes when He says with such earnestness, "If thy hand, if thy foot, if thine eye offend thee pluck it out, cut it off, it is better for thee to enter into life with one eye, one foot, one hand . . . than to be cast into hell fire." And what is the besetting sin? It is different in each one. It is drunkenness, it is fornication, it is secret uncleanness, it is theft, picking and stealing, cheating, fraud, it is slander and backbiting; it is one of the manifold forms of covetousness; it is causeless anger, unrestrained passion, envy, hatred, malice and all uncharitableness. And how is it to be cut off, put away, kept under? By prayer, by constant, assiduous, never-ceasing prayer—by keeping under the body, by fasting, by using the sword of the Spirit, which is the word of God, by constantly turning our thoughts Godward, by remembering the Lord's cross, and the issue of it as described by the Apostle, "They that are Christ's have crucified the flesh, with its affections and lusts." And by confession and absolution. I have known as great miracles of God's grace conferred in confession and its accompanying absolution, as any recorded of the expulsion of evil spirits in the Scriptures.

"And let us run with patience the race that is set before us." Let us run with endurance—enduring to the end. Every Christian has to contend, after the manner of the ancient athletes. He has to strive to win with all his might, but there is this difference; that whereas in the ancient games but one of all the combatants or contenders received the prize, in the Christian contest every one may receive, if each one runs with all his might. To run with endurance is to be careful not to slacken, not to relax prayer, or watchfulness, or self-denial, or looking heavenward to Jesus.

2. "Looking unto Jesus the author and finisher of our faith." "The author," because He it is Who implants faith in us—the Finisher, or Perfecter, because He crowns it as the Judge eternal.

The writer next proceeds to set forth that by which Christ encourages and sustains the faith of which He is the Author. He

him endured the cross, despising the shame, and ᵉis set down at the right hand of the throne of God. 3 'For consider him that endured such contradiction of sinners against himself, ᶠlest ye be wearied and faint in your minds.

ᵉ Ps. cx. 1. ch. i. 3, 13. & viii. 1. 1 Pet. iii. 22.
ᶠ Matt. x. 24, 25. John xv. 20.
ᵍ Gal. vi. 9.

3. "Against himself." So A., P., also K., L., most Cursives; but א, D., E., Arm., Syriac, read, "against themselves."

was made like unto us in all things in which it was possible that He should be so. God encourages us by the reward of glory, honour, and immortality, and though we are not saved by this reward, it is His Will that we should expect it, and work for it. And so with Him. In all His sufferings He looked for His reward. He was to be anointed with the oil of gladness above His fellows, and so

"He endured the cross despising the shame." He endured the unspeakably agonizing pain of it. He despised the ignominy which was attached to its infliction (see my note on Matth. xxvii. 35), because He knew that He must rise again, that He must take His seat at the right hand of God, that He must receive the Spirit not by measure, but in fulness, that He must have all things put under His feet.

"And is set down at the right hand of the throne of God." That is His prize. That was the object to which His human nature looked. "And now, O Father, glorify me with thine own self, with the glory which I had with thee before the world was" (John xvii).

3. "For consider him that endured such contradiction of sinners against himself." Several, as Westcott, read against themselves. It was grievous to the most Holy Saviour to receive the contradiction of sinners against Himself, or to see them opposing their own salvation. The fact was the same whichever way we read the original. They who spake against Him spake against their own mercy—spake against the salvation of their own souls, of which He was the sole Author.

"Lest ye be weary and faint in your minds."

4. "Ye have not yet resisted unto blood striving against sin." Here the Apostle reminds them that many whose names he had

4 ʰ Ye have not yet resisted unto blood, striving against sin.

ʰ 1 Cor x. 13.
ch. x. 32, 33, 34.
ⁱ Job v. 17. Pro. iii. 11.

5 And ye have forgotten the exhortation which speaketh unto you as unto children, ⁱ My son, despise not thou the chastening of the Lord, nor faint when thou art rebuked of him:

---

recounted had been unwearied and fainted not, and had resisted unto blood, as those who were stoned—were sawn asunder, were slain with the sword.

It is clear that those whom the Apostle addressed had not yet resisted unto blood, *i.e.*, unto death, for they were alive yet. Some have gathered from this that the Epistle could not have been addressed to Christian Jews of Jerusalem, for such had been subject to such sharp persecution as those in Stephen's time, or in Herod's: but nothing can be safely gathered from this, as they might have escaped, as the Lord counselled men to flee from one city to another without sin.

"Striving against sin." Not merely striving with persecutors, but against sin. Their persecutors were only the instruments in the hands of one who wielded the power of sin, being its author, and who wielded it against the kingdom of grace and righteousness. When then in the power of Christ they resisted persecution, they strove against sin in its most absolute form and power.

5. "And ye have forgotten the exhortation which speaketh unto you as to sons." All through the Book of Proverbs, and especially in this passage, the Divine Spirit Who inspired the book, speaketh to the Israel of God as if they were His children—and not to the whole body of the people, but to each one; "My son" it says to each.

"Ye have forgotten the exhortation which speaketh unto you," &c. This may be rendered either affirmatively, as in our translation, or interrogatively. "Have ye forgotten?" The latter is less severe.

The persecutions of enemies and unbelievers are here regarded as the loving discipline of a Father in heaven. They forgot the exhortation when they regarded not the distress they were under as a dispensation of God, and rebelled under it, or what was worse, succumbed to it, and were on the way of apostasy.

6 For ᵏ whom the Lord loveth he chasteneth, and scourgeth every son whom he receiveth.

7 ¹ If ye endure chastening, God dealeth with

ᵏ Ps. xciv. 12. & cxix. 75.
Pro. iii. 12.
Jam. i. 12.
Rev. iii. 19.
¹ Deut. viii. 5. 2 Sam. vii. 14. Prov. xiii. 24. & xix. 18. & xxiii. 13.

7. "For chastening" (εἰς παιδίαν). א, A., D., K., L., P., many Cursives, Syr., &c. ιι read by many Cursives. See below.

"Despise not thou"—*i.e.*, regard not lightly.

"Nor faint when thou art rebuked of him." This teaches us that we are to take every distress or persecution as a rebuke from God. A rebuke in the sense of bringing to mind something in our past life, or something in our interior life which requires forgiveness, or acknowledgment, or correction.

I knew one who suffered an apparently most undeserved affliction from the heartless conduct of those brought up by him, and he said to God, "I cannot tax myself with having done anything to bring on this ingratitude and slander which I now suffer, but I take it as a reproof for sins which I have committed in past life, which these persons who are slandering me know not, and which if they knew they would think far worse of me than they do now. 'I became dumb and opened not my mouth, for it was Thy doing.'"

6. "For whom the Lord loveth he chasteneth." One Christian said to another, "My brother, God must love you very much if He brings all this upon you." Now this is literally true. It is hard to believe at the time when we are overwhelmed, but it is literally and actually true, and its truth is abundantly manifested by the conduct of God towards His Incarnate Son; for what Son of God ever endured such pains of body or such distress of mind? "My God, my God, why hast thou forsaken me?" Or what merely human sons could be more in the favour of God than St. Paul and his brother apostles, who yet could say, "I think that God hath set forth us the apostles last, as it were appointed unto death; for we are made a spectacle to the world, and to angels, and to men . . . even unto this present time we both hunger and thirst, and are naked, and are buffeted, and have no certain dwelling-place . . . we are made as the filth of the earth, the offscouring of all things unto this day" (1 Cor. iv. 9, &c.).

7. "If ye endure chastening, God dealeth with you us with sons; for what son," &c. There is considerable difficulty about the

you as with sons; for what son is he whom the father chasteneth not?

<sup>m</sup> Ps. lxxiii. 15; 1 Pet. v. 9.

8 But if ye be without chastisement, <sup>m</sup> whereof all are partakers, then are ye bastards, and not sons.

9 Furthermore we have had fathers of our flesh which corrected *us*, and we gave *them* reverence: shall we not

---

9. "Furthermore we have had fathers of our flesh which corrected us." Revisers translate, "Furthermore we had the fathers of our flesh to chastise us."

reading. The Received Text has little authority. Westcott reads, "It is for chastening ye endure; it is as with sons God dealeth with you." So Revisers. The Vulgate, "In disciplinâ perseverate!" The meaning under all differences is obvious, and is fixed by the next verse.

8. "But if ye be without chastisement, whereof all are partakers," &c. "All" probably alludes to the examples of faith in the last chapter. All these had to wait long to experience the enmity and persecutions of the world, and in numberless other ways to be made to feel that this is not their home.

It is said of some great saint of the Church, I think St. Ambrose, that on a journey he stopped for the night at a nobleman's house, who thought to entertain him by the accounts of his prosperous life. He had had no sickness worth speaking of, his income increased, he added house to house, and field to field, he lost no children, they were all married and were as prosperous as himself. "Let us arise, and leave this house at once," exclaimed the saint, "the favour of God cannot rest here."

"Then are ye bastards, and not sons." "Just as in families," says Chrysostom, "fathers care not for bastards, though they learn nothing, though they be not distinguished, but fear for their legitimate sons, lest they should be indolent." (So here.) If then not to be chastised is a mark of bastards, we ought to rejoice at chastisement if this be a sign of legitimacy.

9. "Furthermore we have had fathers of our flesh which corrected us, and we gave them reverence .... Father of spirits." This seems to teach a deep philosophical truth, that while the body with its mere animal life is derived from our parents, the spirit

much rather be in subjection unto ⁿ the Father of spirits, and live?

10 For they verily for a few days chastened *us* ‖ after their own pleasure; but he for *our* profit, º that *we* might be partakers of his holiness.

11 Now no chastening for the present seemeth to be joyous, but grievous: nevertheless afterward

ⁿ Nu. xvi. 22. & xxvii. 16. Job xii. 10. Eccles. xii. 7. Is. xlii. 5. & lvii. 16. Zech. xii. 1.
‖ Or, *as seemed good*, or, *meet to them*.
º Lev. xi. 44. & xix. 2. 1 Pet. i. 15, 16.

---

comes directly from God, the paternity of the natural father being contrasted with that of the spiritual Father. There is a parallel place in Eccles. xii. 7: "Then shall the dust return to the earth, as it was, and the spirit shall return to God who gave it."

We have no right, however, to treat the words of the sacred writer as if he had in his mind certain philosophical theories. Wordsworth says well: "God is the creator of our bodies, souls, and spirits, but He is not the Father of the carnal corruptions of our nature, which we inherit through our parents from Adam, who (our parents) are therefore here called 'fathers of our flesh,' as contrasted with the pneuma or highest faculty in man."

"Shall we not much rather be in subjection unto the Father of spirits, and live?" Conscious subjection to God the Father of spirits is life, because all the dispensations of His providence towards us are with a view to our enjoying eternal life in His presence.

10. "For they verily for a few days chastened us after their own pleasure," &c. For a short time, the times of our infancy and youth, they chastened us, according to their own wills or impulses, or passions. Not always having our own well-being in view, and by no means with a view to our progress in goodness, and very seldom, indeed, with a view to our preparation for eternal life.

"But he for our profit, that we might be partakers of his holiness." As without holiness no man shall see the Lord, and as God desires that all His children should attain to the beatific vision, all His corrective discipline is that we should be like Him by being conformed to the image of His Son.

11. "Now no chastening for the present seemeth to be joyous." If it were joyous it would not be discipline. Pain has a place in God's universe for two purposes, for punishment and for corrective discipline. In the dispensation of God, discipline must be grievous

it yieldeth ᵖ the peaceable fruit of righteousness unto them which are exercised thereby. 12 Wherefore ᑫ lift up the hands which hang down, and the feeble knees; 13 ʳ And make || straight paths for your feet, lest that which is lame be turned out of the way; ˢ but let it rather be healed.

p Jam. iii. 18.
q Job iv. 3, 4. Is. xxxv. 3.
r Prov. iv. 26, 27.
‖ Or, *even*.
s Gal. vi. 1.

---

or it would be no warning against sin, no foretaste of its final punishment.

"Nevertheless afterward it yieldeth the peaceable fruit of righteousness unto them which are exercised thereby," to them that have been trained by means of it.

"Peaceable fruit." Peace after conflict seems the idea, and this fruit righteousness; "peaceable fruit to them that have been exercised thereby, even the fruit of righteousness." So Westcott and Revisers.

12. "Wherefore lift up the hands which hang down, and the feeble knees." This is a quotation from Isaiah xxxv. 3: "Strengthen ye the weak hands, and confirm the feeble knees."

"The hands which hang down." This may be either their own or their brethren's. Either case of strengthening avails for the other. If one member suffers, all the members suffer with it. If one member be honoured, or, which is the same, be strengthened, all rejoice with it. Wesley says: "The hands which hang down, unable to continue the conflict; the feeble knees, unable to continue the race."

13. "And make straight paths for your feet." "Straight paths," that is, even paths, as Delitzch explains, with no ups and downs in them.

"Lest that which is lame be turned out of the way; but let it rather be healed." The thought in the writer's mind in using the figure is first the halting between two opinions, Judaism and Christianity (comp. χωλαίνειν, 1 Kings xviii. 21), in which so many of these Hebrew Christians were involved, and then the turning out of the Christian path altogether into sheer apostasy. Such apostasy on the part of the infirm and wavering members of the Hebrew Church could be prevented, and their eventual healing rendered possible, only by the whole community determining to

14 ᵗFollow peace with all *men*, and holiness, ᵘwithout which no man shall see the Lord:
15 ˣLooking diligently ʸ lest any man ‖ fail of

ᵗ Ps. xxxiv. 14. Rom. xii. 18. & xiv. 19. 2 Tim. ii. 22.
ᵘ Matt. v. 8. 2 Cor. vii. 1. Eph. v. 5.
ˣ 2 Cor. vi. 1.
ʸ Gal. v. 4.
‖ Or, *fall from*.

make their common course of Christian action a straight and level one, avoiding in future those sideward turnings and alternate ups and downs in favour of the synagogue to which they had been accustomed. But the reference must not be confined to this. There were many other dangers besides those from Judaism. The whole Christian community must determine to take a straightforward course in all matters of right and wrong. There must be no connivance at fornication as in the Corinthian Church, or at idleness as in the Thessalonian.

14. "Follow peace with all men." "If it be possible, as much as lieth in you, live peaceably with all men." Among "all" men we must include the unconverted Jews and the heathen. If without compromising the confession of their Christian faith they can be on good terms with the outside world, they must be so. Persecution, though in the cause of Christ it is not to be succumbed to, is yet not to be courted.

Notice the word "follow." It is usually rendered not follow but "pursue," as if earnestness and eagerness must be put forth to attain to it.

"And holiness, without which no man shall see the Lord." *The* holiness (def. art.). Does this mean any particular holiness? It seems to be cognate with the beatitude, "Blessed are the pure in heart, for they shall see God." Who is here meant by the Lord? Not the Lord Jesus, for good and bad alike shall see him at the last day, but that vision of God with the soul's eye, which must be purified before it can attain to such sight of Him. Compare the words of St. John (who, however, refers it to the Son of God): "When he shall appear we shall be like him, for we shall see him as he is, and every man that hath this hope in him purifieth himself even as he is pure." Chrysostom takes it as referring to what is commonly called purity, the avoidance of fornication and all unclean lusts.

15. "Looking diligently lest any man fail of the grace of God." Looking diligently is literally "overseeing," and is the verb used

the grace of God; *lest any root of bitterness springing up trouble *you*, and thereby many be defiled:

16 ᵃ Lest there *be* any fornicator, or profane

<small>ᵗ Deut. xxix. 18. ch. iii. 12.
ᵃ Eph. v. 3. Col. iii. 5. 1 Thess. iv. 3.</small>

<small>15. "Many." So D., K., L., P., most Cursives; but ℵ, A., read, "the many," *i.e.*, the greater number.</small>

for carrying out the duty of the episcopos or overseer. It implies that the words of the Apostle in Phil. ii. 4 be obeyed: "Look not every man on his own things, but every man also on the things of others."

"Lest any man fail of the grace of God." This may be rendered "Lest there be any man that falleth short of the grace of God," that is, that does not proceed to realize that measure of grace which God hath given to him; or it may be rendered, "Lest any man fall back from the grace of God," that is, who receives it altogether in vain. The first translation is given by the Revisers in their text, the other in their margin. Westcott: "Lest there be any man that falleth back from the grace of God." It is one of those many passages in this Epistle which implies that the grace of God may be received in vain. We would fain not have it so, for it is dreadful to contemplate such a thing, but the Epistle is full of it.

"Lest any root of bitterness springing up trouble you, and thereby," &c. This is a citation from Deut. xxix. 18: "Lest there should be among you man, woman, or family, or tribe, whose heart turneth away this day from the Lord our God to go and serve the gods of these nations; lest there should be a root that beareth gall and wormwood."

Chrysostom notices the difference between a bitter root and a root of bitterness in the sense of bearing bitter fruit. "And well, said he, root of bitterness. He said not bitter, but ' of bitterness.' For it is possible that a bitter root might bear sweet fruits, but it is not possible that a root and fountain of bitterness should ever bear sweet fruit."

"And thereby many—the many—be defiled." A declension in a Church or society may very often be traced to one backslider, so that it is necessary that each one animates his brother in the pursuit of peace and holiness.

16. "Lest there be any fornicator, or profane person, as Esau,

person, as Esau, ᵇ who for one morsel of meat sold his birthright.

17 For ye know how that afterward, ᶜ when he would have inherited the blessing, he was rejected:

ᵇ Gen. xxv. 33.
ᶜ Gen. xxvii. 34, 36, 38.

---

"who for one," &c. "Fornicator or profane person," as Esau. Are we to take fornicator as applying to Esau? He does not say this. A professing Christian may fall either through fleshly lust or through profanity, profanely despising the spiritual blessings of which he is an heir.

Chrysostom and others look upon βέβηλος as involving the sin of gluttony, but if a man is faint with hunger (Gen. xxv. 30), surely it is not gluttony for him to desire food.

It is also supposed by some that Esau was reckoned among adulterers because of his marriage with the Hittite women, of whom it was significantly said that they were a grief to Isaac and to Rebecca.

"Who for one morsel of meat (*i.e.*, for a mess of red pottage) sold his birthright."

No greater contempt for the God of Abraham could well have been shewn. He was hungry it is true, but could there be any lack of food in the tents of his father Isaac?

Altogether, taking into account the circumstances of the family as the sole depository of the promises of God, it was as gross a case of profaneness as can be conceived. He did not care a basin of pottage, indeed, we might say he did not care a fig, a button, a halfpenny, for the promises of God.

And so they acted who, after they had come into the inheritance of the promises of God in Christ, surrendered them to avoid persecution. And so we act when we surrender the prospects of eternity for the joys of time, when we throw in our lot with the world rather than with the Crucified.

But was not the birthright Jacob's by the promise of God? Was it not said that the elder should serve the younger? Yes; but the action of Esau, in bartering his birthright, was of his own free will. He cut himself off. And his conduct vindicated the wisdom of God in decreeing that the Messiah should not spring from his race (See Notes on Rom. ix. 12, 13), but from that of Jacob.

17. "For ye know how that afterward, when he would have in-

NO PLACE OF REPENTANCE. [HEBREWS.

<sup>d</sup> ch. vi. 6.
∥ Or, *way to change his mind.*

<sup>d</sup> for he found no ∥ place of repentance, though he sought it carefully with tears.

---

herited the blessing," &c. When he went out to hunt venison and to bring it to his father, assuming that what had passed betwixt himself and his brother was, as it were, in sport, and would not be remembered or taken into account.

" For he found no place of repentance, though he sought it carefully with tears." "No place of repentance " means merely, that Isaac would not annul his own act. That, in fact, he could not do, for in giving the blessing he was entirely the instrument of God. "I have blessed him, yea, and he shall be blessed" (Gen. xxvii. 33).

The repentance in question has reference wholly to the patriarchal blessing in this life, and has nothing to do with the promise of eternal life. If Esau lost that blessing it was because of his profaneness, because of his rooted unbelief in God and in his promises to Abraham. That he had no real repentance, no change of heart towards God, is manifested by his threat to kill his brother as soon as the days of mourning for his father were ended: and yet he seems to have forgiven him, for when he met Jacob "he ran to meet him, and embraced him, and fell on his neck, and kissed him " (Gen. xxxiii. 4).

The example of Esau is cited for one purpose, and one only; to teach us the danger of despising the promises of life given in the Son of God; but though the repentance of Esau has no bearing on *his* own prospect of spiritual and eternal things, it had the most direct bearing on the eternal prospects of the Hebrew Christians. They were members of Christ, children of God, and inheritors of the kingdom of heaven, and their one business was to heartily thank God that He had called them to this state of salvation, and to pray God to give them His grace, that they might continue in the same.

We have, like them, to learn from this that a time will come when repentance will not be available, and we have to look to ourselves (and to our fellow-members in the body of Christ, as well as to ourselves), that we keep our bodies from fleshly lust and our souls in a reverent frame of submission to God through Jesus Christ.

18. " For ye are not come unto the mount that might be touched,

18 For ye are not come unto ᵉ the mount that might be touched, and that burned with fire, nor unto blackness, and darkness, and tempest,

ᵉ Exod. xix. 12, 18, 19, & xx. 18. Deut. iv. 11. & v. 22. Rom. vi. 14. & viii. 15. 2 Tim. i. 7.

18. "Unto the mount." So D. (Gr.), K., L., most Cursives; but ℵ, A., C., 17, 47, d, f, Vulg. (Am.), Sah., Copt., Syr., omit "mount."
"Darkness" (σκότῳ). So L. and most Cursives; but ℵ, A., C., D., P., and a few Cursives, read ζόφῳ, same meaning.

and that burned with fire." There is considerable difficulty in ascertaining the true reading, whether ὄρει is genuine or not. It seems to be required, for the counter privileges of the Christian people, commencing in verse 22, begins with, " Ye are come unto the Mount Sion." The reader will see the authorities for and against retaining it in the critical note. If it is not retained the sentence must be rendered, "Ye are not come unto a fire capable of being touched, and one kindled," &c. But the absurdity of this is sought to be got rid of by rendering "capable of being touched" by "palpable." So Revisers in their margin.

In these and the following words the Apostolic writer contrasts the terrors of the law at its inauguration with the grace of the Gospel state of things. "Ye are not come unto Mount Sinai enveloped in fire, clouds, and darkness, emblematical of its severe and graceless and obscure character; "but ye are (or have) come to the Mount Sion, the city of the living God," &c. But a system, or state of grace, requires as much, or more, sense of responsibility than a system of mere law. So the Apostolic writer concludes, "See that ye refuse not him that speaketh."

We must now consider each clause of this remarkable passage. Your ancestors were led to the foot of Mount Sinai. It was a mountain that might be touched, but at the peril of life; so that bounds were set, lest the people should approach near to it. God more than once giving command that notwithstanding the bounds there should be care taken that there be no approach to it. This was indicative of the Spirit of the whole dispensation. "Stand off;" "Come not nigh;" "Ye are not yet reconciled." And so no Israelite, unless he was a priest or Levite, could enter into the tabernacle, the very high priest only entering into the most sacred part once a year.

"And that burned with fire." Probably, "to a kindled fire," a

19 And the sound of a trumpet, and the voice of words;
which *voice* they that heard intreated that the
word should not be spoken to them any more:

20 (For they could not endure that which was
commanded, And if so much as a beast touch the
mountain, it shall be stoned, or thrust through
with a dart:

f Exod. xx. 19.
Deut. v. 5, 25.
& xviii. 16.

g Exod. xix. 13.

---

20. "Or thrust through with a dart." Omitted by א, A., C., D., K., L., M., P., and most Cursives; retained by only a few Cursives.

fire " was kindled at his presence." When St. John was permitted to see the majesty of God's presence it was not in a consuming fire. (Rev. iv. 2, 5.)

"Nor unto blackness, and darkness, and tempest." There was fire, and yet the mountain itself was shrouded by the smoke of it, betokening the obscurity of the dispensation in contrast with the clear light of that which succeeded it.

19. "And the sound of a trumpet, and the voice of words; which they that heard," &c. Thus Exodus xx. 19. "And they said unto Moses, Speak thou with us, and we will hear: but let not God speak with us, lest we die." How unspeakably different to the accents of Jesus. "All wondered at the gracious words which proceeded out of his mouth." "Never man spake like this man." "Thou hast the words of eternal life."

20. "For they could not endure that which was commanded." Was this because of the terrible sound of the voice, or was it because of the nature of the commands which God gave to them, which condemned them because there was no grace or assistance given to them, whereby they might fulfil the commandment? I think the former, because when God gave utterance to the ten words, then it was that the heads of the people came near, and desired that God would not speak personally to them any more, and that Moses should act as mediator between themselves and God. (Deut. v. 25, 27.)

"For they could not endure that which was commanded, and if so much as a beast," &c. These two clauses have been connected together in a singular way by many commentators, as if, when the command was given that any irrational creature which might

21 ʰ And so terrible was the sight, *that* Moses said, I exceedingly fear and quake:)
22 But ye are come ⁱ unto mount Sion, ᵏ and

ʰ Exod. xix. 16.
ⁱ Gal. iv. 26. Rev. iii. 12. & xxi. 2, 10.
ᵏ Phil. iii. 20.

accidentally touch the Mount should be put to death, the endurance of the Israelites reached its climax, and they could bear it no longer, and *then* asked that Moses should be constituted their mediator; but such an interpretation is altogether contrary to the whole of the narratives in Exodus or Deuteronomy.

According to Exodus xix. 10-13, the command that neither beast nor man should touch, was given to Moses in the usual way in which God held communication with him, and apparently it had no effect upon the children of Israel in the way of increasing their terror, but they received it, and acted upon it; whereas, when the Almighty gave utterance to the ten "words," *then* they could endure it no longer. In the narrative, as it is contained in Deuteronomy, there is not a syllable said respecting any setting of bounds round the Mount, but the fear manifested by the Israelites is altogether ascribed to their hearing the ten commandments. (Deut. v. 23-28.)

The incident of the setting bounds round the Mount, which neither man nor beast was to pass, was given to emphasize the unapproachableness of the presence of God under the Old Covenant, and with this a very large proportion of the Epistle is occupied.

21. "And so terrible was the sight, that Moses said, I exceedingly fear," &c. There is no mention of Moses saying this in so many words anywhere in the narratives of Exodus and Deuteronomy. The place which most nearly approaches to it is Deut. ix. 19. " For I was afraid of this anger and hot displeasure, wherewith the Lord was hot against you to destroy you." But this does not seem to have been said in view of the terrors of Mount Sinai. It is probable that it was in some traditional account which the writer knew and reproduced.

22. " But ye are come unto Mount Sion, and unto the city of the living God, the heavenly Jerusalem." No place in Holy Scripture that I know of requires more faith to apprehend its true significance than this, for it describes what we always account to be things future as if they were actually present, things heavenly as if they were on earth, things spiritual and invisible as if they were things

unto the city of the living God, the heavenly Jerusalem,

---

palpable, things at present infinitely above us as if they were now within our sphere.

And there can be no doubt but that this is the actual intention of the Apostolic writer in thus expressing himself. As literally and truly as the Israelites came to the mountain that might be touched, because they were so near to it, so he would desire to impress upon the Hebrew Christians that the Mount Sion was equally near to them, so that they should be *in* it through having *come* to it.

Two passages of Scripture may be cited to teach us the extreme nearness of the invisible to the visible world. The first, Revelation iv. 2-5, where the Apostle was bid to " go up," and immediately he was " in the Spirit," and " beheld a throne set in heaven, and one sat on the throne, and a rainbow round about it. According to this, to one who is in the Spirit there is no distance, almost one might say, no space. He was in Patmos, and in a moment he became in the Spirit, and the throne of God was before him. The second is in the Second Book of Kings (vi. 17), when the city in which Elisha was staying was encompassed by the hosts of Syria, and the servant of Elisha was in great fear, and the Lord at the prayer of Elisha opened his eyes, and he saw and beheld that the mountain was full of horses and chariots of fire round about Elisha. Now, if under the old dispensation the angels were so near, and in such multitudes, why not under the new?

There are a considerable number of places which are parallel to this, and serve to assert that the Church, or its members whilst on earth, are yet in heaven. Thus Phil. iii. 20: " Our citizenship is in heaven;" Ephes. ii. 19: " Ye are no more strangers and foreigners, but fellow-citizens with the saints .... in whom all the building groweth .... In whom ye also are builded together for an habitation of God." And 2 Corinth. vi. 16: " Ye are the temple of the living God, as God hath said, I will dwell in them and walk in them." So then it seems that there is no difference between the Church militant and the Church triumphant; and in one sense there is not. It is like as if there was a vast procession, some have already passed before the king, and some are wending their way in the footsteps of those who are gone before, but between those who have gone before and are safe and those who are now following

¹ and to an innumerable company of angels.   1 Deut. xxxiii
2. Ps. lxviii.
17. Ju[d]e 14.

them there is a break and a close scrutiny, and numbers are found wanting and are weeded out, and continue not in the body of those who are moving forward ; and yet, notwithstanding this, it is the same procession. Almighty God has pledged Himself that as sure as the first have passed into His presence so shall the last.

22. "But ye are come unto mount Sion, and unto the city of the living God, the heavenly Jerusalem." This is said to those who are losing their part in the earthly Jerusalem, or because the earthly Jerusalem itself is on the eve of destruction. "Care not for this," the Apostolic writer says, "ye have a better Sion, the heavenly Jerusalem from which the living God will never depart, for it is His city." "The Lord hath chosen Sion to be a habitation for Himself, for He hath longed for her. This shall be my rest for ever, here will I dwell, for I have a delight therein."

This mount Sion—this city of the living God—is in heaven and on earth. It is in heaven, for it is *above* (" Jerusalem which is above"), and yet it is on earth, for its functions of begetting children to God and bringing them up for him are exercised on earth, for St. Paul says, "Jerusalem which is above is free, which is the mother of us all." The Church, then, though on earth, is yet heavenly. It is the instrument of a birth from above ; it feeds men with the Flesh and Blood of Him Who is at the right hand of God. Its Head is in heaven, and yet His Life is in all its members.

"And to an innumerable company of angels." Angels, though they are the angels of heaven, have their principal employment upon earth. If each child of God has his guardian angel, their numbers must be great beyond expression. Their presence in Church assemblies, if realized, is assumed by St. Paul to necessitate reverence and submission and to rebuke forwardness (1 Cor. xi. 10). He assumes that the angels are spectators of the Christian conflict (1 Cor. iv. 9): "God hath set forth us the Apostles last, as it were appointed unto death : for we are made a spectacle unto the world, and to angels, and to men." He adjures Timothy to do everything impartially because of the presence of the angels : " I adjure thee before God, and the Lord Jesus Christ, and the elect angels "(1 Tim. v. 21). The angelic world was, then, to this Apostle

> ᵐ Exod. iv. 22. Jam. i. 18. Rev. xiv. 4.
> ⁿ Luke x. 20. Phil. iv. 3. Rev. xiii. 8.
> ‖ Or, *enrolled*.

23 To the general assembly and Church of ᵐ the firstborn, ⁿ which are ‖ written in heaven,

an intense reality. He never for a moment contemplated their sphere of action or duty as being confined to heaven: he rather looked upon them as being on earth, and so Christians had come to this world of angels, and were inexpressibly interested in their good offices.

23. "To the general assembly and Church of the firstborn, which are written." The word translated "general assembly" (πανηγύρει), signifies the assembly of a whole nation on some great national festival. It is taken very frequently with the former clause, "an innumerable company of angels," and is translated in the margin of the Revised, "and to innumerable hosts, the general assembly of angels."

"And Church of the firstborn." This has been explained as if there were an allusion to Esau who was the first-born, but threw away and despised his right. As if it were the Church of the first-born who hold to their right and will not barter it for all that earth can give.

"The firstborn which are written in heaven." Compare "rejoice because your names are written in heaven," Luke x. 20, and Rev. xxi. 27. "There shall in no wise enter into it anything that defileth, neither whatsoever worketh abomination, or maketh a lie, but they that are written in the Lamb's book of life."

It has been made a question whether this general assembly and Church of the first-born refers to the Church in Paradise, or on earth. It seems to us the latter, particularly from the expression, "which are written in heaven." Those who are actually there would not be said to have their names written there. On the other hand, all the other things here enumerated are unseen and are the objects of faith. Still the Mystical Body of Christ, though a visible body, has invisible grace and privileges. The inward grace or inward part of the Sacraments is as much invisible at the moment of reception as any thing in heaven; and yet it is not of earth but of heaven.

"And to God the Judge of all." How is it that a reference to God as judge comes in here? Mr. Blunt supposes that the idea is

and to God º the Judge of all, and to the spirits of just men ᵖ made perfect,

º Gen xviii. 25. Ps. xciv. 2.
ᵖ Phil. iii. 12. ch. xi. 40.

carried on from the mention of names written in heaven. "I saw the dead, small and great, stand before God, and the books were opened"—the books in which the names of all are written.

Delitzsch, however, takes it differently. "The mention of the *ecclesia militans* suggests the thought of her enemies and persecutors, who by allurements and threatenings would make her untrue to her faith, and of the just judge to whom she may confidently commit her cause."

Bishop Westcott translates it, "And to the God of all as judge."

"And to the spirits of just men made perfect." These are the disembodied spirits of the just who are awaiting the consummation when they shall no longer "be unclothed, but clothed upon" (2 Cor. v. 4).

If by having been brought into the Church of Christ we are brought not merely near, but *to* an innumerable company of angels, and "the spirits of just men made perfect," how do we realize and acknowledge this nearness? In the Prayer Book it is acknowledged, but not perhaps sufficiently. Taking up the language of the most ancient liturgies, we unite our voices with the heavenly host (with angels and archangels, and all the company of heaven), as if they and we formed one choir; and in the collect for St. Michael's Day we pray that the angels may succour and defend us on earth, and on the saints' days we pray to God and praise Him for the Apostles and others as if we were yet in their company; and in the prayer for the church militant we bless God's holy name for "all those departed this life in His faith and fear . . . that with them we may be partakers of His heavenly kingdom." But is this sufficient? We answer that it is little, if at all, short of the recognition of their presence and company in that earliest type of liturgy, the Clementine, and in those of St. Mark and St. James where they are not interpolated.[1]

---

[1] In the Canon of the Mass there is confession made to God, to the blessed Virgin, to blessed Michael the Archangel, to blessed John the Baptist, to the Holy Apostles Peter and Paul, &c.; but there is nothing like this in any ancient liturgy.

None of the non-Catholic bodies seem to have any perception of the nearness or minis

q ch. viii. 6. & ix. 15.
|| Or, testament.
r Exod. xxiv. 8. ch. x. 22. 1 Pet. i. 2.
s Gen. iv. 10. ch. xi. 4.

24 And to Jesus [q] the mediator of the new || covenant, and to [r] the blood of sprinkling, that speaketh better things [s] than *that of* Abel.

---

24. "Better things." Scarcely any authority for it; ℵ, A., C., D., K., L., M., P., most Cursives, read, "better."

24. "And to Jesus the mediator of the new covenant." Thanks be to God, all Christians acknowledge His nearness, and that they have been brought to Him, and come to Him, or to God through Him, and that constantly they come to Him in their approaches to God in private prayer, and in the Sacrament of His Body and Blood. But if they have in very deed come to Jesus, they have come to Him as the Head of His Church, and are bound to recognize that He is not alone, but that His Body in all its members is with Him. Some of these are in the unseen state, but they are as truly in Him now and have their life from Him as they did whilst living on earth; and though we do not know how He employs them in His service, yet we may be sure that employ them He does. SS. Peter and Paul cannot have been for eighteen hundred years merely reposing. He has work for them in their present condition, as much as when they were here in the flesh. Some of these members being militant here on earth are sick and suffering; some are persecuted, some are feeble and need strengthening; so that if we truly come to Him, we come to One in Whom as the Second Adam are all Christians, all those who have gone before and are safe in Him, and all those who are in various ways warring on His side, and are suffering with Him.

"And the blood of sprinkling, that speaketh better things than that of Abel." The Blood of Jesus is that which ratifieth the new covenant for all who believe in the efficacy of His Sacrifice. It is the Blood which answers to that with which the old covenant was inaugurated, and with which all the people were sprinkled. It is the Blood of the true Paschal Lamb which must be sprinkled, not on the door-posts but on the inmost heart. It speaketh better

---

trations of angels or spirits of the just, with one notable exception, that of the Swedenborgians; but with them it is mixed up with such absurdities and groundless speculations that their witness seems useless and incapable of making itself felt outside of themselves.

25 See that ye refuse not him that speaketh. For 'if they escaped not who refused him that spake on earth, much more *shall not* we *escape*, if we turn away from him that *speaketh* from heaven:

<sup>t</sup> ch. ii. 2, 3. & iii. 17. & x. 28, 29.

---

things than that of Abel, for the blood of Abel calls for vengeance, but the Blood of Jesus calls for mercy.[1]

25. "See that ye refuse not him that speaketh." Jesus speaks now as God did of old. The epistle begins with "Hath in these last days spoken to us by His Son." He speaks to us in His holy apostles in their writings, and He accompanies the spoken word, the word of preaching, with power: and He speaketh to us from heaven. The previous words (22-24) were written to assure them how near heaven was to them. And so Jesus through the voice of His ministers speaks to them from heaven.

"If they escaped not ... how much more shall not we escape?" The whole dispensation is heavenly. But if it be heavenly must it not constrain us? must it not, of necessity, change our wills so that we cannot help obeying? No, it is not so. It does not take away our free-will. As they turned away, as they turned a deaf ear, as they refused, so can we. We would fain put this from us,

---

[1] The following note is from Alford, following Bengel: "If Moses had blood wherewith to sprinkle the people, much more Jesus, of whom Moses was a shadow. And therefore the writer (of this Epistle), enumerating the great differences of our Sion from their Sinai, though he has not recounted their blood of sprinkling, as not being worthy of mention in the face of the terrors of God's law, mentions ours, by which we were redeemed unto God, and assigns it a place in the heavenly city next to, but separate from, Jesus Himself in His glorified state. If we come to inquire how this can be we enter on an interesting, but high and difficult subject, on which learned and holy men have been much divided. Our Lord's Blood was shed from Him on the cross. And as His Body did not see corruption, it is obvious to suppose that His Blood did not corrupt as that of ordinary men, being as it is so important a portion of the Body. Hence, and because His Resurrection Body seems to have been bloodless (see Luke xxiv. 39; John xx. 27), some have supposed that the Blood of the Lord remains, as it was poured out, incorruptible in the Presence of God. On such a matter I would neither affirm nor deny, but mention, with all reverence, that which seems to suit the requirements of the words before us. By that Blood we live wherever it is; but as here it is mentioned separately from the Lord Himself, as an item in the glories of the heavenly city and as yet speaking, it seems to require some such view to account for the words used." Bengel has here a long excursus on the point in which he takes strongly the above view. He quotes amongst others some remarkable passages from Calvin on the Hebrews (both on xii. 24 and xiii. 12). 'Thus Christ carried His own Blood into the heavenly Sanctuary, to make atonement for the sins of the world.'"

26 <sup>u</sup> Whose voice then shook the earth: but now he hath promised, saying, <sup>x</sup> Yet once more I shake not the earth only, but also heaven. 27 And this *word*, Yet once more, signifieth <sup>y</sup> the removing of those things that ‖ are shaken,

<sup>u</sup> Exod. xix. 18.
<sup>x</sup> Hag. ii. 6.
<sup>y</sup> Ps. cii. 26. Matt. xxiv. 35. 2 Pet. iii. 10. Rev. xxi. 1.
‖ Or, *may be shaken.*

---

26. " I shake." So D., K., L., P., most Cursives; but ℵ, A., C., M., a few Cursives, Vulg., Syriac, Sah., Copt., Æth., read, " I will shake."

but we cannot. And it is not an equal case. It is a case of " much more." " If they escaped not ... how much more shall we not escape."

26. " Whose voice then shook the earth: but now he hath promised, saying." It is said of Mount Sinai (Exod. xix. 18), " And Mount Sinai was altogether on a smoke, the smoke thereof ascended as the smoke of a furnace, and the whole mount quaked greatly."

" But now he hath promised, saying, Yet once more I shake." This is a prophecy out of Haggai, but in the pages of that prophet it seems to refer only to the first Advent, when the desire of all nations shall come. And God, in preparation for it, had marvellously shaken the kingdoms of the world. " The Persian Empire fell before Alexander's. Alexander's Empire was ended by his sudden death in youth ; of his four successors two only continued, and they, too, fell before the Romans. Then came the Roman civil wars, and so the way of the Gospel of Christ was prepared by the whole world being under the sway of one monarch." (Pusey.)

And yet, whatever preludes of fulfilment there were at our Lord's first coming, they were as nothing to the fulfilment which we look for in the second, when " the earth shall be utterly broken down, the earth shall be clean dissolved, the earth moved exceedingly, the earth shall reel to and fro like a drunkard, it shall fall and not rise again " (Isaiah xxiv. 19, 20). Whereon follows an announcement of the final judgment of men and angels, and the everlasting kingdom of the blessed in the presence of God. (Pusey on Haggai ii. 6, 7.)

27. " And this word, Yet once more, signifieth the removing," &c. Does the Apostolic writer here allude to the shaking of the whole heaven and earth, that the new heaven and new earth may

as of things that are made, that those things which cannot be shaken may remain.

28 Wherefore we receiving a kingdom which cannot be moved, ‖ let us have grace, whereby we may serve God accceptably with reverence and godly fear :

‖ Or, *let us hold fast.*

---

28. "With reverence and godly fear." So K., L., most Cursives; but ℵ, A., C., D., a few Cursives (17, 71, 73, 80, 137), Syriac, read, "with reverence and awe" (εὐλαβείας καὶ δέους). Revisers.

---

be revealed, or does he refer to the removal of the old dispensation, that the new may take its place? Probably the latter, because he proceeds to say, "wherefore we receiving a kingdom which cannot be moved." The things of the old state were "made," they were "of this building," whereas the things of the new state are "not of this building."

"That those things which cannot be shaken," *i.e.*, which are not made with hands, which cannot, like the things which they supersede, "grow old, and be ready to vanish away."

28. "Wherefore we receiving a kingdom which cannot be moved, (or shaken)." It is immovable, because it is the everlasting kingdom of our Lord and Saviour, Jesus Christ.

"Let us have grace, whereby we may serve God acceptably with reverence," &c. This may be translated either "Let us hold fast grace," in which it implies, let us persevere in the grace of God ("but hold fast that which thou hast," is κράτει ὃ ἔχεις); or, as in our translation, it may mean simply, "let us have (*i.e.*, procure) grace," that is, by diligently seeking it and praying for it; or it may mean "let us have thankfulness," "let us be thankful. So Chrysostom, "Let us give thanks to God. For we ought not only not to be vexed and desponding on account of our present condition, but even to feel very great gratitude to Him on account of the things to come."

"Let us have grace," seems more in accordance with "whereby we may serve God acceptably." But Bishop Westcott remarks well, "It is the perception and acknowledgement of the Divine glory which is the strength of man. If God sees a man thankful He will give him more grace."

29. "For our God is a consuming fire." He is a consuming fire

*Exod. xxiv.
17. Deut. iv.
24. & ix. 3.
Ps. l. 3, &
xcvii. 3. Is.
lxvi. 15. 2
Thess. i. 8,
ch. x. 27.

29 For ᶻ our God *is* a consuming fire.

in two ways. He consumes His enemies (2 Thess. i. 8), and He consumes that in us which is inimical to Himself. He consumes the dross as he separates it from the precious metal.

## CHAP. XIII.

ᵃ Rom. xii. 10.
1 Thess. iv. 9.
1 Pet. i. 22.
& ii. 17. & iii.
8. & iv. 8. 2
Pet. i. 7. 1
John iii. 11,
&c. & iv. 7,
20, 21.

ᵇ Matt. xxv.
35. Rom. xii.
13. 1 Tim.
iii 2. 1 Pet.
iv. 9.
ᶜ Gen. xviii.
3. & xix. 2.

LET ᵃ brotherly love continue. 2 ᵇ Be not forgetful to entertain strangers: for thereby ᶜ some have entertained angels unawares.

1. "Let brotherly love continue." They were brethren, as begotten of the same Father, and having the same mother. ("Jerusalem, which is above, is free, which is the mother of us all.")

Because the writer uses the word "continue," some suppose that there had been a temporary cessation or interruption of Christian fellowship. St. Paul commends this philadelphia under the figure of the sympathy of the members of the same mystical body one to another. (1 Cor. xii.)

2. "Be not forgetful to entertain strangers: for some," &c. Thus Abraham entertained angels, supposing, no doubt, at first, that they were only his fellow men. (Gen. xviii. 1-10.) It is true that it is said that he bowed himself toward the ground, but this might be because of the extraordinary majesty of the one to whom he spoke as Lord. Lot also entertained two of these angels, not knowing who they were (Gen. xix. 1-23), and also Manoah, in Judges xiii. 1-5. Chrysostom remarks: See how he enjoins them to preserve what they had: he does not add other things thereto. He did not say 'Be loving as brethren,' but 'Let brotherly love continue.' And again, he did not say, 'Be hospitable,' as though

3 ᵈ Remember them that are in bonds, as bound with them; and them which suffer adversity, as being yourselves also in the body.

4 Marriage *is* honourable in all, and the bed undefiled: ᵉ but whoremongers and adulterers God will judge.

5 *Let your* conversation *be* without covetousness;

ᵈ Matt. xxv. 36. Rom. xii. 15. 1 Cor. xii. 26. Col. iv. 18. 1 Pet. iii. 8.
ᵉ 1 Cor. vi. 9. Gal. v. 19, 21. Ephes. v. 5. Col. iii. 5, 6. Rev. xxii. 15.

---

they were not so, but 'Be not forgetful of hospitality,' for this was likely owing to their afflictions."

3. "Remember them that are in bonds, as bound with them; and them which suffer," &c. "Remember," in your prayers, and in your distributions to the needy; them that are in bonds, as bound with them, not merely as if *you were* bound with them (this, though true, is much too cold), but as being one with them, according to the words of the Apostle: "If one member suffer all the members suffer with it."

"As being yourselves also in the body." If you are yet in the natural body, as you are, you are liable at any time to suffer the same adversities, hunger, thirst, cold, penury, disease, pain, accidents, as those are subject to who are in the body.

4. "Marriage is honourable in all, and the bed undefiled." The Greek is very condensed, for there is no substantive verb (ἐστί or ἔστω). Marriage is honourable in all men, or in all respects (ἐν πᾶσι may be rendered in either way); or it may be "Let marriage be (ἔστω) honourable (or had in honour, or respected), in all things."

"And the bed is (or let the bed be) undefiled."

"But whoremongers and adulterers God will judge." Thus St. Paul heads his list of the sins of the flesh with "adultery, fornication, uncleanness, lasciviousness," and then he says, "They which do such things shall not inherit the kingdom of God" (Gal. v. 19, 21). Fornicators are not commonly judged or punished by human tribunals, and very frequently not even adulterers, and on this account it is the more necessary to assert that such will not escape the judgment of God.

5. "Let your conversation be without covetousness; and be content," &c. "Conversation" (τρόπος) has been translated "Let your character be free from the love of money" (Westcott). Or

and *be* content with such things as ye have: for he hath said, ⁵ I will never leave thee, nor forsake thee.

6 So that we may boldly say, ʰ The Lord *is* my helper, and I will not fear what man shall do unto me.

7 ¹Remember them which ‖ have the rule over

---

*ᶠ Matt. vi. 25, 34. Phil. iv. 11, 12. 1 Tim. vi. 6, 8.*
*ᵍ Gen. xxviii. 15. Deut. xxxi. 6, ˙. Josh. i. 5. 1 Chron. xxviii. 20. Ps. xxxvii. 25.*
*ʰ Ps. xxvii. 1. & lvi. 4, 11, 12. & cxviii. 6.*
*ⁱ ver. 17.*
*‖ Or, are the guides.*

6. Revisers translate, " The Lord is my helper. I will not fear: what shall man do unto me?"

simply, " Be ye free from the love of money" (Revisers). The Vulgate, " Sint mores sine avaritia."

" Let it (your conversation) shew forth the philosophical character of your mind. And it will shew it if we do not seek superfluities, if we keep only to what is necessary." (Chrysostom.)

"And be content with such things as ye have: for he hath said, I will never leave thee, nor forsake thee." These words may be a reminiscence of God's words to Jacob in Gen. xxviii. 15, " I will not leave thee until I have done that which I have spoken to thee of," or to Joshua (i. 5), " As I was with Moses, so I will be with thee; I will not fail thee nor forsake thee."

6. " So that we may boldly say, The Lord is my helper, and I will not fear," &c. They can say this who are perfectly contented with what God has allotted to them. The quotation is taken from Ps. cxviii. " The Lord is on my side, I will not fear what man can do unto me." They whose minds are full of covetous desires fear man, because he can hinder them so much in their prospects of gaining wealth or advancement. They who are contented, and leave all to God, have no fear of the world. They have a friend upon whom they cast all their care, knowing that He careth for them. (1 Pet. v. 7.)

7. " Remember them which have the rule over you, who have spoken," &c. This seems to be spoken of the leaders or rulers which have passed away, as verse 17, " Obey them which have the rule over you," is spoken of those then living.

" They which have the rule over you" seems to refer to the leaders in their capacity as guides rather than of rulers, though it includes the latter. As referring to their former rulers or guides,

you, who have spoken unto you the word of God: ᵏ whose faith follow, considering the end of *their* con- ᵏ ch. vi. 12.
versation.

8 Jesus Christ ¹ the same yesterday, and to day, and for ever. ¹ John viii. 58. ch. i. 12. Rev. i. 4.

---

it brings to memory some very illustrious names, St. Stephen, St. James the son of Zebedee, St. James, their first Bishop.

"Who have spoken unto you the word of God." These are those by whom "the word was confirmed unto us by them that heard Him."

"Whose faith follow, considering the end of their conversation." The end of their conversation would be the end of their lives, and in the case of the three great saints before alluded to, that would be by martyrdom. No stronger argument could be presented to those Hebrew Christians who were in danger of falling away from the faith through persecution. This clause is translated by the Revisers, "And considering the issue of their life imitate their faith." They died the most glorious of deaths, but this death was the fruit, the issue of their faith. "If you then, in the providence of God, would win a crown like theirs, imitate their faith."

8. "Jesus Christ, the same yesterday, and to-day, and for ever." The attribute of unchangeableness here attributed to the Lord Jesus could not be ascribed to Him if He were a mere creature, for Jehovah says of Himself, "I am the Lord, I change not, therefore ye sons of Jacob are not consumed" (Mal. iii. 6). The unchangeableness of our Lord rests upon His Divine Nature, but it is more than doubtful whether His Divine Nature is here specifically before the mind of the Apostolic writer. Rather I should say His human Nature in conjunction with His Divine. What we Christians have to realize is that He is the same now as in the days of His flesh. The two prominent features of His existence upon earth are His willingness to receive all, and His willingness to help all.

His willingness to receive all, no matter how they had sinned; He was willing to receive the extortionate, dishonest, disreputable publicans, and the sinners of the city. He says, "I am not come to call the righteous but sinners to repentance." "The Son of man is come to seek and to save that which was lost." His willingness to help all, He went about healing all manner of

9 ᵐ Be not carried about with divers and strange doctrines. For *it is* a good thing that the heart be established with grace; ⁿ not with meats, which have not profited them that have been occupied therein.

ᵐ Ephes. iv. 14. & v. 6. Col. ii. 4, 8. 1 John iv. 1.
ⁿ Rom. xiv. 17. Col. ii. 16. 1 Tim. iv. 3.

---

9. "Be not carried about" (περιφέρεσθε). So K., L.; but ℵ, A., C., D., M., P., most Cursives, d, f, Vulg., Syriac, read, "be not carried away" (παραφέρεσθε).

sickness and all manner of disease. He broke off in the middle of a sermon, when crowds were hanging on His lips, that He might heal a paralytic. When enduring the unutterable agonies of the cross He prayed for His murderers, He absolved the penitent thief, He committed His mother to St. John.

What He was yesterday, now He is to-day, willing to receive all who come to Him, never casting out one who implores His help, and so He will be for ever. Nothing can in the least degree alter His love to man, or His power to help His people.

9. "Be not carried about with divers and strange doctrines. For it is a good thing that the heart be established with grace . . . not with meats," &c. These "divers and strange doctrines" are opposed to the fixedness and truth of Christ. If He is the same yesterday, to-day, and for ever, His doctrine must be the same, for it depends upon the sameness of His Person: the mode of access through Him to the Father must be the same, His Sacraments, the pledges of His love must be the same. He is now and always the ever-abiding Priest and Victim, the never-failing Intercessor, the Living Bread. His Flesh now and ever is meat indeed.

"It is a good thing that the heart be established with grace; not with meats." What were these meats? They have been explained in two ways:

(1st) As meaning sacrificial meats, the feasting on sacrifices, as the Passover and the peace offerings.

(2nd) As alluding to abstinence from some meats which were allowed by the law. Thus Delitzsch, "We know that Jewish asceticism in the Apostolic age dealt largely in precepts and injunctions concerning the use of, and abstinence from, various kinds of food, but not in those concerning sacrificial feasts. The stricter Judaizing Christians in the Roman Church were, we know, scrupulous as distinguishing between clean and unclean in the

10 º We have an altar, whereof they have no right to eat which serve the tabernacle.  º 1 Cor. ix. 13. & x. 13.

---

matter of food; such scrupulosity the Apostle regarded at the time as a pardonable weakness, which those stronger in the faith were to bear with. Upon the whole it seems likely the Apostle here alludes to the partaking of the creatures slain in sacrifice (for it was God's command that these, or portions of them, should be eaten). Whether the mere carnal Jews eat or abstained it was alike unprofitable, because alike unspiritual.

"Which have not profited them that have been occupied therein." Because the eating was merely outward, satisfying the flesh, and the food they eat having no inward part; and the abstinence was mere will worship, performed besides the commandment of God.

10. "We have an altar, whereof they have no right to eat which serve the tabernacle." The connection between this and the preceding verse seems to be something of this sort. He had asserted that "the heart should be established by grace, not with meats," and then it seems to cross His mind that there was an eating which by God's promise was accompanied with grace: the eating of the elements ordained by Christ as a means whereby He should dwell in us and we in Him. It seems difficult to understand how this place could have ever been understood otherwise than as referring to the Eucharistic altar or table. The Sacrifice of Christ, if it was analogous to the Jewish sacrifices, required to be partaken of by the Victim being eaten. The ancient sacrifices had four parts, (1) the offering by the offerer; (2) the killing or mactation; (3) the presenting of the blood, (4) and the consumption. The creature was presented at the door of the tabernacle. It was slain close to the door, its blood was presented by being sprinkled at the bottom of the altar, and its body was consumed from the altar—a part being burnt up to God—a part being consumed in most sacrifices by the worshippers. So that in no case was the altar an instrument of the slaughter or mactation. It was the means of feasting —of partaking of or feasting upon the sacrifice, and so the terms altar and table were interchangeable. Thus Ezekiel xliv. 16, "They shall come near to my table to minister unto me." And Malachi i. 7, "Ye have offered polluted bread upon mine altar," "ye say the table of the Lord is contemptible."

Now, in this sense, the Lord's table of the Christian Church is strictly an altar.[1] It is that from which the Body of the Divine Victim is taken to be partaken of. If the altar was the thing upon which the ancient sacrifice was slain, then there could be nothing which could correspond to an altar in the Christian Church, but if the altar be that from which the victim is consumed, then there must be one, for the Lord ordained the memorial of His Sacrifice in sacrificial terms. He said, "this is my body which is given for you," and (of course) given in sacrifice. He said, "Do this" (τοῦτο ποιεῖτε) using the word always used in ordaining the offering of sacrifices. He used the sacrificial word ἀνάμνησις. He ordained the whole at the Paschal time, seeing that He was the true Paschal Lamb.

We thus have an altar from which we partake of the Lamb of God.[2]

---

[1] Bishop Wordsworth has a very good note on the significance of the word altar. He quotes some very apposite passages in favour of taking the word altar as indicating the Church's Lord's Table from Hooker, Bishop Andrews, Barrow, and Waterland; but, above all, from the Puritan Richard Baxter. I give two passages from the latter: "The naming of the table as an altar, as related to this representative sacrifice, is no more improper than the other." Again: "'We have an altar whereof they have no right to eat,' seems plainly to mean the Sacramental Communion."

[2] May I be permitted to reproduce a passage from my work entitled, "The One Offering," page 38, a. "If we examine the context of these words, 'We have an altar,' we shall see that the only interpretation which makes a tolerable sense is that which refers them to eating from the Eucharistic table.

"In verse 8 the writer warns the Hebrew Christians against diverse and strange doctrines, and it is evident from the next clause, 'it is a good thing that the heart be established with grace, not with meats, which have not profited them that have been occupied therein,' that these doctrines are doctrines respecting distinction of meats which before (in ix. 10) he had shown to be profitless. Thus he lays down that grace, and not meats, establishes the heart and is profitable. But here the Apostolic writer recollects that Christians have a meat which Christ Himself commanded them to eat, a meat which, if received in faith, establishes the heart; and, moreover, being a feeding on Christ the One Sacrifice, is sacrificial, and is only likely to be connected with, or taken from, an altar. It is a meat also of which a server of any other religion has no right to eat; for if not a follower of Christ, he profanes it.

"This meat being, as regards its outward visible sign, material food, must be eaten from a table, which table has been, from the very first, called an altar, and the thing performed on it a Sacrifice, and the Food taken from it the Body of the only real and all-atoning Sacrificial Victim.

"Now what was the function or use of an altar? An altar was not a thing on which animals were slain in sacrifice, but a thing from which their flesh was eaten. No animal was ever slain upon the Jewish altars. How could a bullock be driven up a high flight of steps to the top of an erection covered with a brass grating, there to be killed in the midst of the roaring and crackling of the flames of the portions of perhaps twenty others? No, the altar was the Lord's Table, so an altar is called in Ezekiel xli. 22, and in Malachi i. 7, 12; and so the altars of false gods are called in 1 Cor. x. 20, 21. After the killing

And this is, if possible, rendered still more certain by the words which follow :—

"Whereof they have no right to eat, which serve the tabernacle." If the only eating be spiritual eating, eating by an internal act of faith in Christ, and nothing else ; then all have a right to eat who are able to realize the all-sufficient Atonement. If God works in any one faith in His Son's Sacrifice, then *ipso facto* the man eats of it in the sense of applying it to himself.

But if there be an eating with the mouth as well as with the heart, if the Lord meant us to eat when He said "Take, eat," if there be an outward part as well as an Inward, then they only can lawfully eat who accept the Sacrifice of Christ to the exclusion of all other.

This seems to show that this altar cannot well be the Cross, for the sacrifice on the Cross must be partaken of spiritually to some extent, before we can partake legitimately of the Euchaiist

"Whereof they have no right to eat who serve the tabernacle."

---

of the victim, and after the sprinkling of its blood, and the preparation of the carcase as for a feast, the part which, by the law of the particular sacrifice, was to be burnt up to God was taken to the top of the altar, and there consumed by fire as the portion of God, and the remainder, which was in some cases assigned to the priests—in some cases to the people or offerers as their portion, was feasted upon by the worshippers as food given them from the Lord's table.

"So that the idea of an altar was not that of an instrument of death, but a table on which consecrated food was laid, and from which it was eaten. Christians, in contrast to Jews, have meat which, if devoutly received, establishes and profits; and their's is also from an altar, but an altar from which unbelieving Jews cannot eat. The words, 'they which serve the tabernacle can (*quoad* the Lord's table) only be unbelieving Jews ;' for if any 'server' of the Jewish altar or tabernacle, before the total abolition of the Jewish state of things, turned to Christ, which vast numbers did (Acts vi. 7), he would have a right to eat of Christ's altar-table.

"The reason given for the exclusion of unbelieving Jews meant something of this sort. We Christians are privileged to eat the flesh of our sin-offering, for we eat of the flesh of One Whose Blood was sprinkled not in any earthly Holy of Holies, but in the heavenly One—in the presence of God Himself. Now in the case of that Jewish type, which corresponded to this, *i.e.* the victim slain on the great day of Atonement—not even the High Priest himself was permitted to partake (Levit. xvi. 27); it was burnt without the camp, as an accursed thing on which the sin of Israel rested.

"These expiatory victims were figures of Christ dying as the propitiation of our sins ; hence Jesus Christ, that He might fulfil this figure or type, suffered without the gate of the city of Jerusalem. As, therefore, those under the law were not permitted to eat of the figure, so it was not lawful for them to eat of the Antitype or the thing figured, so long, that is, as they continued only under the Law, and had not accepted the Gospel."

It is incumbent then upon those Hebrews who desired to be partakers of the Christian Sacrifice to go forth out of the camp of the Synagogue, or Old Testament, and enter into the camp of the New, and so to bear the reproach of Christ.

11 For ᵖ the bodies of those beasts, whose blood is brought into the sanctuary by the high priest for sin, are burned without the camp.

12 Wherefore Jesus also, that he might sanctify the people with his own blood, ᑫ suffered without the gate.

13 Let us go forth therefore unto him without the camp, bearing ʳ his reproach.

<small>p Ex. xxix. 14. Lev. iv. 11, 12, 21. & vi. 30. & ix. 11. & xvi. 27. Numb. xix. 3.
q John xix. 17, 18. Acts vii. 58.
r ch. xi. 26. 1 Pet. iv. 14.</small>

---

11. "For the bodies of those beasts whose blood is brought into the sanctuary," &c. This means the Jewish Priests; even the High Priest was not permitted to eat of the most important sin-offering of the Jewish year. After he had taken the blood of his sin-offering into the Holy of Holies, he did not return to partake of the flesh of the victim as in the case of other sacrifices, but the body or carcase of the sin-offering was burnt without the camp, not having been tasted even by the priest. Now this might be taken as an adumbration or illustration of the fact that no one who served the tabernacle merely, no matter in what capacity, either as priest or worshipper, could partake of the all-sufficient Sin-offering. To do this he must go forth from the tabernacle, and from the camp of the fleshly Israel, and go forth, as it were, to Calvary. For God had fulfilled the type of the sin-offering, by not suffering His Son to be crucified or immolated in the city, but without the city on mount Calvary.

12. "Wherefore Jesus also, that he might sanctify the people . . . without the gate." Wherefore Jesus in order that He might fulfil the type or prefigurement ordained by God, and so sanctify the people (not merely the one nation of Israel, but all the people of God scattered abroad) with His own Blood which He Himself took into the heavenly Holy of Holies

"Suffered without the camp." He suffered without the walls of Jerusalem, the city of the great King, in a polluted place; the place of a skull, where notorious criminals were executed.

13. "Let us go forth therefore unto him without the camp, bearing his reproach." This addressed to the Hebrew Christians means, "Let us profess the faith of Christ in the face of our unbelieving countrymen, though it may entail upon us reproach, persecution, and death.

14 ᵗ For here have we no continuing city, but we seek one to come.
15 ᶠ By him therefore let us offer ᵘ the sacrifice

<small>ᵗ Mic. ii. 10.
Phil. iii. 20.
ch. xi. 10, 16.
& xii. 22.
ᶠ Eph. v. 20.
1 Pet. ii. 5.
ᵘ Lev. vii. 12.
Ps. l. 14, 23.
& lxix. 30, 31.
& cvii. 22.
& cxvi. 17.</small>

14. "We seek one to come;" rather, "the one which is to come."
15. "By him therefore." "Therefore" (οὖν), omitted by א, D., P., Syr.; retained by A., C., M., nearly all Cursives, f, Vulg., Cop., Arm., Æth.

But a further question arises, "Does the Apostolic writer mean that those Christian Jews who had hitherto continued the use of the Sacrifice and Ritual of the Law were no longer to do so? Very probably. It is evident that the rites of Judaism could not long continue to be observed in the Christian Church, and the time of the final rupture was perhaps fast approaching.

14. "For here we have no continuing city, but we seek one to come." This seems as if it were said in prophetic view of the swift approaching destruction of the earthly Sion. We are told by Eusebius that the whole body of the Church at Jerusalem, having been commanded by a Divine Revelation given to men of approved piety there, removed from the city before the war, and dwelt in a certain town beyond the Jordan called Pella.

This is true of all dwellers in earthly habitations who know their high calling of God. Our habitations may continue for a short time when we have passed away, but we shall no longer want them, because we are sealed for a mansion in the eternal, immovable, indestructible city, "The city which hath the foundations, whose builder and maker is God."

15. "By him therefore let us offer the sacrifice of praise to God," &c. "By him," that is, by or through the mediation of our Great High Priest.

"Therefore," is doubtful as to its retention. If it is read here it must carry us back, not to the last verse, but to verse 10, "We have an altar," and 12, "Wherefore Jesus, that he might sanctify," &c.

"Let us offer the sacrifice of praise to God continually, that is, the fruit of our lips," &c. The sacrifice of praise seems to refer to Levit. vii. 12, where the thank-offering is distinguished from the peace-offering by the addition of more bread-offerings. "If he offer it for a thanksgiving, then he shall offer with the sacrifice of thanksgiving unleavened cakes mingled with oil, and unleavened

of praise to God continually, that is, *the fruit of *our* lips † giving thanks to his name.

16 ʸ But to do good and to communicate forget

* Hos. xiv. 2.
† Gr. *confessing to.*
ʸ Ro. xii. 13.

wafers anointed with oil, and cakes mingled with oil of pure flour fried. Besides the cakes he shall offer for his offering leavened bread," &c.

This was the Jewish sacrifice of praise or thank-offering. But our thank or praise offering is said to be "the fruit of our lips giving thanks unto his Name." Does this exclude or set aside the Eucharist? On the contrary, it describes it as compared with the Jewish thank-offering. In the accounts of the Jewish thank or praise offering there is not a syllable said of any verbal acts of praise. There may have been such in later times, but there is not the slightest allusion to them in the Law; whereas the Eucharistic service of the Gospel in its earliest forms which have come down to us is mainly an act of praise and thanksgiving. In the earliest type—that represented in the Clementine—there is a long act of praise which begins with the acknowledgment of the attributes of God Himself, then recounts His works in creation—the earth, the ocean, the plants, the animals, and then man; then it recounts His providences, as regards the human race, from the fall to the act of Redemption itself. And then in the commencement of the consecration prayer it has, "Calling, therefore, to remembrance those things which He endured for our sakes we give thanks to Thee, O Almighty God, not as we ought, but as we are able, and fulfil His institution. For on the same night in which He was betrayed, taking bread," &c. Then follows the words of Institution, and afterwards, "We offer to Thee, our King and our God, according to His institution, this bread and this cup, giving thanks to Thee through Him."

Such is the Christian Eucharist, a sacrifice of praise and thanksgiving offered up in the closest connection with the all-prevailing Sacrifice of the Great High Priest, and distinguished from the Jewish in that it is not the offering of flocks and herds, or the fruit of the ground, but "the calves of our lips" (Hosea xiv. 2).

16. "But to do good and to communicate forget not: for with such," &c. "To do good," that is, by rendering all needful assistance to those requiring it.

not: for ᵉ with such sacrifices God is well pleased.

17 ᵃ Obey them that ‖ have the rule over you, and submit yourselves: for ᵇ they watch for your souls, as they that must give account, that they may do it with joy, and not with grief: for that *is* unprofitable for you.

ᵉ 2 Cor. ix. 12. Phil. iv. 18.
ch. vi. 10.
ᵃ Phil. ii. 29. 1 Thes. v. 12. 1 Tim. v. 17. ver. 7.
‖ Or, *guide.*
ᵇ Eze. iii. 17. & xxxiii. 2, 7. Acts xx. 26, 28.

---

"And to communicate," that is, by giving liberally of our substance to those in need.

"Forget not." It is one of the first duties of Christianity. Judged by the Lord's own account of what will take place at the judgment of the great day, it is the first: "I was an hungred and ye gave me meat, .... naked and ye clothed me, sick and ye visited me."

"With such sacrifices God is well pleased." This seems as if Eucharistic offerings were here in the writer's mind, as in 1 Cor. xvi. 2, where St. Paul orders that the alms for the distress in Judæa should be collected on the first day of the week—the day of the weekly celebration.

17. "Obey them that have the rule over you, and submit yourselves," &c. Similarly St. Paul to the Thessalonians (v. 12, 13): "Know them that are over you, .... esteem them very highly in love for their work's sake."

All the exhortations concerning the government of the Church are of this sort. The members of the Church are never exhorted to assert their Christian liberty as against those over them, nor to watch with jealousy against any encroachments of ecclesiastical power—but rather to submit themselves and obey.

And yet, as Delitzsch says, by his exhortations to the members of the Church in the first place, the author warns also the rulers of the same, although only indirectly and in the most delicate manner, of the heavy responsibility resting on them; for the words, "they sleeplessly watch over your souls," is not merely a statement of fact, but is also an enunciation of the obligation involved in their office. They, whose office brings this with it as a duty and a right, watch over the salvation of your souls without allowing any intermission through the sleep of indolence and false security, as those that shall give account when the Chief Shepherd shall appear.

c Ro. xv. 30. Eph. vi. 19. Col. iv. 3. 1 Thess. v. 25. 2 Thess. iii. 1.
d Acts xxiii. 1. & xxiv. 16. 2 Cor. i. 12.
e Philem. 22.

18 [c] Pray for us: for we trust we have [d] a good conscience, in all things willing to live honestly.

19 But I beseech *you* [e] the rather to do this, that I may be restored to you the sooner.

---

18. "We trust" (πεποίθαμεν). So K. and most Cursives, also Vulg. confirms; but (א) A., C., D., M., P., 17, 67**, 137, read, πειθόμεθα, "we are persuaded."

And Chrysostom: "Let those who rule also hear, and not only those who are under their rule; that just as the subjects ought to be obediently disposed, so ought the rulers also to be sober and watchful. What sayest thou? He (the ruler) watches; he imperils his own head. [The heads of the Church were always the first to suffer in a persecution.] He is subject to the punishments of thy sin, and for thy sake is amenable to what is so fearful, and art thou slothful, and affectedly indifferent and at ease?"

18. Pray for us: for we trust we have a good conscience, in all things," &c. No one can ask the prayers of another who is not sincerely desirous of living up to his profession. No one who is harbouring wilful, secret sin, or walking disorderly, can ask for the prayers of a Christian except he be an hypocrite.

"Willing" is too weak a word. It rather signifies desirous, bent upon living the true Christian life.

19. "But I beseech you rather to do this, that I may be restored to you the sooner." This is very like the language of St. Paul to Philemon (verse 22): "I trust that through your prayers I shall be given unto you." But the more the matter is examined the more it seems to leave the mystery of the authorship unsolved.

Supposing the letter is St. Paul's, it could not have well been written till after the first imprisonment in Rome; but after that time he never visited Judæa, nor does he appear to have ever had it in his mind so to do. And yet, as I show in the Introduction, the reasons seem overwhelming against this Epistle having been written to any Hebrew Church out of Palestine, for there is not the smallest allusion to any mixture of Gentiles in the Church, as there must have been if it had been written, as some suppose, to any Church of Jews in Asia Minor.

"That I may be restored to you the sooner," implies that he must have had some sort of permanent relations with them, which St. Paul never had with any purely Jewish Church.

20 Now ᶠthe God of peace, ᵍthat brought again from the dead our Lord Jesus, ʰthat great shepherd of the sheep, ⁱthrough the blood of the everlasting ‖ covenant,

21 ᵏMake you perfect in every good work to do

---

21. "In every good work." "Work" (ἔργῳ), omitted by ℵ, D., d, f, Vulg.; retained by C., K., M., P., most Cursives, Syr., Arm., Æth.

ᶠ Ro. xv. 33.
1 Thes. v. 23.
ᵍ Acts ii. 24,
32. Rom. iv.
24. & viii. 11.
1 Cor. vi. 14.
& xv. 15. 2
Cor. iv. 14.
Gal. i. 1. Col.
ii. 12. 1 Thes.
i. 10. 1 Pet.
i. 21.
ʰ Is. xl. 11.
Eze. xxxiv. 23.
& xxxvii. 24.
John x. 11, 14.
1 Pet. ii. 25.
& v. 4.
ⁱ Zech. ix. 11.
ch. x. 29.
‖ Or, *testament*.
ᵏ 2 Thes. ii.
17. 1 Pet. v.
10.

20, 21. "Now the God of peace, that brought again from the dead .... make you perfect," &c. This is the benedictory conclusion of the Epistle, as in 1 Pet. v. 10: "But the God of all grace, who hath called us," &c., and in Rom. xvi. 25, "Now to him that is of power to establish you according to my Gospel," &c. This conclusion is a prayer of benediction, and it is throughout an expansion of the name of God as the "God of peace."

God is the God of peace, and so He brought from the dead the Lord Jesus in token that He and His creatures, so far as He was concerned, were by the Death of Christ brought into a state of reconciliation.

The Lord is called "the great shepherd of the sheep." He was brought from the dead to be the Shepherd of the flock of God. Of all the things which were committed into His hands by the Father, the Church, which He had redeemed was the most precious, and so the name of Shepherd is given to Him above all others. The God of peace carries out His work of making peace through Him as a Priest—but as a Priest in the character of Shepherd or Pastor. Pastoral guidance underlies all the priestly functions.

"Through the blood of the everlasting covenant." The whole epistle is upon a covenant—the new covenant—the covenant sealed by blood, by the Blood, not of calves or goats, but by the Blood of the Son of God, Who took our nature of flesh and blood that He might shed His Blood to be the ratification of a new and eternal covenant.

21. "Make you perfect in every good work to do His Will." Make you perfect is καταρτίζειν, to join or fit together, and in the New Testament is first used of fishermen mending their nets, which they would do by joining together the strings which com-

his will, ||¹ working in you that which is wellpleasing in his sight, through Jesus Christ; ᵐ to whom *be* glory for ever and ever. Amen.

22 And I beseech you, brethren, suffer the word of exhortation: for ⁿ I have written a letter unto you in few words.

¶ Or, *doing.*
¹ Phil. ii. 13.
ᵐ Gal. i. 5.
² Tim. iv. 18.
Rev. i. 6.
ⁿ 1 Pet. v. 12.

"In you." So A., C., P., most Cursives, d, f, Vulg., Copt., Æth.; but ℵ, D. (Gr.), K., M., twenty Cursives, Syr., read, "in us."

posed the meshes which were broken; then it passes on to various shades of meaning such as fitting persons together so that they may work harmoniously to their proper end in the Catholic Church, as in 1 Cor. i. 10, "that ye be perfectly joined together in the same mind and in the same judgment"; 2 Cor. xiii. 11, "Be perfect," that is, "be perfectly joined together." If applied to perfecting personal religion in individual members, it seems to indicate the harmony of the various faculties of the soul and spirit, which harmony is destroyed by sin and established by holiness.

"Working in you that which is wellpleasing in His sight." Working in you by His Spirit all peace, all love, all purity, all due subordination, all lowliness, meekness, longsuffering, and mutual forbearance.

"Through Jesus Christ; to whom be glory." Similar doxologies are ascribed to Christ, and, if so, this one is ascribed to Him as His Name immediately precedes. As Delitzsch says: "The Doxology is not intended to apply directly to God, but to Him Who, in consequence of His surrender of Himself, is crowned with honour and glory."

22. "And I beseech you, brethren, suffer the word of exhortation, for I have," &c. It is singular that two very different meanings have been given to this place: "Suffer the word of exhortation, for I, who have no Apostolic authority over you, being the Apostle of the Gentiles, have written this letter to you." Or, "Suffer the word of exhortation, for I have written shortly on a theme which demands a far more exhaustive handling than that which I have been able to bestow upon it."

Anyhow, he writes here as one who felt that what he had been

23 Know ye that ᵒ*our* brother Timothy ᵖis set at liberty; with whom, if he come shortly, I will see you.   ᵒ 1 Thes. iii. 2.
ᵖ 1 Ti. vi. 12.

discussing was somewhat unpopular among them, and, as we say, "against the grain." The Jews, even when converted to Christ, were yet "zealous for the law." Let us ask ourselves what would it be for us to surrender at once the ministry and ritual and traditions of fourteen centuries. The step, the initial step, had been taken, for they had embraced the faith of Christ: but they had yet to learn all that was involved in this. They were slowly learning it, and God through the Apostolic writer dealt mercifully with them and besought them to "suffer the word of exhortation."

23. "Know ye that our brother Timothy is set at liberty, with whom," &c. We know nothing whatsoever of any imprisonment of Timothy, or of any visit which he paid to any Church exclusively of Jewish elements, as the Hebrew body to whom the Apostolic writer wrote must have been. The verse, both in diction and sentiment, has been pronounced Pauline: but the more this is examined the less certainly does it seem to favour the Pauline authorship.

For why should the Apostle make his visit to any Church, especially to a Palestinian Church, dependent upon the companionship of Timothy? It is not absolutely impossible, but it is extremely unlikely.

And besides this, the verse seems to imply that he came as the subordinate of Timothy—to use the common expression, "under his wing." This may have been the case with Luke or Apollos, but not with Paul. And it may be asked what particular reason was there for Timothy visiting, far from his usual sphere of labour, a Church merely Jewish; whereas his work was undoubtedly in Asia Minor? We can well understand St. Paul leaving Timothy somewhere to superintend work in progress, but it seems unlikely that he should take him with him to Palestinian work. Whilst St. Paul was at Ephesus or in Greece, he might for some purpose have accompanied Luke, but I do not think that St. Paul would have made his visit to any Church, certainly not one of Palestine, dependent upon the movements of Timothy.

"Salute all them that have the rule over you." This salutation is not according to the custom of St. Paul, who always salutes the

24 Salute all them ᑫthat have the rule over you, and all the saints. They of Italy salute you.

25 ʳ Grace be with you all. Amen.

¶ Written to the Hebrews from Italy by Timothy.

ᑫ ver. 7, 17.
ʳ Tit. iii. 15.

---

Church, never mentioning the rulers or ministers, except in the Epistle to the Philippians, where he writes, "To all the saints in Christ Jesus which are at Philippi with the Bishops and Deacons."

"They of Italy salute you." It is impossible to gather from this anything certain respecting the writer or place of writing. It may have been written from a place in Italy, in which case it would mean "the Christian Italians of this city salute you," or it may have been written from some unknown city where there was a colony of Italians who sent this salutation to the Hebrews to whom the Epistle was addressed.

It seems, however, certain that if the writer had written from Rome, he would not have designated the senders of this salutation as "they of Italy."

"Grace be with you all. Amen." The same salutation as that at the end of the Epistle to Titus, and nearly the same as that to the Colossians.

"The cause of all good things is this, the continual abiding with us of the grace of the Spirit. For this guides us to all good things, just as when it flies away from us it ruins us and leaves us desolate." (Chrysostom.)

# EXCURSUS

## ON THE EPISTLE TO THE HEBREWS AND EUCHARISTIC WORSHIP.

THE Epistle to the Hebrews is mainly occupied with a comparison between two acts of worship, or as they may be called, two functions of ritual.

There is the ritual action of the Jewish High Priest, on his entering once a year into the earthly Holy of Holies with blood of beasts, and there is the ritual action of the Great High Priest of humanity, Jesus Christ, on His entering once for all into the Heavenly Holy of Holies with His own Blood.

All will freely allow that the first of these is an act of ritual, and in fact that throughout the Epistle it is treated of as being the culminating function of the Jewish religion, but the corresponding entrance of the Lord Jesus into Heaven must be also an act of ritual—for what is ritual? It is surely the way in which outward acts of worship, as distinguished from inward acts, are performed. If any worship is confined to the inmost recesses of the soul, then it needs no ritual because it needs no outward form or demonstration; but if any act of worship is public, *i.e.*, is to be performed in the sight of the congregation as their united act, then there must needs be ritual of some sort.

Now the entrance of the great High Priest into the Heavenly Sanctuary must have been the most public possible; it must have been done in the sight of all the inhabitants of heaven, and so if done to God, as it must have been, it must have been an act of ritual in an infinitely greater and higher way than the corresponding Jewish function.

That it is not wrong, or beside the mark, to speak of ritual in heaven is clear from this, that almost all the outward adjuncts of ritual are said to be in heaven. First of all, there is an altar in heaven (Rev. vi. 9; viii. 3). Now what does this imply? It surely must necessitate altar worship—worship to which an altar is a fitting adjunct. If it had been said that St. John saw a pulpit in heaven could there have been a doubt as to his meaning? He must have meant that there was a place of public instruction or of proclamation. If then there be an altar in heaven there must be worship or service answering to such a thing. This service, in our present state of ignorance, may be unknown to us, it may be transcendental, as the saying is, but it must be according to the truth and fitness of an altar as its centre.

Then beside an altar there is the offering of incense (Rev. viii. 3), there is the Trisagion (iv. 8), and the white robes of service; there is even mention made of the ark of the covenant (Rev. xi. 19).

Now it seems only likely that if there is to be any worship in the Church of God it must be a worship which sets forth the all-atoning Death, and pleads it before God. For the ancient worship in its culminating act sets forth this, and the action of the High Priest in heaven, in His highest function of priesthood, sets forth the same atonement, only as accomplished and perfected. Is there anything between the two? Is there any worship upon earth which in its whole idea as well as in its outward celebration, sets forth, pleads, and realizes to us the all-atoning Death. It would seem that in the nature of things there ought to be, if the worship of the Church is to correspond to the typical worship of the temple or tabernacle on the one side, and the entrance of Christ into heaven with His own Blood on the other.

Now such a worship, showing forth His Death and making over to the believer the fullest benefits of it which he can receive in this world, was ordained by Christ Himself on the very eve of His Passion. He ordained it that there should be a perpetual anamnesis or commemoration of His Atoning Work to put away sin, just as in the Jewish system there was a remembrance, an anamnesis, of sin once a year. This remembrance or anamnesis is set forth by St. Paul as delivered to him by the Lord Himself, and afterwards delivered by him to the Corinthians as their means of setting forth the Lord's Death. (1 Cor. xi. 23.) From the Apostolic times it continued to be *the* act of worship in the Christian Church. It is described to be such by Justin Martyr (1 Apol. 85), and by Irenæus ("Against Heresies," iv. 18, 4-6). It may be well to give the central part or consecration prayer as it exists in Liturgies in use in parts of the world as remote from one another as Spain and Alexandria, Abyssinia and Gaul, as showing that these Liturgies could not have been copied from one another; but the various peoples must have received their respective Liturgies, or Communion offices, from the first planting of Christianity among them.

The earliest type of Liturgy is that in the Apostolic constitution commonly called the Clementine. The whole tone of it shows that it dates from Ante-Nicene times, probably in its present form from the second century. The principal prayer, or prayer of consecration, runs:—

"Calling therefore to remembrance these things which he endured for our sakes, we give thanks to Thee, O God Almighty, not as we ought, but as we are able, and fulfil His Institution. For in the same night that He was betrayed, taking bread into His holy and immaculate hands, and looking up to Thee, His God and Father, and breaking it He gave it to His disciples, saying: 'This is the mystery of the New Testament. Take of it, eat. This is My body, which is broken for many for the remission of sins.' Likewise also, having mingled the cup with wine and water, and blessed it, He gave it to them, saying, 'Drink ye all of it. This is My Blood, which is shed for many for the remission of sins. Do this in remembrance of Me. For as oft as ye eat of this bread, and drink of this cup, ye do shew forth My Death till I come.' Wherefore having in remembrance His Passion, Death, and Resurrection from the dead, His Return into heaven, and His Future Second Appearance, when He shall come with Glory and Power, to judge the Quick and the Dead, and to render to every man according to his works; we offer unto Thee, our King and our God, according to His institution, this bread and this cup, giving thanks to Thee through Him."

From St. James's Liturgy used in Palestine: "When the hour was come that He who had no sin was to suffer a voluntary and Life-giving Death upon the cross for us sinners; in the same night that He was offered, or rather offered Himself, for the life and salvation of the world; taking bread into His holy, immaculate, pure, and immortal hands, looking up to heaven, and presenting it to Thee His God and Father, He gave thanks, sanctified and brake it, and gave it to His disciples and Apostles, saying, 'Take, eat, this is My Body, which is broken and given for you.' Likewise after Supper He took the cup, and mixed it with wine and water,' &c. 'Do this in remembrance of Me. For as oft as ye eat this bread, and drink this cup, ye do shew forth the Death of the Son of Man, and confess His Resurrection unto His coming again.' Wherefore, having in remembrance His life-giving Passion, Salutary Cross, Death, Burial, and Resurrection," &c.

From St. Mark, used in the Patriarchate of Alexandria: "Our Lord Himself, our God and supreme King Jesus Christ, in the same night in which He delivered Himself for our sins, and was about to suffer death for mankind, sitting down to supper with His disciples, He took bread in His holy, spotless, and undefiled hands, and looking up to Thee His Father, but our God and the God of all, He gave thanks, He blessed, He sanctified and break it, and gave it to them, saying, 'This is My Body which is broken, and given for the remission of sins,' " &c.

"In like manner He took the cup . . . . 'Drink ye all of it, for this is My Blood of the New Testament which is shed and given for you and for many for the remission of sins. . . . . Showing forth, therefore, O Lord Almighty, Heavenly Father, the Death of thine only begotten Son our Lord, our God and Saviour Jesus Christ, and confessing His Blessed Resurrection from the dead on the third day, His Ascension," &c. &c.

The Ethiopian, used in Abyssinia: "Thy Holy Son Who came down from heaven, and was born of a virgin, that He might perform Thy will and establish an holy people unto Thee, He extended His hands at His Passion, He suffered that He might release those from sufferings who trust in Thee. Of His own free will He delivered Himself up to suffer, that He might destroy death, break the bonds of Satan, that He might establish His Testament (covenant), and manifest His Resurrection. In the same night in which He was betrayed, He took bread into His holy, blessed, and immaculate hands, He looked up to heaven to Thee His Father; He gave thanks, He blessed, sanctified it, and gave it to His disciples, saying, 'Take, eat ye all of this. This bread is My Body, which is broken for you for the remission of sins.' . . . . Likewise He blessed and sanctified the cup of thanksgiving, and said to them, 'Take, drink ye all of this. This is the cup of My Blood which shall be shed for you,' &c. . . . . And now, O Lord, celebrating the memorial of Thy Death and Resurrection, we offer to Thee this bread and this cup, giving thanks to thee," &c.

From the Mozarabic used in Spain, and a branch of what is called the Ephesian Liturgy used in Gaul: "O Jesus, the good high priest, come, come and be in the midst of us, as Thou wast in the midst of Thy disciples; sanctify this oblation, that it being sanctified we may receive it by the hands of Thy holy angel, O holy Lord and eternal Redeemer. Our Lord Jesus Christ, in that night in which He was betrayed, took bread, and giving thanks, He blessed and brake it, and gave it to His disciples, saying, 'Take and eat, this is My Body which shall be delivered for you. Do this as oft as ye eat it in remembrance of Me.' Likewise also the cup after He had supped, saying, 'This is the cup of the New Testament in My Blood which shall be shed for you and for many for the Remission of sins. Do this as oft as ye drink it in remembrance of Me," &c.

From the Roman: "Thy most dearly beloved Son Jesus Christ our Lord Who, the day before He suffered, took bread into His holy and venerable hands, and with His eyes lifted up towards heaven to God His Almighty Father, giving thanks unto Thee, did bless, break, and give to His disciples, saying, 'Take, and eat ye all of this, for this is My Body.' In like manner after He had supped, taking also the glorious chalice into His holy and venerable hands, and giving Thee thanks, He blessed and gave to the disciples, saying, 'Take and drink ye all of this, for this is the chalice of My Blood of the new and eternal testament—the mystery of faith—which shall be shed for you and for many for the remission of sins. As often as ye do these things, ye shall do them in remembrance of Me.' Wherefore, O Lord, we Thy servants, as also Thy holy people, calling to mind the blessed Passion of the same Christ Thy Son our Lord, His Resurrection from hell, and glorious Ascension into heaven, offer unto Thy most excellent Majesty," &c.

In an earlier part of this office there is a prayer founded on Hebrews x. 19: "Take away from us our iniquities, we beseech Thee, O Lord, that we may be worthy with pure minds to enter into the holy of holies through Christ our Lord."

Now in looking over these words of consecration in liturgies used in all parts of the Christian world—in Ethiopia, Jerusalem, Rome, Gaul, or Spain—we notice that the memorial act is not a mere recounting of the Sufferings of Christ, but a repetition of the act in which, as the Great High Priest after the order of Melchisedec, He took bread and He took the cup, and instituted the memorial or representation of His Sufferings before He actually suffered. Thus His Words are always reproduced in the first person singular, as if He himself there and then said them. It is never said that the Lord Jesus . . . took bread, and declared it to be His Body, but the Lord Jesus took bread and said, "This is My Body;" and this in every Liturgy. By this we emphasize the fact that Jesus is the actual High Priest in each and every celebration, for the principal act in celebrating is the use of the Lord's words, not those of the minister, so that the celebrating minister is but the mere instrument in the hands of the One Great Consecrating Priest, and so that when we "enter into the holiest by the Blood of Jesus, by the new and living way which He hath consecrated for us through the veil, that is to say His Flesh," we do, or must do this, realizing that we have " an ever-present high priest over the house of God."

The conception of the Eucharist as held by the Catholic Church is contained in these verses, Heb. x. 19-22.

It is an " entrance into the holiest." To this it may be objected, " Is not this too great a thing to say of any Eucharist celebrated on earth?" No, because in this Epistle in its most mysterious announcement (xii. 22-24) earth and heaven are supposed to be intermingled—to have at least nothing between them : " Ye are come unto mount Sion, the city of the living God, the heavenly Jerusalem, and to an innumerable company of angels . . . . to God the Judge of all, and to the Spirits of just men made perfect, and to Jesus the Mediator of the New Covenant, and to the blood of sprinkling, which speaketh better things than that of Abel." The Eucharist is a way of access to God, in the Holiest, which is very feebly set forth by the Jewish high priest's entrance into the holy of holies. We are called upon to use this entrance with boldness, not with fear, lest we die (Levit. xvi. 13), but with confidence that by it we live. This entrance is by a new and living way which Jesus hath consecrated for us; not for one man once a year, but for all of us. These words, "new and living way, which He hath consecrated for us," demand an outward and visible way of approach. They cannot possibly be satisfied by a mere internal act of faith, however devout.

"Which he hath consecrated for us." He actually did this when He ordained the Eucharist. The ways of approach by Jewish offerings were not new but old, they "waxed old and were ready to vanish away:" neither were they living, but Jesus said, "I am the living bread," and "I am the life."

"Through the veil." The veil is an outward part which veils the Inward Part. It veils the Lord's Flesh or Body which was broken for us on the cross, and which in a mystical sense is broken and given to us, and through which representation of the Lord's Passion we approach.

"Having an high priest over the house of God." Christ is the High Priest over the house of God, not the house of God in heaven only, but the house, that is, the Church of God, on earth. He is present at every Eucharist to fulfil His word when He first ordained it, so that it should always be His Body and His Blood.

Such is the Eucharistic conception. It unites the merely typical and local conception of the Israelites with the transcendent conception of the functions of the Great High Priest in the Heavenly Sanctuary. If any object that it is too heavenly to be realized on earth, I would ask them to consider Heb. xii. 22-24: "Ye are come unto Mount Sion and unto the city of the living God, the heavenly Jerusalem, and to an innumerable company of angels . . . . and to Jesus the Mediator." Ye are come to it by having embraced the Gospel and entered into the Church. But can this be said of things present? Undoubtedly this marvellous text does refer to things in this life, not to things after death. The whole conception is overpowering in its vastness and mystery; and yet is it not in keeping with the Incarnation of the Eternal Son, His Life, His Death, His Resurrection, and His Ascension, all of which took place in this world? Is it not in keeping with, "Lo, I am with you always, even unto the end of the world?" Is it not in keeping with the contrast between the Old and the New—the one local, the other supra-local and universal; the one an entrance by one man, the other by the whole family or Church of the Priests of God; the one with ignoble blood, the other by the Blood of God (Acts xx. 28)? The entrance of the high priest into the most holy place was the culmination of the Jewish ritual. It was the solemn cleansing and hallowing every year of the whole service (altar, tabernacle, priests, and their ministrations), but it did not render useless, rather it necessitated, the ministration of inferior priests daily. Now so it is with the Christian state of things. The Lord is the priest in every Eucharist, and yet He appointed inferior ministers to act for Him, when He said, " This do in remembrance of me," " As my Father sent me, so send I you." In the Eucharist He deputes others to act for Him. He does not break the bread Himself, but He does it by the hands of others. We do not hear Him say the words of institution, but He is invisibly present, so that the Eucharist is always the same as what it was when He first ordained it. It is always fresh from His Hands.

There is another, but kindred view of the Eucharist suggested by some words of this Epistle, that it is a sacrifice of praise and thanksgiving. The Apostle says (xiii. 10) " we have an altar," and this is an altar given to us that we may eat something from it. It is an altar whereof they have no right to *eat* who serve the Tabernacle, *i.e.*, who are unconverted Jews, serving God only through the rites of the decaying religion.

And after saying that if we would serve Him aright we must "bear His reproach," he concludes with " By him therefore let us offer the sacrifice of praise to God continually, *i.e.*, the fruit (or calves) of our lips giving thanks to His Name.

Now the Eucharist has from the first been called a sacrifice of praise. Thus in the Liturgy of St. James (Prayer of the Veil " Send forth, O God, Thy good grace, and hallow our souls, and bodies, and spirits, and change our dispositions to piety, that in a pure conscience we may present to Thee the mercy of peace, the sacrifice of praise." (Neale, " Translation of Primitive Liturgies," p. 43.) Again, in the Clementine, " Calling therefore to remembrance those things which He endured for our sakes, we give thanks to Thee, O God Almighty, not as we ought, but as we are able, and fulfil His institution." Again, "We offer to Thee, our King and our God, according to His Institution, this bread and this cup, giving thanks to Thee through Him," &c. Again in the Roman, " For whom we offer, or themselves offer to thee, this sacrifice of praise for themselves," &c.

Again in our own, " We Thy humble servants entirely desire Thy Fatherly goodness, mercifully to accept this our sacrifice of praise and thanksgiving." Now in what respect is the Eucharist a sacrifice of praise and thanksgiving. Is it because of the verbal acts of praise which form part of the service? It might be thought to be such, and especially if we compare it with the sacrifice of the law, which contain no specific acts of praise or prayer. It is a very remarkable fact that in all the numerous directions in the Book of Leviticus, there are no words of either thanksgiving or prayer ordered. Did not then pious Israelites accompany their sacrifices with praise and prayer? Doubtless, but this formed no necessary part of this service, whereas in all Christian services of Eucharists, there are acts of praise such as the Trisagion and the Gloria in Excelsis, and the recounting of the various stages in the One Great Redeeming Act. But after all, these do not constitute the Eucharist. They are its adjuncts, but not the Eucharist itself. Whereas the consecration and reception *per se* is *the* act of praise, because it is the setting forth before God, and angels, and men, the Redeeming Body and Blood. This cannot be done silently, as were the Jewish sacrifices. The "word" must accompany the act—the words of institution, and the words of recognition of the various stages of the redeeming work, as in St. James, "Wherefore having in remembrance His life-giving Passion, Salutary Cross, Death, Burial, and Resurrection on the third day," &c.

Now here is the difference between the Jewish anamnesis and the Christian. The Jewish was the anamnesis, the commemoration of sin—the Christian the anamnesis of Redemption from sin. The Jewish sacrificial act was not one, but many. It looked forward to the next year's atonement, and the next, and the next, whereas the other is "Jesus Christ . . . who made there by His one oblation of Himself once offered, a full, perfect, and sufficient sacrifice, oblation and satisfaction for the sins of the whole world." "We praise Thee, we bless Thee, we worship Thee, we glorify Thee, we give thanks to Thee for Thy Great Glory, O Lord God, heavenly King, God the Father Almighty."

If against this bright and glorious conception it be said that there is nothing of it in Scripture, we answer that Scripture gives us no directions respecting Christian worship. There is no direction whatsoever respecting the mode in which Christian worship is to be performed. For instance, there is no direction that the services should begin with the singing of a psalm or hymn—that it should proceed to an extempore prayer as among Nonconformists in England, or a prayer read out of a book as on the Continent.

Neither is there any direction that churchmen should have a service resembling our ordinary matins and even-song, beginning with the reading of a verse out of the Psalms, or Ezekiel, or the Gospels, proceeding with a short exhortation to repentance, then a general confession, then an absolution, and so on. The only hints that we have respecting united Church Service require an Eucharistic Service (as Acts xx. 7; 1 Cor. x. 16, compared with verse 20, 21, xi. 20). Were then the earliest Christians without directions on this point of public worship? No, because St. Paul in his Epistles assumes that every Church to which he writes has been instructed orally both in doctrine and practice. There is not a single Epistle which does not postulate that the Church to which it was sent had been so instructed. Take the first to the Corinthians; St. Paul assumes that he had delivered orally to them such apparently minor matters as the conduct of the women in the church, that they should not be uncovered (x. 1-3). Then he proceeded to say that they had been orally instructed by him respecting the Institution of the Eucharist (xi. 23). Then he promises that when he comes he will give fuller directions respecting its celebration (xi. 34). Then he sends Timothy, that he may tell them how he teaches everywhere in every church. Similarly he reminded the Thessalonians to "stand fast and hold the traditions," and "to withdraw themselves from every brother that walketh disorderly and not after the traditions which they received of us" (2 Thess. ii. 15, and iii. 1).

Now it is a singular fact that not a single one of these traditions has come down to us in Scripture, but respecting two or three of them we are quite certain that they have otherwise come down, and one of these is that in the celebration of the Eucharist the Lord's words in ordaining the Eucharist should be recited, and that there should follow immediately upon it a devout enumeration of the principal stages in the work of Redemption. This is clear, because in all parts of the world the oldest forms of Liturgy contain these not in the same words, but in words slightly differing in form, but containing the same substance. These differences are important in this respect, that they show us that the germs of all the Ancient Liturgies were not copied from one another, but date from a time before the books of the New Testament were collected into one volume, for if they dated from a time when the three Synoptic Gospels were in every one's hands, the words of Institution would always be given in the words handed down to us by St. Matthew or St. Luke, which they are not. The only way for accounting for the variation in these Liturgies is their extreme antiquity, extending back quite to the early Apostolic age. Each Apostle or first planter of a Church would impress upon it his own tradition, just as St. Paul did, and one of these traditions would assuredly be the account of the Lord's words and acts when He instituted, as was the case with St. Paul. If it be still asked why there should be differences at all in any such accounts, we simply refer to the Gospel narrative. The account of the words of institution in St. Matthew and St. Mark differs from those in St. Luke and St. Paul in some important particulars.

I need scarcely say that the Epistle to the Hebrews has no bearing whatsoever upon such adjuncts of Ritual as the vestments of the celebrant or his assistants, or the position of the priest with reference to the altar or the congregation, and such things. The vestment or vestments used ought to emphasize the uniqueness of the rite, as not being one ceremony amongst many, but as being the Christ-ordained memorial (anamnesis) of His Passion. It seems wrong that if there is any distinctive dress for those who take part in the service of God, the celebrant of the Eucharist should be habited in the same way as the choir-boy. In these matters, however, each Church should be at liberty to observe its own traditions, or its own traditional practices.

THE END.

New and cheaper Issue in Twelve monthly vols.
Crown 8vo, red edges, 4/6 each.

# CHURCH COMMENTARY

ON THE

## NEW TESTAMENT.

WITH NOTES, CRITICAL AND PRACTICAL,
INTRODUCTIONS, AND EXCURSUSES.

By the Rev. M. F. Sadler,
*Late Rector of Honiton and Prebendary of Wells.*

---

THE GOSPEL OF ST. MATTHEW.   [*Ready.*
THE GOSPEL OF ST. MARK.   [*Ready.*
THE GOSPEL OF ST. LUKE.   [*Ready.*
THE GOSPEL OF ST. JOHN.   [*Ready.*
THE ACTS OF THE APOSTLES.   [*Ready.*
THE EPISTLE TO THE ROMANS.   [*Ready.*
THE EPISTLES TO THE CORINTHIANS.
   [*Ready.*
THE EPISTLES TO THE GALATIANS, EPHESIANS, AND PHILIPPIANS. [*Nov.* 1.
THE EPISTLES TO THE COLOSSIANS, THESSALONIANS, AND TIMOTHY. [*Dec.* 1.
THE EPISTLES TO TITUS, PHILEMON, AND THE HEBREWS.   [*Jan.* 2, 1899.
THE EPISTLES OF SS. JAMES, PETER, JOHN, AND JUDE.   [*Feb.* 1.
THE REVELATION OF ST. JOHN THE DIVINE.   [*March* 1.

LONDON: GEORGE BELL AND SONS.

# OPINIONS OF THE PRESS.

## THE GOSPELS.

*From* THE CHURCH QUARTERLY, *October*, 1883.

"It is far the best practical Commentary that we know, being plain-spoken, fearless, and definite, and containing matter very unlike the milk and water which is often served up in [so-called] practical Commentaries. ... For solid Church teaching it stands unrivalled. Nothing could be better than the notes on the Sermon on the Mount, and the practical lessons drawn with convincing clearness from our Lord's words on the subject of Almsgiving, Prayer, and Fasting. Throughout the whole book the writer is ever on the watch for general principles and teaching applicable to the wants of our own day, which may legitimately be deduced from the Gospel narrative."

*From* THE CHURCH TIMES, *February 23rd*, 1883.

"The question of the origin of the Four Gospels is well treated, and a more succinct account of the real standing of the Evangelists with respect to each other, or to a supposed original document from which all copied, could scarcely be found than that contained in these few pages. Some few pages introductory to the critical portion of the volume, and explaining the elements of textual criticism, bring us to the text of the Commentary itself. Throughout the whole of its pages the same evidence of scholarship and critical acumen, which distinguishes all the author's work, is apparent; while the faculty of conveying such knowledge to the minds of the least learned in a simple and forcible manner, is abundantly preserved, and will procure for this work the position of one of the best of popular commentaries. Many of the notes extend beyond the scope generally implied by the term, and become full explanations of doctrinal subjects such as will prove of immense value to the student as well as to the general reader. We may cite as an instance of this exhaustive process the lengthy note on St. Matt. xvi. 18, and those notes on the Parables, which, severally treated in their entirety, present a more intelligible meaning than when explained in short disjointed notes. Finally, it remains to mention the fact, which, however, goes without saying, that the tone of the Commentary is thoroughly Catholic, so that the reader will find here a firm defence of the supernatural and divine character of the Gospel story, which never condescends to the tone of much of modern criticism, but remains true to primitive Catholic teaching."

*From* CHURCH BELLS, *November 18th*, 1882.

"It is written in a clear and sensible style, with a healthy tone; and its practical portions are devout without being wearisome or 'goody.'"

*From* THE CHURCH REVIEW, *November*, 1883.

"A valuable and substantial contribution to the literature of the New Testament is made by Mr. Sadler in the volume now before us. ... It might be said that every page of the work lights up the grand historical character of the Church as the one supreme authority for the authenticity and interpretation of the books of Scripture."

*From* THE CHURCH TIMES, *December* 21*st*, 1883.

" We have much pleasure in announcing the issue of ' The Gospel according to St. John, with Notes, Critical and Practical,' by the Rev. M. F. Sadler (George Bell and Sons), a companion volume to his gloss on St. Matthew, and a redemption of the pledge he gave therein to carry on his labours to the remaining Gospels. This is admirably done, being exactly what is wanted for that large and increasing class of readers who need the results of genuine scholarship and sound vigorous thought, but who are repelled by any surface display of erudition, and still more by dryness of treatment, . . . . . The admirable lucidity, which is the distinctive quality of Mr. Sadler's style, comes out markedly in his annotations, whether they take the form of pithy clearings up of verbal difficulties or more elaborate dissertations on important points of doctrine; and he is a good judge in selecting the best matter supplied by his precursors, such as Olshausen, Stier, Godet, and, above all, St. Augustine, whose commentary on St. John is one of that Father's ablest works. This is much less of a mere grammatical inquiry than Professor Westcott's volume in the 'Speaker's Commentary,' but it is much more of a theological explanation, and that of a far sounder and deeper school."

*From* THE LITERARY CHURCHMAN, *December* 7*th*, 1883.

". . . Apart from these longer and more continuous glosses, the reader constantly meets with single pithy notes, which by their clear common sense solve a difficulty at once, and satisfy the understanding promptly, so that this is quite the best popular commentary on S. John we know, without implying by that epithet that even advanced students of Biblical literature will not find ample profit in consulting it."

*From* THE CHURCH TIMES, *October* 3*rd*, 1884.

" We gladly chronicle the third instalment of Prebendary Sadler's clear and sensible Commentary on the Gospels, which exactly meets the needs of that large and increasing class, which, without pretending any interest in the more abstruse problems of scholarship in connection with the Greek Testament, is desirous of having in its hands a trustworthy guide to the actual meaning of the sacred writers, and some plain statement of the results accepted by that calmer type of scholars who understand the nature of evidence, and are not disposed to admit the validity of unsupported conjecture, however original and brilliant, as proof. . . . . The notes, as always with Mr. Sadler, are singularly lucid, pithy, and to the point."

*From* CHURCH BELLS, *November* 22*nd*, 1884.

" This is a work of a veteran scholar and divine to whom the Church owes much. Prebendary Sadler's writing is characterized by great clearness of style, and he has a remarkably persuasive way of putting things. His sermons, as well as his ' Church Doctrine Bible Truth,' &c., have done much towards furnishing the parochial clergy with materials for feeding their flocks. In this commentary he aims at a yet more important object, the instruction of the educated classes. He has carefully compared the original Scriptures with the authorized and revised versions, and has set himself to meet objections of scientific sceptics, and he has achieved great success. . . . . The volume is full of thoughts and suggestions for preachers as well as for general readers."

*From* THE SATURDAY REVIEW, *February 21st*, 1885.
" We can recommend his book to devout and cultivated Churchmen who want to read the Gospels for instruction as well as for edification."

*From* THE CHURCH QUARTERLY, *January*, 1885.
"In reading the notes upon the text, the feature which strikes us most is their intensely practical character. Mr. Sadler has a remarkable faculty of bringing the teaching of the incidents of our Lord's life on earth to bear upon the circumstances of our own time. Even where the points brought out are well worn and familiar, there is a freshness in his manner of treating them which adds greatly to the charm and value of the Commentary."

*From* THE CHURCH TIMES, *July 3rd*, 1886.
" Indeed, one great merit in this commentary and its companion volumes is the frequency with which notes are found, which are capable of being each expanded into useful sermons. They are like very strong essences or tinctures, which will bear considerable dilution before being employed medically, though for convenience they are usually kept in the more portable form."

*From* THE CHURCH QUARTERLY, *July*, 1886.
" We must begin our notice of this volume by offering Prebendary Sadler our hearty congratulations on the completion of his work on the four Gospels. The previous volumes were all reviewed in our columns as they appeared, and we have no hesitation in extending the welcome which we gave to them to their present companion. It is no slight distinction for a writer, after having made his reputation by what is confessedly the best popular work on Church doctrine, to have produced what we hold to be the best popular commentary on the Gospel narrative. There is no other occupying quite the same ground, and we cordially recommend these four volumes, in the now familiar blue binding, as for practical purposes the most useful to the general reader."

*From* CHURCH BELLS, *July 2nd*, 1886.
" Mr. Sadler's excellent qualities as a theological writer and expositor are so well known that we need only introduce the reader to this, his last Commentary on the Gospels, completing the series, by saying that it presents the same features as its predecessors. It is somewhat longer than any of the other three, a circumstance quite intelligible to those who consider how a commentator's view of his responsibility must enlarge as he proceeds with his work. To begin at the beginning, the Introduction is excellent, clear, concise, and full. In short, it says all that need be said on the authorship of the Gospel, and says it well."

*From* THE IRISH ECCLESIASTICAL GAZETTE, *Nov. 6th*, 1886.
" Originality of treatment, depth of insight, and thorough grasp of the practical side of Divine truth characterize these commentaries of Mr. Sadler on the four Gospels."

# THE ACTS OF THE HOLY APOSTLES.

## From THE GUARDIAN, *July*, 1887.

"We find, however, in the notes on St. Luke and the Acts the same freshness in thought and style, the same direct and independent consideration of the themes brought up on the sacred pages, the same knowledge of what has been said by others, the same masterly use, alike without subservience and without neglect, of the great and varied stores which our predecessors have left to us of these days who study the New Testament. The result is that Mr. Sadler's Commentary is decidedly one of the most unhackneyed and original of any we have. It will often be found to give help where others quite fail to do so, and its special value will be to the preacher or teacher who has to give oral and practical instruction; Mr. Sadler's strong point being decidedly in pointing the application to contemporary thought and to life, its trials and its duties, of the divine words with which he has to deal."

## From CHURCH BELLS, *July 8th*, 1887.

"We can hardly imagine a commentary better adapted than Mr. Sadler's for giving to the reader an antidote to that unsettling influence which is now going about in the world, making people have a different set of religious opinions every month or so."

## From THE CHURCH QUARTERLY REVIEW.

"There is vigour and freshness about his writings which makes it a pleasure to read them, while there is certain to be much that is instructive, and their tone and tendency are equally certain to be sound and edifying. This short commentary on the Acts of the Apostles is no exception to the rule, and it well supports the established reputation of its author."

## From THE CHURCH TIMES, *August 26th*, 1887.

"Prebendary Sadler's useful commentary on the New Testament is advanced another important stage by the issue of this volume on the Acts of the Apostles, a part of Scripture whose interest and value seems to increase daily, as investigation into the beginnings of the Christian Church are pressed on with fresh vigour, alike by those who wish to prove Christianity a mere human evolution out of materials lying to hand in the Augustan era, and those who accept it as a divine revelation. Much of the work which has been done of late years in connexion with the Acts and other Pauline records has been devoted chiefly to the externals of history, geography, antiquities, and the like, rather than to the religious teaching which they contain; and this fact makes a gloss from a theologian like Mr. Sadler all the more welcome."

# THE EPISTLES.

*From* CHURCH BELLS, *May* 18*th*, 1888.

" Mr. Sadler carries on his work with unabated vigour, and now we have some hope of his being able to give us a commentary on the whole of the New Testament. Undoubtedly such a work when completed will be of great value, as giving a well-thought-out exposition of the whole of the sources from which we derive the history of the founding, as well as the doctrines, of the Christian Church, and this, too, an exposition which supplies, not the mere personal opinions of its writer, although it is everywhere tinged by his individuality, but the historical meaning of the teaching of individual writers and of the Church at large. The 'introduction' to the present volume is excellent, giving all the requisite information without any unnecessary waste of words."

*From* THE CHURCH TIMES, *June*, 1888.

" There are three excursuses at the end of the volume, on Justification, on Election, and on the Christology of St. Paul, all carefully written, but with most pains bestowed upon the second. We do not know a better book than this Commentary to put into the hands of an intelligent Evangelical who is beginning to doubt the soundness of the system he has heretofore accepted, and is striving to find his way out and up into a higher and clearer atmosphere."

*From* THE CHURCH QUARTERLY REVIEW.

" We hail with pleasure this addition to the Commentary on the New Testament. . . . . . We think this volume will certainly sustain the high position which Mr. Sadler has gained as a practical interpreter of Holy Scripture."

*From* THE IRISH ECCLESIASTICAL GAZETTE, *April* 18*th*, 1890.

" Incomparably the best Commentary on the New Testament extant."

*From* THE BANNER, *May* 23*rd*, 1890.

" Ordinary readers could hardly have a better exposition of the sacred books."

*From* THE LITERARY CHURCHMAN, *February* 6*th*, 1891.

" This volume will be found to present all the characteristic excellences of Mr. Sadler's method ; and it would be hard, indeed, to find any points of objection to these terse, thoughtful, Church-like notes."

*Uniform with the Church Commentary.*

*Second edition. Crown 8vo, 5s.*

# SERMON OUTLINES
## FOR THE CLERGY AND LAY-PREACHERS.
### 321 OUTLINES ARRANGED ACCORDING TO THE CHURCH'S YEAR.

This book, a book of suggestions rather than of mere divisions, or skeletons as they were formerly called, has been composed with a view to meeting the objection heard on all sides that sermons at the present day are very deficient in setting forth Christian doctrines.

*From* THE GUARDIAN, *April 12th, 1893.*
"It is easy to prophesy a considerable sale for this volume. . . . We meet here all the well-known characteristics of his writings. The style is straightforward and vigorous. There is never any doubt about his meaning. His remarks are always pointed, and the arrangement of his material is excellent."

*From* THE CHURCH TIMES, *February 17th, 1893.*
"This volume differs in three respects from most similar volumes: (1) It aims, primarily, at supplying sketches of sermons on Christian Doctrine, couched in clear, definite language. (2) It is a book of 'suggestions, rather than of mere divisions or skeletons.' (3) It includes lists of texts and subjects for courses of Lenten and other sermons. The well-earned reputation of its author will be a sufficient guarantee for the soundness and usefulness of the work."

*From* CHURCH BELLS, *December 16th, 1892.*
"They are adequate, and they are helpful; they set forth the elementary teaching of the Church's seasons, the redemption, salvation, and sanctification of mankind. Each Sunday of each Church season has several appropriate texts and heads of discourses, and these are rich in wise suggestions as to helpful teaching. There is much simplicity and strong meat for learners. Prayer-book lines are made the rule throughout—the best rule of all."

*From* THE ROCK, *November 4th, 1892.*
"We should think that it would be difficult to find anywhere such a real help for preachers as these outlines afford. . . . Such depth of spiritual teaching is seldom to be found."

*From* THE IRISH ECCLESIASTICAL GAZETTE, *Nov. 11th, 1892.*
"This should be among the most popular and useful of Prebendary Sadler's writings."

*From* THE CLERGYMAN'S MAGAZINE, *December, 1892.*
"These outlines are both Evangelical and doctrinal. They occupy exactly one page of the book, and therefore afford ample opportunity for the preacher's own powers of expansion."

# WORKS BY THE REV. M. F. SADLER,
### Rector of Honiton and Prebendary of Wells.

*New and cheaper Issue, price 2s.*
## CHURCH DOCTRINE—BIBLE TRUTH. 49th Thousand.

"Mr. Sadler takes Church Doctrine, specifically so called, subject by subject, and elaborately shows its specially marked Scripturalness. The objective nature of the faith, the Athanasian Creed, the Baptismal Services, the Holy Eucharist, Absolution and the Priesthood, Church Government and Confirmation, are some of the more prominent subjects treated. And Mr. Sadler handles each with a marked degree of sound sense, and with a thorough mastery of his subject."—*Guardian.*

*New and cheaper Issue, price 2s.*
## THE CHURCH TEACHER'S MANUAL OF CHRISTIAN INSTRUCTION.
Being the Church Catechism expanded and explained in Question and Answer, for the Use of Clergymen, Parents, and Teachers. 46th Thousand.

"Far the best book of the kind we have ever seen."—*Literary Churchman.*

**Confirmation:** An Extract from the "Church Teacher's Manual." 70th Thousand. Price 1d.

## THE ONE OFFERING: a Treatise on the Sacrificial
Nature of the Eucharist. 11th Thousand. Price 2s. 6d.

"A treatise of singular clearness and force, which gives us what we did not really possess till it appeared."—*Church Times.*

## JUSTIFICATION OF LIFE: its Nature, Antecedents,
and Results. 2nd Edition, Revised. Price 4s. 6d.

## THE SECOND ADAM and THE NEW BIRTH;
or, The Doctrine of Baptism as contained in Holy Scripture. 12th Edition. Price 4s. 6d.

"The most striking peculiarity of this useful little work is that its author argues almost exclusively from the Bible. We commend it most earnestly to Clergy and laity, as containing in a small compass, and at a trifling cost, a body of sound and Scriptural doctrine respecting the New Birth, which cannot be too widely circulated."—*Guardian.*

## THE SACRAMENT OF RESPONSIBILITY;
or, Testimony of the Scripture to the Teaching of the Church on Holy Baptism. Price 2s. 6d.
Cheap Edition. 8th Edition. Price 6d.

## THE COMMUNICANT'S MANUAL; being a Book
of Self-Examination, Prayer, Praise, and Thanksgiving. 32mo. 114th Thousand. Price 1s. 6d.
Cheap Edition for Distribution. Price 8d.
A Larger Edition. Red rubrics. Fcap. 8vo. Price 2s. 6d.

**SERMONS.** Plain Speaking on Deep Truths. 8th Edition. Price 6s.
Abundant Life, and other Sermons. 2nd Edition. Price 6s.

LONDON: G. BELL AND SONS, York Street, Covent Garden.

www.ingramcontent.com/pod-product-compliance
Lightning Source LLC
Chambersburg PA
CBHW022049230426
43672CB00008B/1119